Behavior Settings

Behavior Settings

A Revision and Extension of Roger G. Barker's
Ecological Psychology

PHIL SCHOGGEN
With a chapter by Karl A. Fox

STANFORD UNIVERSITY PRESS · STANFORD, CALIFORNIA · 1989

Stanford University Press
Stanford, California
© 1968, 1989 by the Board of Trustees of the
Leland Stanford Junior University
Printed in the United States of America

CIP data appear at the end of the book

TO LOUISE SHEDD BARKER

whose wisdom, social skill, and dedication
contributed so much to the research program
on which this book is based

Preface

In 1947, Roger G. Barker and his long-time colleague Herbert F. Wright originated an innovative program of research in child psychology at the Midwest Psychological Field Station of the University of Kansas. The earliest published papers from this program (Barker & Wright, 1949, 1951a, 1951b, 1955; Wright & Barker, 1950; Wright et al. 1955) referred to the work as "psychological ecology," inspired in part by the earlier papers by Kurt Lewin (1943, 1944, 1947) that discussed psychological ecology, and by the writings of Egon Brunswik (1947). At the outset, this work focused on the development of extensive direct observational records of the behavior and situation of individual children as they went about their ordinary activities of everyday life at home, in school, and wherever they went in their home communities (Barker & Wright, 1951a).

In their first major research report, *Midwest and Its Children*, Barker and Wright (1955) describe their discovery of behavior settings as arising from their efforts to sample adequately the overwhelming amount of individual child behavior that occurred in Midwest, the code name for Oskaloosa, the small Kansas town where the field station was located. They found that their sample was improved if, in addition to using the usual sampling bases—age, sex, social class, etc.—they sampled individual behavior in "such divergent places as the drug store, the Sunday-School classes, the 4-H Club meeting, and the football game" (p. 7). They discovered that unique and regularly occurring standing patterns of behavior were characteristic of such behavior areas and that they endured despite sometimes frequent turnover of the particular persons involved. The discovery of these extra-individual wave patterns of behavior, tied to particular parts of the physical-temporal-geographic environment, led to the development of the behavior setting method for studying the ecological environment of molar (goal-directed, purposive) behavior. Almost half that book was devoted to Barker and Wright's report of the behavior setting method and the results of its application to the town of Midwest.

Subsequent development of behavior setting theory and method and the presentation of new data from behavior setting surveys of Midwest were reported in Barker's 1968 book, *Ecological Psychology,* widely regarded as the classical formulation of this approach to the study of the environment of molar behavior. This book incorporated the basic theoretical statement on behavior settings that first appeared as "Ecology and Motivation," a paper published in the 1960 *Nebraska Symposium on Motivation.* Both the book and the paper were concerned exclusively with behavior settings.

Increasingly preoccupied with the potentialities of the behavior setting approach, Barker continued to do research on and write about behavior settings. He was greatly impressed with the fact that the laws that govern and regulate the operation of behavior settings are altogether different from and incommensurate with the laws of psychology that govern individual behavior. Yet the evidence is compelling that behavior and behavior settings are interdependent and that they are linked in more than a probabilistic fashion. It was his recognition of this conceptual breach that led Barker, in a 1969 paper, to call for a new science of the ecological environment, an *eco-behavioral science.* He argued that, because the ecological environment is governed by laws that are incommensurate with those of scientific psychology, it is impossible to understand the ecological environment of molar behavior with the concepts and theories of scientific psychology. The new, eco-behavioral science would "look at the environment of behavior as a phenomenon worthy of investigation for itself, not merely as an instrument for unraveling the behavior-relevant programming within persons" (Barker, 1969, p. 35). Barker renewed this call for an eco-behavioral science in 1978 (Barker & Associates, 1978, p. 41; see Chap. 15 below). And so, what began as a study in child psychology gradually developed into the study of environments of molar behavior, an eco-behavioral science independent of psychology. From a psychological ecology, the specialty became an ecological psychology. Finally, the work with behavior settings was separated off into its own specialty that Barker wants to call an eco-behavioral science, no longer a part of any kind of psychology.

Further theoretical and methodological progress in work with behavior settings has been made and published, particularly in *Qualities of Community Life,* by Barker and Schoggen, in 1973. Although primarily an extensive report of empirical findings from the comparative and repeated study of Midwest and Yoredale (a comparable small town in Yorkshire, England) in terms of behavior settings, this volume includes some important conceptual and methodological advances not described in any other publication.

This has meant that, in order to obtain a complete description of behavior setting theory and method, it has been necessary to consult both *Ecological Psychology* and *Qualities of Community Life*. But even this was found by some workers to be inadequate; they still had questions after reading both. There appeared to be a need for a complete presentation of behavior setting theory and method in a single volume.

Upon the suggestion of Barker and with the encouragement of a number of colleagues who are well acquainted with work in this area, I undertook to revise *Ecological Psychology*. I wanted Barker to collaborate with me on the revision, but he preferred to attend to other interests. Although he has given me every encouragement to proceed with the project, he has steadfastly refused to become involved in this revision in any way. He has not even read the work in draft form.

This revision is intended to make it easier for interested workers to find out about behavior settings. My primary goal has been to provide a current and comprehensive description of behavior setting theory and method in sufficient detail and with illustrations adequate to serve as a guide for new research applications. I have tried to preserve Barker's 1968 presentation of theory and method except where changes were required to reflect the theoretical and methodological advances reported in *Qualities of Community Life* and where clarification and new illustrations appeared to be needed. This has involved some reorganization and extensive additions taken largely from *Qualities of Community Life*. The lengthy report in *Ecological Psychology* of empirical findings from the study of behavior settings in Midwest has been replaced with extensive summaries of most of the published reports of research applications of behavior settings currently available. Included also are two special chapters: one written for this volume by an economist, Karl A. Fox, on the use of behavior settings in social system accounting; and the other a reprint of an article by Barker on behavior settings that have figured prominently in his professional career. In addition, there is a chapter devoted to a discussion of behavior settings in relation to a number of other concepts in social science and the field of environment and behavior. The final chapter is taken from two other papers by Barker (1978a, 1978b), only slightly modified for the present purpose.

Acknowledgments

My gratitude to Roger G. Barker for encouraging me to undertake this revision and extension of his classic research monograph is very great but it pales in comparison to my admiration of him and his brilliant work over the 40 years that he has served as my mentor, model, colleague, co-author, and good friend.

Paul V. Gump has given generously of his time and rich experience. Paul has been teaching about behavior settings for years and is a highly productive research investigator in work with behavior settings. He read most of the manuscript and provided many insightful and helpful suggestions at several points over the many months of work on this volume.

The suggestions of Urs Fuhrer and an unidentified reviewer instigated substantial improvements.

Phyllis Moen, my sociologist colleague in Human Development and Family Studies at Cornell, worked hard at educating me about the meaning of role and status in social science. If my treatment of these concepts herein is still flawed, the error is less serious than it would have been without her wise counsel.

My vast and immeasurable obligation is to my best friend, colleague, and wife of 44 years, Maxine (Dikkie) Schoggen, who contributed so much in so many ways to the completion of this work. Countless hours of intellectual discussion of many technical and theoretical issues drew upon her extensive experience in research with behavior settings. Yet no nitty-gritty task was too tedious for her careful, dedicated attention. Money cannot buy the kind of support that she has so generously given to this effort.

I acknowledge with gratitude also the support provided by the Department of Human Development and Family Studies, New York State College of Human Ecology, Cornell University. The understanding and encouragement of Henry Ricciuti, Department Chair, and Jerome Ziegler, Dean, are greatly appreciated.

The generosity of Jossey-Bass, Publishers, in allowing me to draw freely and extensively from Barker and Schoggen's *Qualities of Community Life* (1973) and Barker and Associates' *Habitats, Environments, and Human Behavior* (1978) for inclusion here is gratefully acknowledged.

Chapter 14 is reprinted from the *Journal of Personality and Social Psychology* with the permission of the American Psychological Association.

The Peanuts comic strips are reprinted with the permission of United Features Syndicate.

Stanford University Press Senior Editor Muriel Bell and Production Editor Julia Johnson Zafferano provided splendid editorial supervision that resulted in substantial improvements.

Phil Schoggen
Ithaca, New York
August 1988

Contents

Behavior Settings

1

Introduction

This book presents concepts and methods for studying the environments of human behavior at the molar—that is, goal-oriented or purposive—level. The term *environment* has a broad range of meanings both in everyday usage and in the social sciences (Moos, 1973; Gump, 1975a; Pervin, 1978). It is important, therefore, to state clearly at the beginning how the term is to be used in the present discussion. In this book, we are concerned with the ecological environment of molar human behavior; this is the objective, preperceptual context of behavior, including both social and physical components of the real-life, everyday settings within which people engage in goal-directed, purposive behavior. By "the objective, preperceptual context" we mean the observable environment that exists independent of the psychological processes of any particular individual. The drugstore in which Mrs. Smith has a prescription filled, the vacant lot where Billy digs holes and builds mounds for his toy tractor, the meeting of the school board where Mr. Jones questions the budget for next year, and the band concert where Mr. Willard goes to hear his son play cornet, are examples of the ecological environment at the level in which we are interested.

This definition of the ecological environment differs from the meaning of the term environment in popular usage. In the language of everyday discourse, newspapers, magazines, television, and politics, the term environment usually refers to climate, weather, downtown, the suburbs, traffic congestion, neighborhoods, industrial districts, lakes, rivers, skyscrapers, pollution, acid rain, and many other aspects of the natural and built surroundings. In those relatively rare instances in which behavior is included in such discussions of environment, the representation is usually quite general: for example, an adolescent may be said to have "gotten in with the wrong crowd," or a child may be described as subject to peer pressure.

This popular conception of the environment differs little from the way the term is used in some social science applications, where studies of the environment in relation to behavior are often concerned with the geographical or physical environment. One widely used book of readings in environmental psychology, for example, is entitled *Environmental Psychology: People and Their Physical Settings* (Proshansky, Ittelson, & Rivlin, 1976). It includes major sections on "The Natural Environment" and "The Built Environment." In the words of the editors, "environmental psychology is concerned with establishing empirical and theoretical relationships between behavior and experience and the physical environment" (p. 4). Featured are reports of research on many aspects of the physical and geographical environment in relation to behavior, such as urban playgrounds, housing and architecture, open classrooms, and environmental hazards. Such research has made important contributions to our understanding of environment-behavior relationships.

Another and clearly different conception of the environment is perhaps even more commonly adopted by other social scientists. In this view, the concern is with the environment as it is perceived by particular persons. This conception of the environment is represented in psychology, for example, by the psychological environment of Lewin (1936), the behavioral environment of Koffka (1935), and the beta environmental press of Murray (1938). It is the environment as it exists psychologically for a given person at a given time. It may correspond more or less closely to the objective properties of the physical or geographical environment as these might be agreed upon by disinterested observers. In sociology, this conception of the environment was articulated by W. I. Thomas in the well-known phrase, "If men define situations as real, they are real in their consequences" (Thomas & Thomas, 1928, p. 572). In current literature, this approach to the environment is seen, for example, in studies of environmental perception, cognitive mapping, privacy, territoriality, crowding, personal space, and environmental stressors. Research in this tradition has greatly improved our understanding of many important phenomena.

In contrast, the ecological environment with which we are concerned in this volume differs sharply from both of these conceptions of the environment as found in the literature of social science. The ecological environment shares with the first of these two conceptions a concern for the physical and geographical environment but, more than this, the ecological environment includes also the objectively observable *standing patterns of behavior* of people—that is, specific sequences of people's behavior that regularly occur within particular settings. For example, the standing patterns of behavior in a basketball game include the playing of the players, the watching and cheering of the spectators, the refereeing of the referees, and the recording and posting of the scores by the scorekeepers. For the occupants of a particular setting, the standing patterns of behavior that occur there are as real and as objective as the physical aspects of the setting. Behavior patterns occurring within a specific setting are as much a part of the environment of an individual in the setting as are the physical and temporal components of the setting. The music teacher's instruction and the singing of one's classmates are crucial components of the unit of the ecological environment known as the elementary school music class, just as important as the music room, the piano, and the metronome.

Yet the ecological environment is not equivalent to the psychological environment, which necessarily refers to the subjective representation of the objective environment by a given person at a particular time. In contrast, the ecological environment has a durable existence in the objective, preperceptual world independent of the psychological processes of any particular person. The music class, with its behavior patterns (teaching teacher, singing pupils) and its geographical-physical-temporal properties (music room, piano, metronome, third period of the school day), is in the readily observable, objective environment regardless of its psychological significance for any particular pupil.

Interest in presenting a systematic account of the methods and concepts for investigating the ecological environment stems from the conviction that the ecological environment is a more important phenomenon for the behavior sciences than it has been hitherto. When environments are relatively uniform and stable, *people* are an obvious source of behavior variance, and the dominant scientific problem and the persistent queries from the applied fields are: What are people like? What is the nature and what are the sources of individual differences? How can people be selected and sorted into the slots provided by bureaucracies, schools, businesses, factories, and armies? What are the needs and capacities of people to which highways, curricula, and laws must be adapted? These are the kinds of issues that dominate interest when environments are relatively stable.

Today, however, environments are more varied and unstable than heretofore, and their contribution to the variance of behavior is enhanced. Both science and society ask with greater urgency then previously: What are environments like? How does a person's habitat differ, for example, in developed and developing countries, in large and small schools, in glass-walled and windowless office buildings, in open and traditional class-

rooms, in automated and conventional offices? How do environments select and shape the people who inhabit them? What are the structural and
dynamic properties of the environments to which people must adapt?
These are questions about the ecological environment and its consequences for persons.

One might think that psychology would have become informed about
the fundamental nature of the ecological environment in the course of its
study of the context of behavior. But this is not the case. It is not the case
because psychology—whether physiological, social, or developmental—
has been concerned primarily with those elements of the environment
that are useful in probing intrapersonal processes (the behavior-relevant
circuitry within the skins of its subjects), such as those involved in studies
of tactual stimuli, conformity to group pressure, or attachment to the
mother. Psychology knows much about the physical properties of the environmental probes it uses for this purpose: of distal objects of perception,
for example, and of energy changes at receptor surfaces. But in accordance with the principles of experimental design, psychology has generally preferred to study elements of the environment under the controlled
conditions of the laboratory, in isolation from the complexities of the real-
life settings in which they occur—away from ball games, from symposia
meetings, from freeways, from music classes.

The result is, inevitably, that the science of psychology has had no adequate knowledge of the *psychologist-free* environment of behavior. The
view is not uncommon among psychologists that the naturally occurring
environment of behavior is a relatively unstructured, passive, probabilistic arena of objects and events within which a person behaves in accordance with the programming carried about as part of the person's internal psychological equipment (Brunswik, 1955; Leeper, 1963; Lewin,
1951). But abundant evidence from our own research and that of many
others indicates clearly that when we look at the environment of behavior
as a phenomenon worthy of investigation for itself, and not merely as an
instrument for unraveling the behavior-relevant programming within persons, the situation is quite different. From this viewpoint, the environment is seen to consist of *highly structured, improbable arrangements of
objects and events that coerce behavior in accordance with their own dynamic patterning.*

Observational records of children's behavior over long time periods
(several hours) in the ordinary settings of everyday life reveal that some
attributes of behavior vary less across different children within a given
setting than across different settings for any one child. It is possible to
predict some aspects of children's behavior more adequately from knowl-

edge of the standing patterns of behavior in the drugstores, music classes, and basketball games they inhabit than from knowledge of the behavior tendencies of particular children (Ashton, 1964; Barker & Gump, 1964; Gump, Schoggen, & Redl, 1963; Gump & Sutton-Smith, 1955; Raush, Dittmann, and Taylor, 1959, 1960; Schuster, Murrell & Cook, 1980). Similar findings are reported in studies of adults (Willems & Halstead, 1978). Such evidence provided the inspiration to look more closely at the real-life environments in which behavior occurs. The methodological and theoretical contributions described in this book represent the major yield from these efforts to understand the ecological environment in relation to molar human behavior.

2

The Ecological Environment

One obvious characteristic of human behavior is its variation. Every day of a person's life is marked by wide fluctuations in almost every discriminable attribute of behavior: in the intelligence exhibited, in the speed of movement, in the emotion expressed, in the goals pursued, and in the friendliness shown, energy expended, or anxiety experienced. Even geniuses think ordinary thoughts much of the time; they, too, have to count their change and decide what clothes to wear. Continuous records of the behavior of individual children show that the ever-changing aspect of the child's stream of behavior is one of its most striking features: trouble and well-being, quietude and activity, success and failure, dominance and submission, correct answers and wrong answers, interest and boredom occur in bewildering complexity (Barker & Wright, 1955). Laymen know of this dimension of human variation from their own experiences and observations; novelists, dramatists, and biographers have described it. But it is not prominent in scientific psychology.

Scientific psychology has been more concerned with another dimension of behavior variability, namely, with differences between individuals. It is one of the great achievements of psychology that in spite of the wide variation of every individual's behavior, methods have been devised for identifying and measuring individual behavior constants. An important part of scientific psychology is concerned with the great number of behavior constants that have been measured and the relations between them.

It is unfortunate that these accomplishments have not been accompanied by equal progress in studying naturally occurring, individual behavior variation. But there is an incompatibility here: to achieve stable behavior measurements, stable conditions must be reimposed each time the measurement is repeated. This method provides measures of individual constancies (under the designated conditions), but it eliminates from consideration individual variations (under different conditions), and it destroys the naturally occurring contexts of behavior.

The problem is not peculiar to psychology. The strength of a beam can be measured only under specified conditions, and under the same conditions each time the measurement is made. But a beam has many strengths depending especially on its structural context. A 2-by-4-inch board fitted into a structure is stronger, will support more weight, if it stands vertically than if it is horizontal. The same is true of the meaning of words. Words have a range of meanings, the precise one being determined by the context in which it occurs. A good dictionary gives a number of these meanings, the modal meanings, but for greatest precision it uses the word in revealing contexts. For example, *Webster's Ninth New Collegiate Dictionary* gives (in part) the following definitions and illustrations of the word "govern":

> 1 a: to exercise continuous sovereign authority over; *esp*: to control and direct the making and administration of policy in b: to rule without sovereign power . . . 2 a *archaic*: manipulate b: to control the speed of (as a machine) esp. by automatic means 3 a: to control, direct, or strongly influence the actions and conduct of b: to exert a determining or guiding influence in or over ⟨income must govern expenditure⟩ ⟨availability often governs choice⟩ c: to hold in check : restrain 4: to require (a word) to be in a certain case 5: to serve as a precedent or deciding principle for ⟨habits and customs that govern human decisions⟩. . . .

A person is like a beam or a word: a person has many strengths, many intelligences, many social maturities, many speeds, many degrees of liberality and conservativeness, and many moralities, depending in large part on the particular contexts of the person's behavior. For example, the same person who displays marked obtuseness when confronted with a mechanical problem may show impressive skill and adroitness in dealing with social situations.

The Inside-Outside Problem

The general sources of intra-individual behavior variation are clear. Individual behavior is connected in complicated ways with both the person's inside parts (such as neurons, muscles, hormones) and with the outside context (with the school class where the person is a pupil, the game in which the person is a player, the street on which the person is a pedestrian). The *psychological person* who writes essays, scores points, and crosses streets stands as an identifiable entity between unstable interior parts and exterior contexts; with each the person is both firmly linked and profoundly separated. The separation comes from the fact that the inside parts and the outside contexts of a person involve phenomena that function according to laws that are different from those that govern the person's behavior. Brain lesions, muscle contractions, and hormone concentration are not psychological phenomena. In the present state of our understanding, they involve laws that are utterly incommensurate with those of psychology. The same is true of the environment with which a person is coupled. The school class, the game, and the street all function according to laws that are alien to those that govern the person's behavior. This is the inside-outside problem that Allport (1955) has discussed. It has also drawn the attention of other scholars (Brunswik, 1943; Chein, 1954; Koffka, 1935; Heider, 1958; Lewin, 1951; and more recently, Fuhrer, 1986, in press). The outside context constitutes the *molar ecological environment*. It consists of those naturally occurring phenomena (1) outside the person's skin, (2) with which the person's molar actions are coupled, but (3) which function according to laws that are incommensurate with the laws that govern the person's molar behavior (Barker, 1960).

The ecological environment differs from the psychological environment (or Lewin's life-space) and from the stimulus, as the following discussion will make clear. The fact that behavior varies under the influence of the alien, incommensurate outside contexts of the psychological person places psychology in a serious dilemma. How is a unified science to encompass such diverse phenomena? Physics does not have to cope with psychological inputs to the systems with which it deals—nor does astronomy, nor does botany. How can psychology hope to cope with nonpsychological inputs? This is the core problem of ecological psychology and ecobehavioral science.

The Tautological Problem

In order to study environment-behavior relations on any level, the environment and the behavior must be described and measured independently; otherwise one becomes entangled in a tautological circle from which there is no escape. Thus, for example, three children who were each observed for an entire day were found to interact with 571, 671, and 749 different identifiable objects, respectively (persons, pets, things); the total numbers of interactions with these objects were 1,822, 2,282, and 2,490, respectively, and each of these interactions had a number of attributes (Schoggen, 1951; Barker & Wright, 1955). But these objects did not constitute the ecological environments of the children, because the behavior of the children provided the sole criteria for identifying the objects. When one uses a person's behavior as the only evidence of what constitutes the person's environment, one deals with psychological variables—that is, with life-space phenomena. The naturally occurring life-space deserves investigation, but it is not the ecological environment, and the latter cannot be discovered by using the person's behavior as the sole reference point. This is true not because it is impossible to see all the behavior that occurs, but because the ecological environment comprises a different class of phenomena and can only be identified and understood independently of the behavior with which it is linked.

This confronts us with the essence of the ecological environment in its relation to people. One can easily conceive of the problems of students of light perception if they had no physical description of light, or only a physical description of light at the precise point of contact with the receptor. To understand this point of intersection, it is essential to know the structure of light, for the point of intersection takes part of its characteristics from the total matrix of which it is a part, and this cannot be known from the point of contact (that is, from the stimulus) alone.

This is a general problem in science. When we are concerned with the outside context of any entity, whether a behaving person, a supporting beam, or a word in a sentence (a product of behavior), this context cannot be described in terms of the points of contact with the entity alone. The properties of the points depend on the structure of which they are parts. Take the word "brought" in the succeedingly more inclusive contexts in which it occurs (from Stevenson, 1882):

> brought
> were brought under
> provisions were brought under cover
> fresh provisions were brought under cover of darkness

The immediate points of contact between the word "brought" and its context are clearly insufficient to define this context; the properties of the contact points "were" and "under" depend on the total sentence. That is, "were" and "under" are not the context of the word "brought"; the whole sentence is the context. The contexts of all words in Stevenson's writings, and in all meaningful writings, occur in organized units that are larger than the preceding and succeeding connecting words. Fig. 2.1 is a physical example of this. The supporting beam (a,b) and its momentary context are shown in the succeeding diagrams. The instantaneous behavior of the

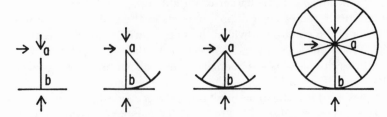

Fig. 2.1. A supporting beam (a, b) and its momentary context.

beam can be completely described in terms of the internal and external structural arrangements and forces existing for it at a particular instant without regard for what is outside of points a and b.

If more than an infinitely small time interval is involved, more is required: it is essential to know the structural and dynamic contexts of the intersection points a and b. The properties of contact point b, in this case, can be defined in terms of its position on the rim of a wheel of a certain diameter and motion, and the properties of point a by its position as the center of the wheel. Knowing, for example, that b is on the rim of a wheel moving forward at 50 miles an hour tells us immediately that there will be a cyclical change in the forward movement of b between zero and 100 miles an hour, with corresponding changes in the strength and direction of the forces and in the behavior of the beam.

This is true of the ecological environment of people, too. A person's momentary behavior is completely determined by his life-space, but if we wish to understand more than the immediate cross-section of the behavior stream, knowledge of the ecological environment is essential. For example, the apparently nonsocial behavior of Billy, a nursery school child, in going into the next room to obtain a particular toy may be seen as highly social through observation of the broader context—that is, the toy, which Billy knows to be a special favorite of Jimmy's, is given to Jimmy who is upset by an unhappy interchange with another child.

As another example, giving and receiving love between mother and child is an important variable in some theories of psychological development. From the developmental viewpoint, such an exchange takes part of its significance from the total context of the mother's and the child's life; for instance, an affectionate display by the mother may have very different significance to the child depending on whether it is a gesture of spontaneous devotion to the child or part of the separation process as mother leaves the child with a caretaker when she goes to her job. It is important to know the larger ecological situation within which the mother-child contact occurs because this is often, technically, the only way to understand what actually happens at the momentary intersection between the person and the ecological environment. But more important, knowledge of the ecological context is essential because development is not a momentary phenomenon (in fact, most behavior in which we are interested is not momentary), and the *course* of the life-space can only be known within the ecological environment in which it is embedded.

The Problem of Structure

Psychology has been predominantly an experimental science. The first psychologists were experimenters who worked in laboratories. Even social, developmental, clinical, and industrial psychologists have, in their research, usually worked as experimenters, arranging and varying the conditions of behavior in order to test hypotheses and hunches. The descriptive, natural history, ecological phase of investigation has had a minor place in psychology, and this has seriously limited the science. Experimental procedures have revealed something about the laws of behavior, but they have not disclosed, nor can they disclose, how the variables of these laws are distributed across the types and conditions of human beings. Experimental work has produced a host of "if . . . then" statements:

If a one-inch red cube is placed on a table before an eight-month-old infant, then the infant will attempt to grasp the cube (Halverson, 1943).

If a person is frustrated, then the person will exhibit aggressive and regressive behavior (Barker, Dembo, & Lewin, 1941; Dollard et al., 1939).

If four-year-olds are asked, "Why do we have houses?" then they will give answers of the following kinds: "To go in," "'Cause it won't rain on us," "To cook in," "To stay in," "To go in and sleep," "To play in," "Because we want to sit down," "To play with them," "This is a house," "In houses we have stoves and we have carpets, too, and we have tinkertoys and we have lots of things, too" (Terman & Merrill, 1962, p. 137).

Psychology knows how people behave under the conditions of experiments, interviews, and clinical procedures, but it knows little about the distribution of these and other conditions, and of their behavior resultants, outside of laboratories, interview situations, and clinics. This historical preoccupation of scientific psychology with experimental methods has contributed to a general neglect of the problem of identifying and describing the naturally occurring structure of the ecological environment.

Indeed, the assumption is not uncommon in scientific psychology that the ecological environment is without structure of its own, that the only structure of concern to us is that imposed upon the ecological environment by the selective and organizing powers of people, which, according to Leeper (1963, pp. 387–88), "yield relatively stable effects out of the kaleidoscopically changing stimulation they receive."

Yet the most primitive, simple, and obvious thing we know about the naturally occurring, ecological environment is that it *does* have structure; it has parts with stable relations between them. One important task is to describe this structure. It is clear that structure cannot be discovered by observing a single part, such as the point of intersection of the environment with a particular person, or by considering the parts separately, one by one, as is commonly done in psychological experiments. For example, a complete description of a single player's behavior in a ball game or the complete statistics of all the plays occurring in the game do not reveal the game of baseball. It is the rules of the game, the arrangement of things, and the behavior of the other players according to the rules, that constitute the essential, unitary, ecological environment of the player; it is these that largely shape the life-space of each player. By dealing with such contexts in terms of their discriminable parts, and by processing them according to probability statistics as in traditional psychological research, we preclude the possibility of discovering the natural structure of the ecological environment. This traditional approach has the value of a filing system, or of a concordance, but we cannot understand a book from its concordance. By these methods, the structure of the context is dismantled and rearranged; the structure is destroyed.

This does not mean, of course, that such investigations are without value. Important information about one level of a functioning system can be obtained when the system is dismantled. All sciences have structure-destroying methods and make valuable use of them. Essential components of the brain can be determined by excising and macerating brain tissue and analyzing it by physical and chemical techniques, even though this ignores or destroys the brain's macrostructure. But most sciences also have special, relatively nondestructive techniques for studying the structure of phenomena. Infrared and temperature-sensitive photography, X-ray analysis, and electrical, magnetic, and resonance techniques are instances. A primary concern of geologists, oceanographers, cytologists, mineralogists, geneticists, and astronomers is precisely with the naturally occurring, unrearranged structure of things: from chromosomes to the solar system and beyond. So it is important for psychology to discover tender-minded, nondestructive techniques for keeping intact naturally occurring behavior and its ecological environment. Based on ecological methodologies found in the biological sciences and translated into terms of behavior phenomena, here are some guidelines for this discovery:

The behavior with which one is concerned must be identified. There are many levels of behavior, each of which has a special environmental context. In the present case we are interested in molar behavior, in the behavior of persons as undivided entities; we are not interested in the behavior of eyelids or glands.

The problem of identifying and describing the ecological environment of behavior is an empirical one. It is necessary to observe and describe the environment on its own terms in order to develop theories that later can guide further empirical investigations.

The identification of the ecological environment is aided by the fact that, unlike the life-space (Lewin's psychological environment), it has an objective reality "out there"; it has observable geographical, physical, and temporal attributes.

Because the geographical-physical-temporal world is not homogeneous but exists in natural parts with definite boundaries, the ecological environment also necessarily occurs in bounded units. Arbitrarily defined physical-temporal units will not, except by chance, constitute an environmental unit. Furthermore, the boundaries and characteristics of the ecological environment cannot be determined by observing only the behavior of the persons within it.

The individual persons within a bounded unit of the ecological environment differ from one another in psychological attributes (needs, goals, perceptions); their behavior in the same environment will, therefore, display some individual differences.

However, because people en masse can be expected to have common attributes, and because the inhabitants of the same ecological unit are subject to inputs and forces characteristic of that particular ecological unit, its inhabitants will exhibit a stable overall extra-individual pattern of behavior; likewise, the inhabitants of different ecological units (each with its own characteristic inputs and forces) will exhibit different overall extra-individual patterns of behavior.

The ecological environment of a person's molar behavior, the molar environment, consists of bounded, geographical-physical-temporal locales and varigated but stable patterns in the behavior of people en masse. These characteristics of the ecological environment and behavior are familiar to laymen. The dictionary defines common ecological units in terms of both their physical-temporal and their extra-individual behavior coordinates. Thus,

> road: a track (physical attribute) for travel or for conveying goods (extra-individual pattern of behavior);
> store: any place where goods (physical attribute) are kept for sale (extra-individual pattern of behavior);
> park: a piece of ground (physical attribute) kept for ornament or recreation (extra-individual pattern of behavior).

An analysis of all descriptions of behavior occurring in one newspaper revealed that about 50 percent of the reports were in terms of ecological units, including their extra-individual behavior patterns (Barker & Wright, 1955); for example, "Ellson Drugstore will hold a sale on Friday and Saturday," "The Midwest High School commencement was held last Tuesday." Such physical-behavioral units are common phenomenal entities, and they are *natural units in no way imposed or created by an investigator.* To laymen they are as objective as rivers and forests, and they can be defined by denotation; they involve, in the beginning, no theories or hypothetical concepts; they are parts of the objective environment that are experienced as directly as rain and sandy beaches are experienced.

Ecological Units

An initial practical problem of ecological research is to identify the natural units of the phenomena studied. The essential nature of the units with which ecology deals is the same whether they are physical, social, biological, or behavioral units: (1) they occur without feedback from the investigator, they are self-generated; (2) each unit has a time-space locus; and (3) an unbroken boundary separates an internal pattern from a differing external pattern. By these criteria, an electron, a person, and a waterfall are ecological units. This is true also of most towns and cities, and within a city it is true of a particular school, of the geometry lesson within the school, and of student Susan Green raising her hand to ask to recite. In contrast, a square mile in the center of a city is not an ecological unit by the criteria given; its boundary is not self-generated. Nor are the Republican voters of the city, the members of the middle-class, the women, or the school system ecological units; they have no continuously bounded time-space locus.

Many ecological units occur in circumjacent-included series, or assemblies. A chick embryo, for example, is a nesting set of organs, cells, nuclei, molecules, atoms, and subatomic particles. In these assemblies the number of included levels is sharply restricted (in the 14-day chick embryo, for example, there are nine or ten levels of units); at each level the number of discriminable varieties of units is also limited (at the level of organs in the chick embryo there are about 40 varieties of units, such as the heart and lungs); and within each variety there are differing numbers of individual units (within the organ variety *heart* there is a single unit; within the organ variety *lungs* there are two units). Within this arrangement, each circumjacent assembly (such as the heart) is reciprocally linked with the included units (the different ventricles of the heart) of which it is composed. This is clearly exemplified by the relation between words, punctuation marks, and sentences: words and punctuation marks form sentences from which, in turn, the words and punctuation marks derive their precise meanings.

This raises the theoretical problem, introduced above, of accounting within a single explanatory theory for the reciprocal relations between different levels of phenomena. How, for example, can we account for the fact that a gas molecule behaves according to the laws of molecular motion and *at the same time* according to the entirely different laws of the jet of gas of which it is a part? How can the explanations of the movement of a train of wheat across the Kansas plains by an economist (a scientist of circumjacent assemblies—farms, grain markets, financial institutions) and by an engineer (a scientist of interjacent units—cylinders, pistons, fuel) ever be incorporated into a single theory? Both the laws of economics and the laws of engineering are true; both operate in predictable ways on the train, but they are as utterly incommensurate as the price of wheat in Chicago and the horsepower of the engine. In behavior science, analogously, how can we ever subsume the laws of individual motivation and the principles of institutional and organizational operation within one system of concepts?

The difficulty in all of these cases resides in the fact that the "laws" that govern individual units are different from those applicable to the compound, circumjacent series or assemblies of units; yet units and unit assemblies are closely coupled. Ecological psychology is concerned with molar behavior and the ecological contexts in which it occurs. The problem can be illustrated by an example.

Anne Matson was 10 years and 11 months of age and in the sixth grade of the Midwest public school. It was 2:09 P.M. and time for the daily music lessons with Miss Madison. The first three minutes of the record, made at the time (March 8, 1951), reported Anne's behavior as follows (Barker et al., 1961):

Mrs. Nelson said in a businesslike manner, "All right, the class will pass."

Anne picked up her music book from her desk.

She stood.

Anne motioned urgently to her row, indicating that they should follow her around the front of the room.

The class filed out, carrying their music books.

Anne walked quickly to the music room; she was near the end of the single-file line.

2:10. The children seated themselves in a semicircle across the front of the music room.

Anne sat with Opal Bennett directly on her right and Rex Graw on her left. Alvin Stone was one seat over from Rex.

Miss Madison said briskly, "All right, let's open our books to page 27."

Anne watched Miss Madison solemnly.

Anne licked her finger.

She turned to the correct page.

Miss Madison asked the class, "How would you conduct this song?"

Immediately Anne raised her hand urgently, eager to be called on.

2:11. Miss Madison called on Ellen Thomas to show how she would conduct this song.

Ellen waved her right arm in three-four rhythm.

Miss Madison watched Ellen critically.

With her hand still partway in the air, Anne watched earnestly.

Someone in the class objected that Ellen's beat wasn't quite right.

Persistently, Anne put her hand up higher, wishing to be called on.

Miss Madison called on Stella Townsend.

Anne put her hand down with disappointment showing in her facial expression.

Intently she watched Stella demonstrate the pattern for conducting the song.

Miss Madison called on Opal Bennett.

Anne didn't raise her hand.

(*There was really no opportunity for hand-raising.*)

She turned to her right.

With interest she watched Opal demonstrate the way to lead the song.

Miss Madison demonstrated how three-four time should be led.

Anne watched with an interested expression.

2:12. She started to practice, moving her arms in the demonstrated pattern.

Some of the other children also started practicing.

Miss Madison said pedagogically, "All right, let's all do it together."

She stood sideways in a businesslike way so that the children could see her hands.

She led the children as they all practiced conducting three-four time.

Anne let her fingers hang loosely in a consciously graceful manner.

With restraint and enjoyment she moved her arm up, down, and across in the correct pattern.

2:13. Miss Madison said, "Now we want one person to get up in front of the class and conduct."

Anne immediately raised her hand very eagerly straight up into the air.

On her face was a look of expectancy.

She held her hand in the air until Miss Madison called on Ellen Thomas.

This excerpt illustrates the kinds of dependent variables with which we are concerned, namely, a child's molar actions: for example, watching teacher demonstrate three-four time, practicing three-four time, raising hand to be called on, looking at Opal. For ecological psychology, the question becomes: What are the ecological contexts of such behavior?

There are an infinite number of discriminable phenomena external to any individual's behavior. In the case of Anne Matson during the music class there were, for example, her neighbors Opal and Rex, the music book, the song on page 27, the piano, the fifth and sixth grade classroom across the hall, the entire elementary school, the cool overcast day, the town of Midwest, the country of the United States, Anne's hand, the windows of the room, Andrea French sitting five seats away, Ellen's smile, and so on without limit. With which of these innumerable exterior phenomena was Anne's behavior linked? And were these phenomena related only via their links with Anne, or did they have a stable independent structure; were they an ecological assembly of units independent of Anne and her behavior? These are the central questions of ecological psychology.

How does one identify and describe the environment of behavior? Students of perception have been centrally concerned with this problem, and they have had some success in dealing with it. When perception psychologists have turned from the nature of perception to the *preperceptual* nature of light and sound, they have discovered something very important about the ecological environment of vision and hearing: it is not random; it involves bounded manifolds of individual elements with varied and unusual patterns. The environment of vision and hearing has a structure that is independent of its connections with perceptual mechanisms. All science reveals that nature is not uniform; the environments of atoms and molecules, of cells and organs, of trees and forests are patterned and structured, and this greatly facilitates the identification and analysis of these environments.

It would appear that students of molar behavior might profitably emulate this approach by students of perception and consider the ecological environment of the behavior with which they are concerned entirely aside from its connection with behavior. This requires, in fact, a new science that stands with respect to molar behavior as the physics of light and sound stand with respect to vision and hearing. An analogy may help to make the problem clear.

If a novice from England wished to understand the environment of a first baseman in a game of American baseball, the visitor might set about to observe the interactions of the player with his surroundings. To do this with utmost precision, the novice might view the first baseman through field glasses, so focused that the player would be centered in the field of the glasses with just enough of the environment included to encompass all the player's contacts with the environment, all inputs and outputs: all balls caught, balls thrown, players tagged, etc. Despite the commendable observational care, however, this method would never provide the novice with an understanding of "the game" that gives meaning to a first baseman's transactions with his surroundings and that, in fact, constitutes the environment of his baseball-playing behavior. By observing a player in this way, the novice would, in fact, fragment the game and destroy the very phenomenon of interest. So, also, might observations and interviews be used to construct the player's life-space during the game: his achievements, aspirations, successes, failures, and conflicts; his judgments of the speed of the ball, of the fairness of the umpire, and of the errors of his teammates. But this would only substitute for the former fragmented picture of "the game" the psychological consequences of the fragments, and thus remove the novice even further from the goal of understanding the ecological environment. Finally, the novice might perform innumerable correlations between the first baseman's achievements (balls caught, etc.) and particular attributes of the ecological environment involved (speed of balls thrown to him, distance of throw, weight of bat, curve of balls, etc.). But an understanding of the phenomenon known as a baseball game could never be achieved by this means. It would seem clear that a novice would learn more about the ecological environment of a first baseman by blotting out the player and observing the game around him. This would be analogous to what the student of light and sound does with elaborate instrumentation, and it is the approach taken in ecological psychology. This is reflected even in the title of one early paper, referring to ecological psychology as "the psychology of the absent organism" (Barker, 1962). But it is only the particular individual person that is left out, not the standing patterns of behavior characteristic of that setting. In ecological psychology, attention shifts from concern with the individual person's molar behavior to the immediate *context* of that behavior, and that context clearly includes the patterns of molar behavior of people in general.

It is not easy, at first, to leave the person out of observations of the environment of molar behavior. Our perceptual apparatus is adjusted by our long training with the person-centered viewing glasses of observations, interviews, and questionnaires to see *individuals* whenever we see behavior. But with some effort and experience the extra-individual assemblies of behavior episodes, behavior objects, and place that surround persons can be observed and described. Their nonrandom distribution and bounded character are crucial aids. To illustrate, consider ordinary school classes. As an environmental unit, as a unit of the ecological environment of molar behavior, a fifth-grade academic subjects class has the following readily apparent characteristics:

It is a natural phenomenon; it is not created by an experimenter for scientific purposes.

It has a specific, denotable space-time locus.

A boundary surrounds the class.

The boundary is self-generated (not imposed by the research investigator); it changes as the class changes in size and in the nature of its activity.

The class is objective in the sense that it exists independent of any particular person's perception of it, qua class; it is a preperceptual ecological entity.

It has two sets of components: people displaying behavior patterns (such as reciting, discussing, writing, sitting); and physical objects with which behavior is transacted (such as chairs, desks, chalkboards, paper, pencils, books).

The unit, the class, is circumjacent to its components; the class surrounds or encloses the behavior patterns and the objects; the pupils are *in* the class.

The behavior patterns and physical objects that constitute the unit fifth-grade academic subjects class are internally organized and arranged to form a configuration that is by no means random.

The configuration of behavior patterns and physical objects within the boundary of the class is easily discriminated from that outside the boundary.

There is a synomorphic relation—that is, a similarity in structure, form, or shape—between the behavior patterns occurring within the class and the characteristics and arrangement of the physical objects. The desks and chairs are shaped to fit sitting and writing behavior; the seats face the teacher's desk, and the children face the teacher.

The unity of the class is not due to the similarity of its parts at any moment; for example, speaking occurs in one part and listening in another. The unity is based, rather, on the interdependence of the parts; events in different parts of the class have a greater effect on each other than equivalent events beyond its boundary.

The people who inhabit the class are to a considerable degree inter-changeable and replaceable. Pupils come and go; even the teacher may be replaced. But the class as an entity with its different components continues as serenely as an old car with new piston rings and the right front wheel now carried as the spare.

The behavior patterns of this entity cannot, however, be greatly changed without destroying it: there must be teaching, there must be study, there must be verbal interaction.

A pupil has two positions in the class: first, the person is a component of the supra-individual unit (the class), and second, the person is an in-dividual with psychological needs and personal goals whose life-space is partly formed within the constraints imposed by the very entity of which the person is a part.

Such entities are readily recognizable; they are common phenomena of everyday life. We have called them behavior settings (frequently short-ened to settings). Studies of behavior settings provide evidence that they are stable, extra-individual units with great coercive power over the be-havior that occurs within them (Ashton, 1964; Barker, 1960; Barker & As-sociates, 1978; Barker & Gump, 1964; Barker & Schoggen, 1973; Barker & Wright, 1955; Gump, Schoggen, & Redl, 1957, 1963; Gump & Sutton-Smith, 1955; Jordan, 1963; Ragle, Johnson, & Barker, 1967; Raush, Dittman, & Taylor, 1959, 1960; Schoggen & Barker, 1974, 1977; Schuster, Murrell, & Cook, 1980; Soskin & John, 1963; Wicker, 1967, 1968, 1969a; Wicker & Kirmeyer, 1976, 1977; Willems, 1967; Willems & Halstead, 1978; see also Chaps. 10 and 11 below).

There are other sources of information about behavior settings, for they are ubiquitous phenomena of everyday life; they are frequently portrayed in nonscientific writings, pictorial displays, and photographs. Drawing on such sources, we next present some illustrations of behavior settings in more complete detail.

Examples of Behavior Settings

Here are three items of information found in the December 12, 1963, issue of the *Midwest Weekly*, the local paper in the small Kansas town that we have studied:

Midwest County Barracks and Auxiliary, Veterans of WWI, met Nov. 21 in the Legion Hall in Midwest. Fifty-eight members were there to enjoy Thanksgiving festivities. Officers elected will be installed next month. Owing to our regular meeting date being too close to Christmas, we will meet Dec. 19 at 6:30 in the Legion Hall at Midwest. The ladies auxiliary will serve two turkeys. You bring the trimmings and a 25 cent gift and we will have a Merry Christmas party.

On Saturday, Dec. 7, seventeen MHS Latin students and Miss Hoffer attended the Foreign Language Christmas Festival at Ellton State College. They began the day by registering in Albert Taylor Hall, the main building. They practiced Christmas carols in Latin, saw a motion picture in Latin, and listened to tapes of "Interviews on Mt. Olympus." They attended the Festival in the afternoon and sang their carols along with students of other languages. The program closed with the breaking of the pinata.

Watches—Diamonds
EXPERT REPAIR
Ruttley's Jewelry
Midwest, Kansas

These are glimpses of three behavior settings that occurred in Midwest during the year 1963–64, namely, American Legion World War I Barracks and Auxiliary Meeting and Dinner, High School Latin Class Trip to Convention at state college, and Ruttley's Jewelry and Watch Repair Shop. This issue of the *Midwest Weekly* was in no way unusual; it described the week in Midwest in terms of 106 behavior settings similar to the three above. In 79 of the 106 behavior setting reports, one or more individuals were identified as participants (usually as performers or leaders), as in the second and third items above; the other 27 reports describe standing patterns of settings, or fragments of them, without identifying any inhabitant, as in the first news item. In addition to the 106 items about behavior settings within the town, there were 2 reports of behavior in unspecified settings, 11 reports of out-of-town activities in the behavior settings of other communities, 26 reports of activities within behavior settings of private homes in town, and 14 reports of visits of residents to homes outside of Midwest.

The *Midwest Weekly* exemplifies the importance of behavior settings in the everyday lives of Midwest residents; settings are, in fact, their most common means of describing the town's behavior and environment. The hybrid, eco-behavioral character of behavior settings appears to present Midwest's inhabitants with no difficulty; nouns that combine milieu and standing behavior pattern are common: for example, oyster supper, basketball game, church dinner, golden gavel ceremony, car wash, gift exchange, livestock auction, and auto repair.

Next we present more detailed descriptions of two other behavior settings from the Midwest study, Basketball Game and Household Auction Sale. In each case, three different views of the setting are included: a brief summary of the essential elements of the program; a photograph; and a news report or public announcement.

BASKETBALL GAME

(1) *Rules for High School Boys Basketball Game—program for the players and officials* (adapted from *The New Book of Knowledge* and *Encyclopedia Americana*, both Danbury, Conn.: Grolier, 1984). Two teams of five players each compete for scores by putting the ball through the baskets at opposite ends of the court. On each team, the *center* and two *forwards* are referred to as front-court players and two *guards* as back-court players. Each team has a *coach*, who sits on the bench with the substitutes and directs play.

A *basket* or *field goal* counts two or three points. A *free throw* is worth one point. Both are made by throwing the ball into the hoop (basket) from above: for a two-point basket, from the floor *within* the three-point line against the efforts of defenders; for a three-point basket, from the floor *outside* the three-point line against defenders; and for a free throw, from the free-throw line without interference.

A basketball is spherical, 30 inches in circumference (diameter about 9.5 inches), and weighs from 20 to 22 ounces. Its cover may be of leather or of comparable synthetic material and is inflated with air.

The dimensions of the *court* are 84 feet long and 50 feet wide. At the midpoint of each end of the court, a *basket* is suspended so that its rim is 10 feet above the floor level and about 4 feet in from a point above the end line of the court called the *base line*.

The basket itself is a metal ring, called the *hoop*, 18 inches in diameter, with its plane parallel to the floor. It is attached to a *backboard*, a surface of glass or wood hung perpendicular to the floor. The backboard is usually rectangular, six feet wide and four feet high, but a smaller fan-shaped board may be used instead. Suspended from the hoop is a funnel-shaped net of cord to slow down the ball as it passes through the basket, making its passage more visible.

The playing area is divided in half by a centerline midway between the baskets. At the middle of this line is a circle where the *center jump* takes place at the start of the game and at certain other times.

The most important floor markings are in front of each basket. Parallel to the backboard and 15 feet from it is the *free-throw line*, from which a player makes his free throws after he has been fouled. From the ends of the foul line to the base line run two lines that form the *free-throw lane* 12 feet wide. The inside of this foul lane area is a restricted zone. No offensive player may remain in it for longer than three seconds; players must keep moving through this zone and must make their *shots* at the basket and *passes* to teammates while on the run.

The team that scores more points in regulation time wins the game. Teams play for 32 minutes, divided into eight-minute quarters. One-minute rest periods occur at the end of the first and third quarters with ten minutes between halves. If the score is tied when the regulation time ends, *overtime periods*, of three-minute duration, are played until a decision is reached.

Two officials equipped with whistles, the *referee* and the *umpire*, control play. Both move all around the court, calling infractions, putting the ball in play, ruling on the legality of the scoring, and enforcing discipline. An *official scorekeeper* and a *timer* sit at a table alongside the court.

A player may not run with the ball in his possession. He may pass the ball to a teammate, shoot it at the basket, or move it around the court himself by using the *dribble*, that is, bouncing the ball continuously with only one hand while running, walking, or standing. Once a player stops dribbling, he may not start again; he must pass the ball or shoot it. If he breaks this rule, he is called for a *traveling* violation. Infractions that do not involve physical contact, such as traveling, remaining too long in the three-second zone, delaying the game, or entering the court illegally, are called *technical fouls* and are punished by awarding possession of the ball to the other team.

Infractions that involve physical contact are termed *personal fouls*. No physical contact is allowed as a deliberate means of defense. The defender may not push, pull, trip, tackle, or in any other physical manner interfere with his opponent; in return, offensive players may not use body blocks or similar maneuvers to aid their teammates. A player who is fouled is awarded one or two free throws, depending on the seriousness of the infraction. The player who committed the infraction is charged with a personal foul. When a player has been charged with five fouls, he must leave the game permanently.

When the ball goes out of bounds, possession of it is considered lost by the team that last touched it in bounds and the ball is awarded to the other team. When there is a *held ball* (that is, when players from opposing teams are each firmly holding it), a *jump ball* is required. The referee tosses the ball straight up between two opposing players who try to tap it to a teammate and are forbidden to catch it or to interfere with each other.

When a score is made, the team scored upon puts the ball in play from out-of-bounds under the basket in which the points were scored. This ap-

Fig. 2.2. High School Boys Basketball Game

plies to free throws as well as to baskets. The offensive team has ten seconds in which to move the ball beyond the court centerline. This rule prevents an offensive team from *stalling*. When a shot at the basket fails to go in, the *rebound* is in play and may be recovered by either team.

The game begins with a *center jump*—a jump ball held in the center circle. The team that gains possession works for a basket until it either makes one, is fouled, or loses the ball out of bounds, on a violation, or by having it stolen by an opponent. Then the other team follows the same procedure. Time is "out" during all free throws or when there is any abnormal delay caused, for example, by an injury or by retrieving a ball from out-of-bounds. Teams may call a limited number of *time outs* during a game for strategic reasons or to rest.

(2) *Photograph of Basketball Game.* The photograph is a 0.004-second record of one occurrence of the Midwest behavior setting High School Boys Basketball Game. In spite of its extreme brevity (0.0000015 of the total time of an occurrence), a number of the behavior setting attributes described above are revealed. (See picture, p. 24.)

(a) The picture demonstrates that this behavior setting is an objective, preperceptual phenomenon; it is photographable. It indicates that, on a continuum from empirical objects to abstract concepts, High School Boys Basketball Game falls toward the object end of the scale.

(b) The two kinds of behavior setting components can be seen: people and milieu (physical, geographical) objects such as balls, goals, and bleachers.

(c) Parts of the boundary of the setting are pictured (walls, doors).

(d) The ordered and organized nature of this setting's standing patterns of behavior (playing, refereeing, cheerleading, sitting, watching) and milieu are shown; it is unlikely indeed that the components of the setting would by chance fall into the pattern recorded by the photograph.

(e) The synomorphic relation between the standing behavior patterns and the structure or arrangement of milieu parts is displayed; for example, the sitting behavior fits the bleachers, the spectators face the court, and the players face the ball.

(f) The circumjacency of the milieu of the game (walls, doors) to the standing patterns of behavior is shown; the players, officials, cheerleaders, and spectators are *within* the milieu.

(g) The picture shows that the parts of this behavior setting are not uniform and iterative but multiform and nonrepetitive; different inhabitants of the setting engaging in different kinds of behavior—for example, players playing, referee refereeing, cheerleaders leading a cheer, and spectators watching—are recorded.

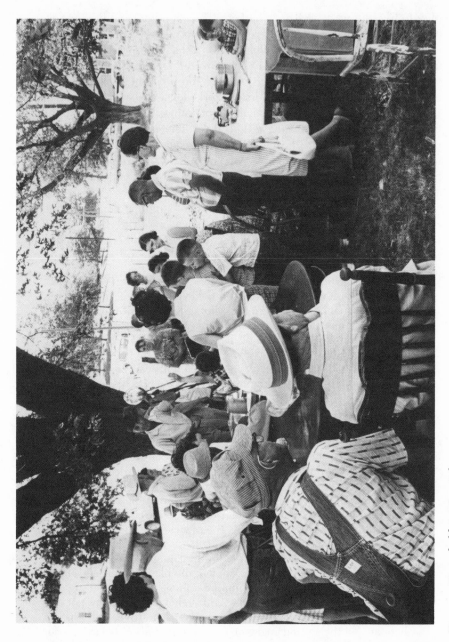

Fig. 2.3. Household Auction Sale

(h) The interchangeability of parts of the setting is suggested; substitute players are on the bench.

(i) Differences in amount of power over the setting held by different inhabitants can be inferred from the picture: coaches, players, officials, referees, and spectators occupy very different power positions.

(3) *News Report of Basketball Game from the Midwest High School Cub Reporter*

Bears Stun Patton

The slow, control Midwest team of last year turned run and gun, and showed promise for a good year with a stunning upset over the Kaws of Patton, 66–64.

The "stars" were abandoned for the first game, but Ken Kelcey and Ron Barton were the most formidable. Ken, whose great uncle was a kangaroo, poured in 24 points on his patented turnabout-explosion shot. He kept Midwest in reach at the first of the game as the Bears had a bad case of the jitters.

Patton took an early lead but couldn't hold the pace against the Bears' full court press and pressure offense. The Bears went to the lockers at half time down one point.

The fans were not downhearted and gave the Bears tremendous support.

In the second half the Bears turned it on and took a 10-point lead. About this time the reserves made their debut. Jim Auburn, who made three fouls in the first quarter, fouled out. Vern Day came in and made his presence known; Allen Bertram and Vern got nine points between them to keep the Bears in the lead. Coach substituted freely during this time as Ron Barton had four fouls and the Bears were weakening.

It looked as if Midwest was out of it when they were down four points with less than two minutes to play. The Bears put the pressure on and tied it when Ron Barton was fouled from behind with three seconds left. The 5'3" senior coolly stepped to the line and hit both tosses of a 1 and 1 to assure the Bears of the victory.

Frank Nading, who likes to rest his elbows on opponents' noses, was instrumental in the win. He and Ken rebounded with the taller Patton foes.

The game was a classic affair, and it pointed out the strength in Midwest this year.

AUCTION SALE

(1) *Program for Household Auction Sale.* Samuel Baker, founder in 1744 of the London auction house of Messrs. Sotheby and Company, drew up a set of five conditions for sale, four of which constitute the es-

sential elements of auction sale programs in Midwest. (Baker started as a bookseller; hence the reference to books [Brough, 1963].) They are as follows:

(a) That he who Bids most is the Buyer, but if any Dispute arises, the Book or Books to be put to Sale again.
(b) That no Person advances less than Sixpence each bidding, and after the Book arises to One Pound, no less than One Shilling. [The principle that the advance in bidding is in proportion to the amount bid applies in Midwest.]
(c) The Books are in most elegant Condition, and supposed to be Perfect, but if any appear otherwise before taken away, the Buyer is at his Choice to take or leave them. [The buyer in Midwest has two minutes to examine an article; if it is not as represented by the auctioneer it may be returned.]
(d) The Books must be taken away at the Buyer's Expence, and the Money paid at the Place of Sale, within Three Days after each sale is ended. [Articles must be paid for on the day of the sale in Midwest.]

(2) *Photograph of Auction Sale.* The photograph is a record of the Midwest behavior setting Household Auction Sale. (See picture, p. 26.) It exhibits most of the behavior setting characteristics shown in the photograph of High School Boys Basketball Game. Differences between these behavior settings as revealed in the photographs are:

(a) The physical-geographical boundary of Auction Sale is less definite than the boundary of Basketball Game; it is not marked by a physical structure as it is in the latter setting. However, a definite boundary zone can be seen within which the standing pattern of Auction Sale changes to the different patterns of the adjacent settings (such as Trafficways and nonpublic, family behavior settings).
(b) The shape of the standing pattern of Auction Sale is very different from that of Basketball Game; it resembles the pattern of iron filings in a magnetic field, whereas the pattern of the game reminds one of a cell with partitioned, internal subparts.
(c) The synomorphy of the milieu and behavior is evident in both pictures, but the synomorphy of the auction is in the nature of behaving inhabitants infiltrating the milieu, whereas that of the game appears to involve tensions between salient milieu parts (for example, the playing court) and inhabitants (spectators) that separate but position inhabitants vis-à-vis the milieu.
(d) According to the pictures, the pattern of Auction Sale is more uniform and repetitive than that of Basketball Game; less variety is evident in the behavior of the auction inhabitants than in the behavior of the game inhabitants.

PUBLIC SALE

At the John English home on north corner of Warren and Chero-
kee St. One block north and one block west of the Baptist Church
in Midwest, Kansas.

SATURDAY, JUNE 25

STARTING AT 2:00 O'CLOCK P.M.

Electric Cook Stove	2—Stand Tables
Refrigerator	Bookcase
	Small stand
China closet	2—Dressers
Buffet	Chest of drawers
Round dining table	3—Iron beds, springs & matt-
2—Gas heating stoves	resses
Ironing board	Floor Lamp
Divan	Maytag Washing Machine
2—Rocking Chairs	Few dishes and misc. items.

JOHN ENGLISH

Terms: Cash   Not responsible for accidents
Jack Mund, Auctioneer   Darlene Romney, Clerk

(3) *Public Notice of Auction Sale.* (See above.)

These descriptions of Basketball Game and Auction Sale illustrate units
of the ecological environment of human molar behavior as discovered in
our research in Midwest in the mid-1960's. In the next chapter, we turn
from this general discussion and illustration of behavior settings to the
presentation and explication of the defining properties of behavior
settings.

3
The Defining Properties of Behavior Settings

A behavior setting is defined in terms of two kinds of properties: structural and dynamic. On the structural side, a behavior setting consists of one or more *standing patterns of behavior-and-milieu*, with the milieu circumjacent and synomorphic to the behavior. On the dynamic side, the behavior-milieu parts of a behavior setting—that is, the synomorphs that comprise the setting—have a *specified degree of interdependence among themselves* that is greater than their interdependence with parts of other behavior settings. These are the essential properties of a behavior setting; the crucial terms will now be defined, elaborated, and illustrated.

(1) Standing patterns of behavior. A behavior setting consists of at least one but usually several integrated standing patterns of behavior. In the literature of the behavioral and social sciences, many different kinds of behavior units have been identified and used for various purposes in work at different levels: reflex, actone, molar unit, group activity, custom, and role are examples. A standing pattern of behavior is another behavior unit. It is a *bounded pattern in the behavior of persons, en masse.* In a high school basketball game, for example, several standing patterns of behavior—such as the game playing of the team members, the refereeing of the officials, the time-keeping of the time-keepers, the leading of the crowd in cheers by the cheerleaders, and the sitting, standing, and cheering of the spectators—together with other standing patterns make up the integrated complex of behavior patterns that identify the setting. Analogously, a church worship service displays a number of constituent standing patterns in the behavior of its inhabitants; the preaching of the pastor, the sitting, listening, standing, and hymn singing of members of the congregation, the anthem singing of the choir, the collecting of the offering by

ushers, and the music playing of the organist, all illustrate standing behavior patterns that make up the behavior setting. Although fewer people
are involved, a piano lesson consists of analogous patterns in the behavior
of its participants.

A standing pattern of behavior is not a common behavior element
among disparate behavior elements, such as the twang in Midwestern
speech or the custom in small American towns of greeting others, including strangers, when they are encountered on the street. A standing pattern of behavior is a discrete behavior entity with specific temporal-spatial
coordinates; a basketball game, a worship service, or a piano lesson has, in
each case, a precise and delimited position (location) in time and space.
Furthermore, a standing pattern of behavior is not a characteristic of the
particular individuals involved; it is an *extra-individual* behavior phenomenon; it has unique and stable characteristics that persist even when
current inhabitants of the setting are replaced by others. For example,
when a given year's seniors on the basketball team graduate, other players
take their places in the setting High School Boys Basketball Game, but
the standing pattern of basketball playing behavior remains intact.

As we will see in Chap. 13, standing patterns of behavior as behavior
units have much in common with the concept of role as used in sociology;
the chief difference is that a role defines a position a person occupies
within the social structure of society, whereas a standing pattern of behavior is defined as part of a particular environmental entity, a behavior setting, with a specific locus in time and space. A role does not have such a
temporal-geographical locus.

(2) Standing patterns of behavior-and-milieu. The behavior patterns
that constitute a behavior setting are attached to particular constellations
of nonbehavioral (physical, geographical) parts of the setting. Both constructed parts of the environment (buildings, streets, baseball diamonds,
bleachers, basketballs, scoreboards, whistles, hymn books, pipe-organs)
and natural features (hills, trees, flowers, grass, sunshine, rain) can constitute the milieu, or soma, of a behavior setting. In a basketball game, for
example, the playing behavior is focused on the ball, the baskets, and
the playing-court boundaries; the refereeing is attached to the referee's
whistle; the scorekeeping pattern of behavior is centered on the score-
sheets and writing or other recording instruments; the timekeeping is
linked to the timing device, and so forth.

Typically, the milieu of a behavior setting is an intricate complex of
times, places, and things. The milieu of the setting 4-H Club Meeting is a
constellation of a particular room in a particular residence at a particular

time with particular objects arranged in a particular pattern. The milieu parts of a setting exist independently of the standing patterns of behavior and independently of anyone's perception of the setting. During the interval between meetings, the behavior setting 4-H Club Meeting is nonexistent, qua setting, but the milieu parts—the meeting place, club constitution and by-laws, minutes book, roll of members, etc.—continue to exist, although usually in a different configuration. This is true regardless of whether any person happens to think about or even to discuss the 4-H Club with other persons.

(3) The milieu is *circumjacent* to the behavior pattern. Circumjacent means surrounding (enclosing, environing, encompassing); it describes an essential property of the physical-geographical-temporal milieu of a behavior setting. The milieu of a setting is circumjacent to the standing patterns of behavior. The physical-geographical-temporal boundaries of the milieu surround the behavior patterns usually without a break, as in the case of a store that opens at 8:00 A.M. and closes at 6:00 P.M.

(4) The milieu is *synomorphic* with the behavior pattern. Synomorphic means similar in shape, form, or structure; it describes an essential feature of the relationship between the behavior patterns and the milieu of a behavior setting.

At the level of the behavior setting as a whole, the synomorphy of the boundary of the behavior pattern and of the boundary of the milieu is striking and fundamental: the boundary of the football field is the boundary of the game; the beginning and end of the school music period mark the limits of the pattern of music class behavior; the walls and doors of the barbershop and the hours of operation constitute the boundaries of the hair-dressing behavior pattern in that setting.

The synomorphy of behavior and milieu also extends to the fine, interior structure of a behavior setting. There is similarity in the structure of the milieu and the structure of the standing patterns of behavior within the setting. Basketball, for example, requires its own peculiarly shaped ball; the game cannot be played with a football. In a barbershop, the barber chair, the mirrors, and the special sink for shampooing (milieu) are all designed, shaped, and constructed to fit and support the standing patterns of behavior—hair cutting, styling, and shampooing. In the case of a worship service, both the pews (milieu) and the listening congregation (behavior pattern) face the pulpit (milieu) and the preaching pastor (behavior pattern). The behavioral and milieu components of a behavior setting are not independently arranged; there is an essential fittingness between them. See, for example, Fig. 3.1.

Architects, designers, and engineers are often at great pains to create

© United Feature Syndicate, Inc., 1966

Fig. 3.1. Charlie Brown deals with a problem of synomorphy.

physical structures that fit, support, and facilitate particular patterns of behavior. Once these structures are created, they subsequently elicit and shape the patterns of behavior. Sir Winston Churchill's famous remark to the House of Commons recognized this: "We shape our buildings and they shape us" (quoted in Hall, 1966, p. 106).

(5) The behavior-milieu parts are called *synomorphs*. The physical sciences have avoided phenomena with behavior as a component, and the behavioral sciences have avoided phenomena with physical things and conditions as essential elements. So we have sciences of behavior-free objects and events (ponds, glaciers, lightning flashes), and we have sciences of phenomena without geophysical loci and attributes (organizations, social classes, roles). We lack a science of things and occurrences that have both physical and behavioral attributes. Behavior settings are such phenomena; they consist of *behavior-and-circumjacent-synomorphic-milieu entities*.

The synomorphic relation between milieu parts and standing patterns of behavior identifies the basic elements upon which behavior settings are built. To find such a relationship provides the first clue that a behavior setting may be at hand. Without such a relationship, there is no possibility that a behavior setting exists. From the adjectival form—synomorphic relation—is derived the noun—synomorph—to refer to an instance of congruence or fittingness between a particular behavior pattern and specific parts of the milieu. For example, we identify as a synomorph the behavior-milieu configuration of the pastor reading or preaching from the pulpit, the physical dimensions and shape of which fit and support the behavior patterns: reading from the Bible or notes for the sermon. The ushers' taking the offering in plates of size and shape convenient for passing among the congregation and receiving contributions of money or pledge envelopes constitutes another synomorph. The playing of the organ fits and is supported by the design and construction of the organ console, bench, footpedals, and music rack. Most behavior settings include a number of such behavior-milieu synomorphs.

In some instances, the behavior-milieu synomorphs involve milieu parts that do not surround or enclose the behavior: the preaching pastor is not surrounded by the pulpit, the shampooing hair-dresser is not enclosed by the sink, the collection plates are not circumjacent to the taking of the offering. Although the synomorphic relation (that is, the similarity in structure between the behavior patterns and the milieu parts) is clear in such cases, the lack of circumjacency of the milieu to the behavior pattern means that they cannot themselves meet the defining criteria for behavior settings; rather, they will be part of some more inclusive set of synomorphs that together constitute a behavior setting.

Synomorphs in which the milieu part is circumjacent to the behavior pattern may or may not stand alone as behavior settings, depending on their degree of interdependence with other synomorphs.

(6) The synomorphs of a given behavior setting have a specified degree of interdependence. Within any given community or institution, it is generally understood that behavior-milieu synomorphs are more or less interdependent. A college, for example, may maintain a master schedule of activities to avoid conflicts between events likely to require the same resources. A high school varsity club will not plan to hold a fund-raising auction on the same night as a varsity basketball game. In Midwest, the functionaries of the High School Senior Class Food Sale know that this affair should not be arranged for the same day as the 4-H Club Food Sale; they know that its standing pattern of behavior would not be vigorous. It is common knowledge, too, that the Boy Scout Pop Stand thrives when it coincides in time with the Old Settlers Reunion Midway. On the other

hand, the Pintner Abstract and Title Company office is not affected by the occurrence or nonoccurrence of the Parent-Teacher Association Carnival. Merchants, teachers, and organization leaders in Midwest as in other communities and institutions are astute judges of such interrelations.

The fact that the synomorphs of a community such as Midwest constitute a more or less interconnected network makes it possible to identify those with any specified degree of interdependence. This may be clarified by an analogy. The climate of a country can be described in terms of climatic areas and the economy in terms of economic regions. There are two common ways of defining the extent of such areas and regions: first, in terms of a defined amount of intra-area variability (for example, an average rainfall differential of two inches might be established as the limit of the territory to be included in a climatic area), and second, in terms of a defined degree of interdependence (for example, a correlation of 0.70 between indexes of economic change might be fixed as the limit of the domain included in an economic region). We have used this second kind of criterion as a basis for identifying the unitary sets of synomorphs called behavior settings.

The nature of this interdependence criterion was stated with precision by Lewin (1951). He pointed out that in all interdependent systems, whether they involve physiological, physical, or economic systems (or behavior settings), a unit can be defined in terms of any degree of interdependence desired. Thus we might divide the population of Midwest into economic units on the basis of financial interdependence. Such an economic unit can be defined as follows: individuals A, B, C, . . . N make up an economic unit if a change in the economic state of A of (x) amount is accompanied by a change of Kx in the economic state of B, C, . . . N, in which the symbol K represents a proportion of x arbitrarily chosen as an index of interdependence. If a high value of K is chosen, 0.9 for example, the town would be divided into many economic units because only the incomes of immediate family members—husband, wife, and minor children—are likely to be so highly interdependent as to change by as much as 90 percent of the change received by another member. An interdependence index, K, of 0.5 would undoubtedly combine some immediate family units with extended family units, and perhaps some business associates and their families would fall within the same unit; hence the town would have fewer economic units. If the degree were placed very low, such as 0.01, the community might turn out to be a single economic unit.

This can be exemplified by the hypothetical case of Mr. Joe Lamprey and what might happen if he were to inherit an annuity of $500 a month.

Community members	Previous monthly income	Subsequent monthly income	Percentage change
Mr. Joe Lamprey	$ 500	$1,000	100
Mrs. Joe Lamprey	300	575	92
George Lamprey, son	10	20	100
Mary Lamprey, daughter	5	15	200
Mrs. Ella Lamprey, mother	200	250	25
James Hill, business partner	400	424	6
Jack Rolf, insurance agent	300	312	4
10 Midwesterners (average)	200	206	3
115 Midwesterners (average)	1,500	1,500	0

Detailed study of the monthly income of a number of people might reveal information contained in the tabulation. In terms of an interdependence index, K, of 0.90, the economic unit with reference to Joe Lamprey contains the first four persons on the list, because an increase of 100 percent in Joe's income is accompanied by an increase of 90 percent or more in their income. If this relationship were mutual for all the members of this group of four, and if this were the average number of persons with an economic interdependence index of 0.90, there would be 187 such economic units in a total population of 750. An interdependence index of 0.25 would increase the unit centering about Joe to five persons, and again if this were general, it would reduce the number of economic units to 150. An interdependence index of 0.03 would, according to the data of the tabulation, include 17 persons in Joe's economic unit, dividing the town population of 750 into 44 such units. With an index of 0.003 there would be only six economic units in the community.

The same principles of interdependence can be used to define such diverse community units as friendship groups, ground water or air pollution units, information units, and sets of behavior-milieu synomorphs. In the next chapter, we discuss the specific operations involved in applying these principles to the task of determining whether different synomorphs and synomorph complexes constitute single or multiple behavior settings.

(7) The synomorphs of a given behavior setting have a greater degree of interdependence among themselves than with parts of other behavior settings. Dynamic interdependence or functional dependence between synomorphs determines which synomorphs combine to form one behavior setting and which belong to another. If the degree of interdependence is at or above the specified amount, two or more synomorphs constitute a single behavior setting. But if the degree of interdependence is less than the specified amount—that is, if the two synomorphs are sufficiently independent—each stands alone as a behavior setting or, possibly, as a part

of another behavior setting with which it is more interdependent. (The amount specified is represented by the *K* test for interdependence, which is considered in detail in the next chapter.)

From the study of Midwest, an example of the required degree of internal unity is found in the setting Ellson Drugstore. The fountain, the pharmacy, and the variety department are different synomorphs within the drugstore. Structurally each is discrete and separate from the others, but dynamically they are so interdependent in their functioning that, by the criteria used, they are parts of the single behavior setting Ellson Drugstore. In contrast, the Junior High Class, the Intermediate Class, and the Primary Class, which are also synomorphs that are structurally separate from each other but are all included within the Baptist Church Vacation Church School, are so independent in their functioning that, by the criteria used, they are discrete behavior settings. A fundamental property of a behavior setting is internal unity. However, the Baptist Church Vacation Church School does not have the required degree of internal unity; it is a multisetting synomorph. Like the schools, the churches, and the court house, the Baptist Church Vacation Church School is not itself a behavior setting but rather a host for several behavior settings.

The same criterion, dynamic interdependence, applies to synomorphs that are structurally not a part of any other synomorph—that is, synomorphs that are physically and geographically separate. An example is found in the behavior setting Chaco Garage and Service Station. Structurally, Chaco garage and Chaco service station are separate synomorphs; a wall and doors clearly separate the garage from the service station. Unlike the fountain, pharmacy, and variety department of Ellson Drugstore, the garage and the service station are not located within any larger, circumjacent synomorph; they are structurally independent. But dynamically they are not independent; small changes in the functioning of the garage (such as the number of its customers) are accompanied by changes in the functioning of the service station, and vice versa. These two structurally separate synomorphs are so interdependent functionally that, by the index we have used, they become the single synomorph complex, or behavior setting, Chaco Garage and Service Station. On the other hand, the synomorphs Chaco Garage and Service Station and Eastman Garage, which are also structurally separate, are dynamically almost completely independent. Even quite large changes in the functioning of Chaco Garage and Service Station are accompanied by only small changes in the functioning of Eastman Garage. These two synomorphs are dynamically so independent in their operations that they are separate behavior settings.

Structure and Dynamic Tests for Behavior Settings

Implicit in these structural and dynamic attributes of a behavior setting are two tests for evaluating any part of a community or institution as a possible behavior setting. Here we introduce and illustrate these tests briefly; in the next chapter, we demonstrate the operational procedures involved in using these tests in empirical applications.

Structure test. Is the community part in question a behavior-milieu synomorph or synomorph complex with the specified properties? Only parts of the community or institution that display certain properties, particularly a synomorphic relation with standing patterns of behavior, meet this test. This criterion serves to exclude as behavior settings such discriminable community features as mores and customs, social classes, organizations, ethnic groups, geographical areas, roles, legal codes, and educational systems.

Dynamic interdependence test. For community parts that pass the structure test—that is, for parts that are synomorphs or synomorph complexes—the next queston concerns their dynamic interdependence among themselves. Does the synomorph in question have the specified degree of interdependence, K, in relation to other synomorphs? (The specified empirical operations used in measuring degree of dynamic interdependence are described in detail in the next chapter.)

In the case of synomorph complexes—two or more structurally interrelated synomorphs such as the pharmacy, the fountain, and the variety department of Ellson Drugstore—the several interrelated synomorphs must show the specified degree of interdependence with each other and with the complex as a whole, the drugstore. If any such structurally interrelated synomorph is too independent of the others or of the total synomorph complex, that synomorph complex is, by definition, more than a single behavior setting. If, for example, the fountain showed too little functional interdependence with the other parts of the drugstore and the drugstore as a whole, it would qualify as a behavior setting independent of the other synomorphs. This criterion serves, in Midwest, to exclude as behavior settings such synomorphs as the churches, the schools, and the courthouse; these behavior-milieu structures are not behavior settings, but multiple-setting synomorph complexes, institutions that serve as hosts for several behavior settings (with K set at 21, as explained in the next chapter).

In the case of synomorphs that are structurally unrelated (when their physical and temporal boundaries do not intersect), the test of dynamic interdependence asks whether the synomorph is sufficiently independent of other synomorphs ($K \geqq 21$). If such a synomorph is not sufficiently independent of other synomorphs—that is, if it is too interdependent ($K < 21$) with one or more other synomorphs—then that synomorph is, by definition, a constituent part of a more inclusive complex of synomorphs, a behavior setting. This criterion serves, in Midwest, to exclude as a discrete behavior setting the Presbyterian church worship service on June 19; this worship service is, by the criterion used, a part (a single occurrence) of the recurring, multisynomorph behavior setting Presbyterian Church Worship Service.

When research was initiated in Midwest, we were confronted with the discouraging task of selecting from the countless parts of the town those that were relevant to our efforts to describe the living conditions of the residents, especially the children. The endless list included such varied features of Midwest as the weather vane on the Courthouse, the upper social class, Delaware Street, the Methodist Church, the Old Settlers Reunion Amateur Show, the County Commissioners' Meeting on February 3, the Black residents, the Culver family, the Stop-for-Pedestrians signs, the Volunteer Fire Department, a school tax of 12 mills, May Day, the North Precinct Polling Place, Mrs. Arla Grainger, a bonded indebtedness of $8,500, the *Midwest Weekly*, and the prevailing southwest wind. The discovery of behavior settings gave us a new understanding of the environment of Midwest. For example, the two tests for behavior settings reduce this sample list of community parts to two behavior settings: Old Settlers Reunion Amateur Show and North Precinct Polling Place. Some parts are excluded because they fail the structure test; they are not behavior-milieu synomorphs. This is true of

the weather vane	the upper social class
the Black residents	the Culver family
the Stop-for-Pedestrians signs	the Volunteer Fire Department
the school tax	May Day
Mrs. Grainger	the bonded indebtedness
the *Midwest Weekly*	the prevailing winds

Another part is excluded because there is less than the requisite degree of dynamic interdependence with and among its structurally interrelated synomorphs, namely, the Methodist Church; it is a multisetting synomorph that hosts several behavior settings. Still other potential settings on the list are excluded because their interdependence with structurally external synomorphs is too great; this is true of Delaware Street (which is part of the behavior setting Trafficways) and of the February 3 meeting of

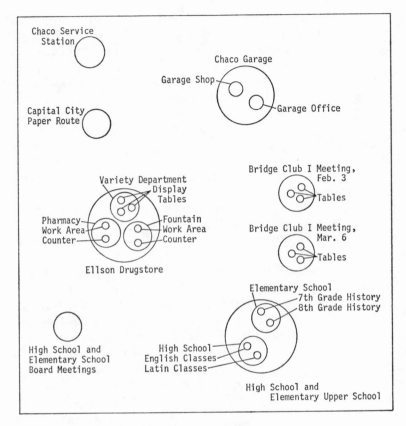

Fig. 3.2. Synomorphic structure of a part of Midwest.

the County Commissioners (which is part of the multiple-synomorph behavior setting County Commissioners' Meeting that occurs weekly).

Description of a community or an institution in terms of behavior settings includes all of its discriminable parts, because either the discriminable parts that are not behavior settings are parts or attributes of more inclusive behavior settings or they are multisetting units. The complicated *synomorphic* structure of a part of Midwest is represented in Fig. 3.2; the *behavior setting* structure of the same part, as determined by the two tests, is represented in Fig. 3.3.

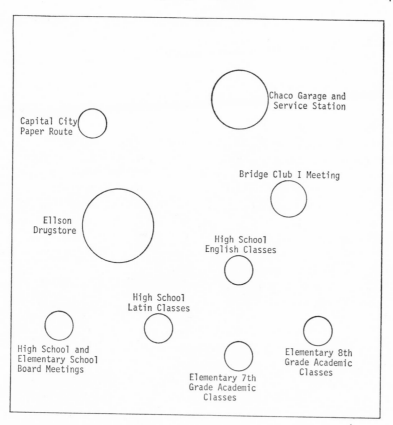

Fig. 3.3. Behavior setting structure of the part of Midwest shown in Fig. 3.2.

Sources of Our Knowledge of Behavior Settings

The structural attributes of behavior settings are directly perceived by any observer. One sees, for example, that the behavior patterns involved in the setting Elementary School Eighth Grade Graduation Party and Dance (dancing, conversing, eating, playing musical instruments, etc.) occur inside, not outside, the setting (the boundaries of which coincide with the scheduled time and the walls and doors of the high school gymnasium); one sees directly that the geographical arrangement of the chairs, the open floor area, the refreshment tables, the band, the loudspeakers, the lights, and the decorations is congruent with the patterns of behavior. But the dynamic attributes of behavior settings, their internal unity, and the forces that arrange persons, behavior, and objects into the shape and order required by the setting are apprehended only indirectly. We next consider some evidence on the dynamics of behavior settings.

INFLUENCE OF BEHAVIOR SETTINGS ON THE BEHAVIOR OF SETTING INHABITANTS

The influence of behavior settings on behavior occurring in the settings is exhibited in natural experiments that occur in any community. In these experiments, behavior settings are independent variables and the behavior of the setting inhabitants dependent variables. Data from one such experiment are presented in Table 3.1, where some aspects of the behavior of Midwest children of the second grade are summarized as they passed from one behavior setting to another during the school day. The same children exhibit these different patterns of behavior day after day, and the experiment is repeated each year with a new group, with the same results. *The changes observed in the behavior of children as they change from one setting to another can only be ascribed to forces operating within the behavior settings.*

Some aspects of the behavior of different persons within the same behavior setting, however, may differ widely: one person may enter a drugstore to buy medicine for a friend, another to buy poison for an enemy; one person may go to church for spiritual satisfaction, another for social advantage; one patient in the doctor's office may receive reassurance, another may learn the worst; one pupil in a class may experience great success, another profound failure. Yet all these people will conform to the

TABLE 3.1
Behavior of the Same Children in Different Behavior Settings

	Behavior setting		
	Second-Grade Academic Class	Playground	Second-Grade Music Class
Behavior pattern	Organized activity; little change in position; slow tempo; serious mood; limited variety of behavior, with sitting, reading, writing, and reciting predominant.	Unorganized or partly organized activity; fast tempo; exuberant mood; large variety of behavior, with games predominant.	Organized activity, variation in tempo; medium cheerfulness; little variety of behavior, singing predominant.

standing pattern characteristic of behavior in the several settings. In other words, the content and structure of a person's psychological world or life-space are by no means determined entirely by the behavior setting.

SOURCES OF BEHAVIOR-MILIEU SYNOMORPHY

Evidence of the internal unity and coerciveness of behavior settings, and of some of the mechanisms involved, is revealed when the sources of the behavior-milieu synomorphy are considered. Eight possible sources of the synomorphy of standing patterns of behavior and the physical-geographical milieu are identified next.

(1) *Physical forces.* Physical arrangements can enforce some patterns of behavior and prevent others. School corridors, for example, allow loco-motion in certain directions only, their narrowness prevents the playing of circle games, and the absence of chairs or ledges encourages standing and walking and discourages sitting or lying. The layout of streets and side-walks, the size and arrangement of rooms, and the distribution of fur-niture and equipment are often important factors in coercing certain features of standing patterns of behavior and in restricting others. The physical forces impelling and hindering behavior do not have to be abso-lute, like a wall that cannot be breached; they can be effective by making actions of some kinds easier than others. It is physically easier to walk on the streets and sidewalks of a town than to cut through vacant lots; even dogs follow the streets and sidewalks much of the time. In these cases, physical forces from the milieu mold behavior to conform to its shape.

The physical properties of objects also elicit and induce certain patterns of behavior. A ball will be rolled, thrown, and bounced. A swing elicits swinging behavior. Given a hammer, a young child sees everything as in need of hammering. Crayon and paper encourage drawing; fingerpaints are equally coercive for many children. The advent of the microcomputer has spawned new behavior patterns in many people; users often find it a highly seductive behavior object. Many of the behavior-milieu syno-morphs that constitute a behavior setting derive from the coerciveness of the physical properties of behavior objects within the setting.

(2) *Social forces.* Social forces can be strongly coercive. The power at-taching to a teacher, organization president, or store manager to enforce a particular pattern of behavior is well known. In addition, social forces to conform to the standing pattern issue from the behavior pattern itself. Thus a child who holds back as the third and fourth grades rush pell-mell through the school halls to the playground for recess is pushed along by the tide of behavior: by physical forces in the form of crowding and shov-

ing, but also by social forces in the form of behavioral contagion or even threats and promises.

Social forces to conform stemming from the behavior pattern itself elicit from the setting's inhabitants certain kinds of behavior and exclude others. The forces upon a person to rise when the church congregation rises, to sit when it sits, and to be silent when it is silent are strong indeed. The social pressures to be affable at a cocktail party, businesslike at the annual school meeting, and sad at a funeral cannot be ignored. In a college class, lecturing, demonstrating, discussing, listening, and questioning are virtully required. It is equally certain that none of the students will rise and break into song from the latest hit record. Should such an event occur despite the strong coercions against it, the originator would be regarded as engaged in a prank or as showing emotional instability.

(3) *Physiological processes.* Without question there are built-in behavior mechanisms in human beings that respond with mechanical compulsiveness to some features of the geographical-physical milieu. A brisk, cold wind puts spring in one's step and discourages dawdling. An overheated classroom induces lethargy, even drowsiness. Research has shown that noise interferes with cognitive development (Cohen, Glass, & Singer, 1973; Wachs & Gruen, 1982).

(4) *Physiognomic perception.* An important factor in molding standing patterns of behavior within behavior settings is the coercive influence on perception of some configurations of stimuli originating in the geographical-physical milieu. Children everywhere appear to see a smooth, level area free of obstructions, such as a long, shiny corridor, a school gymnasium, or a bare or closely mowed field, as a place for running and romping in unorganized, exuberant activity. These milieu features appear via perception to demand this kind of behavior. Open spaces seduce children; just as a ball induces rolling, throwing, and bouncing behavior, smooth open spaces elicit running and romping freely. The environment is well endowed with these perceived, seductive characteristics. Displays and arrangements of merchandise in stores, the order of church worship services, the ceremony at weddings, the guidelines painted on the streets, the furnishings in homes, all are calculated to coerce behavior to the appropriate patterns.

(5) *Learning.* The learning of behavior suitable for particular behavior-milieu synomorphs is an important source of the conformity of persons to the standing patterns of behavior. The process of teaching children to conform, to be quiet in church, to eat at mealtime, to sit still in school, proceeds continuously. Wicker (1972, 1979a) presents a more extended discussion of the contribution of operant, observational, and instructional

learning processes to the development of synomorphy, or behavior/ environment congruence as he calls it.

(6) *Selection of settings by persons.* There is an affinity between the standing pattern of a behavior setting and the behavior repertoires of the persons who enter it. This occurs partly via the discriminative and selective behavior of different persons. An adolescent boy who finds the behavior pattern of a Sunday school class intolerable will refuse to attend. A girl who dislikes tasks requiring fine motor coordination will probably avoid a club devoted to needlepoint. Those who remain will, therefore, be self-selected for their ability to conform to the standing pattern of behavior.

(7) *Selection of persons by behavior settings.* Some behavior settings have entrance requirements that exclude persons whose behavior does not readily conform to that of the standing pattern and to the requirements of the milieu. Boys younger than 11 years cannot join the Boy Scouts; a child is not eligible to attend nursery school until age three; persons wishing to have a part in a play must audition; high school football is not open to females (in most schools at present); candidates for membership in the Masonic Lodge are examined to make sure that they can abide by the behavioral requirements of the lodge. Furthermore, settings often eject persons who do not conform to the standing pattern of behavior: a crying child may be taken out of the worship service, "incorrigible" boys are expelled from school, members who miss more than three meetings are dropped from the student council, choir members who cannot master the music are discouraged from continuing in the choir.

(8) *Influence of behavior on the milieu.* The channels so far mentioned by which the synomorphy of behavior pattern and milieu arises have been via direct physical and social forces acting on behavior, via the native or learned reactions to the milieu through perception, or via selection of persons with appropriate behavior possibilities. Another source is the effect of behavior on milieu. Often, as noted above, this occurs through deliberate intent, as when designers and architects plan homes, buildings, or playgrounds. But it can and does occur also as an incidental, unintended result of behavior. For example, there was a time when the now well-worn footpath across a particular vacant lot did not exist. The first persons to cross the lot diagonally shaped that part of the environment in line with their need to reduce the amount of required walking. Yet the path that they created was not completely straight but curved and bent around clumps of bushes, mounds, and muddy depressions. Once established, however, that path shaped the behavior of countless pedestrians, nearly all of whom now follow its curves and bends as faithfully as a train on steel rails.

The synomorphy of milieu and behavior arises, too, from the explicit demand of behavior for a particular milieu. Midwest children and their parents wanted to have opportunities for swimming instruction and recreation, but the required facilities were not available in the town. Through a series of fund-raising efforts, the use of loaned equipment, and a great deal of volunteer labor over a period of years, the necessary milieu was constructed and the appropriate behavior objects were assembled. Midwesterners are justly proud of the newly created behavior-milieu synomorph, the swimming pool in the city park. In another community, a number of persons became concerned with issues in good government. Finding no suitable vehicle for work on these problems, they formed a local chapter of a nonpartisan lobby that holds regular meetings with presentations and discussions on priority issues such as campaign finance, arms buildup, and nuclear weapons. They created new behavior-milieu synomorphs in line with their values. Indeed, much of the behavior in modern society is concerned with creating new milieu arrangements to support new standing patterns of behavior, or altering old milieu features to conform to changes in old patterns of behavior (Sarason, 1972).

INITIATION AND TERMINATION OF
BEHAVIOR SETTING OCCURRENCES

Still other evidence of the internal unity and coerciveness of behavior settings is found in the functional interconnectedness of their parts. When any principal part of a setting is changed—for example, when the teacher is absent from the setting Elementary School First to Fourth Grade Music Class—all aspects of the setting are affected; this is true, too, if the heat or the lights fail. The internal interdependence of behavior settings is nowhere shown more clearly than in the beginning and end of a behavior setting occurrence. Characteristically, all parts of a setting begin and cease simultaneously. In Midwest, the department store as a behavior setting ceases to exist, in toto, at 5:30 P.M.; it recurs, fully accessible, at 8:00 the following morning. The drugstore is open until 6:30 P.M., when it suddenly ceases; it rejoins the public behavior areas at 7:30 A.M. Different behavior settings of Midwest have different schedules of opening and closing, and the schedules combine in such a way that the town slowly expands in the morning and slowly closes down at night. But almost every setting opens and closes as a unit; in this respect settings almost always function in an all-or-none manner, that is, as units. Larger stores in cities may appear to function less as a total unit: some sections of a large store may be open for business on Saturday while other parts of the store, such as the business office and the restaurant, are closed. In such cases, however, these different parts of the store probably constitute behavior settings separate from the store as a whole; thus the principle of unitary operation of behavior settings holds here as well.

NONTRANSPOSABILITY OF STANDING PATTERNS OF BEHAVIOR

The unity and coerciveness of behavior settings is further demonstrated by the fact that behavior frequently cannot be transposed between them. Midwest residents cannot telephone at the behavior setting United States Post Office or deposit mail in the setting Telephone Booth; they would not weld a bearing in High School Latin Class or recite a Latin lesson in the setting County Garage and Machine Shop. The objects, equipment, and other conditions obtaining in particular settings are as essential for some kinds of behavior as are persons with the requisite motives and skills. Behavior settings are not neutral, geographical-temporal regions to which any behavior can be freely added; the behavior pattern and the milieu are dynamically inseparable.

We turn now from this consideration of how behavior settings are defined and the sources of synomorphy between standing patterns of behavior and milieu parts to the empirical operations utilized in identifying behavior settings in a particular community or institution.

4

Identifying Behavior Settings

In the previous chapter, the defining properties of behavior settings were presented and illustrated. In this and the next three chapters, we describe the processes involved in making a *behavior setting survey*, a comprehensive inventory and description of all the public behavior settings of a community or institution. This chapter is devoted to the first stage in completing such a survey, the process of identifying the behavior settings. Our objective is to describe the processes involved in analyzing the ecological environment in terms of behavior settings in sufficient detail and with enough illustrations to enable others to use this chapter as a comprehensive guide in empirical research applications. The task is to divide the total ecological environment of the community or institution into parts that qualify as behavior settings according to the definition discussed in the previous chapter. We refer to this process of identifying behavior settings as making a behavior setting *inventory*. These units, the behavior settings, are equivalent in their defining properties but differ widely in many other respects. These variable attributes and properties of behavior settings are addressed in the second stage of a behavior setting survey. That stage is considered in the three chapters following this one; they are devoted to presentations of some of the ways that have been used to describe a number of such variable attributes of behavior settings.

The Behavior Setting Inventory

The behavior setting has found its greatest usefulness in studies of public areas of whole small towns as environments for behavior and child development and in studies of institutions such as high schools, churches, hospitals, colleges, supermarkets, and even mining camps and military installations in remote locations. Although these studies differ in important respects, they have all faced the common task of identifying behavior settings. This process involves two steps: (1) identifying and listing all potential behavior settings, and (2) discarding potential settings that upon closer examination do not meet the defining criteria of behavior settings—that is, they do not pass the tests for structure and dynamic interdependence.

Making a behavior setting inventory of a community (town, neighborhood, institution) is a precise operation, and a detailed technical exposition is required to describe the procedures involved. The apparent complexity of the procedures should not discourage one from undertaking a behavior setting inventory, however, because experience with the procedures soon teaches a fieldworker to recognize most community units that possess the structural and dynamic properties of behavior settings. This is facilitated by the fact that behavior setting criteria were established, in part, so that they will identify commonly perceived community units. In borderline cases, a few simple calculations usually suffice to eliminate uncertainties. However, this should not obscure the fact that behavior settings are precisely defined, that there are reliable procedures for identifying behavior settings in the field, and that even an experienced fieldworker regularly has to make detailed judgments and careful computations.

IDENTIFYING POTENTIAL BEHAVIOR SETTINGS

The first task is to discover every possible behavior setting that occurs in the public arena of the community during the period to be covered by the inventory. The best way to begin is to walk the streets and halls of the community or institution and observe and record the walled, fenced, and otherwise bounded areas; almost all of these are the exoskeletons of behavior-milieu synomorphs and many of them are the loci of behavior settings. Frequently the name of a setting or a complex of settings is inscribed on a door, a window, or a sign on the premises, such as First Methodist Church, Ellson Drugstore, Principal's Office, J. Wiley Attorney-at-Law, Kiwanis Club Meets Here Noon Wednesday. Detailed maps and plans of areas and buildings may be useful but are not usually available.

Excellent sources of potential settings are the local newspapers, telephone and other classified directories, rosters of social agencies, school schedules, organization programs, membership lists, church bulletins, placards, handbills, announcements, and other public documents. They suggest many potential settings for inclusion in a preliminary list. Here is an example of an item from the *Midwest Weekly* that provides a number of potential settings:

Box Social

Wednesday, October 15, at 7:30 P.M. the Senior High Class of
M.H.S. will sponsor a Box Social in the high school gym.
Come and play Bingo, walk for a cake, eat pie and ice cream.
Girls: Be sure to bring a box!
Boys: Be sure to bring plenty of money!

In this item there are the following possible settings: Box Social, Senior Class, Midwest High School, High School Gym, Bingo, Walk for a Cake.

In addition to direct observation through visitation in the field and reference to public documents, informants selected for their knowledge of particular community areas and institutions can be extremely useful in building the list of potential settings. Most behavior settings of a community are in the public domain and are well known to many citizens. A technical definition of behavior settings is not required to give an informant an adequate idea of what is wanted; a sample list of settings is usually enough. Field work in identifying behavior settings has been effectively carried out by high school students.

The initial inventory should aim to include all public parts of the community that might fit the definition of a behavior setting, and it should be organized into an efficient working list. In the first inventory of Midwest, the items were grouped into six broad categories: Business, Church, Government, Voluntary Association, School, and Miscellaneous, as shown in Table 4.1. This classification had no systematic significance, but it served as a convenient way to locate items in the inventory. Different but analogous categories would be appropriate in studies of other environments, such as colleges, hospitals, and high schools.

DISCARDING NONSETTINGS

The second step in completing an inventory is to eliminate from the list of potential settings those items that do not meet the criteria for a behavior setting. To qualify as a behavior setting, a community part must pass the two behavior setting tests introduced briefly above in Chap. 3: the tests for structure and dynamic interdependence.

The structure test. First, the potential setting must pass the structure test; it must be a behavior-milieu synomorph with all five of the following characteristics:

TABLE 4.1
*Sample List of Potential Settings with Results of Structure
and Dynamic Interdependence Tests*

Category	Setting
Business	1. *Drugstore
	2. Fountain of Drugstore
	3. Pharmacy of Drugstore
	4. Variety Department of Drugstore
	5. *J. Wiley, Attorney's Office
	6. *Barber Shop
	7. *J. Wiley, Music Lessons
Church	8. Methodist Church
	9. *Joash Worship Service at Methodist Church
	10. *Adult Choir Practice at Methodist Church
	11. Presbyterian Church
	12. *Worship Service at Presbyterian Church
	13. Anthem by Presbyterian Church Choir
Government	14. *County Treasurer's Office
	15. *Payment of Taxes at County Treasurer's Office*
	16. *Courthouse Square
	17. *Sitting on Benches of Courthouse Square*
Voluntary	18. *Boy Scout Troop 72 Meeting
Association	19. Tenderfoot Test at Scout Meeting
	20. Beaver Patrol Activities at Scout Meeting
	21. *4-H Club*
	22. *Skating Party of 4-H Club
	23. *Regular Meeting of 4-H Club
	24. Election of 4-H Club Officers
	25. *Achievement Banquet of 4-H Club
	26. *Hopscotch Games*
	27. March 3 Meeting of Couples Bridge Club
	28. April 1 Meeting of Couples Bridge Club
	29. May 2 Meeting of Couples Bridge Club
School	30. High School
	31. *High School Senior Class*
	32. *Box Social by Senior Class
	33. Bingo Game
	34. Walk for a Cake
	35. *High School Gym*
	36. *Girls Locker Room
	37. *Brick-paved Area in Front of High School*
Miscellaneous	38. *Trafficways
	39. *State Highway*

*Behavior settings—that is, community parts that pass both the structure and the dynamic interdependence tests.

Items in italics are not behavior-milieu synomorphs according to the structure test; they are not tested by the dynamics test.

The *structural* relationships of these potential behavior settings are indicated by the indent, as follows:

   11. Presbyterian Church (a community part that stands alone, that is interjacent to no other potential setting in the list)

   12. Worship Service at Presbyterian Church (first nesting level; a part that is interjacent to a community part that stands alone)

   13. Anthem by Presbyterian Church Choir (second nesting level; a part that is interjacent to an interjacent part)

(a) a standing pattern or complex of patterns of behavior (bounded patterns in the behavior of persons en masse that occur independently of the particular persons involved at any one time) that is
(b) anchored to a particular milieu complex
(c) at particular time-space loci
(d) with behavior and milieu synomorphic
(e) and with milieu circumjacent to behavior.

If a community part does not display all five of these structural characteristics, the part is not a behavior-milieu synomorph with the defining properties of a behavior setting. One asks about each item on the list whether the community part named possesses all of the essential structural characteristics. On the basis of answers to this question, some items are eliminated from the original list of potential settings. This is true of the following items in Table 4.1 (the main structural inadequacies of these items are indicated in brackets):

15. Payment of taxes at County Treasurer's Office [(a) there is no bounded pattern of behavior distinct from the total pattern of the County Treasurer's Office];
17. Sitting on benches of Courthouse Square [(e) the milieu—the benches—is not circumjacent to the behavior];
21. 4-H Club [(a) the 4-H Club exhibits highly varied patterns of behavior, (b) it is anchored to many different milieu complexes, (c) at unpredictable times and places. The 4-H Club appears in many forms in meetings, parties, banquets, cooking classes; it turns out to be a multisetting phenomenon];
26. Hopscotch Games [(c) occur at almost any time and place. A particular game would be a synomorph];
31. High School Senior Class [see comments for item 21];
35. High School Gym [(a) a great variety of behavior patterns are anchored to the gym, such as basketball games, dances, banquets, and PTA meetings; it is the site of a number of behavior settings];
37. Brick-paved Area in Front of High School [(d) no synomorphic pattern of behavior and milieu; the boundary of the bricked area is not the boundary of any pattern of behavior. The bricked area is a behaviorally nonsignificant part of the behavior setting Trafficways];
39. State Highway [see comments for item 37].

The application of the structure test as above to the items of the initial inventory as shown in Table 4.1 indicates that, of the 39 items in the exemplifying list, 31 remain as behavior-milieu synomorphs that qualify as behavior settings on the basis of their structural characteristics.

Dynamic interdependence test. These 31 synomorphs must also pass the test for dynamic interdependence using the K test, the application of which is described in detail in the next section of this chapter. This test is applied first to synomorphs that are structurally interjacent to other synomorphs—that is, synomorphs with intersecting physical or temporal boundaries. In Table 4.1, such interjacent synomorphs are indicated by the indentations. This involves testing the degree of interdependence of:

2. Fountain, 3. Pharmacy, and 4. Variety Department with each other and of each with 1. Drugstore;
9. Joash Service and 10. Adult Choir Practice with each other and of each with 8. Methodist Church;
12. Worship Service with 11. Presbyterian Church;
13. Anthem with 12. Worship Service;
19. Tenderfoot Test and 20. Beaver Patrol Activities with each other and of each with 18. Boy Scout Meeting;
24. Election of 4-H Club Officers with 23. Regular Meeting of 4-H Club;
32. Box Social and 36. Girls Locker Room with each other and of each with 30. High School;
33. Bingo Game and 34. Walk for a Cake with each other and of each with 32. Box Social.

The application of the K test for interdependence in the comparisons listed above shows that the following synomorphs pass the test for dynamic interdependence. That is, these structurally interrelated synomorphs have the degree of internal unity (K-21) specified for behavior settings:

1. Drugstore (includes 2. Fountain, 3. Pharmacy, and 4. Variety Department);
9. Joash Worship Service at Methodist Church;
10. Adult Choir Practice at Methodist Church;
12. Worship Service at Presbysterian Church (includes 13. Anthem by Presbyterian Church Choir);
18. Boy Scout Troop 72 Meeting (includes 19. Tenderfoot Test at Scout Meeting and 20. Beaver Patrol Activities at Scout Meeting);
23. Regular Meeting of 4-H Club (includes 24. Election of 4-H Club Officers);
32. Box Social by Senior Class (includes 33. Bingo Game and 34. Walk for a Cake);
36. Girls Locker Room in High School.

By the same test, three of the potential settings in Table 4.1—namely, 8. Methodist Church, 11. Presbyterian Church, and 30. High School—are synomorph complexes, not behavior settings, because their structurally interrelated synomorphs do not have the specified degree of interdependence; their interjacent synomorphs are too independent of each other and of the including synomorph itself. They are multiple setting synomorphs; that is, they are not themselves behavior settings but rather physical/geographical and organizational hosts for behavior settings such as 9. Joash Worship Service at Methodist Church, 13. Anthem by Presbyterian Church Choir, and 32. Box Social by Senior Class.

From the application of the structure test and the test for dynamic interdependence to the structurally interrelated synomorphs and synomorph complexes shown in Table 4.1, we have determined that 8 of the original 39 items on the list of potential settings satisfy the criteria for a behavior setting and that 20 of them do not. The remaining 11 items are synomorphs that are structurally independent of the other synomorphs, since they do not coincide in time and space with any other synomorph on the list. They are:

    5. J. Wiley, Attorney's Office
    6. Barbershop
    7. J. Wiley, Music Lessons
   14. County Treasurer's Office
   16. Courthouse Square
   22. Skating Party of 4-H Club
   25. Achievement Banquet of 4-H Club
   27. March 3 Meeting of Couples Bridge Club
   28. April 1 Meeting of Couples Bridge Club
   29. May 2 Meeting of Couples Bridge Club
   38. Trafficways

Application of the *K* test for interdependence shows that all except three of these potential behavior settings are sufficiently independent of each other to qualify as behavior settings. The exceptions, the three monthly meetings of the Couples Bridge Club (27, 28, and 29), are interdependent synomorphs that constitute the behavior setting Couples Bridge Club Meeting.

In summary, testing of the 39 potential settings on the exemplary list shown in Table 4.1 indicates that 8 of them fail the structure test, 15 fail the test for dynamic interdependence at the level specified (*K*-21), and 16 pass both tests as behavior settings.

The Index of Interdependence, *K*

In this section we present a detailed description of the operations involved in assessing the degree of interdependence between any two behavior-milieu synomorphs or synomorph complexes. The *K* test for interdependence may at first appear formidable and tedious, but experience with the process soon shows that it is not difficult to use. For one thing, formal application of the full K test is necessary in only a small proportion of the possible comparisons; in most cases, the outcome is obvious before any detailed ratings are made. For anyone acquainted with the assumptions underlying the index of interdependence, there would be no need to run a formal K test to discover that, for example, synomorphs as obviously independent as High School Latin Classes and Ruttley's Jewelry and Watch Repair Shop would, if tested on the K test, prove to be independent at the level specified. In the early stages of work on an inventory, one usually needs to run quite a few K tests, but this becomes increasingly unnecessary as work progresses. For another thing, raters soon become adept at applying the K test; K values are quickly and easily obtained.

The operations for determining the interdependence index K of pairs of synomorphs are based on two sets of assumptions:

(1) Interdependence between synomorphs occurs:

    (a) via behavior, which has effects across synomorphs;
    (b) via inhabitants, who migrate between synomorphs; and
    (c) via leaders, who are common to synomorphs.

(2) The amount of interdependence that occurs via these channels is a direct function of:

    (a) the amount of behavior, the number of inhabitants, and the number of leaders that span the synomorphs;
    (b) the closeness of the synomorphs in space and time; and
    (c) the extent to which the synomorphs use the same or similar behavior objects and behavior mechanisms (verbalization, listening, gross motor).

In consequence, the value of K for any pair of synomorphs consists of ratings of the degree to which:

(1) Behavior or its consequences span the synomorphs.

(2) The same inhabitants occupy the synomorphs.

(3) The same persons are active as leaders and operatives in the synomorphs.

(4) The synomorphs use the same physical space or spaces that are close together.

(5) The synomorphs occur at the same time or at times that are close together.

(6) The synomorphs use the same or similar behavior objects.

(7) The same kinds of behavior mechanisms occur in the synomorphs.

Two meetings of Mrs. Smith's Elementary School First Grade Academic Subjects class on different days are structurally discrete synomorphs that have almost the same inhabitants and leaders, occupy the same space, and use the same behavior objects by means of the same behavior mechanisms; they are virtually identical with respect to five of the seven measures of K. Two meetings of different First Grade Academic Subjects classes, such as Mrs. Smith's and Mrs. Brown's, on the other hand, are not identical on any of the seven measures of K but do use behavior objects (desks, books, chalkboards) of the same kinds by means of much the same behavior mechanisms (writing, listening, reading, thinking). Therefore, according to the assumptions on which the index K is based, the two meetings of Mrs. Smith's class have greater interdependence than the two meetings of the different classes. In fact, according to the rating of K, the two meetings of Mrs. Smith's class constitute two occurrences of a single behavior setting, whereas the two meetings of the different classes are single occurrences of entirely different behavior settings.

The degree of interdependence of two synomorphs is estimated by rating them with respect to each of the seven measures on 7-point scales. A rating of 1 represents the greatest and a rating of 7 the least influence, commonality, connectedness, or similarity between the synomorphs on the measure in question. The interdependence index of the pair of synomorphs equals the sum of the ratings of the seven measures. The total interdependence scale, then, ranges from a score of 7, indicating maximal interdependence, to a score of 49, indicating minimal interdependence.

Before looking closely at the details of the seven scales, consider the pair of synomorphs mentioned above, High School Latin Classes and Ruttley's Jewelry and Watch Repair Shop, in terms of the kinds of questions the scales of the K test for dynamic interdependence ask:

Behavior. Little if any behavior or its consequences spans these two synomorphs; events in one have little or no impact on events in the other.

Population. During the period of the inventory only a few of the members of the Latin class entered Ruttley's jewelry shop and no one on the staff of the jewelry shop entered Latin class.

Leaders. The Latin teacher and the jewelry store staff are different people; there is no overlap in leaders or other operatives.

Space. The shop and the high school are separated by several blocks.

Time. There is some simultaneity of occurrence: Latin class meets for one hour in the morning, five days a week during the school year, but the shop is open during business hours daily except Sunday.

Objects. The behavior objects used in the two synomorphs are different and of different kinds with few exceptions.

Mechanisms. Different kinds of behavior mechanisms are prominent in the two synomorphs—for example, thinking, talking, and writing in Latin class, and fine motor manipulation in the shop.

Thus it is apparent that these two synomorphs are quite independent of each other on six of the seven dimensions. This rough consideration of the pair on these scales confirms what common sense suggests: there is little interdependence between these two synomorphs. Systematic application of the seven scales of the *K* test as described below merely yields a more precise, quantified estimate of just how little interdependence there is between Latin class and the jewelry shop; the value of *K* for this pair exceeds 30, well above 21, which is the cutting point selected to establish two synomorphs as separate K-21 behavior settings (see the next major section for explanation of the K-21 cutting point).

Next, each of the seven interdependence scales is described and illustrated.

(1) *Behavioral interdependence*: the degree to which behavior in synomorph A has direct consequences in synomorph B, and vice versa. Behavior may interconnect synomorphs in two ways: (a) molar actions begun in A may be continued or completed in B, and vice versa; for example, the English class may be interrupted by an announcement over the speaker from the principal's office, a customer at the drugstore fountain may speak directly to someone in the pharmacy, or a shortage of currency in the jewelry shop may send a staff member to the bank next door for fresh supplies; (b) the physical resultants of behavior in A may spread to B, and vice versa; for example, the film shown to one class in an open school may attract the attention of students in another class, loud music from a portable stereo in the hallway may distract students in the Algebra class, the roar of the crowd at the basketball game may interfere with business in the concession stand, or cooking odors from the kitchen of the school cafeteria may spread to the classrooms, generating eagerness for lunch dismissal. Scale 4.1 provides for both kinds of behavioral interdependence. The highest percentage that applies is used; if both kinds of behavioral interdependence occur, the average of the two ratings is the final rating.

(2) *Population (inhabitant) interdependence:* the degree to which the people who enter synomorph A also enter synomorph B, and vice versa. The percentage of population overlap is determined by the following formula:

$$\text{Percentage overlap} = \frac{2P_{ab}}{P_a + P_b} \times 100$$

where P_a = Number of people who enter synomorph A, P_b = Number of people who enter synomorph B, and P_{ab} = Number of people who enter both A and B. See Scale 4.2 for converting the percentage overlap to an interdependence rating.

This rating requires that the identities of the people who enter the synomorphs be known. Wherever possible, membership lists and rosters of participants and officers supplement knowledge of fieldworkers from direct observation in the community. In settings with large numbers of participants, such as basketball games, stores, and drama performances, estimates are based on direct observation in multiple visits, usually by several different fieldworkers. In many instances, such direct observational information is supplemented by reports from informants who know the settings well.

(3) *Leadership interdependence:* the degree to which the leaders and other operatives of synomorph A are also the leaders and operatives of synomorph B, and vice versa. This includes all operatives, persons who

SCALE 4.1

Rating	Percentage of molar actions beginning in A that is complete in B, or vice versa (highest percentage counts)	Percentage of behavior in A having physical consequences in B, or vice versa (highest percentage counts)
1	95–100	95–100
2	67–94	67–94
3	34–66	34–66
4	5–33	5–33
5	2–4	2–4
6	trace–1	trace–1
7	none	none

SCALE 4.2

Rating	Percentage overlap
1	95–100
2	67–94
3	33–66
4	6–32
5	2–5
6	trace–1
7	none

penetrate the synomorphs to zones 6, 5, and 4 (see Chap. 7 for definitions and discussion of penetrations zones). Ratings are done in the same way as for population interdependence using Scale 4.2.

(4) *Spatial interdependence:* the degree to which synomorphs A and B use the same or proximate spatial areas (see Scale 4.3). In case both "same space" and "proximate space" scales apply, the one that indicates the greater interdependence is used. The descriptions listed under the "proximate space" column are appropriate for studies of small towns such as Midwest. Studies of other communities, institutions, and sections of cities may need to make some modifications in wording to reflect the analogous levels of spatial interdependence.

(5) *Interdependence based on temporal contiguity:* the degree to which synomorphs A and B occur at the same time, or at proximate times. Synomorphs may occur temporally close together on some occasions and be temporally separated at other times. For example, the American Legion Post in Midwest meets monthly, whereas the Boy Scout Troop meets weekly; once a month, therefore, their meetings occur during the same week and once a month their meetings are more than two weeks apart. Temporal contiguity is rated using Scale 4.4. The "closest temporal proximity" of synomorphs A and B determines the column to enter (Simultaneous, Same Part of Day, Same Day, etc.). The percentage of all contacts with "closest temporal proximity" is the number of such contacts for A plus the number for B divided by the total number of occurrences of both synomorphs multiplied by 100.

For example, the Boy Scout Troop met every Monday night during the year covered by the behavior setting inventory, 1963–64. The American

SCALE 4.3

Rating	Same space Percentage of space common to A and B	Proximate space
1	95–100	
2	50–94	
3	10–49	or A and B use different parts of same room or small area
4	5–9	or A and B use different parts of same building or lot
5	2–4	or A and B use areas in same part of town
6	trace–1	or A and B use areas in same town but different parts of the town
7	none	or A in town, B out of town

SCALE 4.4

Interde-pendence rating	Percentage of contacts with closest temporal proximity					
	Simulta-neous	Same part of day	Same day	Same week	Same month	Same year
1	75–100					
2	50–74	75–100				
3	25–49	50–74	75–100			
4	5–24	25–49	50–74	75–100		
5	0–4	5–24	25–49	50–74	75–100	
6		0–4	5–24	25–49	50–74	50–100
7			0–4	0–24	0–49	0–49

Legion Post met the first Wednesday of every month. The closest temporal proximity of these synomorphs was "Same Week" in Scale 4.4. The 12 Scout and the 12 Legion meetings that occurred in this close contact are added and the sum divided by the sum of the 12 Legion meetings and the 52 Scout meetings, as follows:

$$\frac{12 \text{ Scout Meetings} + 12 \text{ Legion Meetings}}{52 \text{ Scout Meetings} + 12 \text{ Legion Meetings}} = 24/64 = .37 \times 100 = 37\%$$

In column "Same Week," 37 falls at scale point 6. The temporal contiguity rating for these two synomorphs, then, is 6.

Scale 4.4 is intended to allow recording of the "closest temporal proximity" of the synomorphs being compared. The column headings, therefore, mean that the two synomorphs coincide in time within the interval named: "Same Part of Day" means that both occurred in the morning, in the afternoon, or in the evening; "Same Day" means, for example, that both occurred on Tuesday but one in the morning and one in the afternoon; "Same Week" means that both occurred within any 7-day period; "Same Month" means any 30-day period; and "Same Year" means more than 30 days apart but within the year of the inventory.

(6) *Interdependence based on behavior objects*: the degree to which synomorphs A and B use identical or similar objects. See Scale 4.5. In case both scales apply, the scale that indicates the greater interdependence is used.

(7) *Interdependence based on commonality of behavior mechanisms*: the degree to which the behavior mechanisms occurring in synomorph A also occur in synomorph B. The interdependence score is determined by the number of the following behavior mechanisms that are present at the required level in one synomorph and not in the other:

Gross Motor Activity	Listening	Writing
Manipulation (Fine Motor)	Thinking	Observing
Talking	Eating	Affective Behavior
Singing	Reading	Tactual Feeling

The interdependence rating is given in Scale 4.6.

In judging whether a mechanism is "present at the required level," the question is whether the behavior occurs with sufficient regularity, frequency, and salience to be recognized as an integral and important part of the standing pattern of behavior of the synomorph. As a practical guide, if the mechanism is associated with 25 percent or more of the person-hours

SCALE 4.5

Rating	Identical objects	Similar objects
1	Identical objects used in A and B; i.e., all behavior objects shared	
2	More than half of the objects shared by A and B	or Virtually all objects in A and B of same kind[a]
3	Half of the objects shared by A and B	or More than half of the objects in A and B of the same kind[a]
4	Less than half the objects shared by A and B	or Half the objects in A and B of same kind[a]
5	Few behavior objects in A and B identical	or Less than half the objects of A and B of same kind[a]
6	Almost no objects shared by A and B	or Few behavior objects of same kind[a] in A and B
7	No objects shared	or Almost no similarity between objects in A and B

[a] Objects of the same kind are objects that have the same dictionary definition; for example, spoons are used in the behavior setting School Lunchroom and the setting Clifford's Drugstore Fountain, but they are different spoons.

SCALE 4.6

Inter-dependence rating	Number of mechanisms present in one setting and absent in the other
1	0–1
2	2–3
3	4–6
4	7–8
5	9–10
6	11
7	12

spent in the synomorph, the mechanism should be considered as "present at the required level." Thus, at a basketball game some writing behavior occurs (scorekeeping), but such behavior does not occupy 25 percent or more of the total person-hours spent in the synomorph. The same would hold for several of the other mechanisms, such as Manipulation (Fine Motor), Singing, Eating, Reading, and Tactual Feeling. In Latin class, Talking, Writing, Observing, Listening, Thinking, and Reading would pass the test. In the jewelry shop, Manipulation (Fine Motor), Talking, Observing, Listening, and Thinking would be rated as present at the required level.

THE *K*-21 CUTTING POINT: BEHAVIOR SETTINGS

A set of synomorphs with *K* values, inter se, of 20 or less constitutes a single behavior setting; synomorphs with *K* values of 21 or greater are discrete behavior settings or parts of discrete settings.

It was pointed out above (Chap. 3) that when the units of a system are defined in terms of degree of interdependence, the units can be made larger or smaller by varying the degree of interdependence by which the units are defined; one is at liberty to select any degree whatever, depending on one's purposes. In the Midwest study, the critical value of *K* for identifying separate behavior settings was originally set at 21 (on the scale ranging from 7 to 49) on an empirical basis; this value appeared to identify community parts with phenomenal reality and with dynamic significance for behavior. Higher and lower values of *K* would identify units with different properties and might be appropriate for particular problems. A higher critical *K* value would identify fewer community units, each with a lower degree of interdependence among its included synomorphs. A cutting point of 31, for example, would place together in the same unit all garages and service stations of Midwest; similarly the grocery stores would constitute a single unit as would other classes of businesses and professions, such as the drugstores, hardware stores, and lawyers' offices. A cutting point lower than 21 would identify more community units, each with a higher degree of interdependence among its included synomorphs. A critical *K* value of 14 would separate the fountain, pharmacy, and variety department of Ellson drugstore into separate units; it would detach Chaco service station from Chaco garage.

The arbitrariness of the *K*-21 cutting point may appear to be inconsistent with our stated purpose of studying the ecological environment in terms of natural units—that is, units not created by the investigator but units as they occur in nature without intervention by the investigator. In what sense are *K*-21 behavior settings natural units if the cutting point is chosen so arbitrarily? Are they not just space-time tesserae (fragments, particles) selected and arranged by the investigator? The problem is analogous to that of a census in which the number of rooms in dwellings must be assessed. How many rooms has a house? Are walled areas joined by doorways without doors, double doors, or archways, one room or two? What about open areas separated by different floor levels, railings, counters, or curtains? The census design must provide a definition of the degree of separation an area must have to be identified as a room and that definition is arbitrary in that the degree of separation can be set at any desired level depending on the purposes of the census. But once that degree has been established, the number of rooms in different houses is determined by the houses, not by the censustaker. The situation is similar in the case of behavior settings.

ILLUSTRATIONS OF *K*-TEST APPLICATION

At Meadowview, a high school we have studied in central New York state, the student council sponsored an all-school dance to raise money for its various projects for the year. The dance was held in the school gymnasium with the five-piece band and elaborate amplification equipment placed near the center of the room. About 200 students attended the dance, and seven teachers and parents supervised as chaperones. Four members of the student council took turns at the entrance desk monitoring admissions. Refreshments were served at a snack bar adjoining the lounge/lobby area separated from the gym by a partition with two doorways.

Observation by a fieldworker on site and the subsequent application of the structure test identified the following synomorphs that should be considered as possible *K*-21 behavior settings:

The admission table. Two student council members sit at a table and collect money or tickets from students as they enter the lounge/lobby area from the entrance hall; they also note departing students and give occasional reminders that re-entering the building is not allowed.

The lounge/lobby area. Patrons sit at tables eating and drinking, conversing, and laughing; adult chaperones stand about, visit among themselves and with students, and move between lounge/lobby and gym, keeping watch on student behavior and intervening if necessary; they also monitor the comings and goings of students.

The snack bar. Attendants take orders from patrons, serve snacks, and collect money; patrons approach snack bar, place orders, pay, receive snacks, and leave snack bar.

The dance in the gym. Band plays, singer sings, sound amplification crew operates sound equipment and lights; patrons dance, sit on the bleachers along opposite wall, watch the band perform, visit informally with other students.

Announcement of dress contest winners. Band stops regular music, plays fanfare, and president of student council takes the microphone to report the results of the voting for costume competition among the classes of the high school; patrons gather near microphone, listen, cheer results.

The application of the K test begins with a comparison of any two of these synomorphs. For example, if we examine first the lounge/lobby area versus the dance in the gym, the following estimates are obtained:

Behavior. Rating = 2 (Scale 4.1). The continual movement between the synomorphs of dancers and chaperones and the loud music that dominates both synomorphs are the main bases.

Population. Rating = 1 (Scale 4.2). All persons who enter either synomorph also enter *both* synomorphs.

Leaders. Rating = 2 (Scale 4.2). The seven chaperones and the president of the student council have major responsibility in both synomorphs; in the dance, five band members and two technicians are added; $2 \times 8 = 16/8 + 15 = .70 \times 100 = 70$ percent.

Space. Rating = 3 (Scale 4.3). The spaces used by the two synomorphs are separated only by a folding partition with two open doorways to encourage traffic flow.

Time. Rating = 1 (Scale 4.4). The two synomorphs occur simultaneously throughout their entire duration.

Objects. Rating = 5 (Scale 4.5). The dance in the gym has many objects not found in the lobby/lounge and vice versa, such as musical instruments, sound system, lights, and bleachers in the gym; tables, chairs, food, and drinks in the lounge/lobby. Objects in common to the two synomorphs include the costumes of the dancers.

Mechanisms. Rating = 3 (Scale 4.6). Eating is unique to the lobby/lounge, while singing, emoting, and gross motor actions are largely limited to the dance floor.

The sum of these seven ratings equals 17, indicating a degree of interdependence that is sufficient to keep the two synomorphs together as parts of a single K-21 behavior setting. Similar comparisons of the other possible pairings of all the synomorphs found at the dance show that the obtained values of K are in the same range as the two summarized just above; none of them reach the K-21 cutting point. The same is true when each of the synomorphs is tested against all of the others combined. Thus they are interdependent among themselves at the level specified (K of 21 or less) and hence belong together in a single behavior setting, Student Council Dance.

As another example, consider an ordinary college course. Is it a single behavior setting or more than one? The freshman/sophomore-level course entitled "Observational Methods" met three days each week at 11:15 A.M. during a certain fall semester in Room 114, Academic Hall, State College. Professor Jones lectured, presented a film, or brought a guest lecturer on Mondays and Wednesdays; Fridays were reserved for meetings of the 36 undergraduate students in three small discussion groups with graduate student assistants in charge of two of them and Professor Jones in charge of the other. A number of synomorphs and synomorph complexes that pass the structure test are readily apparent:

(1) Any one class meeting on Monday or Wednesday with its pattern of Professor Jones presenting lecture, film, or guest lecturer and students sitting, listening, taking notes, asking questions.

(2) Any one Friday meeting of one of the three discussion sections with its pattern of 12 or so students holding discussions among themselves with the discussion leader serving as one who poses questions, steers the discussion, draws out quiet members, and helps find answers to students' questions about readings, lectures, films.

(3) The one-hour midterm examination held during the regular Friday meeting time on October 14, in the rooms regularly used by the discussion sections, with its pattern of quiet concentration on writing answers to the exam questions by the students and the discussion leader handing out exams and monitoring the student activity.

(4) The two-hour final examination held in a larger room in the same building during the officially scheduled time for all college final exams about two weeks after the last class. The behavior pattern is similar to that in the midterm exam.

The comparisons in this case might begin with testing any one regular lecture session against any other. Suppose we begin by comparing September 12 and November 7.

Behavior. Rating = 5. There is little influence from the earlier to the later class meeting. Professor Jones does continue in the November meeting development of some points presented in the September meeting, but this is a minor part of the behavior pattern in November.

Population. Rating = 1. The few absences do not bring the percentage of overlap below 95.

Leaders. Rating = 1. Professor Jones is the single leader (zone 6) and the graduate student teaching assistants occupy zone 4 in both synomorphs; the overlap is 100 percent. (Zones of penetration are discussed in Chap. 7.)

Space. Rating = 1. Both synomorphs occur in the same space, Room 114, Academic Hall.

Time. Rating = 6. In the closest point of contact between these two synomorphs, they are separated by more than 30 days.

Objects. Rating = 2. Most of the objects (chairs, chalkboard, projector) in the two synomorphs are the same; only a few (books, papers, illustrations) are different.

Mechanisms. Rating = 1. All mechanisms occurring in one synomorph also occur in the other.

These estimates total 17, indicating that regular lecture class meetings separated by more than a month are sufficiently interdependent that they belong to one behavior setting. But what about the discussion sections that meet on Fridays? Are they behavior settings separate from each other and separate from the lectures? First, in view of the low value of *K* just obtained in comparing two regular lecture sessions, we may safely assume that a similar result would be found if we compared two sessions of one discussion group—same population, leader, space, objects, and mechanisms. But with different populations and different persons in charge, two different discussion sections will be less interdependent. Next, let us look at the ratings in comparing two discussion sections led by the two graduate teaching assistants, Ms. Green and Mr. Williams.

Behavior. Rating = 5. There is little evidence that behavior beginning in either of these discussions sessions ends in the other. Consultation between the two discussion leaders no doubt produces some such behavior, but it is clearly limited.

Population. Rating = 4. Only Professor Jones, who visits both discussion sections during the semester, is common to both. Thus the calculation called for in the formula is $2/(14 + 14) = 1/14 = .07 \times 100 = 7$ percent.

Leaders. Rating = 3. The only person in penetration zone 4 or higher in *both* synomorphs is Professor Jones, thus the values for the formula are $2/(2 + 2) = 1/2 = .50 \times 100 = 50$ percent.

Space. Rating = 4. The two synomorphs occupy spaces in different parts of the same building.

Time. Rating = 1. Both occur at the same time every time they meet.

Objects. Rating = 2. Most of the objects appearing in one section are of the same kind as those appearing in the other.

Mechanisms. Rating = 1. None of the mechanisms is unique to either of the two synomorphs.

These values sum to a total of 20, just below the level (21) specified as the criterion for a behavior setting. The two discussion sections tested, Ms. Green's and Mr. Williams', come close to qualifying as separate behavior settings. Such borderline cases are considered in relation to obtained *K* values in related decisions. In this case, the *K* of 20 is higher than the value obtained by comparing either of these student-led discussion sections with that led by Professor Jones. This argues for leaving all three of the discussion sections together. Another consideration concerns the obtained *K* value in comparing this combination of the three discussion sections considered as a single synomorph complex with the lectures as another. Here are the ratings:

Behavior. Rating = 3. Given that the discussion section leaders are asked to use the discussion sessions to clarify and elaborate on issues raised in the lectures, films, demonstrations, and readings assigned in the lecture sessions, many molar actions that begin in the lectures are continued and completed in the discussion sessions; similarly, questions and unresolved issues arising in the discussion sessions are often brought to the lecture session for clarification.

Population. Rating = 1. All persons (except a few visitors and guest lecturers) entering either synomorph also enter the other.

Leaders. Rating = 2. Professor Jones and the two graduate assistants are occupants of penetration zones 6, 5, and 4 (see Chap. 7) in both synomorphs. Two guest lecturers during the semester are unique to the lectures. Therefore, the calculations are $2 \times 3 = 6/8 = .75$ or 75 percent.

Space. Rating = 3. The lectures occur in Room 114; one of the discussion sections meets in the same room, the others in nearby rooms in the same building; one-third of the space used by both is common to both.

Time. Rating = 4. The closest temporal proximity of these two synomorphs is the same week, and it holds for all occurrences.

Objects. Rating = 2. Many of the objects are identical in the two synomorphs.

Mechanisms. Rating = 1. All mechanisms occurring in one also occur in the other synomorph.

These ratings produce a total *K* value of 16, indicating that these two synomorph complexes are quite interdependent and therefore constitute parts of a single *K*-21 behavior setting. This low *K* value between the synomorph complex including the three discussion sections and the lectures as another synomorph complex also provides the basis for deciding that the question of the borderline value (20) found in testing the two discussion sections should be resolved in the same direction; that is, the discussion sections do not stand as separate behavior settings but belong together. We conclude, therefore, that the lecture meetings and the discussion group meetings belong together as parts of a single *K*-21 behavior setting.

The remaining question concerns the midterm and final examinations.

Are they behavior settings separate from each other and from the rest of the course? Comparing the two exams, we obtain the following ratings:

Behavior. Rating = 4. Although many of the substantive issues of concern are common to both the midterm and the final examinations, few of the molar actions beginning in the midterm are completed in the final exam.

Population. Rating = 1. Nearly all persons entering the midterm also enter the final.

Leaders. Rating = 1. The two synomorphs have the same leaders, Professor Jones and the two graduate assistants.

Space. Rating = 4. The midterm exam occurs in the regular classrooms in which the discussion sections meet; the final occurs in another, larger room in the same building.

Time. Rating = 6. The closest (and only) point of temporal contact is more than 30 days.

Objects. Rating = 2. Many of the objects are identical in the two synomorphs and virtually all are of the same kind.

Mechanisms. Rating = 1. All mechanisms occurring in one also occur in the other synomorph.

These ratings total 19, which places these two synomorphs in the borderline region requiring review and consideration in relation to other decisions. Relevant here is the question whether the two exams taken together as one complex of synomorphs are sufficiently independent to stand as a separate behavior setting or whether the exams belong with the lectures and the discussion sections in the same setting. The next *K* test, therefore, compares the exams with the rest of the course. Here are the ratings:

Behavior. Rating = 3. Many of the molar actions beginning in the lectures and discussion section meetings continue or are completed in the midterm or final examinations.

Population. Rating = 1. Nearly all of the persons entering one of the synomorphs also enter the other.

Leaders. Rating = 1. The synomorphs have the same leaders.

Space. Rating = 2. More than half the total space is common to the two synomorphs; the only space unique to one synomorph is the large room in which the final exam is held.

Time. Rating = 7. The closest temporal proximity between these two synomorphs is within the same week; 3 of the 42 class meetings and the midterm exam occur within the same seven-day period: $4/43 = .09 \times 100 = 9$ percent of the contacts between these two synomorphs are within this period.

Objects. Rating = 2. Few objects are unique to one of the synomorphs; nearly all are of the same kind.

Mechanisms. Rating = 2. Verbalization and listening that are characteristic of the behavior pattern in the lectures are present but in only a small fraction of the behavior occurring in the exams.

These ratings total a K value of 18, indicating that the exams should be considered as part of the same K-21 behavior setting as the rest of the course. This finding also indicates that the borderline K of 19 between the two exams should be interpreted in the same direction, that the two exams are too interdependent to stand as separate settings.

We conclude, therefore, that all of the synomorphs and synomorph complexes identified at the beginning of this illustration are, by the K test and at the level specified (21), sufficiently interdependent among themselves to constitute a single behavior setting, the course as a whole, "Observational Methods."

In addition to these detailed comparisons involved in applying the K test for interdependence to specific synomorph pairs, Table 4.2 shows examples from the Midwest study of sets of synomorphs with different ranges of K values among themselves and the behavior settings they form.

TABLE 4.2
Examples of K *Values from Midwest Study*

Synomorph sets	K values	Behavior settings
Third Grade Reading Class Third Grade Writing Class Third Grade Arithmetic Class	14–16	Third Grade Academic Subjects
Drugstore Fountain Drugstore Pharmacy Drugstore Variety Department	19–20	Drugstore
Twelve Monthly Meetings of Womens Club I	18–20	Womens Club I Meeting
Third Grade Academic Subjects Fourth Grade Academic Subjects Fifth Grade Academic Subjects	28–30	Third Grade Academic Subjects Fourth Grade Academic Subjects Fifth Grade Academic Subjects

Presbyterian Church Worship
  Service
Presbyterian Church Sunday
  School Opening Exercises
Presbyterian Church Members
  Meeting
Presbyterian Church Martha Circle
  Study Group
	22–37	Presbyterian Church Worship
		  Service
		Presbyterian Church Sunday
		  School Opening Exercises
		Presbyterian Church Members
		  Meeting
		Presbyterian Church Martha Circle
		  Study Group

VARIATION IN K VALUES WITH TIME PERIOD COVERED

The K test for dynamic interdependence was initially developed in studies of whole small towns for periods of one year. The cutting point of 21 was selected on the basis of empirical findings in such year-long studies. Reflection suggests and empirical testing reveals that obtained values of K are markedly influenced by the total time period included in the study. Investigations that span periods either much shorter or much longer than one year may require modifications in the use of the K test.

To illustrate, recall the Midwest setting Ellson Drugstore and its included synomorph complexes: the pharmacy, the fountain, and the variety department. Over the year of the study, the K test showed the three included synomorphs to be so interdependent that they were not separate K-21 settings but parts of the setting Ellson Drugstore. In part the value of K was determined by the overlap in population, which, over the full year of the study, was quite high: observation showed that most of the persons entering any one of the three synomorph complexes of the drugstore would, at some time during the year, also enter the others. However, if the period included in the study is substantially reduced, say to six months or to three months, this percentage of overlap will obviously be reduced, yielding a higher value of K indicating lesser interdependence. A period of but one week would show a yet smaller amount of overlap. Similar differences, although usually to a lesser degree, may be found on the other interdependence ratings of the K test.

Analogous problems are encountered when time periods much longer than the standard one year are considered. The aim to differentiate units on the basis of a defined degree of functional interdependence remains intact, but the evidence of interdependence is different for long periods of time; the overlap of leaders and members between occurrences separated by years is always, finally, reduced to zero, and connections via temporal contiguity are inevitably attenuated. Although the value of K between any two occurrences of the Midwest behavior setting Presbyterian Church Worship Service during the one-year period studied was clearly below the selected cutting point of 21, indicating that they were two occurrences of the same setting, that value would certainly rise with each passing year and ultimately would substantially exceed 21. Are they still two occurrences of the same behavior setting? This problem and practical solutions for it are considered in greater detail in Barker and Schoggen (1973, pp. 42–44), where viability of behavior settings over a decade is given empirical measurement.

RELIABILITY OF INTERDEPENDENCE SCALE RATINGS

The reliability of ratings using the interdependence scale was investigated by having three judges compute K values for a stratified sample of 100 synomorph pairs from the Midwest study analogous to the comparisons demonstrated above. The sample was selected to represent every kind of relation between synomorphs. In the case of 79 of these pairs, the K values of all judges were 21 or above, and for 10 of the pairs the K values of all judges were 20 or below; thus the three judges agreed that 89 percent of the synomorphs were or were not behavior settings at the level specified. This agreement was better than chance at the .001 level of confidence. Correlations between the ratings of pairs of judges were .93, .93, and .92.

In a more recent investigation on a smaller scale, Prull (1976) tested the agreement of independent raters and found somewhat lower levels of agreement; three judges agreed that 74 percent of the 27 synomorph pairs in the sample either were or were not K-21 behavior settings. The interjudge correlations were reported as .61, .68, and .72. Prull's study, a dissertation, was limited to certain kinds of settings on the campus of one college. The ratings were made by persons familiar with the college but with no prior experience with behavior setting inventory procedures. Perhaps agreement levels in this study would have been higher if a larger sample of synomorphs had been included.

Prull also presents interesting and valuable data on interjudge agreement on each of the seven scales of the K test. Although he found substantial differences in agreement across the seven scales, he concludes that the relatively low agreement on some of the scales—such as behavioral interdependence and leadership interdependence—was due to the relative lack of good information in this study rather than to any deficiencies in the scales themselves (Prull, 1976, p. 136).

LeCompte (1972a) reports tests of reliability of the unitization procedure among three judges in a year-long study of behavior settings in a rehabilitation hospital. Using two different statistical techniques, agreement among the three judges in identifying 122 behavior settings was found to be 90 percent or better (pp. 4.2.1–2).

In view of the less-than-perfect agreement with which the value of K is judged, synomorph pairs with K values between 18 and 22 in practical fieldwork should, as indicated above, always be reconsidered and compared with previous judgments for similar synomorph pairs. If the obtained K value is not in accord with previous determinations, the scale ratings should be carefully checked and new ratings made if errors are discovered. K values less than 18 and greater than 22 normally are not reconsidered.

Nomenclature of Behavior Settings

The nomenclature of behavior settings presents difficulties. Although a behavior setting is the total, extra-individual pattern of behavior and milieu, the common names of settings often refer to only one of these aspects. Although the name of the behavior setting City Park in Midwest specifies its physical side, the pattern of the behaving persons and objects is an essential part of the setting. The physical park, per se, without the behavior and objects, is not a behavior setting. In contrast, the name of the setting Presbyterian Sunday School Exercises stresses the behavior, when actually this setting is composed of the integrated functioning of the members, superintendent, auditorium, piano, song leader, pews, songbooks, and so forth. Again, the name of the behavior setting County Superintendent of Schools' Office implicates at any particular time a particular person; in fact, this setting is the behavior-milieu complex associated with a number of different individuals over a period of time and certain persisting parts of the community (a suite of offices labeled "County Superintendent of Schools," a certificate of election, etc.). The inhabitants of a community understand this verbal shorthand.

Conclusion

This completes our presentation on the definition and identification of behavior settings. It is important to note that all behavior settings identified through the processes described above have the same defining attributes, and that in terms of these attributes they are equivalent entities. It is this that makes it legitimate to enumerate them and perform arithmetical manipulations with respect to measures of their common attributes. Any two behavior settings will differ in many respects, but in their defining properties they are identical. Although, as we have seen, High School Latin Classes and Ruttley's Jewelry and Watch Repair Shop are different behavior settings and obviously have many very different characteristics, they are equivalent in terms of their defining properties. This equivalence makes it possible to compare different environments in terms of behavior settings; behavior settings as defined give us a stable, constant unit for the comparative study of different environments at a given time and for the same environment at different times.

In the case of the definition of a room in the example mentioned above, two rooms—spaces that meet the definition of a room as specified—are identical in their defining properties. Homes and other dwellings can be compared in terms of number of rooms with assurance that a common unit is the subject of investigation. But in addition to their common defining properties, rooms have many characteristics that vary widely from room to room, such as height of ceiling, square footage, color of walls, number of windows and doors, and material used for the floor.

Behavior settings also have many characteristics or properties that vary from setting to setting, such as frequency of occurrence, duration, identities of inhabitants and their manifold characteristics, interests served, activities supported, and autonomy. These are relatively stable, idiosyncratic characteristics that are defined by the program of the setting and are maintained by the homeostatic control mechanisms of the setting. These enduring, whole-entity characteristics of the behavior settings of a town or institution make it possible to describe the kind of habitat the town or institution provides for its inhabitants. In the next three chapters, we consider methods of measuring and describing a number of these relatively stable, distinctive attributes of the behavior settings of a town or institution.

5
Measuring Habitat Extent and Habitat Variety

Behavior settings have been used in empirical applications most frequently to measure and describe important characteristics of whole environmental entities, such as small towns and institutions as habitats for human behavior and development. However, behavior settings are also useful in less extensive studies (see Chap. 11). After completion of the inventory of all the behavior settings occurring one or more times during the time period covered by the study in the particular environmental entity under investigation, attention can be directed to questions about the variable qualities or attributes of the habitat as reflected in the characteristics of its behavior settings. In this and the next two chapters, we describe a number of such variables that have been included in previous investigations.

Questions of primary importance about any ecological environment concern habitat size (how big is this entity?) and habitat variety (how homogeneous or variegated are the behavior settings in this entity?). Comparing towns in terms of acres or population size tells us little about habitat size in terms of opportunities and obligations for molar human behavior. Big schools are obviously different from small schools in many ways, but size of student body alone tells little about the richness and variety of behavioral opportunities and obligations provided by the schools. In this chapter, we consider theoretical and methodological issues involved in measuring habitat extent and habitat variety in whole environmental units.

In the discussion below, it will be convenient to draw for illustration on investigations of behavior settings in the two small towns that we have studied: Midwest, Kansas, and a comparable town in Yorkshire, England, called Yoredale. Substantive findings about these towns in terms of their behavior settings are fully reported elsewhere (Barker & Schoggen, 1973) and will not concern us here, where our interest is exclusively method-ological and theoretical.

Theory of Habitat Extent

The primary whole-entity attribute of a behavior setting is *existence* (occurrence, happening). A list of the behavior settings occurring during a stated period—such as a year—in a town, a part of a town, or an institu-tion is a roster of its habitat regions—that is, parts of the environment that provide inhabitants with opportunities and obligations for engaging in dif-ferent kinds of molar behavior. Three direct enumerations of the extent of this habitat are: the number of behavior settings in the roster, the sum of the daily occurrences of the settings in the roster, and the total hours of duration of the behavior settings in the roster.

Number. The number (N) is simply the total number of different K-21 behavior settings that occurred one or more times during the period cov-ered by the inventory as identified by the procedures described in previ-ous chapters.

Occurrence. The occurrence (O) of a behavior setting is the number of days in the period under study, usually a year, on which the setting occurs for any length of time. In a year-long study, then, the maximum occur-rence of a setting is 365 days (366 in a leap year), or one occurrence a day. This is true for behavior settings that function for less than an hour, for those that continue for 24 hours, and for settings that suspend operations for a period during a day (the Midwest Bank and many offices in Midwest cease for an hour at noon; a court session may convene for an hour in the morning, be dismissed for three hours, and reconvene in the afternoon). In all of these cases, a setting is credited with a single occurrence per day. Behavior settings that can be initiated by anyone at any time without spe-cial arrangement have an occurrence of 365 even though there may be days when they are uninhabited—for example, a telephone booth, a ceme-tery, or a park.

Duration. The duration (D) of a behavior setting is the total number of hours it functions during the period of the study. In the ordinary case, duration in hours per occurrence (d) and number of occurrences (O) are stable and well-known attributes of behavior settings, so that duration (D) is the product of hours per occurrence and number of occurrences (Od); this is true of school classes, church worship services, and grocery stores, for example. But when the length of the occurrence varies (auction sales, committee meetings), and when the setting is available at any time but is actually occupied only intermittently (cemetery, telephone booth), detailed information must be obtained or estimates made of separate occurrences and their durations.

Data concerning the occurrence and duration of most behavior settings are readily available; they are often posted on the doors of businesses and offices, announced in newspapers and organization bulletins, and recorded in minutes of meetings. The occurrence and duration of settings with irregular schedules such as auction sales must be obtained through on-site observation and consultation with informants.

In the earliest attempts to measure habitat extent, we relied mainly on the one measure, N, number of settings per year (Barker & Wright, 1955). Setting duration and frequency of occurrence were treated primarily as attributes of individual settings, not as contributors to overall habitat size. Later experience, however, showed that using number of settings per year as the only measure of habitat extent does not represent habitat size adequately, as the discussion below will demonstrate. Comparative studies of different communities, and of the same community at different times, showed us that all three of these direct measures of habitat extent (N, O, D) need to be considered.

In our studies of the behavior settings of Midwest and Yoredale for periods of one year at a time, these three direct enumerations of behavior settings were used to derive a single measure of habitat extent, which is called an *urb*. For convenience in practical computations, however, we have used the *centiurb*, defined as 1 percent of an urb. Next we discuss the issues that led us to the centiurb as a better measure of habitat extent than any one of the three direct measures.

RELATIONS BETWEEN NUMBER, OCCURRENCE, AND DURATION OF BEHAVIOR SETTINGS

On Tuesday, October 22, 1963, between 10 and 11 A.M., there were 148 behavior settings available in Yoredale and 126 settings in Midwest. In Yoredale, there were two places for banking behavior (compared with one in Midwest); seven places for "hallwaying" (four in Midwest); four places to engage in beauty-shop behavior (one in Midwest); and three places to place bets (none in Midwest). This ratio, in general, holds true; the mean number of behavior settings occurring in Midwest in an average hour in 1963–64 was 88 percent of the number occurring in Yoredale. But the story is different for a year-long period. During 1963–64, 884 behavior settings occurred (one or more times) in Midwest and 758 settings in

Yoredale; that is, by the year, in 1963–64 the number of behavior settings in Midwest was 117 percent of the number in Yoredale.

These data are surprising and confusing; they raise some fundamental questions: Is there a basic temporal interval for enumerating behavior settings? Are years more basic for this purpose than hours? When is a behavior setting a region of the habitat? When is it "at hand" for inhabiting? Finally, is there, in fact, a univocal measure of the extent of the environment? Some examples reveal the generality of the situation from which these questions arise.

First, an institutional example. A philanthropist endows a number of display galleries in four museums and fills them with art treasures. These permanent exhibits amount to 13, 15, 18, and 22 percent, respectively, of the exhibit galleries in the fortunate museums. The museum directors, for administrative reasons, place restrictions on the days the galleries are open to the public. Counting each day a gallery is open to the public as one gallery-day, it turns out that the philanthropist's galleries are open for 4.5, 5.0, 3.6, and 7.0 percent, respectively, of the museums' total gallery-days. But the galleries, when open, are not always open for full days, so that the philanthropist's galleries account for 0.7, 0.9, 0.8, and 1.7 percent, respectively, of the museums' total gallery-hours. The question is: What is the extent of the philanthropist's contributions to these museums?

To the museum directors, who see themselves as conservators of art treasures, the contribution ranges from 13 to 22 percent of their collections. But to museum visitors, the philanthropist contributed 3.6 to 7.0 percent of the exhibits; for, wandering freely through the open galleries on their occasional visits, they would find these proportions of the galleries acknowledging this gift. To museum guards, the philanthropist's gifts account for 0.7 to 1.7 percent of their work hours.

So, to the question of the extent of the philanthropist's contributions to the museums, there are three answers: the gifts amount to (a) between 13 and 22 percent of the museums' resources, (b) 3.6 to 7.0 percent of the museums' daily accessible exhibits, and (c) 0.7 to 1.7 percent of the gallery-hours of operation. Is one of these answers more true than the others? Are there ways to combine them into a single measure of extent of museum environment?

Here is another institutional example. One college offers 450 different classes in a particular semester; there are 418 meetings of these classes during an average week, 260 during an average school day, and 35 during an average hour. Another college offers 500 classes, with 400 meetings during an average week, 200 during an average day, and 50 during an average hour. Which college is larger in terms of classes that are at hand for attending? The second school is 111 percent as large as the first in terms of classes per semester, 96 percent as large by the week (it has more less-than-weekly classes), 77 percent as large by the day (it has more classes that meet only once or twice a week, and fewer that meet four or five times a week), and 143 percent as large by the hour (it has more multi-hour classes).

Finally, a biological example. Tidepools are important ecological features of the shore environment. Like behavior settings, some tidepools are year-round, continuous fixtures, whereas others have limited durations. Tidepools that are not continuous may be reconstituted each day by the tides, or they may be reconstituted only occasionally, during periods of conjunction of high tides and winds; they then last for varying times. A tidepool, like a behavior setting, has an identity that can be specified by spatial-temporal coordinates; it can be denoted by pointing; it can be examined and re-examined. One can enumerate precisely those present during any period of time: 45 minutes, 7 hours, 13 days, 9.5 months, or a full year. But what period? One might find the following numbers of tidepools on two shore areas: (a) total number of pools during a year—884 in area 1 and 758 in area 2; (b) mean number of pools during random days—146 in area 1 and 178 in area 2; (c) mean number of pools during random hours—33 in area 1 and 37 in area 2. In this conjectural example, the actual 1963–64 data for the behavior settings of Midwest and Yoredale have been used; they are, in fact, data that might be duplicated on a shore region. It is obvious that the different measures of tidepool extent would have different consequences for different animal species. Measure (c) indicates that both areas are meager habitats for rapidly migrating birds; neither area is rich in pools for short-time visitors, but area 2 is more favorable for them than area 1. Measure (b) shows that both areas have more extensive tidepool environments for slower migrants, or for long-time residents that are day-long feeders, and that area 2 is more extensive than area 1. But for the staff of a permanent marine laboratory, size measurement (a) is salient; over the seasons, area 1 is richer in tidepool collection sites than area 2.

These examples show that our discovery that Midwest and Yoredale are of different relative extents when their behavior settings are enumerated by the year, day, and hour is not peculiar to them. This equivocal relation occurs in all cases where the rate of recurrence of the entities enumerated is not the same in the localities compared. We conclude, therefore, that the same enumerating time interval must be used when comparisons are made, and it must be chosen for its relevance to the problem under consideration. So the question arises: What is the relevant interval for determining the extents of habitats such as those provided by Midwest and Yoredale? Some fundamental facts about human action are relevant to this question.

TEMPORAL RELATIONS BETWEEN BEHAVIOR AND BEHAVIOR SETTINGS

Our concern is primarily with the environment of molar behavior. In the present connection it is of great importance that molar actions extend over varying lengths of time. "Doing the family shopping" may continue for an hour, whereas "getting married next June" extends for months. Intentions (Lewin, 1951), plans (Miller, Galanter, & Pribram, 1960), cognitive maps (Tolman, 1932), scripts (Schank & Abelson, 1977), and social episodes (Forgas, 1979) are stable states that have been postulated to account on the organism side for the elementary fact that behavior occurs in units that persist over time. A molar action takes place within behavior settings that are at hand during its time span, and our investigations show that the number of settings at hand varies with the duration of the span. "Doing the family shopping" occurs within a smaller time span and smaller habitat (number of behavior settings) than "getting married next June." If we knew the durations of the molar actions that occur in particular environments such as Midwest and Yoredale, these would provide the necessary temporal frames for determining the extents of the towns' habitats.

We have some bases for estimating the durations of molar actions, for they are governed by the segments into which time is divided by clocks and calendars, by sunrise and sunset, by noon whistles and the 6:00 news. Time is marked off by hours, days, weeks, months, and years as clearly as space is marked off by inches, feet, and miles (or centimeters, meters, and kilometers). Engagement books, diaries, programs of organizations and institutions, and schedules of events are as ubiquitous in Midwest and Yoredale as elsewhere in Western society, and they are almost all segmented by hours, days, months, and years. In consequence, the actions of the inhabitants of Midwest and Yoredale, their plans and intentions, are arranged in terms of hourly, daily, monthly, and yearly periods as inevitably as they are arranged in accordance with the towns' physical spaces and their temperatures, precipitations, and terrains.

However, another elementary attribute of molar behavior attenuates for individual actions the coerciveness of these imposed time intervals: molar behavior is goal-directed. When environmental circumstances change, alterations occur in the molar actions underway so that they usually maintain their goal directions until they are completed. An important environmental change is the periodic termination and initiation of the behavior settings of a community. Molar actions have a special property that maintains their directions under these circumstances: flexible duration. If the behavior setting Grocery Store shows signs of terminating its daily occurrence at 5:30 instead of the expected 6:00 P.M., the action of "doing the family shopping," which usually continues for an hour, is either telescoped and completed before 5:30 or extended into the next day, when Grocery Store again occurs. In either case, "doing the family shopping" continues and is completed; the absence of Grocery Store between 5:30 P.M. and 8:00 A.M. the next day is not crucial to the completion of this molar action. Most molar actions have this flexibility, and it makes their completion independent, to some degree, of the temporal schedules of the behavior settings they require for their completion. This means that a behavior setting is almost equally at hand for many molar actions if it occurs this hour, this day, tomorrow, or on following days.

In the absence of data on the relative frequencies of molar actions of different durations, we assume that the behavioral present—the time interval within which intentions are carried out—is distributed with about equal frequency around the modal intervals *during this hour, during this day*, and *during this year*. On this basis, the most general single measure of relative habitat extent is one that weights equally the number of behavior settings that occur within these three periods. When we do this for Midwest and Yoredale in 1963–64, we find that Midwest has $884/758 = 1.17$ as many behavior settings per year as Yoredale, it has $146/178 = 0.82$ as many settings per day, and it has $32.6/37.2 = 0.88$ as many settings per hour (Table 5.1). The mean of these ratios, which weights them equally, is 0.95. For a sample of molar actions centering with equal frequency on completion during this hour, during this day, and during this year, there are 95 percent as many behavior settings at hand in Midwest as in Yoredale.

STANDARD TOWN

In order to make general comparisons of habitat extent across different ecological environments or of the same environment at different times, a common base of comparison would be useful. Ideally, we would wish for a composite measure based on previous studies of a number of different communities so that habitat extent could be expressed in values that would show size of community in relation to an established and known standard. Unfortunately, no such composite measure is available; commu-

TABLE 5.1
Habitat Extent in Terms of Behavior Settings and Centiurbs

| | 1954–55 | | | | 1963–64 | | | |
| | Midwest | | Yoredale | | Midwest | | Yoredale | |
Measure	No. (1a)	%[a] (1b)	No. (2a)	%[a] (2b)	No. (3a)	%[a] (3b)	No. (4a)	%[a] (4b)
(1) Behavior settings per year	576	85	504	74	884	130	758	111
(2) Mean BS per day	136	90	144	95	146	97	178	118
(3) Mean BS per hour	32.4	95	34.3	101	32.6	95	37.2	109
(4) Extent in centiurbs (mean of rows 1, 2, 3)		90		90		107		113

SOURCE: Reprinted from Barker and Schoggen, 1973, table 3.1.
[a] Percentage of standard town.

nity size measures appear to be limited to size of population, physical area, and numbers of structures, all useful for many purposes but not for measuring the numbers of opportunities and obligations for engaging in different kinds of molar behavior.

In the Midwest-Yoredale studies, therefore, we made a first effort to establish such a composite measure. We created for this purpose a hypothetical standard town whose dimensions in terms of number of behavior settings per year, mean number per day, and mean number per hour are measured by obtaining in each of these dimensions the mean of four values: Midwest in 1954–55 and 1963–64 and Yoredale in 1954–55 and 1963–64. From the data of Table 5.1, the dimensional values of this standard town are calculated to be:

(a) behavior settings per year, 680.5 (Row 1, Cols. [1a+2a+3a+4a]/4)
(b) mean behavior settings per day, 151.0 (R 2, C [1a+2a+3a+4a]/4)
(c) mean behavior settings per hour, 34.1 (R 3, C [1a+2a+3a+4a]/4)

The resulting standard town with these dimensions is called an urb. The dimensional values of the towns, or parts of the towns, and of individual behavior settings can be calculated and reported, for convenience, in terms of percentages of the urb values, or centiurbs (cu). Here, as an example, are the dimensional values and extent in centiurbs of Midwest's habitat in 1963–64:

(a) behavior settings per year as percentage of urb,
     $100(884/680.5) = 130.0$ (T 5.1, R 1, C 3b)
(b) mean behavior settings per day as percentage of urb,
     $100(146/151) = 96.7$ (T 5.1, R 2, C 3b)

(c)   mean behavior settings per hour as percentage of urb,
100(32.6/34.1) = 95.6 (T 5.1, R 3, C 3b)

The extent of whole town in centiurbs (the mean of a, b, and c) equals 107
(T 5.1, R 4, C 3b). By the same process, the habitat extent of Yoredale in
the same year turns out to be 113 cu (T 5.1, R 4, C 4b).

Many combinations of the dimensional values sum to the same habitat
extent. Relatively few behavior settings per year may be compensated—
as far as habitat extent is concerned—by relatively many per day or per
hour and vice versa. This is an aspect of behavior-habitat reality; it is in
accord with the fundamental nature of molar action (flexible means and
stable goal direction), and it is in accord with the fundamental nature of
the human habitat (particular parts present and absent on regular or irregular schedules). This feature of habitat extent is illustrated by the data
in Table 5.2 regarding Midwest's 1963–64 habitat within its different *authority systems* (classes of behavior settings under the aegis of the town's
churches, government agencies, private enterprises, schools, and voluntary associations; authority systems are discussed in detail in Chap. 6).

The values in Table 5.2 were obtained as follows: Taking the first row of
the first column (28.4 percent) as an example, the inventory found that
193 behavior settings under the aegis of the town's churches occurred at
least once during 1963–64 (Barker & Schoggen, 1973, table 6.1, p. 195).
As stated above, the urb value for behavior settings per year is 680.5. The
tabled value, then, is 100(193/680.5) = 28.4 percent.

Churches and Voluntary Associations have authority over almost the
same extent of Midwest's habitat, 12.2 and 12.3 cu respectively, even
though the authority of the Churches extends to fewer settings in the
year. However, Church settings occur on more days than settings of Volun-

TABLE 5.2
*Measures of Midwest's Habitat Within Its Authority Systems, 1963–64:
Number of Behavior Settings per Year, per Day, and per Hour as
Percentages of Urb Values; Extent in Centiurbs*

Measure	Churches	Government Agencies	Private Enterprises	Schools	Voluntary Associations
Behavior settings per year	28.4%	16.8%	19.4%	34.2%	31.2%
BS per day	6.6	14.9	43.5	27.7	3.8
BS per hour	1.8	20.8	58.9	12.3	1.8
Extent (mean of rows 1, 2, 3)	12.2 cu	17.5 cu	40.6 cu	24.8 cu	12.3 cu

SOURCE: Reprinted from Barker and Schoggen, 1973, table 2.1.

tary Associations, and this compensates almost precisely for the Churches' fewer settings per year. Midwest's Private Enterprises have authority over fewer behavior settings per year than do its Schools, but their much greater daily and hourly occurrence results in 164 percent as much Private Enterprise habitat as School habitat.

STANDARD BEHAVIOR SETTING

In practical applications, the calculations of habitat extent are greatly simplified by the use of values for a hypothetical standard behavior setting, defined as one that occurs every hour of each day during the year covered by the inventory. These values serve as convenient weights for determining the measurement in centiurbs of any town, part of town, or single behavior setting. The dimensional values of this standard setting in terms of percentages of the values for standard town (urbs) are shown in Table 5.3, and an example of the use of the values as weights is given in Table 5.4, which illustrates the calculation of the extent of Midwest's Primary Aesthetic Habitat, one of eleven *action patterns* discussed in Chap. 7.

REGULAR AND OCCASIONAL HABITATS

A distinction of importance for some analyses is that between regular and occasional behavior settings. Regular settings recur on many days in a year for many hours per occurrence. Vista Cafe in Yoredale and Skelly Service Station in Midwest are regular behavior settings; they recur day in and day out. Such settings constitute a town's regular habitat; they are routinely at hand. Occasional settings recur on one or a few days in a year for one or a few hours per occurrence; Church of England Garden Fete in

TABLE 5.3
Standard Behavior Setting: Dimensional Values and Extent in Centiurbs

Dimensions	No. of settings	Dimensional values
Behavior settings		
per year	1	$100(1/680.5) = 0.147\%$
Mean BS per day	1	$100(1/151.0) = 0.662$
Mean BS per hour	1	$100(1/34.1) = 2.932$
Extent		1.25 cu

SOURCE: Reprinted from Barker and Schoggen, 1973, table 2.2.
NOTE: A standard behavior setting is one that occurs continuously throughout a survey year.

TABLE 5.4
Dimensional Values of Standard Behavior Setting (SBS) Used as Weights for Determining Extent of Midwest's Primary Aesthetic Habitat (PAH) in 1963–64

Dimensions	Number of settings in PAH	Dimensional values of SBS as weights	Dimensional values of PAH (Col. 1 × Col. 2)
Behavior settings per year	75	0.147%	11.025%
Mean BS per day	5.8	0.662	3.845
Mean BS per hour	0.4	2.932	1.173
Extent			5.35 cu

SOURCE: Reprinted from Barker and Schoggen, 1973, table 2.3.
NOTE: Primary aesthetic habitat consists of behavior settings where the action pattern Aesthetics is prominent.

Yoredale and Parent-Teacher Association Carnival in Midwest are occasional behavior settings. Such settings constitute a town's occasional habitat; plans and advance arrangements must be made to inhabit them, for if missed, they are not at hand again for a long time.

In measurement by centiurbs (Tables 5.3 and 5.4), the first dimension, "behavior settings per year," contributes equally to all behavior settings, whether regular or occasional; if a behavior setting occurs 365 days for 24 hours per day or only once during the year for one hour, it is one setting with a weight of 0.147, and the first dimension contributes 0.147/3 to the centiurb measure of habitat extent. But the second dimension, "mean number of behavior settings per day," contributes more to the extent of a regular setting than to that of an occasional setting; to a regular setting that occurs every day it contributes 0.662/3 to the centiurb measure, whereas to an occasional behavior setting that occurs once during the year for one hour it contributed, in 1963–64 (a leap year), 1/366 of this amount. The third dimension of the centiurb measure, "mean number of behavior settings per hour," contributes still more to the centiurb measure of the extent of regular settings than of occasional settings; to a regular setting that occurs continuously throughout the year, the third dimension contributes 2.932, whereas to an occasional setting occurring once during the year for one hour (of 8,784 hours in leap year) it contributed 1/8,784 as much in 1963–64.

For these reasons, the relative contribution of behavior settings per year, per day, and per hour to the centiurb measure is an indication of the relative presence of regular and occasional behavior settings in the habitat. It may be noted, for example, in Table 5.2, that Private Enterprises and Government Agencies receive greater proportions of their overall centiurb value from behavior settings per hour than from behavior settings per year, whereas the reverse is true for Churches, Schools, and Voluntary Associations. These data show that the habitats controlled by Private Enterprise and Government Agencies have relatively more regular and fewer occasional behavior settings than the habitats controlled by Churches, Schools, and Voluntary Associations.

HABITAT EXTENT AS A MEASURE OF RESOURCES FOR MOLAR ACTIONS

Many kinds of molar actions occur only within particular kinds of settings; sentencing a man to jail takes place only in settings of the District or County Courts (not in Grocery Stores or Worship Services); getting a haircut occurs only in Barbershops (not in Business Meetings or Basketball Games); filling a tooth is carried out only in Dentists' Offices (not in Garages or Dances). Where this relation holds, molar actions for which there are no appropriate settings do not occur: cricket is not played in Midwest, there is no behavior setting Cricket Game; Latin is not taught in Yoredale, there is no setting Latin Class.

Because of this relation between behavior settings and molar actions, number of behavior settings is a more important component of the extent of the habitat of molar actions than number of behavior setting occurrences or number of hours' duration. This is obvious when one considers the more limited behavior resources of the 12 monthly occurrences of the single Midwest recreational setting Women's Bridge Club II in comparison with 12 occurrences of a wider sample of different recreational settings: three meetings of Women's Bridge Club II, High School Home Economics Club Christmas Party, Old Settlers Pet Parade, Garland Lanes Bowling Exhibition, American Legion Auxiliary Card Party for March of Dimes, Married Couples Bridge Club Meetings in March, Elementary School Operetta, Tractor Pulling Contest, Women's Bridge Club III May Meeting, and Women's Bridge Club IV September Meeting. In terms of centiurbs, the 12 monthly occurrences of Women's Bridge Club II have a habitat extent of 0.06 cu, and the 12 settings (including three meetings of Women's Bridge Club II) have a habitat extent of 0.50 cu. According to the centiurb measurement, the availability of opportunities to set goals and attempt to achieve satisfactions (molar behavior resources) are more than eight times as great in the latter case as in the former. Measurement of habitat extent by centiurbs weights an additional behavior setting 365 (or 366) times greater than an additional occurrence of an existing behavior setting, and it weights an additional behavior setting 8,760 (or 8,784) times greater than an additional hour of an existing setting.

Measurement of habitat extent in terms of centiurbs is a measure of the "at-handness" of habitat supports and coercions for molar actions; it is a temporal-spatial proximity measure. The larger the centiurb measure of habitat extent, the greater the number of molar behavior opportunities and requirements within the normal time perspective—that is, the greater the number of goal possibilities and obligations immediately at hand.

It should be clear that measuring habitat extent provided by a town, a part of town, or an institution in terms of behavior settings and centiurbs does not include the total universe of habitat resources available to the inhabitants but is limited to those that occur within the boundaries of the community selected for study. The measurement of the resources concerned with physical health in Midwest and Yoredale, for example, included only the doctors' offices and other health-related behavior settings located within the towns. Regional hospitals were also available within an hour's drive of both towns, and medical specialists could be consulted in larger cities at greater distances. In one of the small high schools in our studies, there is no swimming program because the school does not have its own pool. The beautiful, Olympic-size pool of a nearby larger school is a valued resource for some students from the pool-less school who arrange to have access to it, but it is a weak substitute for a swimming program as a regular part of the small school's habitat readily at hand for all the school's students.

Resources such as these and countless others would, of course, need to be represented in any effort to study in a comprehensive way *all* resources available to particular persons. A behavior setting inventory of a community has a different objective: to measure the at-handness of habitat supports and coercions for molar actions within the community. The centiurb measure of habitat extent is a temporal-spatial proximity measure of a given community, not an assessment of all resources potentially available regardless of location.

PHYSICAL MILIEU AND HABITAT EXTENT

It will be noted that amount of space is not included in determinations of habitat extent, which is based entirely on the number, occurrence, and duration of behavior settings. This does not imply that extent of physical space is not a factor of importance in the programs of behavior settings, including the behavior of their human components. It means only that habitat extent as we have defined it and measured it in centiurbs is independent of the amount of physical space. In fact, many habitat regions of the same extent in centiurbs are geographically larger, as is often the case in Midwest as compared with Yoredale. They normally differ in some other physical properties, too; they are usually warmer in Midwest, and have boundary walls that are less solid and less well insulated against sound transmission. All of these differences in the physical properties of the towns' settings are undoubtedly causally interrelated with their standing patterns of behavior, and they deserve investigation, but we judge them to have no systematic relation to the extent—the temporal-geographical proximity, or at-handness—of the towns' habitats. When the area of Ellson Drugstore was doubled by taking over adjacent store space, it did not appreciably change its temporal-geographical proximity to the inhabitants of Midwest; it was still a single 7:30 A.M.-to-6 P.M. Monday-through-Saturday locus, no more and no less at hand within the time perspective of Midwesterners for planning and engaging in drugstore behavior. However, when the Midwest behavior setting Dentons Drugstore went out of business, leaving only Ellson Drugstore, the extent of the *genotype* (see p. 90) Drugstores decreased in Midwest from two loci to one locus, from 365 to 300 days, and from 5,110 to 2,400 total hours of occurrence during the year. After this happened, travelers stopping for an hour in Midwest and day-long visitors to the town were more likely to find no resources for drugstore behavior, and the plans of the town's inhabitants for drugstore behavior had to be plotted within a future with drugstore settings less immediately accessible in time and space. According to the measurement by centiurbs, the extent of the genotype Drugstores decreased from 2.5 cu before the demise of Dentons Drugstore to 1.4 cu after its demise, a decrease of 44 percent.

Ellson Drugstore's program was immediately changed by the loss of its genotype mate in complex ways, one being the production of more person-hours of behavior. This, in fact, was an important factor behind the spatial expansion of the setting. Reduction in the extent of the genotype Drugstores caused an expansion of the spatial dimension of the remaining drugstore, but it did not increase its extent as measured in centiurbs—its geo-temporal proximity.

A new recreational facility, a bowling alley, was constructed in Midwest in the interval between the two surveys reported in Barker and Schoggen (1973). When completed, a fine new building had been added to the town but recreational habitat extent as measured by centiurbs did not increase until the lanes opened for business, bowlers began using the lanes, and leagues began to form. By the time of the survey in 1963–64, the new facility was serving as a host institution for 25 behavior settings (such as

Garland Lanes Saturday Junior (13–17) Girls League Bowling Game) with a total habitat extent of 2.02 centiurbs, an important increase in the availability of opportunities and coercions (league members are obligated to participate on regularly scheduled occasions) for engaging in goal-directed (molar) behavior.

Although it is true that the centiurb measure of habitat extent is not dependent on amount of physical space in behavior settings, there are, of course, minimum space requirements for every behavior setting; without the building, the 25 bowling settings would not exist. The centiurb measure only assumes that such minimum space requirements are met; it includes no specific representation of such minimal requirements.

It is also true, as Wicker, McGrath, and Armstrong (1972) have pointed out, that the amount of physical space or capacity sets an upper limit on the number of persons a setting can accommodate: Keith Barbershop with two barber chairs but only one barber can accommodate just a few customers at a time—one in the chair and two or three others waiting; Presbyterian Church Annual Public Dinner and Bazaar held in the church basement has seating for about 100 persons at one time. Although such upper limits clearly exist, they are not incorporated in any way into the centiurb measure of habitat extent largely because such limits are practically not important in the behavior settings of towns such as Midwest; careful scrutiny of all the 885 settings in Midwest in 1963–64 (listed in Barker & Schoggen, 1973, app. A) revealed only a few for which setting capacity may have affected the number of persons inhabiting the setting— that is, the physical capacity of almost all settings far exceeds the number of setting inhabitants. Given that human molar behavior has constancy of goal direction but flexibility of means, the limits imposed by the physical capacity of behavior settings can be circumvented by a variety of techniques. Potential customers of Keith Barbershop learn to avoid certain times when the shop is unusually busy; at the Presbyterian Church Annual Public Dinner and Bazaar, plates are cleared as diners finish so that others can be served; Dr. Sterne Dental Service Office operates by appointment only.

Wicker, McGrath, and Armstrong (1972), in a questionnaire study of 107 churches in Illinois, demonstrated the importance of the capacity variable in determining attendance at Sunday morning worship services in these churches; they found that seating capacity of the room accounted for more of the variance in church attendance than did size of church membership. This was true even though one technique of reducing the limitation imposed by capacity—holding two and even three services each Sunday morning—was frequently employed by these churches.

Thus physical capacity of behavior settings can be important in certain kinds of settings, such as Sunday morning worship services, telephone booths, rock concerts, and popular restaurants on Saturday night. However, our study of *all* the settings of small towns like Midwest and Yoredale leads us to believe that setting capacity rarely has a significant influence on behavior setting participation.

GENERALIZABILITY OF CENTIURB MEASURE OF HABITAT EXTENT

As we have seen, the centiurb measure was developed in connection with our studies of two small towns. Immediately, however, the question arises concerning applicability of the centiurb measure in studies of other ecological environments, such as other towns, institutions, and parts of cities. The principles utilized in the centiurb measure seem fully transferable and applicable in studies of other environments. The centiurb values based on number of settings per year, mean number per day, and mean number per hour should be as useful in studies of colleges, hospitals, or sections of cities as they are in studies of small towns. The centiurb assessment of habitat extent would appear to be just as superior to other measures of the environment (square footage, number of rooms, size of population) in studies of the at-handness of opportunities and obligations for engaging in purposive, goal-directed behavior in other ecological environments as it is in studies of small towns. How different quantitatively the actual centiurb values might turn out to be in such studies as compared with those reported for Midwest and Yoredale is simply an empirical question to be answered by research. The usefulness of the centiurb measure in studies of community change is nicely demonstrated in the study of the impact of the construction of a major flood control and recreational reservoir on six small towns in the vicinity (Harloff, Gump, & Campbell, 1981).

Measuring Habitat Variety: Behavior Setting Genotypes

The problem of classifying behavior settings poses difficulties comparable to that of classifying organisms or minerals. The outward appearance of the standing patterns of the settings Pintner Abstract and Title Company and of Wolf Attorney Office are so similar that a stranger might easily confuse them and attempt to transact lawyer's business in an abstract office, and vice versa. The surface aspects of the Midwest School Principal's Office changed so much between 1954 and 1964 that a returning student might not recognize it. It is widely understood, however, that such superficial similarities and differences are adventitious and that among the perplexing multiplicity of behavior settings on this level there are a smaller number of more fundamental types.

A community has common names, or code words, that identify types of behavior settings. Four people at a card table with cards before them do not know how to initiate the behavior setting until the code word is known: bridge, pinochle, poker, hearts, etc. A patron inquires about the standing pattern of behavior by using the appropriate code word: Is this a bank? No, this is a real estate office. Code words of these kinds identify behavior settings with such fundamental similarities that we have called them *behavior setting genotypes*.

Organisms of the same genotype have the same coded programs stored in their nuclei, and behavior settings of the same genotype have the same coded programs stored in their most central performance (leadership) zones: zone 6 if the most central region has a single inhabitant, zone 5 if it has multiple inhabitants (see pp. 127–29 for discussion of zones of penetration). Sometimes this program is coded via written language; a printout of the program of baseball games is available in a baseball rule book. In these cases, the programs of different settings can be compared, item by item, to determine their degree of equivalence. However, written programs are not usually available; for most behavior settings, therefore, other evidence of their genotypic equivalence is essential.

A central problem of behavior setting operation is to get the proper program stored within performance zone inhabitants, and especially within the occupants of zones 6/5. This is accomplished by formal training and/or experience in the setting, and it requires time. But when the program of a setting is incorporated within a person, it is one of the person's relatively permanent attributes, and the code name of the program is often used as personal reference, such as attorney, postmaster, grocer, pharmacist, teacher. It is especially important in the present connection to note that a longer time is usually required for a person to become the *carrier of the program* of a setting than to become the *carrier of input* to the setting. A person can generate a problem for an attorney in much less time than it takes to generate the know-how of an attorney.

These facts provide a practical basis for judging whether different behavior settings are of the same or different genotypes even when details of their programs are not known. If settings A and B continue to function without change when their zone 6/5 inhabitants are interchanged, then A and B have the same program and are identical in genotype. The behavior setting Wolf Attorney Office would continue to function effectively if attorney Wiley displaced attorney Wolf in zone 6—if Wiley purchased Wolf's practice, for example. Transpositions of this kind occur not infrequently. And they can occur because the programs of general law offices are the same: the laws, the princples, the forms, the know-how are identical. It is the particular legal cases and the problems of particular clients that differ. These are the inputs. Attorney Wiley would have to be briefed on attorney Wolf's cases, but the functioning of the setting would scarcely miss a beat. On the other hand, if attorney Wiley were to transfer to zone 6 of County Engineer's Office, the setting would stop short; the general law office program that has been incorporated within attorney Wiley by long schooling and experience could not process the inputs to County Engineer's Office.

Thus there are persons who carry the program brand of a particular behavior setting genotype upon them, and all such behavior settings in which they function effectively as zone 6/5 performers are of the same genotype. In this connection it is important to recognize that some individuals store a number of programs, that is, some people are versatile. The test, therefore, is not whether a particular person is interchangeable between zone 6/5 of different settings but whether the program the person possesses as a performer in a particular behavior setting is transposable to other behavior settings.

The transposability of *programmed* performers between zone 6/5 of different behavior settings is the most crucial evidence of their genotypic equivalence. But there is other evidence of considerable value in borderline cases.

(1) In judging the transposability of stored programs, the inhabitants of all zones are relevant, though their diagnostic significance increases with their depth of penetration into the central zones of the settings. The part of a behavior setting program stored by a zone 2 inhabitant (audience, invited guest) is widely interchangeable among zone 2 of other behavior settings, the program of a zone 3 inhabitant (member, customer) is less widely transferable, and the program of a minor functionary in zone 4 (bookkeeper, mechanic) has restricted transposability, whereas the total program stored by occupants of zones 6 and 5 (piano teacher, cafe operator) are transposable only between settings with the same total program. In marginal cases, the total picture of inhabitant transposability may be of diagnostic significance.

(2) The program of a behavior setting requires "hardware" (behavior objects, an exoskeleton) of a particular kind. When a program functions with inappropriate hardware, the result can be disastrous or ridiculous. Donkey baseball, with the players riding donkeys, is an example of the

latter; the point of this amusing exhibition is that the baseball program cannot function effectively when donkeys are involved as behavior objects. Behavior settings with the same genotype have, in general, interchangeable classes of inhabitants, behavior objects, and milieu properties.

(3) The program of a setting is responsive to a limited range of inputs. The setting Dr. Sterne Dental Service Office will not receive the input "Treat my sick dog," or "I want a quart of milk," but for appropriate inputs—"I have a toothache"—the setting exhibits zero or minimal resistance. Settings with the same programs accept the same kinds of inputs.

OPERATIONS FOR IDENTIFYING BEHAVIOR SETTING
GENOTYPES

Whatever program criterion is used, the question arises: What degree of program difference places settings in different genotypes? Is the program of a baseball game sufficiently different from that of a softball game to signify that they are of different genotypes? A cutting point is obviously required, and we have set it as follows: Two behavior settings are of the same genotype if, when their zone 6/5 performers are interchanged, they receive and process the same inputs as formerly, in the same way, and without delay.

The requirement "without delay" is important, for given enough time almost all behavior settings have interchangeable performers. A librarian could become the proprietor of a grocery store, and vice versa, if enough time were devoted to learning the new program; a dentist could operate a law office, and vice versa, if the dentist and the lawyer returned to school for a number of years. The rule is, therefore, that two settings are of the same genotype if both operate without delay when their most central inhabitants are interchanged. "Without delay" is interpreted as follows:

(a) if X is the time required to incorporate the program of behavior setting A into a naive person—to make the person a skilled zone 6/5 performer—and
(b) if the time required to incorporate the program of behavior setting A into a person *who already has the program of setting B* is between 0 percent and 25 percent of X, and
(c) if statements (a) and (b), above, hold also for behavior setting B,
(d) then settings A and B are of the same genotype; the programs are transferable.

The 25 percent delay in achieving effectiveness is allowed to accommodate differences in inputs and some "retooling" of the transposed program.

Here are examples: An experienced zone 6 performer in the behavior setting Presbyterian Church Worship Service—a Presbyterian pastor, with no training or experience in the setting Methodist Church Worship Service—could nevertheless function efficiently in the latter with almost no delay. Evidence: (a) this has been observed to occur; and (b) the training programs and curricula that imprint the programs of the setting Methodist Church Worship Service and the setting Presbyterian Church Worship Service on the respective pastors are almost identical. But an experienced zone 6 performer in the setting Presbyterian Church Worship Service with no training or experience in the behavior setting Garland Lanes Monday Mens League Bowling Game could *not* transfer efficiently to zone 5, team manager, of the latter even with a full 25 percent allowance; the worship service program possessed by the pastor would afford no advantage over an entirely naive person in becoming programmed for bowling. Evidence: (a) a Presbyterian pastor has been observed to bowl without any advantage over other naive bowlers; and (b) the curriculum for training a Presbyterian pastor has virtually no elements in common with the lessons of a bowling school or the experience of a bowling team manager.

Some complications arise when the test is applied to behavior settings with more than one program—that is, to settings with multiple synomorphs (see Chap. 3). Some programs of such paired settings may be interchangeable and not others. The variety store–programmed proprietor of Kane Variety Store could function effectively in only one of the three programs of Ellson Drugstore, namely, the variety department. Having the variety store program would give no advantage in becoming programmed for the pharmacy or the fountain. In contrast, the druggist, being programmed for the variety department of Ellson Drugstore as well as the pharmacy and the fountain, could function effectively in zone 6 of Kane Variety Store. But because transferability of programs must be mutual, Kane Variety Store and Ellson Drugstore belong to different genotypes.

The process of determining whether any two behavior settings belong to the same or different genotypes is often simple and quickly completed. No special analysis is required to know that the programs of many settings cannot be interchanged without serious disruption. But in other cases, the two settings must be carefully compared using a standardized form called a *genotype comparator* (see Table 5.5). The six steps involved are as follows:

(1) Identify via the structure test (pp. 50–52) the synomorph programs included within setting A and setting B and list them in columns (1) and

TABLE 5.5
Genotype Comparator

	Setting A			vs.		Setting B		
(1) Synomorph programs of A	(2) Time to program novice	(3) Time to program B-performer	(4) Percentage of A's OT[a]	(5) Synomorph programs of B	(6) Time to program novice	(7) Time to program A-performer	(8) Percentage of B's OT[a]

Total percentage of OT devoted to nontransferable programs (9) _____

Total percentage of OT devoted to nontransferable programs (10) _____

[a]For nontransferable programs.

(5), respectively, of the comparator. The included synomorph programs should meet all the criteria of the structure test except the last; the milieu may not always be circumjacent to the standing pattern of behavior.

(2) Estimate the time required to incorporate each of these programs into a novice—that is, the time required via training and experience to enable a novice to become an effective performer at the deepest levels of penetration—and record these times is columns (2) and (6).

The time required to incorporate some programs into performers is officially documented: nine months for a barber, three years for a dentist. The course of training required for licensing these performers is prescribed. In cases where there is no recognized training curriculum, the time is estimated, such as for the proprietor of a grocery store, the carrier of a paper route, or the teacher of a Sunday School class. In all cases the incorporation time is the time required in addition to the essential general education.

(3) Estimate the time required to incorporate each program of setting A into an efficient performer of setting B, and vice versa; record these times in columns (3) and (7).

The first question in connection with step 3 is: What performers incorporate into themselves the total program of the synomorph? The second question is: What is the essential curriculum or training experience for mastering this program? Some performers must master specialized "content"; the mathematics teacher must know mathematics as well as teaching methods, and the mathematics teacher is *not* transferable to an English class. But the chairperson of a golf club business meeting does not need to know in detail about the "content" of golf club business (greens, membership, buldings); the chairperson must, however, know about conducting a business meeting, and part of this is making sure that the experts with the needed information are present. The same is true of the chairperson of a city council meeting. It is the business meeting program that is essential, and this can be learned in any business meeting irrespective of the particular business transacted.

In judging transferability of a performer, the question is: How effective in behavior setting A would be a person programmed for behavior setting B, and vice versa? The program of setting A may be wide or narrow, simple or complex. The program of Third Grade Academic Subjects is wide and simple in comparison with Swine Producers' School. A third grade teacher is able to transfer to the similarly wide and simple program of other elementary school academic classes, but the teacher of the swine class might or might not be effective in other animal husbandry courses; the general breadth of the training required for the particular course must be considered.

It is essential to be empirical in making these estimates. The best evidence is instances within the community where a similar transfer has occurred and the time to "retool" is known. But there is other evidence. The amount of duplication in the training curricula of the two settings is one kind of evidence. Whether different licenses are required to function in the performance zones of setting A and setting B (chiropractor versus school administrator), whether different examinations are set for performers of setting A than for performers of setting B (barbers versus beauticians), and whether experience in performance zones of setting A is generally accepted as qualifying a person for the performance zones of setting B are other sorts of evidence.

(4) Identify nontransferable programs—that is, programs for which time recorded in column 3 (and 7) divided by time recorded in column 2 (and 6) is between 0.26 and 1.0.

(5) Estimate the percentage of the total occupancy time (OT; see p. 141) devoted to each nontransferable program and record in columns (4) and (8). The occupancy time of a synomorph corresponding to one of the programs of a behavior setting is determined in the same way as the total OT of the setting (see p. 142 for description of method), and it is then expressed as a percentage of the total OT. The OT of some synomorphs is available in official records, such as the dinner synomorph and the business meeting synomorph of Farm Bureau Annual County Dinner and Program. The OT of other synomorphs has to be estimated on the basis of observational visits to the settings and information from records and informants.

(6) Sum the percentages in columns (4) and (8) and record in spaces (9) and (10). If the nontransferable programs recorded in space (9) *or* in space (10) amount to more than 25 percent of the OT, settings A and B are *not* of the same genotype; if they amount to less than 25 percent of the OT of *both* A and B, they are of the same genotype.

VARIETY WITHIN AND DIFFERENCES BETWEEN
BEHAVIOR SETTING GENOTYPES

The fact that behavior settings of each genotype have transposable programs among themselves does not mean that all genotypes have the same variety and complication within their programs, or that there is the same difference between programs of different genotypes.

A nonbehavioral example will illustrate this. Take two Briggs and Stratton one-cylinder gasoline motors, two Rolls-Royce eight-cylinder automobile engines, and two IBM 370/68 computers. The programs and parts involved in the operation of these pairs of machines are completely interchangeable; by this test each pair is of the same "genotype." But the variety and complication *within* the programs of each of the three genotypes is very different; each Briggs and Stratton motor may have 50 different parts, the Rolls-Royce engines may have 500 parts each, and each computer may have 5,000 different parts. In addition, the degree of difference *between* the genotypes is high: the Briggs and Stratton motors and the Rolls-Royce engines have greater similarity than either one has with the computers. Some big engines of the Rolls-Royce type incorporate small motors of the Briggs and Stratton type within them; in this respect, they are identical.

So it is with behavior settings. Behavior setting genotypes are empirically determined classes of settings. One genotype may be limited and rigid in its programs (such as Refreshment Stands); another genotype may be much broader and, indeed, may incorporate subparts that, alone, are separate genotypes (such as Carnivals).

A description of the genotypes of a town or institution portrays the varieties of standing patterns within its environment, and the number of genotypes in a town or institution is a measure of its habitat variety—the diversity of molar behavior resources and the range of molar behavior opportunities.

The usefulness of behavior setting genotypes in representing habitat variety is demonstrated in the comparison of Midwest and Yoredale (Barker & Schoggen, 1973). That report (pp. 64–80) also describes the use of genotypes and centiurbs to measure the extent of change in habitat variety over a decade. Crucial questions in comparative studies are: How similar are the habitats? What do they have in common? Barker and Schoggen also identified (pp. 32–34) seven degree-of-commonality genotype categories, ranging from genotypes fully common to both towns, through genotypes that are intermittently common or partly common, to those unique to one town.

6
Habitat Variables I:
Relationships Between and Among Settings

In previous chapters, we have considered methods for discriminating habitat units (behavior settings), of measuring habitat extent (centiurbs), and of measuring habitat variety (genotypes). We have not, however, discussed methods of describing the habitat units and of measuring the degree to which they possess various *qualities* or *attributes*. What we have done so far is analogous to presenting ways of identifying trees, measuring the extent of a forest, and counting the varieties of trees that compose it, but without presenting methods of describing the trees themselves. We turn next to methods of describing a number of variable qualities, attributes, or properties of behavior settings.

Behavior settings differ on many dimensions. They can be classified, for example, into settings of short and long duration, settings with male, female, and mixed gender population, settings where work predominates, settings where education, play, or socializing are prominent, settings that welcome or exclude children, and settings that are controlled locally or by remote authority. Which of these and many other dimensions of behavior settings one chooses to study will depend on one's interests and purposes. The variables discussed in this and the next chapter are those that have been included most frequently in empirical studies using behavior settings. They were developed for their relevance to the particular concerns of the original studies. Other qualities of settings might well have been chosen even in these studies, and future investigations need not include, much less be limited to, the variables described below. Wicker (1979b, 1981, 1987) and Stokols (1978) have proposed a number of promising new dimensions for the study of environments in terms of behavior settings. Flexibility and innovation are needed in the future development of research with behavior settings.

In the previous chapter, we were concerned with the use of behavior settings to measure broad features of an ecological environment—habitat size and habitat variability. In the present chapter, we consider two variables that measure external relationships between and among behavior settings, namely, *authority systems* and *behavior setting autonomy*. Although these two variables provide important information about interrelationships between and among the behavior settings of the town, they constitute only a limited effort to examine such interrelationships or the more extended range of contexts called for by Bronfenbrenner (1979). Other important dimensions, such as overlap of leaders and members across settings, economic interdependencies, and hierarchical linkages among settings, remain largely unexplored. Wicker (1979a, 1987) has suggested some specific ways of analyzing linkages among settings in terms of resource inputs, social influence channels, and product outputs. Such work is for the future; in this chapter, consideration is limited to the variables of relationships among settings that have been utilized in empirical applications of the behavior setting approach: authority systems and behavior setting autonomy.

In the next chapter, the focus shifts to individual behavior settings and some of their internal attributes or properties, such as action patterns, behavior mechanisms, penetration, and person-hours or occupancy time.

Behavior Setting Authority Systems

A behavior setting may have power over a number of other settings or over no other setting. In Midwest, High School and Elementary School Board Meeting is an important behavior setting because it has great authority over a considerable number of the town's behavior settings—for example, over Elementary Upper and Lower School Principal's Office, and through it over Sixth Grade Academic Subjects Class, and through it over Sixth Grade Hike and Picnic. In fact, School Board Meeting has some authority over 227 other behavior settings in the town. In contrast, Burgess Beauty Shop is not under the authority of the school board or any other setting, and it has no authority over any other Midwest behavior setting. Both School Board Meeting and Burgess Beauty Shop are authority systems, the former involving 228 settings and the latter only one.

The test of the authority of a behavior setting is whether or not it determines the standing pattern of other settings via directed, intentional intervention either immediately or through intermediary settings. Excluded by this test are the nonselective interdependencies that diffuse settings without direction; the interdependencies involved in the index *K* are of this kind. Behavior settings within the same authority system may have lower degrees of functional interdependence than settings in different authority systems. For example, there is almost no diffusion of influence between Elementary School Principal's Office and Sixth Grade Academic Subjects Class. The communications that do take place are of short duration, are irregular in occurrence, have in each case a particular content, are usually in one direction only, and are dominated by Principal's Office. But there is much more diffusion of influence between Sixth Grade Academic Subjects Class and Methodist Church Junior Department Sunday School Class, which is within a different authority system. The diffusion in this case is largely via many common inhabitants.

Arbitrarily excluded from consideration in connection with classifying settings by the authority systems to which they belong are controls exerted by governmental behavior settings over other, nongovernmental settings via legal regulations. For example, the power of the government via the county health department to close a restaurant for health code violations is not considered under the authority system categorization.

A behavior setting authority system is identified by the controlling setting, such as School Board Meeting or Baseball Association Committee Meeting. The controlling setting of an authority system is frequently a committee meeting. Each behavior setting of a town occurs in only one authority system.

The behavior settings of the different authority systems are grouped into the five classes described below; these five classes control all public behavior settings of a town. The classes of authority systems are based on the following characteristics of the controlling settings:

Private Enterprises: includes all settings under the control of behavior settings operated by private citizens in order to earn a living;

Churches: comprises those settings that are controlled by central administrative settings of churches;

Government Agencies: embraces all behavior settings managed by executive settings of town, county, state, or federal governments, excluding school-controlled settings;

Schools: includes the settings under the aegis of executive settings operated by private or public educational agencies (town, district, county, state, or national school boards and committees);

Voluntary Associations: comprises all settings other than those in the first four classes—that is, comprises settings organized by the citizens for the pursuit of interests other than those addressed by settings in other authority system classes (such as Bowling Association

Womens Executive Committee Meeting, Civic Club Meeting, Civic Club Rummage Sale).

The authority system to which a behavior setting belongs identifies one category of influence on its program. For example, many aspects of the Midwest behavior setting Methodist Church Worship Service are controlled by the setting Methodist Church Official Board Meeting, the local executive setting of the Midwest Methodist Church. The Methodist Church Official Board can determine the aesthetic attributes of Methodist Church Worship Service, and it has this power over the action patterns of all settings under its aegis. The latter settings constitute the Methodist Church authority system in Midwest. The executive settings of all churches of a town, and all the behavior settings they control, constitute the Church authority system class of the town. On a similar basis, all the other settings of the town belong to one or another of the other authority system classes: Government, School, Private Enterprise, and Voluntary Association classes.

Descriptions of towns in terms of the authority system classes to which their settings belong are based on the assumption that differences in the extents to which these classes of executive settings control the towns' habitats constitute significant differences for inhabitant behavior. We assume, for example, that among all behavior settings of the genotype Parties, the programs of those under the aegis of the Church authority system are different in common, subtle ways from those under the aegis of the nonchurch Voluntary Associations. One clear difference is that the influence routes to be followed in effecting changes in habitats vary according to their authority system affiliations. Persons interested in the relative power of, say, churches or government agencies over the towns' habitats should find results from such descriptions directly meaningful.

Behavior Setting Autonomy

Behavior settings differ in the extent to which their functioning is influenced by occurrences in other behavior settings located within the community and at different geographical distances from it. For example, crucial features of the program of the Yoredale behavior setting British Railways Freight Office and Delivery are subject to control from the national level by executive settings located outside of Yoredale, outside of the surrounding rural district, and outside of the surrounding dale region; its performers (leaders and other operatives) are appointed, and its program is determined at a great distance from Yoredale. British Railways Freight Office and Delivery has, therefore, a low degree of local autonomy. In contrast, the performers and program of the Yoredale behavior setting Dramatic Society Reception are determined almost entirely by the executive setting Dramatic Society Committee Meeting, which is located in Yoredale; therefore Dramatic Society Reception has a high degree of local autonomy. The extent of a town's behavior settings that are locally autonomous is a measure of the degree to which the town's inhabitants control the environment in which they live.

The autonomy measures described below were developed in the Midwest and Yoredale studies on the assumption that it makes a difference to the behavior and experience of the towns' inhabitants whether decisions with respect to officers, membership rules, agendas, meeting places, space, equipment, budgets, etc., of the settings they inhabit are made within the local community, where the inhabitants can continually participate directly, or whether the settings operate under directives that come from headquarters located at varying distances, such as the county seat or the state or national capital, where continual, direct participation by local setting inhabitants is all but impossible. Geographical closeness of such control centers of behavior settings is assumed to be positively correlated with power of inhabitants over their ecological environments. In Midwest, for example, Betsons Sewing Service is subject to almost no influences from outside the town, but Midwest Bank is strongly influenced by regulations originating at the state and national levels. We describe below the autonomy scale as it has been used in the Midwest and Yoredale studies; some modifications would be appropriate for use in other kinds of environments, such as institutions or sections of cities.

The autonomy of a behavior setting is a rating of the degree to which four decisions regarding the operations of the setting—namely, appointment of performers, admittance of members, determination of fees and prices, and establishment of programs and schedules—occur within five geographical areas with differing proximities to the setting as follows: within the town, outside the town but within the school district, outside the district but within the county, outside the county but within the state, and ouside the state but within the nation.

The highest local autonomy proximity rating is 9; it indicates that the four decisions are made entirely within the boundaries of the town, that the setting has complete local autonomy. Proximity ratings vary between 9 and 1; a rating of 7 means that the four decisions are made outside the town but within the local school district; other ratings signify that the de-

TABLE 6.1
Illustrative Calculations on Decisions for Autonomy Ratings

Behavior setting: Bridge Club I, 1963–64
Decision: appointment of performers

Locus of decision	Proximity rating of locus (PR)	Relative weight of locus (RW)	Weighted rating of locus (PR × RW)
Within town	9	1.00	9
Within school district	7	0	0
Within county	5	0	0
Within state	3	0	0
Within nation	1	0	0
		Local autonomy: Σ (PR × RW)	9

Behavior setting: Presbyterian Church Quarterly Presbytery Meeting
Decision: appointment of performers

Locus of decision	Proximity rating of locus (PR)	Relative weight of locus (RW)	Weighted rating of locus (PR × RW)
Within town	9	0	0
Within school district	7	0	0
Within county	5	0	0
Within state	3	0.75	2.25
Within nation	1	0.25	0.25
		Local autonomy: Σ (PR × RW)	2.50

Behavior setting: Presbyterian Church Quarterly Presbytery Meeting
Decision: finances

Locus of decision	Proximity rating of locus (PR)	Relative weight of locus (RW)	Weighted rating of locus (PR × RW)
Within town	9	0.15	1.35
Within school district	7	0	0
Within county	5	0	0
Within state	3	0.85	2.55
Within nation	1	0	0
		Local autonomy: Σ (PR × RW)	3.90

cisions are made at the county (rating 5), the state (rating 3), and national (rating 1) levels.

The local autonomy of each of the four decisions is rated using a rating form such as the one shown in the three illustrative decisions presented in Table 6.1.

Because the proximity ratings (PR, 9-7-5-3-1) are constant across all decisions and settings, they are printed as part of the form itself. The ratings call for judgments as to (a) the loci of all persons or agencies involved in the decision under consideration, and (b) how to allocate the relative weights (RW) appropriate to the different loci involved in this decision. The relative-weight allocation permits the judgment to reflect the common situation in which power to affect the decision being rated is distributed among persons located in loci at different distances from the setting. The rater enters the appropriate relative weights in the (RW) column of the form, making sure that the values total 1.00 for each decision. Following are some explanatory comments about the examples of rating decisions shown in Table 6.1.

Women's Bridge Club I: appointment of performers. The performers in this behavior setting are all chosen within the borders of Midwest; no person or agency in the district, county, state, or nation has any influence over the decision regarding who shall be the performers (president, host, etc.). On the decision concerning performers, therefore, the locus "within the town" receives the entire relative weight value of 1.00, and all other loci a weight of 0. Women's Bridge Club I in Midwest has complete local autonomy in the appointment of performers. Similar processes (not shown in Table 6.1) with respect to the other three decisions in determining the autonomy of this setting—decisions concerning admission of members, financial policies, and club programs and schedules—produce the same result; the autonomy rating is also 9 for each of these decisions. The local autonomy rating for the setting as a whole, therefore, is the mean of the local autonomy ratings for the four decisions: $36/4 = 9$.

Presbyterian Church Quarterly Presbytery Delegates Meeting: appointment of performers. The main decisions concerning appointment of performers in this behavior setting are at the state level, but national committees and nationally determined policies have some weight; relative weight of these loci is judged to be 0.75 and 0.25, respectively, and the other two loci receive ratings of 0. The ratings regarding admission of members (not shown in Table 6.1) are judged to be the same as for performers, so the same allocation of relative weights is appropriate to the ratings on this decision as well.

Presbyterian Church Quarterly Presbytery Delegates Meeting: finances. Decisions about both the finances of this behavior setting and its programs and schedules are made almost entirely at the state level, but with some influence within the town, such as the price of the meal served the delegates and the scheduling of the program. State and town loci are judged, therefore, to have weights of 0.85 and 0.15, respectively, in these decisions. The form for the decision regarding fees and prices is as shown

TABLE 6.2
Overall Autonomy Rating of the Setting Presbyterian Church
Quarterly Presbytery Delegates Meeting

Decisions	Autonomy rating
Appointment of performers	2.5
Admittance of members	2.5
Determination of fees and prices	3.9
Establishment of programs and schedules	3.9
Mean autonomy rating	12.8/4 = 3.2

TABLE 6.3
Local Autonomy Ratings for Selected
Midwest Behavior Settings

Setting	Autonomy rating
High School Senior Car Wash	9
American Legion Auxiliary Card Party for March of Dimes	9
Garland Lanes Bowling Exhibition	8
High School Award Assembly	7
County Superintendent of Schools Office	6
County Engineers Office	5
State Primary Election South Midwest Polling Place	4
U.S. Farmers Home Administration Office	3
U.S. Army Corps of Engineers Office	2
U.S. Post Office	1

in the final example in Table 6.1. The same values apply to the decision concerning programs and schedules (which is not shown).

The overall rating on autonomy of this entire behavior setting Presbyterian Church Quarterly Presbytery Delegates Meeting combines the results of the four decisions, calculated in Table 6.2. The final rating value of 3.2 indicates that this setting is controlled largely at the level of the state, with relatively little local autonomy. Examples of the local autonomy ratings of a number of Midwest behavior settings are given in Table 6.3. These autonomy ratings were calculated following the procedure illustrated in Table 6.2. (The final ratings are rounded to the nearest integer.)

Each behavior setting is, of course, local; it is located within the town under investigation. (Some local settings include out-of-town trips or excursions, but they are organized and start and end within the town.) Almost every behavior setting has within it penetration zone 6 or 5 performers, who exercise control over the program of the setting (penetration zones are discussed on pp. 127–29). But people become zone 6/5 performers via power that has a locus. The locus may be (a) within the 6/5 zone itself (for example, a proprietor "opens" a real estate office); (b) outside of zone 6/5 but within the setting (the president of PTA Meeting is elected by the members); or (c) outside of the setting but within the town (City Council appoints the Fire Marshal, who presides over City Firefighters' Meeting). All of these loci receive an autonomy rating of 9, indicating maximum local autonomy in determining zone 6/5 performers in these settings. However, zone 6/5 performers may be appointed by powers that reside (d) outside the town but within the immediately surrounding district (sixth grade teacher); (e) outside the district but within the county (manager of County Cooperative Feed Mill); or (f) outside the county but within the state (judge of District Court); or (g) outside the state but within the nation (manager of U.S. Army Corps of Engineers Office). Loci (d) through (g) receive local autonomy ratings of 7, 5, 3, and 1, respectively, as indicated in the rating illustrations given in Tables 6.2 and 6.3.

The zone 6/5 performers operate the programs of the settings. But one can ask: What power establishes the programs of the settings? The performers themselves may do so, as in the case of partners in a privately owned store; but this power may reside at any location. In our rating scale, three attributes of behavior setting programs—membership regulations, finances, and other policy matters—are rated according to the same directives that govern the appointment of 6/5 leaders.

In judging power over any of these attributes of behavior settings, only the next most inclusive region is considered. For example, local service stations in Midwest get their gasoline prices and other information from "headquarters" at the state level; it in turn is controlled by other centers outside the state. Only the nearest headquarters, the state in this example, is considered in rating locus of power.

In the case of stores, the customers are the members. Here the question concerning admittance of members is: Who determines what kinds of customers the store will seek to attract? Males or females? Teenagers or adults? Local patrons or transients?

Where a local merchant's main business is based on a franchise granted by a firm outside the town, such as an automobile dealership or a chain store outlet, the power to appoint 6/5 performers is shared equally within the town and at the locus of the firm's nearest headquarters. Where an individual is hired and paid from a distance, such as a teacher or gas company representative, one should rate power as located solely at the agency's headquarters.

In the case of finances, where an out-of-town authority decides what the prices or fees are and the local people determine whether they will pay them, one should count local and foreign power as equal. Similarly, in rating games and competitions with distant schools, the performers, members, finances, and policies are decided jointly by the local and visiting schools, so one should rate the power of each as equal.

7
Habitat Variables II:
Attributes of Individual Settings

Action Patterns: Rating Scales

The standing patterns of behavior settings have many discriminable features; in the Midwest and Yoredale studies, the settings were rated on the following 11 variables called *action patterns*: Aesthetics (making the environment more beautiful); Business (exchanging goods, services, or privileges for money); Education (formal education of any kind); Government (making, implementing, and evaluating government regulations); Nutrition (eating and drinking); Personal Appearance (improving appearance via clothing, grooming, and adornments); Physical Health (promoting health); Professional Involvement (paid rather than voluntary performance in a setting); Recreation (play, sports, and games); Religion (behavior concerned with worship); and Social Contact (interpersonal interaction).

The degree to which each action pattern occurs in a behavior setting can be categorized as prominent, secondary, or absent. A prominent action pattern is one that occurs in connection with 80 percent or more of the standing pattern of a behavior setting; it is a major component, a definitive attribute of a setting. For example, the action pattern attribute Recreation is present in almost the entire standing pattern of Midwest's behavior setting High School Boys Basketball Game; it is present in the running players, in the bouncing ball, in the performing band, in the cheering spectators. Recreation is, therefore, prominent in that setting. On the other hand, the action pattern Business is present in only a small part of the standing pattern of High School Boys Basketball Game, in buying and selling tickets and refreshments. Business is, therefore, a secondary action pattern of this setting; it is present but not prominent.

The reverse situation occurs with respect to these action patterns in the Midwest behavior setting Household Auction Sale. Here Recreation occurs to only a minor degree; it is a secondary attribute. But Business is present in almost all the standing pattern: it is present in the patter of the auctioneer, in the display of household goods, in the bidding of the buyers, and in the conditions of sale. Business is, therefore, prominent in Household Auction Sale. Basketball games are *for* recreation; auction sales are *for* buying and selling.

More than one action pattern can be prominent in a behavior setting. Social Contact is prominent in High School Boys Basketball Game in addition to Recreation, and it is prominent in Household Auction Sale in addition to Business.

The behavior settings of a town where an action pattern is prominent are the primary environmental loci of the action pattern; they make up its *primary habitat*, and their extent is a measure of a town's major habitat resources for generating behavior possessing the action pattern. For example, the behavior settings of a town where Education is prominent make up its primary educational habitat (PEH); in Yoredale in 1963–64 the PEH is 14.2 cu in extent and constitutes 12.6 percent of the town's total habitat. This means that 12.6 percent of Yoredale's habitat consists of behavior settings made up of classrooms, lesson plans, enrolled students, textbooks, certified teachers, and so forth, that produce educational actions (formal teaching and learning) when they function in accordance with their prescribed programs of events. The behavior generated by a town's PEH is the town's output of educational behavior. When we speak of a town's output of educational behavior, aesthetic behavior, or religious behavior, we refer to the outputs of the town's primary educational, aesthetic, or religious habitats.

A quality is secondary within a setting if it occurs in some but less than 80 percent of the standing pattern of the setting. An attribute is absent if it does not occur with sufficient regularity or frequency to qualify as secondary. The *territorial range* of an attribute is the sum of its prominent and secondary extents.

The extent of the presence of each action pattern can simply be estimated as primary, secondary, or absent, as described and illustrated above. In the Midwest and Yoredale studies, however, detailed calculations on action pattern subscales were carried out in the interest of more precise measurements. These procedures are described below and are followed by more explicit definitions of the action patterns.

The degree to which each action pattern occurs in a setting is rated on a scale made up of four subscales: participation, supply, evaluation-appreciation, and teaching-learning. In all cases, ratings are made in accordance with local perceptions and values as seen by fieldworkers. Two of the action patterns, Personal Appearance and Professional Involvement, are rated on special scales given in connection with the definitions of these patterns.

PARTICIPATION SUBSCALE

Definition: Behaving within the setting in ways that are described in the definition of the action pattern.

Rating: The percentage of the total occupancy time (OT) of the setting (OT is discussed on pp. 141–42 below) that involves the action patterns is judged and converted to a rating on Scale 7.1.

Example: It is judged that normally 81–100 percent of all the OT of the setting Mrs. Wiley, Music Lesson involves the action pattern Education—that is, formal teaching by Mrs. Wiley and learning by the pupil. This setting is, therefore, rated 5 (maximum) for participation in the action pattern Education.

SUPPLY SUBSCALE

Definition: Providing materials for carrying out the action pattern in another setting. To receive a rating for supply, there must be either (a) a product that is exported to another setting, or (b) a person especially prepared within the setting for contributions to the action patterns of another setting. Examples of the latter are choir practice and drama rehearsal, which contribute specially trained persons for performance in other settings: worship services and plays. General education does not count as contributing to another setting.

Rating: Supply is rated on the same scale as participation, but note that the total OT of the setting is divided between the participation and the supply ratings; that is, the maximum rating for participation and supply

SCALE 7.1

Rating	Participation subscale
0	The action pattern does not occur in the setting
1	The action pattern occurs in 1–20 percent of the OT
2	The action pattern occurs in 21–40 percent of the OT
3	The action pattern occurs in 41–60 percent of the OT
4	The action pattern occurs in 61–80 percent of the OT
5	The action pattern occurs in 81–100 percent of the OT

combined is 6 because the total OT cannot exceed 100 percent. For example, if a setting is rated 5 for 85 percent OT on participation, it cannot be given more than 1 on supply.

Examples: Buying and eating ice cream at Ellson Drugstore soda fountain is judged on the participation subscale on the action pattern Nutrition, but buying ice cream to take home is judged on the supply scale. The OT of Kanes Grocery Store is mostly devoted to obtaining food for use in other settings (judged 81–100 percent); only a small amount of the time is devoted to eating or preparing food for eating in the setting (judged 1–20 percent).

EVALUATION AND APPRECIATION SUBSCALE

Definition: Refers to behavior that explicitly recognizes the values of the action pattern, whether good or bad, or tests its effectiveness. Applauding at a play is an evaluation of the action patterns Aesthetics and Recreation; presenting attendance pins in Sunday school for a year's perfect attendance is a recognition of the action pattern Religion; giving tests in school is evaluation of the action pattern Education.

Appraisal that is merely conventional or part of the general conversation is not rated. This is necessary, for in every setting there is some evaluation of action patterns, but unless open and explicit, it cannot be rated. To receive a rating, there must usually be a place in the program for appreciation and evaluation: a vote of thanks, an examination, a prayer, applause, a cheer.

In settings such as Church Worship Service, where it is inappropriate to openly express appreciation, a rating for evaluation can, nevertheless, be made if there is clear evidence of evaluation that is more than merely the polite thing to do. In other settings, too, where it is clear from the comments of individuals that the evaluation is more than casual, a rating is indicated. This comes down to the rule that conventional or polite evaluation of a setting receives no rating; there must be evidence of greater evaluative involvement in the setting by the participants (see Scale 7.2).

Example: Public recognition of educational achievement is judged to constitute less than half of the OT of the setting Eighth Grade Graduation; Education is, therefore, rated 1 on this subscale.

TEACHING AND LEARNING SUBSCALE

Definition: Explicit learning and teaching of the action pattern; does not include incidental learning.

Rating: Rate as on the evaluation and appreciation subscale.

SCALE 7.2

Rating	Evaluation and appreciation subscale
0	No behavior in the setting explicitly evaluates or appreciates the action pattern
1	Less than half of the OT of the setting is devoted to evaluation or appreciation of the action pattern
2	More than half of the OT of the setting is devoted to evaluation or appreciation of the action pattern

TABLE 7.1
Sample Ratings of Selected Behavior Settings on the Action Pattern Recreation

	Rating on subscale				
Behavior setting	Partici-pation	Supply	Appreci-ation	Learning	Total
Cemetery Board Meeting	0	0	0	0	0
Trafficways	2	0	0	0	2
Midwest Theater	5	0	1	1	7
Wesley Lumber Yard	1	0	0	0	1
Midwest Town Team Baseball Game	5	0	2	2	9

Example: School Teachers' County Institute is a setting where teachers not only participate in being educated but learn how to educate. This is rated 2 (maximum) for learning about the action pattern Education.

The rating of an action pattern of a setting is the sum of the ratings on the participation, supply, appreciation, and learning subscales. The total rating ranges from 0 to 10. Illustrative ratings of a number of Midwest behavior settings are in Table 7.1.

An action pattern rating is, in most cases, an indication of the proportion of the total OT of a behavior setting that is devoted to the action pattern. However, this basis is not appropriate with Personal Appearance and Professional Involvement, and the basis of the ratings of these action patterns is, accordingly, modified. In these cases, however, the rating values appear to be harmonious with the interpretation of action pattern ratings as indicating the actual importance of action patterns relative to their total possible range of importance in the setting.

Action Patterns: Definitions

(1) *Aesthetics*. Any artistic activity; any behavior aimed at making the environment more beautiful, as this is locally defined.

Participation: doing artistic work of any kind (painting, decorating, landscaping, singing, dancing, etc.) and removing the unsightly. A purely functional setting such as a machine shop is rated 0. A setting such as a store, where there is even a minimal effort to make it attractive, is rated 1 (OT 1–20 percent).

Supply: supplying art, cleaning, landscaping, and musical materials and equipment. Key question: Does the setting provide materials for beautifying another setting? The setting Dent and Company, Decorators, besides doing artistic things itself, provides beautification of other settings.

Evaluation and appreciation: assessing products of art or persons with aesthetic talents or accomplishments.

Learning: teaching art, learning art. Key question: Is music, home decoration, painting, or other artistic activity formally taught here? Incidental learning about art is not considered.

Beautifying the self (Personal Appearance) is *not* included under Aesthetics. For example, in rating a beauty shop, beautification of the customers is not included in the rating on Aesthetics. This applies to worship services, parties, and to other settings where both "dressing up" and making the setting beautiful occur. In other words, the action patterns Aesthetics and Personal Appearance can be summed to get the total hours for all beautification.

If time is spent making a setting beautiful *before* the setting officially begins—such as decorating for a party—these hours are included in the total OT, and they are counted as Aesthetic participation. When the setting has permanent beauty, the process of keeping it in a beautiful state contributes to participation in Aesthetics. Often in such cases, there will also be time spent in evaluation. In fact, the *choice* of a beautiful rather than an unbeautiful locus for a setting in itself constitutes an evaluation.

Putting things in order, or in accordance with an accepted or established standard (such as the spacing of a letter on a page), is *not* included under Aesthetics.

Some patterns of behavior are purely utilitarian or functional, such as making a tool box; other patterns are purely aesthetic, such as painting a picture or singing a song; still other activities are a mixture, such as making bookshelves or tables. In rating Aesthetics, judge the proportion of the OT concerned with aesthetic aspects of the activity.

At a concert, the audience is included as participating in aesthetic behavior. In addition, there are often some hours for evaluation.

(2) *Business.* The exchange of goods, services, or privileges where payment is obligatory. Does not include gifts of money or service or hiring out for wages (see Professional Involvement, pp. 120–21).

Participation: exchanging merchandise, services, or privileges for money; transporting persons or goods for a fee; processing raw materials into salable form. That part of the OT of a setting that is occupied with the sale of goods, services, or privileges.

Supply: supplying objects and materials necessary for the execution of business in other settings. That part of the OT of a setting that is involved in supplying goods to support business in other settings within or outside of the town.

Evaluation and appreciation: examining and appreciating the achievements or values of business, businessmen, or business institutions.

Learning: learning and teaching how to do business; serving as an apprentice where there is explicit instruction in business practices; the extent to which the OT of the setting is devoted to instructing and learning the methods and skills of business.

Buying and selling means that payment is obligatory, whether or not payment is made on the spot. However, it must be understood that a "business" transaction has been made and that an obligation to pay is assumed by the buyer. This does *not* include time spent in working for wages, but it does include the time spent in seeking employment and collecting wages. The highest participation in Business is found in an efficient store where practically all the behavior is concerned with trying to sell and buy. Low participation is found in a football game, where payment of the entrance fee is almost incidental to watching and playing. School classrooms and church worship services receive no rating for Business. The hiring of teachers and preachers occurs in executive settings such as meetings of the school board and the church committee meetings.

In rating, estimate the time involved in actual transactions of buying and selling. If time is spent in the setting thereafter, using what has been purchased, do not include this. Thus, when admission is charged to an event, only the short time in purchasing tickets is included in the OT of Business participation, not the time spent in attendance at the event.

Every commercial setting, where prices are set competitively, receives some rating for evaluation. A bookkeeper who looks after payment of accounts is rated as participating in buying and selling, as are clerks when they are stocking shelves and preparing goods. Business is not merely waiting on customers. The purpose of the buying and selling is not taken into consideration. A church bazaar gets as high a rating for Business as a grocery store. Any social organization with a *regular* obligatory entrance fee rates 1–20 percent for Business. This is true of a school board meeting that hires teachers and of a meeting of a church congregation that sets the pay of a minister. But a church committee that deals only with "stewardship," collecting gifts from the members, is not a business setting.

(3) *Education.* Formal education of any kind; does not include incidental learning or teaching. The crucial question is: Does someone take the role of teacher and others the role of pupils, with the intent to teach in the first case and to learn in the second?

Participation: teaching individuals or classes of students, and learning in individual or group lessons. The OT of both teacher and pupils is included in the participation rating.

Supply: supplying materials for teaching or learning in other settings.

Evaluation and appreciation: approving of education or of persons who have completed a course of study and evaluating educational achievements (examinations, graduations).

Learning: teaching or learning procedures of education or stimulating people to increase education.

In almost every setting there is probably teaching by someone and learning by someone. At a bridge club someone might say, "Tell me how to count this hand according to Goren," and the one addressed might reply, "I would be glad to." This kind of incidental learning is not included in the ratings on the action pattern Education. The teaching position and the learning positions have to be regular, planned parts of the setting. For this to occur there is usually someone with professional training (a teacher, a doctor, a pastor), though in some settings, such as seminars, members may alternate in the instructional position. But there is always someone in a teaching position and there is always a pupil or a class.

Adolescent apprentices are pupils and their supervisors are teachers; a setting with apprentices receives a rating for Education. But a store with an adolescent clerk or shop assistant does *not* receive an Education rating. Giving information about coming events is not Education. Lectures and films at cultural and religious meetings are often instructional, but for the present purpose they do not count as Education. On the other hand, a driving school and an adult Sunday school class are Education because the formal instructional positions of teachers and learners are clearly recognized by the participants. A class that involves much individual work, such as a woodwork or typing class, in which the teacher walks about giving individual instruction, is rated as 81–100 percent participation in Education—the teacher is teaching and the pupils are learning virtually all of the time.

(4) *Government.* Behavior that has to do with government at any level.

Participation: engaging in civic affairs or in behavior that is controlled by government regulations. Key question: What proportion of the total OT is devoted to carrying out governmental orders or governmental functions? Note that government activities are defined strictly as law making, law interpretation, and law execution; they do not include, for example, using the streets and sidewalks (which are entirely government controlled) or getting mail at the post office. Only the OT of the performers (police, city maintenance workers, postal clerks) in these settings contributes to the Government rating.

Supply: supplying materials for governing activities, such as printing ballots at a print shop or providing income tax forms in a bank lobby.

Evaluation and appreciation: recognition of patriotic people, government officials, or governmental events; evaluating laws.

Learning: teaching or learning about government or legal procedures.

The essential question: To what degree does this setting involve activities directly controlled by a *primary* government agency? A store that collects a state tax on each sale carries out a governmental activity, with low OT, however. The meeting of an elected or appointed school board involves almost 100 percent governmental OT. But the school that the board sets up and turns over to administrators and teachers to operate is *not* a primary government agency, and it receives no rating for participation in the Government action pattern. However, if the school board makes special demands at the level of behavior settings in the schools—such as requiring fire drills or particular courses of study, or setting the dates of opening and closing—it takes this behavior out of the hands of the intermediary administrator, and this behavior *is* governmental. Settings requiring a license that must be regularly renewed from a primary governmental agency are rated at least 1 percent on participation in Government. This is true, too, if there are any legal restrictions, such as that which prohibits the presence of dogs in restaurants or food stores.

However, regulations that influence behavior only once, and then become a permanent part of the background of the setting, are not rated. This is true of building codes, such as standards of electrical wiring or fire-door regulations. The argument is that these do not influence the ordinary behavior pattern of the setting. All businesses with paid employees receive some Government rating because of government controls on wages, benefits, and working conditions.

Behavior settings where government is involved in instigating or restraining behavior to no greater extent than that required to cope with illegal activity receive no Government rating. These settings start, stop, and function without any government participation or reference to government at any level. The behavior settings of organizations with government charters, such as the Red Cross and Boy Scouts, do *not* for this reason receive a Government rating; neither do the settings of voluntary professional associations of government employees, such as an association of school principals. However, if evaluation of government occurs in behavior settings of such organizations, some Government rating is required.

Behavior settings that *may* occur at a location that has government regulations, such as Past Matrons Club Meeting at Country Kitchen where taxes were paid, receive no Government rating. The Government rating goes to the restaurant and not to the club meeting. This applies also to organization dances that occur in buildings with occupancy regulations, for example.

The difference between Government ratings 0 and 1 is crucial. Rating 0 means that government activities are not involved in any degree in the behavior pattern of the setting, whereas ratings 1 and above mean that there is at least a minimum of government involvement (greater than the general police powers that apply to all public settings). The minimum is exemplified in church worship services where there is regularly a prayer for government officials, and by 4-H Cooking Class, which is instigated by a government organization (the Agricultural Extension Service).

Note that behavior settings without government employees may require Government ratings. This is true of lawyers' offices, for example, where almost all the OT is concerned with influencing the making, execution, enforcement, and interpretation of government activities for clients.

Note, too, that the Government rating makes no distinction between public and private settings. A lawyer's office (private) receives a Government rating of 6, whereas the city park (public) receives a rating of 1. This is true because in the lawyer's office almost 100 percent of the OT of the lawyer and clients is spent participating in and evaluating the operation of government laws and regulations; in the city park, however, the OT of the one government employee who carries out the regulations of the city council amounts to less than 20 percent of the total OT of the park, most of whose occupants are concerned not with government regulations but with recreation, picnicking, and playing.

(5) *Nutrition.* Behavior that has to do with eating or drinking for nutritional purposes (including soft drinks and alcoholic beverages).

Participation: eating, drinking, preparing, or serving food. Key question: Does anyone eat or drink or prepare food or beverages in the setting?

Supply: acquiring food, beverages, and eating utensils, or preparing food for use in another setting.

Evaluation and appreciation: judging or appreciating the values of nutrition, of ways and means of serving food, or recognizing persons who excel in the preparation of meals.

Learning: teaching or learning ways and means of preparing and serving meals.

Following are some nutritional properties of behavior settings that receive different total ratings for Nutrition and some examples of different kinds of such settings:

Rating = 0: no eating, and no involvement with nutrition via supply, evaluation, or learning. Examples: music classes, executive committee meetings, plays and programs, machine shops, Sunday school classes, post offices, Boy Scout meetings.

Rating = 1: snacks, coffee, tea consumed, or small amount of supply, evaluation, and learning. Examples: academic classes, games, trafficways.

Rating = 2: light refreshments served. Examples: lodge meetings, parties, bridge club meetings, receptions.

Rating = 3: meetings with supper and/or continuous light eating. Examples: bowling club matches, ice cream socials, picnics.

Rating = 4: meetings with meals. Examples: Easter service with breakfast, Rotary Club meeting, alumni reunion with dinner, dramatic society dinner-dance.

Rating = 5: dinners with meetings. Example: annual dinners of organizations.

Rating = 6: food supply and/or consummation 80 percent plus of OT. Examples: food sales, restaurants, cooking classes, grocery stores, market day (Yoredale).

(6) *Personal Appearance.* Behavior concerned with improving personal appearance via clothing, grooming, and adornment.

Participation: getting well dressed, well groomed, looking one's best.

Supply: supplying materials for personal adornment and grooming.

Evaluation and appreciation: recognizing well-groomed persons; appreciating clothing or equipment for grooming.

Learning: teaching or learning ways and means of proper grooming and personal appearance.

The action pattern Personal Appearance is concerned with adornment, not with utility. Dress that is purely for functional purposes, as in wearing warm clothing for cold weather, receives no ratings for Personal Appearance. However, many work clothes have some aesthetic aspects. In any case, Personal Appearance is concerned with aesthetics applied to personal appearance; in this connection, see the definition of Aesthetics (pp. 112–13). The basic or zero level for Personal Appearance is house clothing—that is, what is acceptable within the privacy of one's home. Scale 7.3 is applicable.

SCALE 7.3

Rating	Personal appearance
0	House clothing and adornment
1	Street, school, ordinary, or everyday clothing
2	Clothing for well-dressed occasions, such as church
3	Dress for semiformal party
4	Formal dress affairs
5	Ceremonial dress for fancy dress ball

Jewelry and adornments count as Personal Appearance. But insignia that only identify a person's role (such as a police badge) do not count. Often, of course, insignia have adornment properties; in this case, judge the beauty of the insignia. Uniforms and ceremonial and symbolic dress and adornment are evidence of participation in Personal Appearance. The rating varies with the elaborateness, elegance, and care devoted to the costume and adornment. In general, wearing uniforms and ceremonial or formal dress receives a rating one or two points above a similar setting without uniforms or ceremonial dress. Thus, school settings where the students wear uniforms receive a rating of 2 instead of 1. A confirmation service with the girls in veils and the bishop in robes receives a rating of 4 instead of 2, as for an ordinary church service. To receive the extra bonus, the number of specially dressed persons must be substantial. In cases where only some people in a setting are specially dressed, as at a church service where only the minister and choir wear robes, or at a fashion show, a proportional allowance must be made. In some of these cases there may be some rating for evaluation and appreciation, too. The highest ratings for Personal Appearance are for fancy dress balls, parades, costume parties, and lodge meetings where ceremonial dress is worn and admired by everyone.

(7) *Physical Health.* Behavior that promotes or evaluates physical health. Applies specifically to physical, not mental health.

Participation: caring medically for people in any way, promoting physical health; includes athletic or physical activities concerned with improving physical health.

Supply: supplying medicines and medical or athletic equipment; books and money for promoting physical health elsewhere are included.

Evaluation and appreciation: recognizing healthy people and judging health (physical examinations, athletic awards).

Learning: teaching or learning ways and means of being healthy, stimulating healthful ways of living, learning medical skills (Red Cross CPR course, home economics class).

Physical Health does not include sale of food for ordinary nutrition, but it includes special health foods and dietary supplements such as vitamins. It refers only to the active promotion of health, not to prevention of accidents or illness. Behavior settings that operate under government health regulations, such as restaurants, barber shops, and grocery stores, do not receive a Physical Health rating. Only human health is rated; animal health is not included. Fund drives for particular health purposes (Heart, Cancer, etc.) are rated for Physical Health, but those behavior settings of organizations concerned with general welfare, with health only implicit, are not rated (Red Cross, Children's Service League). Types of behavior settings that receive high ratings on Physical Health are physical education classes, offices of medical practitioners, and fund drives for health causes.

(8) *Professional Involvement*. The degree to which the performers (leaders and other operatives) in the setting are paid rather than voluntary. All ratings are based on the OT of the *performers*, that is, inhabitants of zones 6, 5, and 4 (penetration zones are discussed on pp. 127–29).

Participation: receiving wages or profits for performing in the setting; the proportion of the OT of *all* the performers of the setting that is *paid* time. The OT of the performers is judged on the usual participation scale (see Scale 7.4).

Supply: providing materials for paid work by performers in another setting. Judge on Scale 7.4. For example, the clerks in a builder's supply store spend a substantial percentage of their time supplying materials for builders to make a profit in other settings.

Evaluation and appreciation: evaluating paid performers. But note that evaluation by members, customers, and audience is *not* counted as professional evaluation; only evaluation by superiors is counted: persons with power to determine the future employment of a performer (selection

SCALE 7.4

Rating	Professional involvement participation
0	The performers receive no pay
1	1–20 percent of the OT of the performers is paid
2	21–40 percent of the OT of the performers is paid
3	41–60 percent of the OT of the performers is paid
4	61–80 percent of the OT of the performers is paid
5	81–100 percent of the OT of the performers is paid

committee, employer, principal). Judge on usual evaluation scale with *total* OT as base.

Learning: providing education in classes or via apprenticeship for eventual paid work (school computer classes, garage with apprentices). Judge on usual learning and teaching scale with *total* OT as base.

In cases where the performers get only a nominal fee, much of the OT is voluntary; therefore the occupancy hours should be reduced accordingly, such as for jurors (who are semivoluntary) or members of volunteer fire departments. Payment of expenses of entertainers is *not* considered payment for services. Every business with employees receives some rating for evaluation, because the employer judges the employees as paid performers.

Teaching and learning that involve progress toward a certificate or examination for entrance to or promotion in a profession or vocation receive some rating under evaluation and appreciation. Where the professional is present in the setting but not as a performer, as a biology teacher might be at a basketball game, no rating on Professional Involvement is made. A performer is counted as performing during the whole setting occurrence even though the performance lasts only part of the time; for example, the church organist is counted as being in the role of performer at all times during the worship service. But in the case of settings with multiple occurrences, if a performer takes part in only some of the occurrences, the performance time is reduced accordingly. Also, if there is in the setting a single *performance period* after which the performer leaves, then only the time of the performance itself is counted. But when a person is in the role of performer for the whole time, as is the organist, but is active only part of the time, the whole period is counted.

(9) *Recreation*. Behavior that gives immediate gratification; consummatory behavior; play, sport, games.

Participation: playing, having fun, reading for enjoyment, relaxing, being entertained. Recreational behavior is guided by the person's own needs; there is little compulsion. The Recreation rating is decreased to the degree that such serious action patterns as Business, Education, Government, and Religion share the OT of a setting.

Supply: supplying materials and objects for recreation in other settings.

Evaluation and appreciation: recognizing and appreciating entertainment or entertainers.

Learning: teaching or learning about ways and means of recreation; stimulating the use of facilities for entertainment.

Not all behavior that is enjoyable is Recreation. Social contacts that are incidental to a business or religious setting may be enjoyable but do not count as recreation unless recreation is the purpose of the social contact. *Immediate gratification* must be the primary function of the behavior. This means that to receive a rating for Recreation, (a) a setting must have a time, such as a coffee break; (b) a setting must have a place, such as a reading nook, expressly for recreation; or (c) the standing pattern of the setting must be free enough that it can be shifted from serious to recreational behavior at any time, such as a snack bar. The whole setting may, of course, be a time and place for recreation (as in a party); in this case the participation rating is 81–100 percent.

Films in a theater count as Recreation; instructional films do not. Selling gasoline for recreational use of cars is supply for Recreation. A concert of sacred music in a church is not Recreation; a concert of secular songs in a church *is* recreational. One indication of whether a setting is a recreational setting is the presence of joyful applause—that is, applause that suggests, "I am enjoying myself," not applause for achievement.

Behavior settings in which 80 percent of the OT is concerned seriously and purposefully with reality, and with no supply, evaluation, or learning of recreation, receive a 0 rating for Recreation; this includes most laundry services, lumberyards, real estate offices, government offices, banks, attorneys' offices, court sessions, school academic classes, and worship services.

Behavior settings with 80+ percent of the OT devoted to enjoyment, relaxation, consummatory behavior, and some evaluation of recreation receive high (6+) ratings for Recreation: for example, parties, movies, dances, organization dinners and banquets, parades, picnics, bowling games, and football games and practices. Behavior settings rated in the intermediate range (1–5) in Recreation include restaurants, school classroom free time, hardware stores, and religious fellowship meetings.

(10) *Religion.* Behavior that has to do with worship.

Participation: engaging in religious exercises.

Supply: supplying religious artifacts or materials for purposes of worship.

Evaluation and appreciation: criticizing and appreciating religion and religious behavior.

Learning: teaching or learning about religion or ways to practice religion. There must be formal teaching in classes.

Behavior settings with no religious behavior whatever—no participation, supply, evaluation, or learning—receive a 0 rating; settings with perfunctory, often formal religious behavior, such as saying Grace at an otherwise nonreligious setting, receive a 1 rating. Behavior settings with a combination of substantial religious behavior and substantial nonreligious behavior—youth fellowship meetings, Easter sunrise service with breakfast—receive 2–5 ratings. Settings with 80+ percent OT devoted to religious behavior and with some evaluation receive a 6+ rating. This includes church committees that open with a prayer and then consider church problems exclusively.

(11) *Social Contact.* Having interpersonal relations of any kind.

Participation: engaging in social interactions.

Supply: supplying materials and equipment for engaging in social interaction.

Evaluation and appreciation: recognizing sociable persons or values of sociability.

Learning: teaching and learning social techniques.

Calculate the proportion of the total OT in which there is actual social interaction. When a teacher calls a school class to order and all the pupils respond, all are engaging in social contact. If the pupils are doing individual desk work and the teacher is speaking to one child and only that child is listening, the proportion engaging in social contact is $2/N$, where N is the number in the class.

A concert involves social contact to the degree that the musicians are communicating with the audience. In Midwest, none of the behavior settings received an overall rating of 0 on Social Contact. Ratings of 1 to 3 include behavior settings with some occupants who function for considerable periods of time in isolation; nonsocial functioning is possible in these settings, and in some cases it is enforced. Ratings 1, 2, and 3 include some single-person shops, settings where mechanics do much work alone, offices with routine, and single-person jobs such as typing, word-processing, computing, filing, examinations, and delivery routes. High Social Contact ratings occur in meetings, classes, card clubs, worship services, taverns, weddings, concerts, and plays.

Behavior Mechanisms: Rating Scales

The standing behavior patterns of behavior settings have been rated on four variables called *behavior mechanisms*: Affective Behavior, Gross Motor Activity, Manipulation, and Talking. The extent to which these mechanisms occur in a behavior setting is judged by a rating method similar to that used with the action patterns. There are three subscales.

SCALE 7.5

Rating	Behavior mechanism: participation
0	The mechanism occurs in less than 10 percent of the OT of the setting
1	The mechanism occurs in 10–33 percent of the OT of the setting
2	The mechanism occurs in 34–66 percent of the OT of the setting
3	The mechanism occurs in 67–90 percent of the OT of the setting
4	The mechanism occurs in more than 90 percent of the OT of setting

PARTICIPATION SUBSCALE

Definition: The degree of occurrence of the mechanism in the standing behavior pattern of the setting; see Scale 7.5.

Example: Talking, including singing, was judged to be involved in 34–66 percent of the total OT of the Midwest setting Primary School Music Classes; hence it was rated 2 for the mechanism Talking.

TEMPO SUBSCALE

Definition: The maximum speed with which the mechanism normally occurs in the setting; the unusual, abnormal burst of speed is not rated. In rating tempo and also intensity, consider the average maximum speed or degree of occurrence in the setting. An analogy may help here: a single index of the height of the range of mountains is the average height of the peaks of the range. A curve representing the tempo or intensity of behavior patterns in a behavior setting is in most cases a fluctuating curve, and the "height" of the curve can similarly be indicated by a single index—the average height of its peaks. This is what is meant by the maximum normal speed and intensity.

In the behavior mechanism ratings, ratings of the peak speeds with which the mechanisms occur (during the time that they do occur) and ratings of the peak intensities with which they occur (when they do occur) are added to ratings of the extent to which the mechanisms occur in the standing patterns of behavior. These are not, therefore, "volumetric" ratings. A mechanism that is expressed in only 1 percent of the OT of the setting but that is expressed at top speed and intensity when it does occur receives a rating only 40 percent less than if it occurred at those high speeds and intensities during the whole time: it would receive in the latter case a rating of 10 and in the former case a rating of 6. There are other combinations that add to 6; for example, the mechanism occurs in 100 percent of the OT (rating 4) at average speed (rating 1) and average intensity (rating 1). See Scale 7.6.

Examples: In the setting Manor Bakery Route, the maximal speed of Gross Motor Activity is regularly more rapid than the median rate of gross motor movement, the delivery person hurries, rating 2. High School Boys Basketball Practice involves Gross Motor Activity at top speed, rating 3. The setting High School Commercial Classes includes instruction in touch typing requiring manipulation (fine motor skills) at speeds faster than the median range, rating 2.

INTENSITY SUBSCALE

Definition: The usual, maximal rate of energy expenditure via the mechanism; see Scale 7.7.

Examples: The events in High School Track Meet regularly involve a maximal energy expenditure via Gross Motor Activity, rating 3; in Midwest City Library, the maximal normal energy expenditure involved in the mechanism Talking is very low, rating 0.

A behavior setting mechanism rating is the sum of the ratings on these three subscales. The range of ratings is from 0 to 10.

SCALE 7.6

Rating	Behavior mechanism: tempo
0	When the mechanism occurs, its maximal normal speed is slow; reaction times are long
1	The maximal normal speed of the mechanism is in the median range, neither fast nor slow
2	The maximal normal speed of the mechanism is above the median range
3	The maximal normal speed of the mechanism is near the physiological limit

SCALE 7.7

Rating	Behavior mechanism: intensity
0	When the mechanism occurs, the maximal normal rate of energy expenditure is very low
1	Maximal normal energy expenditure is in the median range
2	Maximal normal energy expenditure is above the median range
3	Maximal normal energy exerted is near the physiological limit

Behavior Mechanisms: Definitions

(1) *Affective Behavior*: Overt emotional behavior of any kind.

Participation: the percentage of the total OT of the setting in which overt emotionality occurs.

Tempo: refers to rate of change in emotionality, to speed of mood changes, to swiftness of alteration in emotional expression. Rate the highest, *normal* rate of variation in affective behavior.

Intensity: the greatest normal intensity of overt emotionality that regularly occurs in the setting.

To receive a rating for participation in the case of Affective Behavior, the emotional aspect of behavior must deviate from the degree of expressiveness that occurs when behavior is described as calm, placid, unemotional. Deviation from this norm may be shown by (a) unusual quietness, restraint, or self-control; (b) excessive expressiveness, such as cheering, yelling, hearty singing, kicking, or running; and (c) verbal description of feelings, such as "We are profoundly saddened. . . ." The degree of deviation via any of these routes is the basis of the rating of intensity.

In church services the prayers and songs are means of expressing emotion overtly. An organ concert in a church where there is no overt emotional expression, except by the organist as performer, receives an additional rating for Affective Behavior insofar as the audience is attentive— that is, participates in the mood of the music.

(2) *Gross Motor Activity*. Involvement of the large muscles, limbs, and trunk of the body in the standing behavior pattern of a setting; opposed to sedentary behavior.

Participation: degree to which movements involving the large muscles occur in the standing behavior pattern of the setting.

Tempo: maximal, normal speed of large muscle, limb, and trunk movements in the setting.

Intensity: greatest force regularly used in gross motor activity when it occurs.

With athletic events, note that the number of spectators in relation to the players is an important factor. Usually, only the players participate in gross motor activity of any intensity. Standing upright is counted as Gross Motor Activity of 0 speed and 0 intensity.

(3) *Manipulation*. Involvement of the hands in the standing behavior pattern of the setting.

Participation: the proportion of the total OT in which the hands are used to grasp, manipulate, push, pull, tap, clap, etc.
Tempo: maximal normal rate of hand movement.
Intensity: maximal, regular force exerted by the hands in behavior.

(4) *Talking*: All forms of verbalizing, including singing, yelling, crying, cheering.
Participation: the percentage of the total OT of a setting that involves verbalization of any kind.
Tempo: maximal, normal speed of verbalizing.
Intensity: maximal, ordinary loudness of verbalizing.

At a cocktail party where almost everyone talks most of the time, Talking is rated 67–90 percent of OT; during a normal conversation between two people, Talking is rated 100 percent of OT. This is reduced as the conversing group becomes larger. In a formal lecture, only the lecturer talks. In a committee meeting of five persons, usually about two will be talking.

Penetration of Behavior Settings

Behavior settings have internal structural and dynamic arrangements. One important feature of these arrangements is the power that different parts of a setting exercise over the entire setting. This ranges from parts with virtually no power over the setting (such as the part "sidewalk superintendants" occupy in the setting High School Construction Project) to those with control over the entire behavior setting (such as the part occupied by the single teacher of the setting First to Fourth Grades Music Classes). This dimension of behavior settings has been called the *penetration dimension*, and it includes seven zones of penetration from 6, the central and most powerful zone of penetration, to 0, the most peripheral zone and the one with least power over the setting. These zones are defined as follows:

Zone 6: Single leader. Zone 6 is the most central zone. Included here are the positions of all persons who serve as single leaders of behavior settings. Persons in zone 6 have immediate authority over the whole setting during one or more regular occurrences of the setting. This authority is not shared during such an occurrence, though zone 6 single leaders may have helpers or subordinate leaders in zone 4. Different persons may occupy zone 6 of a given setting during different occurrences of one setting during the survey year, as when a guest minister substitutes for the regular pastor in Methodist Church Worship Service or when a new president of the High School Student Council takes office during the year. Examples: the teacher in Second Grade Academic Subjects; the scoutmaster at Boy Scout Troop Meeting; the band leader in City Summer Band Practice.

Zone 5: Joint leaders. Persons who enter zone 5 lead the setting jointly with others in this zone during a single occurrence of a behavior setting. Persons in zone 5 have immediate authority over the whole setting, but their power is shared more or less simultaneously with others during one occurrence of the setting. (Zones 5 and 6 normally are mutually exclusive.) Examples: Mr. and Mrs. Cabell, who jointly own and operate Cabells Department Store; the president of the High School Drama Club Variety Show and the teacher who sponsors the club.

Zone 4: Active functionary. Inhabitants of this zone have power over a part of a setting, but they do not lead it. The people in this zone have direct power over a limited part of the setting. Examples: cast of the Junior Class Play; witness at District Court Session; usher in Methodist Church Worship Service.

Zones 6, 5, and 4: Operatives or performers. Inhabitants penetrating to any of these zones are referred to as behavior setting operatives or performers. These are the operating zones of the setting, the loci of the power to control the central operations of the entire behavior setting. (See additional remarks on zones 6–4, below, p. 132.)

Zone 3: Member or customer. Occupants of zone 3 have great potential power but usually little immediate power. They are the voting members, the paying customers who ultimately make or break the setting. Examples: member at Rotary Club Meeting; pupil in First Grade Academic Subjects; customer in Blanchard Hardware Store.

Zone 2: Audience or invited guest. The inhabitants of this zone have a definite place; they are welcome, but they have little power in the setting; at most they can applaud or express disapproval. Examples: spectators at Old Settlers Reunion Pet Parade; visitors (nonmembers) at Presbyterian Church Worship Service; guests at Civil Weddings.

Zone 1: Onlookers. This is the most peripheral zone within the setting. Persons in this zone take no active part in the standing pattern of behavior; at most they are onlookers. They are tolerated but not welcomed; they have no power within the setting. Examples: the infant who accompanies its mother to Weylens Grocery; loafers at United States Post Office; a child waiting at Dr. Sterne Dental Service Office while her friend receives treatment.

Zone 0: Potential inhabitants. Persons outside the setting itself but who occupy regions surrounding the setting are in zone 0; they are potential inhabitants. Examples: a passerby noticing the window display at Cabells Department Store; a citizen reading a poster announcing High School Christmas Program; a person reading the invitation to attend Republican Women's Club County Meeting.

Penetration is rated in terms of the maximum depth of penetration into a behavior setting achieved by individuals or members of population subgroups. The maximum depth of penetration is the most central zone any individual or member of a population subgroup enters during the survey year. If one preschool child sings in the program of the setting Parent-Teacher Association Meeting during one occurrence of the setting, and no preschool child penetrates further on any occurrence of the setting throughout the survey year, the preschool population subgroup receives a maximum penetration rating of 4, active functionary, for this behavior setting.

Information on the maximum depth of penetration of individuals and of members of population subgroups is available from the records of many behavior settings, such as school and Sunday school settings, some behavior settings connected with government agencies (court sessions, committee meetings), and some voluntary organization settings (Boy Scout Troop Meeting). Some penetration data are published in newspapers and other publications (church bulletins, school yearbooks); such data are supplemented and confirmed by fieldworkers via direct observation in the settings and through informants.

Attributes and nomenclature of the penetration zones are described in Table 7.2. Several terms of the table—in particular, habitat-claims, human components, and implemented habitat-claims—require definition and explanation.

Habitat-claims for human components. The behavior settings that constitute the habitat of a town or an institution specify human components for certain loci (slots, positions) within them. These are habitat-claims for human components. The position of secretary of 4-H Club, Regular Meeting is such a habitat-claim; this position requires an appropriate human component, one with the necessary knowledge and skills, in order to become operational. Habitat-claims are stable structural and dynamic features of the habitat provided by a community or an institution. The number of habitat-claims of a behavior setting for operatives (penetration zones 6, 5, and 4) is the number of positions of responsibility that must be filled (operatives that must be present) for the normal occurrence of the

TABLE 7.2

Penetration Zones of Behavior Settings: Their Functions, Power, Habitat-Claims, and Human Components; Examples of Implemented Habitat-Claims

Penetration zone	Functions	Power	Habitat-claims	Human components	Implemented habitat-claims
6	Control and implementation of program and maintenance circuits	Direct control of entire setting	Single leaderships	Single leaders	Claim-leader actions: club president presiding at meeting
5	Control and implementation of program and maintenance circuits	Direct, but shared, control of entire setting	Multiple leaderships	Multiple leaders	Claim-leader actions: team captain conferring with coach
4	Joint control (with zone 5 or 6) and implementation of subsystems of program and maintenance circuits	Direct, shared control of part of setting	Factorships	Factors (functionaries, assistants, etc.)	Claim-factor actions: church organist playing for worship service
6–4	Control and operation of program and maintenance circuits	Direct control of entire setting	Habitat-claims for operatives; positions of responsibility	Operatives	Claim-operations or claim-operator actions (responsible actions): lawyer or his secretary answering query of client
3	Implementation of major goal and emergency maintenance circuits	Indirect control of most of setting	Memberships	Members (customers, clients, etc.)	Claim-member actions: store customer making purchase
2	Implementation of minor goal and emergency maintenance circuits	Some influence on part of setting	Spectatorships	Spectators (audience, invited guests, etc.)	Claim-spectator actions: parade viewer watching parade
1	No functions	Almost no power	None; neutral places	Onlookers (loafers, etc.)	Claim-onlooker actions: infant accompanying mother in grocery store
0	Recruiting and dissuading potential inhabitants	Region of influence external to setting	None; potential places	Potential inhabitants	Potential guest reading invitation

SOURCE: Reprinted from Barker and Schoggen, 1973, table 2.4.

setting. For example, Presbyterian Church Worship Service in Midwest requires 20 operatives: 1 minister (zone 6, single leader) and 19 other operatives in zone 4 (functionaries, factors, assistants—1 organist, 12 choir members, 2 ushers, 2 candlelighters, 2 greeters). In the English village of Yoredale in 1963–64, there were 7,764 habitat-claims for human components within the operating zones of all the town's behavior settings combined—that is, habitat-claims for operatives. If all of Yoredale's behavior settings were to occur simultaneously, it would require 7,764 human components—different people—to operate the town's habitat.

The *operational range* of a class of inhabitants is the extent in centiurbs of the behavior settings in which members of the class are operatives or performers (zones 6, 5, or 4). For example, in 1963–64 persons in the aged population subgroup in Yoredale were operatives in 18.3 cu, or 16 percent of the town's total habitat measured in centiurbs (113 cu).

Similarly, the *territorial range* of a class of inhabitants is the extent in centiurbs of the behavior settings that members of the class enter at any level of penetration, 6 through 1. For example, the aged population subgroup in Yoredale were inhabitants of 80.1 cu, or 71 percent, of the town's total habitat; this means that one or more members of the aged subgroup entered one or more times during the survey year settings that totaled 80.1 cu of the town's 113 cu.

Human components. Single leaders (zone 6), multiple leaders (zone 5), functionaries (zone 4), operatives (zones 6–4), members (zone 3), spectators (zone 2), onlookers (zone 1), and potential inhabitants (zone 0) identify the human components of the indicated penetration zones of behavior settings.

Implemented habitat-claims. These are habitat-claims in operation—that is, habitat-claims *and* their human components. The Yoredale behavior setting Women's Luncheon Club Meeting has a habitat-claim in its program called vote-of-thanks (to the speaker), and the setting is incomplete without a particular human component to fill this slot. When Mrs. Shields moves the vote-of-thanks at the March meeting, at the request of the president, this is one claim-factor action. The vote-of-thanks is analogous to the motor-compressor assembly of a refrigerator: without the compressor and without the motor, the assembly is nonfunctional and the refrigerator is incomplete; without the vote-of-thanks in the program and without the mover, the Women's Luncheon Club Meeting is incomplete.

Habitat-claims, human components, and implemented habitat-claims are all attributes of the habitat of the community or institution under study; they are whole-entity properties, created by the component behavior settings of the habitat. The Women's Luncheon Club Meeting determines who shall implement the event; Mrs. Shields is a functionary (she transacts business) of the setting.

Penetration zone o requires special comment. It is the region surrounding a behavior setting within which the forces of the setting operate to impel people and materials into it or to repel them from it. Zone o is the zone of *potential* inhabitants of the setting. It is the region where advertisements urging attendance circulate and where warnings such as "No Minors Allowed" are posted; it overlaps with zones 1 to 6 of other behavior settings. For example, if a client in the Yoredale behavior setting Blacketts Ladies Hairdresser reads a notice on the counter stating that the annual Church of England Jumble [rummage] Sale is being held and soliciting attendance, the client is simultaneously in zone 3 of Blacketts Ladies Hairdresser and in zone o of Church of England Jumble Sale. The o penetration zones of a number of behavior settings overlap: the client of Blacketts Ladies Hairdresser may not only be invited by the notice to become an inhabitant of Church of England Jumble Sale, but she may also be urged by a fellow client to take advantage of the good values in the setting Harbough and Lawerne, General Draper. In towns the size of Midwest and Yoredale, almost all town inhabitants are, over a survey year, occupants of zone o of most of the town's behavior settings—that is, the population of zone o of most settings is the population of the town. Still others from out of town would increase the population of zone o even more.

Penetration zones 6, 5, and 4, the operating zones, are particularly important. Their human components, the operatives, are the most immediately essential inhabitants of a behavior setting; they staff its program and maintenance circuits (see Chap. 8), where they are responsible for maintaining the setting as a structural unit and operating its program. This responsibility entails power over the setting, but it also involves coercion of the inhabitants by the setting, for along with the greater power of the more central penetration zones over a behavior setting there is greater power over the inhabitants. Behavior setting operatives are more strongly constrained by the homeostatic controls of the settings they implement than are members, spectators, or onlookers (inhabitants of zones 3–1). The strength of the forces acting on the chairperson of a meeting, the proprietor of a store, the lead in a play, or the minister in a worship service to enter the setting and behave in accordance with its program are greater than those on the typical member, customer, playgoer, or parishioner. The more central the penetration zone, the more essential is each inhabitant to the occurrence of the setting. In behavior settings of the genotypes Baseball Games, Business Meetings, and Attorneys' Offices, for example, larger proportions of their claims for operatives than of their normal complements of members and spectators must be filled for adequate functioning on any occasion.

Operatives fill positions of responsibility within behavior settings; they are the human components of the habitat-claims that are most crucial for the normal operation of settings, and these habitat-claims are located within stronger force fields than other habitat-claims. In psychological language, the inhabitants of the operating zones of behavior settings carry out important and difficult actions; they are important, hard-working people; they control the setting and are controlled by it. They are the setting's most responsible inhabitants.

This does not mean that the inhabitants of penetration zones 3–0 are not important components of the habitat of the community or institution. In the long run, they are the sine qua non of behavior settings; without them, a setting is like a kindled fire without a supply of fuel. Furthermore they, along with operatives, staff the maintenance circuits in emergencies; when behavior settings of the habitat are less than optimally habitable, the homeostatic controls of these settings pressure the inhabitants of all the penetration zones into the maintenance circuits. For example, a town with relatively few inhabitants per centiurb falls below its optimally habitable state relatively frequently, and when it does so, pressures per available component toward maintenance circuits are relatively great. On the average, therefore, the inhabitants of such towns are more important to its survival as a human habitat than are the inhabitants of towns with high inhabitant/centiurb ratios. These issues are considered in more detail in Chap. 9.

Further documentation of penetration ratings is available in appendixes A and B of Barker and Schoggen (1973), where all behavior settings of both Midwest and Yoredale are listed according to genotype to which they belong. The genotype descriptions include penetration ratings of all human components of the settings.

Attendance

Behavior settings differ in the degree to which they bring to bear pressure on different population subgroups to inhabit or avoid them. In Midwest, as in most towns in the United States, six-year-old children are required by law to inhabit the behavior setting First Grade Academic Subjects (or an equivalent setting), and they are prevented from inhabiting the behavior setting Boy Scout Troop Meeting. Measures of the attendance selectivity of behavior settings with respect to different population subgroups indicate the degrees of freedom and restriction of the subgroups. Because of our special interest in the ecological environments of children and adolescents, the Midwest and Yoredale studies included measures of the attendance selectivity of the settings of the town with respect to children and adolescents. This property of behavior settings was originally called "Pressure" (Barker & Wright, 1955; Barker, 1968) but was later changed to "Attendance" (Barker & Schoggen, 1973).

Five classes of behavior settings, differing with respect to their pressures on children and adolescents to attend (inhabit) them, were identified in the Midwest and Yoredale studies. The definitions of these classes are given below for the child population subgroup, but they are applicable to the adolescent or any other subgroup with appropriate substitutions.

Attendance Required. These are the settings about which children have virtually no choice. Children have to go to these settings; all the pressure of the family, in most cases, and if necessary of the police force of the community requires child attendance. These are in most communities almost exclusively school settings.

Attendance Encouraged. These settings bring pressure to bear on the eligible children to attend, yet the children have some choice. For example, boys are invited but not required to participate in the setting Boy Scout Cub Pack Meeting. Children are singled out from other age groups as the special targets of attendance pressures generated by these settings. The pressures apply specifically to children to a greater degree than to members of other age subgroups.

Attendance Pressures Neutral. These behavior settings generate no special pressures on children either to enter or to stay out of them. Children as an age group are not singled out in any way as targets for special pressure to enter or not enter these settings. Examples are Trafficways and Reids Grocery Store.

Attendance Discouraged. These behavior settings resist and discourage, but do not prohibit, the entrance and participation of children; they discriminate against children as an age group. For example, children are discouraged from entering Attorneys' Offices in Midwest and Commission (betting) Agents' offices in Yoredale.

Attendance Prohibited. These behavior settings actively exclude children as an age group; pressures against entrance of children (except temporarily, in emergencies) are virtually irresistible. The presence of children is not tolerated, for example, in Yoredale's King's Arm Pub or in Midwest's Odd Fellows Lodge Meetings.

The attendance selectivity of a behavior setting is the degree to which forces stemming from the environment act on members of the subgroup to approach and enter or to withdraw from and avoid it. Attendance selectivity does *not* refer to the positive or negative valence (attractiveness or repulsiveness) of a setting for particular persons; it refers to environmental pressures that bear on members of the subgroup.

If a setting is scheduled at a time when children cannot inhabit it, such as during school hours, this signifies some resistance to school-age children. When a behavior setting simultaneously involves forces on some children to attend and on other children to avoid the setting, a decision has to be made as to which kind of pressure is most significant for children as a single category. For example, some children (six-year-olds) receive strong forces to attend First Grade Academic Subjects, whereas other children (those under six years of age) receive strong forces not to attend this setting. A court session may require the attendance of some children as witnesses, for example, and exclude others. At the installation of new members in a club, the newly elected members are urged to attend, whereas the attendance of those not elected is resisted. There is usually little difficulty in choosing the most salient attendance rating for the setting. In the above cases it seems clear that for the wide age-range of children it is crucial that schools require children to attend, that courts require child witnesses to be present, and that clubs urge child members to come to installation meetings (even though schools also prevent some children from attending, courts may reject some children from their proceedings, and clubs may exclude children who are not members). For the child population subgroup, the attendance rating for the school setting and the courts would be Attendance Required and, for the installation meeting, Attendance Encouraged.

The attendance selectivity of a setting in encouraging or discouraging entrance and participation by members of the child population subgroup is not rated on an absolute scale; it is rated relative to the selectivity of the setting with regard to other age subgroups. The rating Attendance Pressures Neutral means that children are not singled out in any way for greater pressure than other age groups to enter or not enter the setting. In Midwest, both Trafficways and Country Kitchen (a restaurant), for example, receive the neutral attendance rating for this reason; although Trafficways brings very little pressure regarding entrance on any age subgroup and Country Kitchen brings considerably more (via signs, advertisements, etc.), neither setting discriminates selectively against children from other population subgroups to pressure them to enter and participate—they treat all subgroups equally.

The forces that operate on children to enter settings rated Attendance

Encouraged are greater than those that operate on some other age groups, but the forces are not irresistible; children have a choice of entering or not entering. Children are invited, urged, and encouraged to enter these settings to a greater degree than some other age subgroups; children are singled out as a focus of the forces into these settings. But a setting does not receive an Attendance Encouraged rating for children if the pressure is on a particular person who happens to be a child. It is sometimes difficult to determine, for example, whether the proprietor of a store has searched for and secured "a child helper" or has hired John Doe because he is a good worker who just happens also to be a child. To avoid this difficulty in the most frequent case, family businesses in which children are involved as helpers are rated Attendance Pressures Neutral, *not* Attendance Encouraged.

The basis of the rating Attendance Required is the same as that for Attendance Encouraged, except that here the forces operating on members of the subgroup are all but irresistible. In the case of Attendance Encouraged, the setting suffers and may cease to operate if the forces from the setting are not sufficiently strong to bring the necessary children into it. This regularly occurs with Cub Scout packs, school clubs, and Sunday school classes, for example. But in the case of some behavior settings this is not allowed to happen; outside forces from the community require that these settings continue to function at an effective level. Community forces are added to behavior setting claim forces to overcome all child resistance to entering these settings, most of which are school related.

Settings are given a rating of Attendance Discouraged when the forces that operate on children *not to enter* them are stronger than those that operate on some other age groups, but the forces are not irresistible. Children are discouraged from entering these settings; impediments are placed in their paths; doors are closed; the "Not Welcome" sign is displayed in many ways. The programs of these settings are disturbed and delayed by children more than by the presence of some other age groups; the removal of children and their replacement by older people contributes to the smooth operation of these settings.

The basis of the rating Attendance Prohibited is the same as that of Attendance Discouraged, except that here the forces on children are much stronger; they are virtually irresistible. In the case of Attendance Discouraged, the behavior setting programs continue to function with more or less disturbance and drag when children are present. This regularly occurs in Midwest in such settings as Presbyterian Senior Choir Practice and Women's Club I Meeting, where children are more or less in the way but are tolerated when necessary. There are, however, some settings that cease functioning if children are regularly present, such as High School Driver Education Class. In these cases there is usually an arbitrary cut-off, or safety factor, which stops operations when children are present; this may be an article of the constitution or a bylaw of the organization that operates the setting.

There is almost always an exception to the absolute exclusion of children from behavior settings. Emergencies arise, such as when an essential person cannot attend the setting without bringing a child; in these cases, the setting will usually continue temporarily with the offending child more or less isolated from the operation of the setting.

The "No Admittance" signs on these settings take many forms via rules and regulations, meeting times when children cannot attend, and so forth. One common bit of evidence is that a member of such a setting will usually not attend the setting if other child-care arrangements are not possible and the member must either take the child along or not attend.

It should be noted that selective pressure on children toward or away from a setting does not mean that the same behavior setting does not exert pressure on other age subgroups. There is pressure on adults (teachers) to enter First Grade Academic Subjects, for example. But at the same time, there is no pressure on adolescents or aged persons to enter this setting; in fact, members of these age subgroups are discouraged from entering this setting. If First Grade Academic Subjects would function without noticeable disruption with a random sample of 30 Midwest inhabitants, the attendance rating on children would be Attendance Pressures Neutral. But this is not true, of course; the program of First Grade Academic Subjects requires children as one of its components.

There are in general two sources of evidence regarding the forces on children to enter behavior settings: children are actually observed to receive more and/or stronger forces than other groups in the way of requests, invitations, urging, and orders; and the behavior setting is observed to falter more in its functioning if its child members are removed (and replaced by older people) than if members of some other age subgroups are removed.

An effective procedure for rating behavior settings on attendance is to answer the following questions in order:

(1) Are children *required* to enter this behavior setting? If there are laws requiring it, or (a) if the setting would cease to function if it had no child inhabitants and (b) if the community would not allow this to happen, rating = 1. If these statements are *not* true, consider question (2).

(2) Are children *prohibited* from entering this behavior setting except in emergency? If children are such foreign bodies in this setting that the

program ceases if they are regularly present, rating = 5. In practice, the following classes of behavior settings receive a rating of 5.

Behavior settings inhabited by trained professionals with training and/or experience requirements that preclude children, such as meetings of a teacher's association or an insurance salesperson's meeting.

Boards and committees of adult organizations (even when children are not excluded from the organization meeting), such as a meeting of the PTA executive committee.

Business and vocational association meetings, such as a meeting of a chamber of commerce.

Meetings of adult lodges.

Adult organization special meetings (even when children attend regular meetings), such as Home Demonstration Unit Trip to Capitol City.

Meetings of adult organization delegates from a large area (even if children are not excluded from local meetings), such as Farm Bureau District Meeting.

Settings from which children are excluded by law, such as taverns, bars, and cocktail lounges.

Behavior settings that are age-graded (especially when age-appropriate settings occur simultaneously), such as High School Latin Class.

If children are not prohibited, consider question (3).

(3) Is this behavior setting neutral to entrance and participation by children? Would older people be as effective to the program of this behavior setting as children? If the answer is yes, rating = 3; if no, consider question (4).

(4) Is the program of this behavior setting supported by children? Does the setting welcome and invite children? Does the absence of children interfere with the functioning of this behavior setting? If the answer is yes, rating = 2.

(5) If none of the above questions are answered yes, rating = 4.

Beneficence

Most of a town's behavior settings serve all or several of the population subgroups more or less equally, but some settings are designed specifically to benefit particular subgroups more than others. In the Midwest and Yoredale studies, the special interest in children and adolescents resulted in the identification of behavior settings that were intended to benefit selectively the children and adolescents of the towns and settings in which children and adolescents serve the interests of other age subgroups. Initially this property of behavior settings carried the title "Welfare" (Barker & Wright, 1955) and was later changed to "Beneficence" (Barker & Schoggen, 1973).

The intended beneficiary of each behavior setting was judged using the following four categories. As in the case of attendance, above, these definitions are stated with respect to children as beneficiaries of settings but, with appropriate substitutions, they could apply to any population subgroup.

Children benefited directly. These are behavior settings that serve the welfare of their child inhabitants particularly; they are designed and intended specifically to influence child inhabitants in a particular beneficial way, such as to educate, provide recreation for, entertain, or feed them. School classes, meetings of the Cub Scouts, and Santa's visit to the town square are examples of the kinds of settings for which children are the intended beneficiaries. Included here are only those settings that benefit children selectively; settings that serve all age subgroups indiscriminately, such as most businesses, are excluded.

Children benefited indirectly. This category is for behavior settings that promote the welfare of the child inhabitants of *other* behavior settings. These settings have no child members; rather, they instigate, support, and control other settings that do benefit their child members. For example, Midwest's Elementary School Faculty Meeting has no child members, but its central purpose is to provide for the educational well-being of children in other behavior settings. This category does not include settings that, as only one function among others, foster children's behavior settings; for instance, Women's Institute Meeting may arrange a children's Christmas party, but that is only one small part of the work of that setting. Only adult settings that would cease if the child settings they foster should cease—such as Kindergarten Parents' Association Meeting—are included in this category.

Unconcerned with children. Behavior settings whose primary purposes are not specifically and selectively related to the welfare of children as a group are placed in this category. It includes settings, such as stores, that are unselective with respect to children—that is, they have no more interest in children than in other population subgroups. It also includes settings that focus specifically on the interests of other age subgroups, even to the point of discouraging or prohibiting entrance by children, such as High School Latin Class.

Children benefit others. In this category are placed those settings that are implemented by child operatives for the benefit of members of other age subgroups. The child inhabitants of these settings have responsible positions where they educate, entertain, provide recreation for, or other-

TABLE 7.3

Characteristics of Inhabitant Subgroups in Midwest and Yoredale

Subgroups	Definition
Age subgroups	
Infants	Under 2 years of age
Preschool children	2 to 5:11 years of age
Younger School ages	6 to 8:11 years of age
Older school ages	9 to 11:11 years of age
Adolescents	12 to 17:11 years of age
Adults	18 to 64:11 years of age
Aged	65 years and over
Sex subgroups	
Male	
Female	
Social class subgroups	Social classes I, II, and III correspond
Social class I	fairly well to Warner's upper-middle,
Social class II	lower-middle, and upper-lower classes,
Social class III	and G to Warner's upper-upper class
Social class G (Gentry)	(Warner, Meeker, & Eells, 1949).
Race subgroups	
White	
Black	

wise benefit people of other age groups, as in Elementary School Christmas Program.

Inhabitant Attributes

A behavior setting has a determinant number of inhabitants during any specified period of time. This is an important attribute of the habitat constituted by a town's behavior settings. The inhabitants can be identified with respect to whatever inhabitant characteristics may be relevant to particular problems. Table 7.3 lists the characteristics of inhabitant subgroups as identified in the Midwest and Yoredale studies.

Behavior Output of Habitats

DESCRIBING BEHAVIOR OUTPUT

We have pointed out earlier (Chap. 5) that particular kinds of molar actions occur only in particular behavior settings and that this fact provides a basis for determining the habitat resources of a town for stated molar actions. Contrariwise, behavior settings with particular habitat resources inevitably produce behavior appropriate to the resources; this is the case because the inhabitants of a behavior setting have two positions within it. On the one hand, they are habitat components; they are parts of the machinery of the setting, functioning according to its programs of operation. On the other hand, they are persons, each with her or his own unique perceptions and intentions. This dichotomous, incommensurate condition is discussed in some detail in Chap. 8. But we can state here that it provides the basis for the fact that the habitat attributes of a behavior setting describe its behavior output, too. If District Court Sessions, Barbershops, Dentists' Offices, Cricket Games, and Latin Classes are present in a town, then sentencing-to-jail, hair-cutting, tooth-filling, cricket-playing, and Latin-teaching inevitably occur. If the action pattern Religion is an attribute of the standing pattern of a behavior setting, religious actions are among the actions of its inhabitants (in the same way, a factory with facilities and a program for manufacturing phosphate fertilizer actually produces phosphate fertilizer when it is in operation). However, the habitat characteristics of a behavior setting where the action pattern Religion is present (and of the facilities and program of a phosphate factory) do not reveal the *amount* of output of religious actions (or of phosphate fertilizer); they reveal only the programmed *kind* of output. The amount of output is a function of the amount and nature of the input—of the human components, in the case of behavior settings.

MEASURING BEHAVIOR OUTPUT

In the Midwest-Yoredale studies, five measures of behavior output were developed and used in the Barker and Schoggen (1973) report: person-hours, which is the same as occupancy time (OT); inhabitant-setting intersections; claim-operations; leader acts; and leaders. The different output measures are useful because in some cases they measure the same phenomena with different degrees of precision via different operations, thereby providing checks on the findings; in other cases, they measure different output phenomena. We describe below the three measures that have figured most prominently in previous research: person-hours or occupancy time, inhabitant-setting intersections, and claim-operations. The interested reader is referred to Barker and Schoggen (1973, p. 48) for description of leader acts and leaders.

Person-hours/occupancy time (OT) of behavior. The inhabitants of a behavior setting act continuously in accordance with its standing pattern; therefore, the sum of the times all inhabitants spend in it is a measure of the amount of behavior with the attributes of its standing pattern. This sum for a survey year is the OT it produces. This is the most comprehensive measure we have used to determine the amounts of behavior generated by the total habitats of the towns studied. Examples: In Midwest in 1963–64, the 830 inhabitants occupied the town's public behavior settings for a grand total of 1,125,134 hours. This total OT can be partitioned among classes of inhabitants (children, adults, aged), among genotypes (Worship Services, Basketball Games, Funerals), among authority systems (Private Enterprises, Schools), and among action patterns (Religion, Education) for many analytical purposes. For example, 27,000 (2.4 percent) of the Midwest hours occur in behavior settings where the action pattern Religion is prominent—that is, the town's primary religious habitat. In the Midwest-Yoredale studies, it was also useful to report data separately on the person-hours of behavior generated via all inhabitants of the settings and the person-hours generated via residents of the towns.

Calculating person-hours/occupancy time (OT). The OT is the product of the number of occurrences of a setting (O), the average number of inhabitants per occurrence (p), and the average duration per occurrence in hours (d). The product, person-hours-per-year (Opd), is the OT of the behavior setting. Examples of behavior setting OTs from Midwest in 1963–64 are given in Table 7.4. The calculation of separate estimates of OT for the 14 population subgroups of Midwest is illustrated in Table 7.5, which shows the computation of OT of Midwest residents for the behavior setting Methodist Church Mother-Daughter Banquet.

TABLE 7.4
Behavior Setting Occupancy Times, 1963–64

(person-hours-per-year)

Behavior setting	Midwest residents OT	Total OT
Elementary School Third Grade Academic Subjects	7,280	18,430
Burgess Beauty Shop	12,750	15,750
Elementary Lower School Lunchroom	10,103	15,500
Chaco Garage and Service Station	9,542	14,000
Blanchard Hardware Store	6,822	8,322
High School A Team Football Game	2,710	7,467
Presbyterian Church Worship Service	4,015	5,918
Keith Barber Shop	1,540	4,290
Rotary Club Meeting	2,083	2,341
Presbyterian Church Funeral	320	605
Halloween Dance	150	213
Methodist Church Kindergarten Sunday School Class	111	146

TABLE 7.5
*Methodist Church Mother-Daughter Banquet Occupancy Times
of Subgroups of Midwest Residents, 1963–64*

Population subgroup	Occurrence O	Population p	Duration in hours d	Occupancy Time Opd
Infant (under 2 yrs.)	1	1	2	2
Preschool (2:0–5:11)	1	5	2	10
Younger School (6:0–8:11)	1	11	2	22
Older School (9:0–11:11)	1	7	2	14
Adolescent (12:0–17:11)	1	17	1.75[a]	29
Adult (18:0–64:11)	1	51	2.1[a]	109
Aged (65:0 and over)	1	20	2.5[a]	60
Male	1	7	1[a]	7
Female	1	105	2	237
Social class I	1	20	2	40
Social class II	1	81	2.2	176
Social class III	1	11	2.75	30
White	1	112	2.2	246
Black	1	0	0	0
Total	1	112	2.2	246

[a]The male adolescents waited on tables only. Some of the adult and aged women cooked the dinner and prepared the tables.

In studies over long time spans such as one year that include settings with sizeable populations, the numerical values of OT become unwieldy. For example, the total OT of Midwest settings in 1963–64 varied from 94,145 person-hours-per-year for the setting Trafficways to only 6 for Cemetery Board Meeting. For settings with large numbers of inhabitants, such as High School Football Game, errors in estimating OT are certain to be larger than for settings with few inhabitants. For these reasons, a geometric coding system was developed for recording OT. This coding system is described below in the Appendix.

Precise records of occurrence, duration, and population are available for a considerable number of behavior settings. This is true of most school and Sunday school settings and many social organization settings. Data for other behavior settings must be secured by means of observation by fieldworkers or from informants. Such data are not private in the case of almost all community settings.

Inhabitant-setting intersections. An inhabitant-setting intersection (ISI) consists of a unique combination of *a particular behavior setting* in any of its occurrences and *a specific human component* in any penetration zone of the setting during one or more of its occurrences. If Jane White attends the Presbyterian Church Worship Service once during 1963–64, this is one ISI; if she attends the Methodist Church Worship Service 30 times during the year, this also counts as one ISI. The ISI of a behavior setting is the number of different persons through which it generates behavior during all of its occurrences in the year. The ISI of Yoredale's Middle Juniors Academic Class in 1963–64, is, for example, 30; this is the total number of different persons, 3 teachers and 27 children, in attendance for one or more days. For a town, or a part of a town, the number of inhabitant-setting intersections is the sum of the ISI of all of its behavior settings; it is equivalent, for example, to the number of class enrollments in a school. The ISI is a less precise, operationally independent measure of the output phenomena measured by OT. Whereas the ISI output measures for Midwest's Presbyterian Church Worship Service and Methodist Church Worship Service via Jane White are both one, the OT output measures are 1 and 30, respectively.

Claim-operations. A claim-operation is a special type of ISI; it is an ISI in the operating zones (6–4) of a behavior setting—that is, a unique combination of a particular behavior setting, a specific habitat-claim in penetration zones 6–4 of the setting, and a particular human component implementing the claim. Table 7.6 gives some examples from Midwest. Claim-operations such as these keep the towns habitable for shoppers, pupils, golfers, taxpayers, diners, etc.; they implement the programs of behavior settings and maintain their milieux, and they are crucial for the continuance of the towns as human habitats. The number of claim-operations is a measure of the essential operations a town's habitat requires of its human components; it includes the actions of both leaders and functionaries. In psychological language, the number of claim-operations is a measure of the responsible, important, and difficult actions a town's in-

TABLE 7.6
Examples of Claim-Operations in Midwest

Behavior setting	Habitat-claim	Human component	Claim-operation
English Class	Position of teacher	Jane White	English Teacher White teaching
Saddle Club Organization Meeting	Position of secretary	Jane White	Saddle Club Secretary White recording
Saddle Club Organization Meeting	Chairmanship	George Smith	Saddle Club Chairman Smith presiding
Presbyterian Church Worship Service	Pastorate	George Smith	Presbyterian Pastor Smith preaching
Presbyterian Church Worship Service	Pastorate	Walter Jones	Presbyterian Pastor Jones preaching

SOURCE: Reprinted from Barker and Schoggen, 1973, table 2.5.

habitants perform in the process of operating and maintaining the settings of the town as a human habitat.

Claim-operations implement habitat-claims in all *operating* zones of behavior settings: in zones of single leadership (zone 6; for instance, bank presidencies); in zones of multiple leaderships (zone 5; for instance, joint proprietorship of stores); and in zones of functionaries (zone 4; for instance, office clerkships). They occur only in the program and maintenance circuits (see Chap. 8) of behavior settings.

Interjudge Agreement on Behavior Setting Ratings and Classifications

The degree of agreement among independent judges' ratings of the action patterns, behavior mechanisms, *K* values, occupancy times, and penetration of behavior settings has been investigated and reported (Barker & Wright, 1955). In all cases the degree of agreement is well above that usually accepted as adequate for studies of distributions of ratings and differences in central tendencies. However, these data are valid only for the studies of Midwest and Yoredale, where special conditions prevailed: these communities were the sites of intensive and continuing observation for long periods of time by the same investigators, some of whom were established town residents. New assessments of agreement are required for other studies in which the judges may be less familiar with the environment of interest. As noted above (Chap. 4), this has been done in some other investigations (Prull, 1976; LeCompte, 1972a).

Studies of agreement in judging the other variables described above—authority systems, autonomy, occurrence, duration, population, attendance, and beneficence—were not carried out as part of the Midwest and Yoredale studies. There are several reasons for this: (a) When ratings are involved in these assessments, they are not more difficult to make than ratings on which interjudge agreement has been investigated, and there is no reason to expect that agreement on the former would be lower than on the latter. (b) A number of the assessments (occurrence, duration, population) are based wholly on census-type information obtained from public records, publications, informants, and direct observation. Maximal accuracy is obtained in these cases by double-checking clerical work, by obtaining information from more than one informant or observer, and by cross-checking the findings against other variables with known relations to the variable being assessed; for example, if the duration and population of a setting are relatively high, the occupancy time must be relatively high, also. (c) The remaining assessments require the evaluation of less-than-complete information in terms of the judges' knowledge of their sources and of the community. For instance, in judging attendance, assessing the direction and degree of pressure on children to attend or to avoid the behavior setting Kindergarten Parents' Association Meeting requires careful fieldwork to secure information from inhabitants of this setting, and it requires judgment in evaluating what may be meager or perhaps contradictory information from fallible informants. Maximal accuracy in cases such as this is obtained by using multiple information sources and cross-checking against other variables.

In the Midwest and Yoredale studies, efforts toward obtaining adequate data were focused on careful field and clerical work of the kinds mentioned under (b) and (c), above. In this connection, it is apparent that permanent or long-term field stations such as those in Midwest and Yoredale with staff members well informed about the community and with archives of verified community data have great advantages. Even so, confidence in the findings of these studies would be enhanced by more adequate assessments of interjudge agreement, particularly on the variables requiring more difficult judgments, such as attendance. This limitation on the Midwest-Yoredale studies should be avoided in other investigations using these variables; this is especially true in studies that cannot achieve the high level of rich and comprehensive information about the communities that characterized the Midwest-Yoredale investigations.

8

A Theory of Behavior Settings

Psychology is a complex of overlapping, interdependent sciences encompassing widely disparate phenomena, methods, and theories. An explication of any part of psychology requires that the position of the part on the main dimensions of the total complex be set forth. We shall do this, briefly, for the phenomena and the methods of ecological psychology and, in some detail, for its theory. In doing this, we shall reconsider in wider contexts some of the topics already covered.

Phenomena of Ecological Psychology

The range of phenomena with which psychologists have dealt is encompassed by the round of events that extends from distal objects in the ecological environment (for example, a fly ball in a baseball game), to proximal events at receptor surfaces (the image of the moving ball on a player's retinas), to afferent, central, and efferent processes within the silent intrapersonal sector of the circuit (perceiving the ball), to molecular acts (raising the hands), and finally to molar actions that alter the ecological environment (catching the ball). The three major sectors of this unit are marked on the diagram of Fig. 8.1; namely, the ecological sector of objects and physical events that become stimuli; the organism or intrapersonal sector of receptive, central, and effector processes; and the behavioral sector of actones (molecular acts) and achievements (molar behavior) that occur, again, in the ecological environment. Brunswik (1955) convincingly demonstrated the value of this environment-organism-environment continuum (E-O-E arc, psychological unit, behavior unit) for identifying and appraising many facets of psychological science, and he placed representative

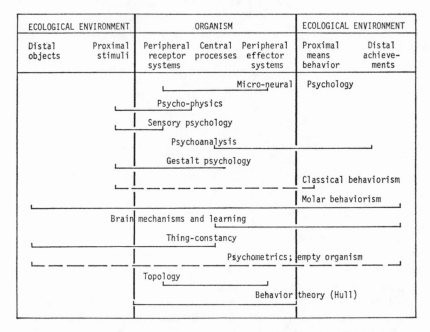

Fig. 8.1. The place of representative schools and problems of psychology on the basic psychological unit defined by Brunswik. All phenomena considered (——); only initial and terminal phenomena considered (- - -), such as stimulus and response.

schools and problems of psychology upon this basic unit, as shown in the figure. From this it appears that psychologists have ranged in their prospecting along the length of this mother lode of psychological ore, usually staking out claims in limited sectors; a few have gone so far as to claim the whole arc from its origin to its termination as the province of psychology (see, for example, Brunswik, 1955; Miller, Galanter, & Pribram, 1960; Murray, 1959; Zener & Gaffron, 1962).

Ecological psychology encompasses the whole E-O-E arc; in addition, it encompasses certain phenomena within the ecological environment which transmit and shape influences that extend from the termination of one arc to the origins of others. For example, ecological psychology deals not only with events involved in a player's catching a ball in a ball game, but also with the playing field (its size and shape), the other players (their number and skill), the rules of the game, and other ecological phenomena that affect the consequences for subsequent behavior of catching or not catching the ball. The subject matter of ecological psychology cannot be

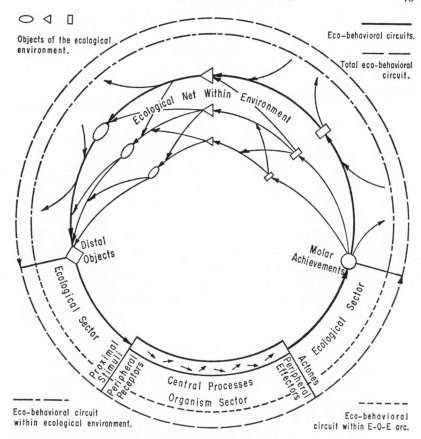

Fig. 8.2. Eco-behavioral circuits. The solid, directed lines represent the circuits; the broken lines are labeling guides.

represented by an arc joining—via receptor, central, and effector systems—ecological objects and events on the afferent and efferent sides of persons; it must be represented by circuits that incorporate the behavior of persons with objects and events of the ecological environment to form interdependent units (Fig. 8.2). Ecological psychology is more than a behavior science; it is an eco-behavioral science.

Methods of Ecological Psychology

The phenomena of a science occur without benefit of scientists, but the data of a science are the joint product of scientists and phenomena coupled within specially contrived data-generating systems. The characteristics of the data-generating systems of psychology, including the details of the couplings between psychologists and phenomena, are almost limitless; they are the province of psychological methodology and cannot be considered here. However, the great diversity of couplings between psychologists and psychological phenomena can be divided into two types, which produce data of crucially different significance.

PSYCHOLOGISTS AS TRANSDUCERS: T DATA

One type of data-generating system is represented in Fig. 8.3. It is characterized by a transitive connection between phenomena and data extending from psychological phenomena to psychologist and from psychologist to data. Psychological phenomena are scanned by the psychologist who functions with respect to them as a transducer, transforming them in accordance with coding categories into data. This data-generating system is, in effect, a translating machine; it translates psychological phenomena into data. The data it generates are operative images of the phenomena, prepared in retrievable form for storage and further analysis. Here is an early example of this type of data, gathered by Isaacs (1930) on July 19, 1926:

> When Mrs. I. lifted up the smouldering rubbish in the bonfire to put more paper under it and make it flame, Dan (5:2) said, "Oh, you *are* brave!" Later on, Jessica used the word "brave" without appearing to understand it and Dan corrected her, telling her, "'Brave' is when you stand close to something you don't like, and don't go away" [p. 112].

Psychological phenomena dominate this data-generating system: they are the operators; the psychologist is a docile receiver, coder, and transmitter of information about the input, interior conditions, and output of psychological units. The data as they issue from the system answer the question, "What goes on here?"; en masse, they report the abundance and distribution of psychological phenomena with varying input, interior, and output attributes.

Transducer data can be translated back into psychological phenomena, and the agreement between the original phenomena and the reconstituted phenomena is the ultimate test of the adequacy of T data. In fact, psychological phenomena are infrequently completely reconstituted in psychological science, but often intermediate steps of the first translation are reconstituted in the course of data analysis. This is the case when ratings of the content or quality of the original phenomena are made from T data. In court proceedings, behavior phenomena are sometimes re-

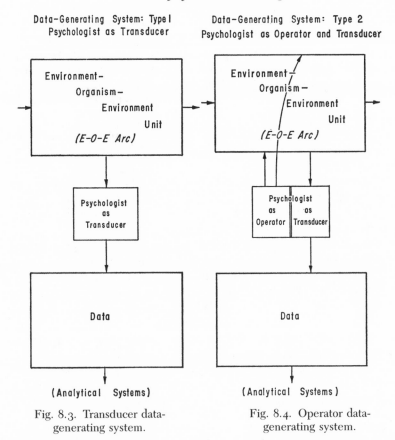

Fig. 8.3. Transducer data-
generating system.

Fig. 8.4. Operator data-
generating system.

enacted from data supplied by witnesses, and most of the so-called performing arts are based on the possibility of reconstituting behavior from
coded records. See, for example, Wiener (1962) and Ashby (1956).

Following are examples of analyses of T data:

(1)(a) Sixty-six percent of the behavior units of the children of Midwest
receive some input from persons or animals, that is, they are social units;
in 60 percent of these social units the person providing the input is an
adult, and in 66 percent of the units, a female; animals are the source of 3
percent of the social inputs. (b) Adults dominate children in about 33 percent of the units to which they supply input; children dominate children
in 17 percent of the units to which they provide input. (c) The input to 66
percent of the social units is compatible with the child's behavior in the
unit (Barker & Wright, 1955; Wright, 1967).

(2) Mothers direct social actions neither more nor less frequently to chil-

dren with physical impairments than to nondisabled children (Schoggen, 1978).

(3) Disturbances—that is, unpleasant disruptions in a child's experience as indicated by the child's expressive behavior—occur at a median rate of 5.4 disturbances per hour; half of these disturbances are evoked by adults, and 5 percent of them are occasioned by the loss of something the child values (Fawl, 1978).

(4) The units of Midwest children's behavior are of shorter duration, on the average, than those of comparable Yoredale children (Schoggen, Barker, & Barker, 1978).

(5) Yoredale adults provide children with devaluative social inputs four times as frequently as Midwest adults (Barker & Barker, 1978).

This data-generating system provides information about psychological phenomena in terms of transformations made by a psychologist; the transformations constitute the psychologist's *only* contribution to the data of the system. By using the psychologist as a transducer only, and not as operator, this system produces data that denote a world the psychologist did not make in any respect; they signal behavior and its conditions, in situ.

Data-generating systems of this type have no commonly accepted name, so we have called them, after the psychologist's role, *transducer data systems*—T systems, for short. We shall also use the terms transducer methods (T methods) and transducer data (T data).

PSYCHOLOGISTS AS OPERATORS: O DATA

The other type of data-generating system is represented in Fig. 8.4. In it there are two kinds of couplings between psychological phenomena and psychologist: in addition to functioning as transducer, as in the first type, the psychologist is coupled with the psychological unit as an operative part of it, regulating input, and/or influencing interior conditions, and/or constraining output. The psychologist dominates this system; psychologist as operator sends via the unit to psychologist as receiver and transducer. The data answer the question, "What goes on here, under the conditions of input, interior conditions, and output that I impose?" Here is an example of this type of data from the WISC-R test (Wechsler, 1974, pp. 90, 166):

Psychologist as operator: Listen carefully. What does Brave mean?

Subject: You have courage to do things by yourself.

The crucial feature of this data-generating system is that by becoming involved as an operator in the units being investigated, the psychologist achieves control that permits the research to focus on segments and processes of particular concern, via data that refer to events contrived in part by the psychologist.

Data-generating systems of this type may be appropriately called, after the psychologist's role, *operator data systems*; we shall also use the terms O method and O data. These are, in essence, experimental methods. We have not used that term, however, because of its common restriction in psychology to operations carried out in laboratories, and hence its exclusion of interview, questionnaire, and clinical methods, a restriction and an exclusion that do not apply in any degree to O methods generally.

ECOLOGICAL METHODS

We are now in a position to locate ecological psychology with respect to this methodological dichotomy as follows: ecological psychology is a transducer science; in it, research psychologists function as sensors and transducers, and its data record behavior and its conditions in situ.

One may well ask: Why should ecological psychology be satisfied with less than the most rigorously defined and controlled data-generating arrangements? Why bother with the role of transducer? Similar questions have been asked in connection with a motley class of methods variously called field methods, naturalistic approaches, and observational techniques. These methods have not infrequently been judged and found wanting. It is commonly said of them that almost anything they can do, experiments can do better. Their advantage is said to lie in their relative simplicity, which makes them useful as rough-and-ready methods for reconnoitering new problems. It is not easy to evaluate these judgments about the untidy class of methods to which they refer, but it is clear that they are not relevant to an understanding of the scientific value of transducer as contrasted with operator methods.

The models show that T data refer to psychological phenomena that are explicitly excluded when the psychologist functions as operator. Indeed, the primary task of the psychologist as transducer is carefully to preserve phenomena that the psychologist as operator carefully alters—namely, psychologist-free units. We have to say, therefore, that what T methods do, O methods cannot do at all: O methods cannot signal behavior and its conditions unaltered by the system that generates the data.

The models show, too, that O data refer to phenomena that psychologists as transducers explicitly exclude, namely, psychological units arranged in accordance with the curiosities of the psychologist. The primary task of the operator is to alter, in ways that are crucial to the operator's interests, phenomena that the psychologist as transducer leaves intact. It should be noted, however, that an investigator can sometimes select T data that refer to psychological units with the particular attributes of interest at the time. We have to say, therefore, that what O methods do, T methods usually cannot do at all, or can do less efficiently: T methods cannot focus so clearly on the particular events within psychological units that interest the investigator.

It is obvious that, in concrete cases, the data which psychologists produce as operators and as transducers differ in ways that are of fundamental significance for the science. Take intelligence, for example. Millions of reliable and valid intelligence tests have been administered, scored, and reported, thus providing a vast store of O data, for psychologists are strong operators in test situations, supplying input ("What does Brave mean?"), regulating interior conditions ("Try to work as quickly as you can"), and constraining output ("Now make one just like mine"). These data provide basic information about intellectual functioning within test-score generating systems and about intellectual processes and their constants: about IQ, about general factors, about verbal factors, and so forth. But this great and successful scientific assault on the problem of intelligence has provided almost no information about the intellectual demands the environments of life make on people or about how people respond to the "test items" with which they are confronted in the course of living. The science of psychology provides virtually no information about the intelligence of people outside of data-generating systems operated by psychologists.

Take frustration as another example. Experiments have provided basic information about the consequences for children of frustration, as defined and contrived in experiments such as those by Barker, Dembo, and Lewin (1941). But Fawl (1978) did *not* contrive frustration for his subjects; instead he studied it in transducer records of children's everyday behavior. Using "goal blockage" as a working definition of frustration, Fawl reported:

> The results . . . were surprising in two respects. First, even with a liberal interpretation of blockage fewer blocked goals were detected than we expected. . . . Second, frustration . . . usually failed to produce an apparent state of disturbance on the part of the child. Meaningful relationships could not be found between blockage . . . and consequent behaviors such as aggression, regression . . . and other theoretically relevant behavioral manifestations [p. 147].

In other words, frustration was rare in children's days, and when it did occur it did not have the behavioral consequences observed in the laboratory. It appears that the earlier experiments simulated frustration very well as defined and prescribed in theories, but the experiments did not simulate frustration as life prescribes it for children.

The conclusion is inescapable that psychologists as operators and as transducers are not analogous and that the data they produce have fundamentally different uses within the science. One may contend that the phenomena denoted by T data are unimportant, or that they are not psychology. One may argue that O data refer, potentially at least, to more fundamental, universal, invariant psychological processes than T data. But, however the phenomena denoted by T data are classified and evaluated, they comprise a realm of phenomena forever inaccessible via O data. The data that psychologists produce as transducers are not horse-and-buggy versions of the data they produce as operators. If one wishes to know, for example, such information as the duration of behavior units, the sources of social input, or the frequency of disturbances, only T data will provide the answers.

This state of affairs is most surprising in view of the situation in the old, prestigeful sciences that psychology so admires and emulates in other respects. In these sciences, the quest for the phenomena of science as they occur unaltered by the techniques of search and discovery is a central, continuing task; the development of techniques for identifying entities and signaling processes without altering them (within organisms, within cells, within physical systems, and within machines) is among the sciences' most valued achievements. Handbooks and encyclopedias attest to the success of these efforts. We read, for example, that potassium (K) ranks seventh in order of abundance of elements, and constitutes about 2.59 percent of the igneous rocks of the earth's crust; that its compounds are widely distributed in the primary rocks, the oceans, the soil, plants, and animals; and that soluble potassium salts are present in all fertile soils (*Encyclopaedia Britannica*, 1962). The fact that there is no equivalent information in the literature of scientific psychology (about playing, about laughing, about talking, about being valued and devalued, about conflict, about failure) confronts psychologists with a monumental incompleted task. This is the task of ecological psychology, and for it T methods are essential.

Discovery of Behavior Settings

In the Midwest research, we were confronted with the practical problem of what to record, as transducers, and what to count as analysts of T data. What *is* a unit of a person's unbroken behavior stream? This question is ordinarily settled quickly: a unit is an answer to a questionnaire item (the investigator's item); it is a trial on a maze (the investigator's maze); it is the completion of a sentence (the investigator's sentence). But when an investigator's units are not imposed on the stream of behavior, what are *its* units?

MOLAR UNITS OF INDIVIDUAL BEHAVIOR

When observers approach subjects' behavior streams as sensors and transducers, signaling in ordinary language what they see, structural-dynamic units are always found. Here is an example of transducer data denoting two such units; these data refer to five-year-old Maud Pintner in Clifford's Drugstore in Midwest on December 5, 1950, as Maud sat at the fountain waiting to order the treat her mother had promised her. The two units occurred successively and they occupied, together, less than half a minute.

2:48 P.M. From her jeans pocket Maud now took an orange crayon. She brushed it across her lips as if it were a lipstick.

Maud then leaned over, sliding her arms along the counter, as she watched a man serve a strawberry soda to his blond, curly-headed, three-year-old girl. Maud seemed fascinated by the procedure; she took in every detail of the situation.

The analyst titled these units Pretending to Use Lipstick and Watching Girl Eat Soda (Barker & Wright, 1951c, p. 248).

Wright and others have studied these units, called behavior episodes, in great detail and have discovered some of their attributes (Barker & Wright, 1955; Barker, 1963b; Dickman, 1963; Wright, 1967)—namely, constancy of direction, equal potency throughout their parts, and limited size-range. Like crystals and cells that also have distinguishing attributes and limited size-ranges, behavior episodes have as clear a position in the hierarchy of behavior units as the former have in the hierarchies of physical and organic units. It is impressive that empirically identified behavior episodes should agree so well with Brunswik's independent, theoretical formulation of the E-O-E unit of psychological phenomena (see p. 147).

The discovery of behavior episodes, and the accumulation of evidence that they are fundamental molar units of the behavior stream, solved the problem of what to record as transducers and what to count as analysts of T data. But we were then confronted with the questions: What is the environment of behavior episodes? How are episodes and their environments related? The search for answers to these questions led to the discovery of behavior settings. And during the search we learned some things about naturally occurring behavior and its environment that must be reported.

ENVIRONMENT OF MOLAR BEHAVIOR UNITS

On the basis of Brunswik's model of the E-O-E arc and of operator data-generating systems, we expected congruence between environmental inputs and behavior episodes. We expected behavior episodes to march along single file preceded by inputs from the environment and terminating in outputs to the environment, as they do when psychologists are operators in psychophysics experiments (stimulus with response), in intelligence tests (problem with attempted solution), and in polling interviews (question with answer). We expected to be able to predict with some accuracy from ecological inputs to behavioral outputs. But we were wrong.

According to T data, the behavior episodes of everyday life do not move along single file, but rather, one, two, or three abreast quite irregularly. In the upper row of Fig. 8.5, the structure of Maud's behavior in the corner drugstore is represented in terms of episodes. During this 11-minute period Maud engaged in 25 episodes of behavior, including Pretending to Use Lipstick and Watching Girl Eat Soda. Ten of these episodes occurred

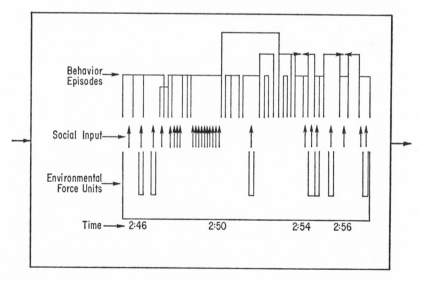

Fig. 8.5. Behavior setting: Clifford's Drugstore. Maud is Treated to Ice Cream Cone.

singly, but 15 of them occurred simultaneously with other episodes, and in one case there was a triple overlap, namely, Eating Ice Cream Cone, Watching Girl Eat Soda (on another occasion), and Trying to Get Her Mother's Attention. This segment of behavior is by no means atypical; in over 200 hours of children's behavior as recorded in specimen records, including 18 day-long records, 73 percent (median) of Midwest children's episodes overlap simultaneously with one or more other episodes (Barker & Wright, 1955). Furthermore, according to T data, units of environmental input and units of behavior are not regularly coupled and congruent, and prediction of behavior episodes from ecological inputs is poor. The 26 social inputs Maud received in the drugstore, as they occurred in temporal order, are listed below (the source of the input is given first in each case).

1. Mother: "We'll all go to the drugstore."
2. Mother: "Not now; you're not having a comic now."
3. Mother: "Leave things [Christmas cards] alone."
4. Mother: "Come on now, get your coat off."
5. Mother: "Maud, come back and sit down."
6. Mother: Pushes Maud toward the stool.
7. Mother: "Now you sit here."
8. Mother: "What do you want, Maud?"
9. Mother: "*Oh*, you don't want a *soda!*"
10. Mother: "No, you don't get a soda."
11. Mother: "What do you want?"
12. Mother: "You don't want a soda. Besides you wouldn't drink it if you had it."
13. Mother: "Do you want a coke?"
14. Mother: "Do you want an ice cream cone?"
15. Mother: "*Do* you want an ice cream cone?"
16. Clerk: "What flavor, Maud?"
17. Clerk: "Vanilla, that's the white one."
18. Clerk: "Don't eat Fred's cone."
19. Mother: "Come on, get your coat on, Maud."
20. Mother: Refuses Maud's whispered request.
21. Fred: Snatches Maud's coat.
22. Clerk: "Hi Maud," as she ruffles Maud's hair.
23. Mother: "Come on."
24. Mother: Pushes Maud toward her coat.
25. Fred: Asks Maud for gum (from gum machine).
26. Mother: Urges children from store with words and motions.

Like the stem of an incomplete sentence that might be given Maud in a test, each social input could serve as the origin of a congruent behavior episode, or of a limited range of episodes, in Maud's behavior stream. For example, there is only one action by Maud that is congruent with the mother's first input, "We'll all go to the drugstore," namely, the episode Entering Drugstore. But there are a number of congruent completions for the eighth input, "What do you want, Maud?," such as Asking for Ice Cream Cone, Asking for Coke, and Asking for Soda. A social input has a requirement, or direction, with respect to the behavior of the receiver, and the particular input chosen reflects the originator's presumption, on the basis of experience or primitive theory, that it is the one most likely to be effective—that is, to initiate the desired episode from the recipient. The ensuing behavior of the recipient provides an immediate test of the correctness of the presumption. Table 8.1 shows some of the social inputs to Maud in the drugstore, the episodes that are congruent with them, and the actual, ensuing episodes.

Three of the table's inputs were the instigation of congruent behavior in Maud's behavior stream, and three were not. In all, about one-third of the social inputs to Maud in the drugstore elicited congruent behavior episodes from her, namely, inputs 1, 6, 7, 8, 15, 17, 20, 25, and 26. In large samples of children's behavior, about half of all social inputs elicit congruent behavior episodes (Barker & Wright, 1955; Hall, 1965).

This finding was discouraging to us; it seemed to foreclose the possibility of discovering lawfulness between ecological inputs and behavior episodes within the undisturbed stream of behavior. Although it is true, according to Brunswik, that the prediction of behavior from input can only be made "probabilistically," predictions with only a 50 percent accuracy

TABLE 8.1
Social Input and Behavior Episodes

Social input	Congruent episode	Ensuing episode
(1) We'll all go to the drugstore.	Entering drugstore	Entering drugstore
(2) Not now; you're not having a comic now.	Returning comic to shelf	Looking at comic (continuation of ongoing episode)
(6) Pushes Maud toward stool.	Moving toward stool	Moving toward stool
(8) What do you want, Maud?	Choosing treat	Choosing treat (soda)
(9) *Oh*, you don't want a *soda*!	Choosing different treat	Choosing treat (continuation of ongoing episode)
(21) Fred snatches Maud's coat.	Retrieving coat	Ignoring Fred

are not impressive. And although it is true, too, that the associates of children are not scientists with explicitly formulated theories to guide them, they are nonetheless experts in the art of providing effective inputs, and it does not appear likely that their record can be greatly improved.

Despite this evidence, we were loath to abandon the precision of exactly identified, reliably described, and correctly enumerated inputs and episodes; they satisfied the first requirement of good research: replicable data. They seemed to provide firm ground in an unfirm region. So we persisted in the effort to find lawfulness between inputs and behavior episodes. We were encouraged in this by the theories and traditions of psychology which affirmed that lawfulness, if it existed, would be discovered between points of the E-O-E arc. These traditions and theories strongly indicated that ecological phenomena more remote than the distal objects at the origins and terminations of the arcs were not lawfully related to behavior.

WHY PSYCHOLOGY HAS TRADITIONALLY EXCLUDED THE ECOLOGICAL ENVIRONMENT BEYOND THE E-O-E ARC

From these traditions and theories—the conventional wisdom of scientific psychology—we identified four barriers to including within psychological science more of the ecological environment than that which lies along the E-O-E arc.

The ecological environment is said to be disordered. One reason for not venturing beyond the limits of the E-O-E arc is found in the fact that psychologists who have considered the problem have found the ecological environment on the afferent side of the person to be unstable and to exhibit at best only statistical regularities. This has confronted students of the total E-O-E arc with the difficult problem of making precise derivations and predictions on the basis of unstable, disordered independent variables. In consequence, the selective and organizing powers of the intrapersonal segment of the arc—which, to quote Leeper (1963, pp. 387–88), "yield relatively stable effects out of the kaleidoscopically changing stimulation they receive"—have claimed the greatest efforts of psychologists. It is here that the problems of perception and learning fall. This is one reason for the predominance of operator data-generating systems in psychological science: in this way the investigator is able to impose order upon the ecological input and so bypass the problem of its presumed intrinsic disorderedness.

The ecological environment is thought to lack direction with respect to behavior. It is widely believed that nonsocial components of the ecological environment do not demand behavior, that they enter psychology only as permissive, supportive, or resistive circumstances, and that the intrapersonal sector of the E-O-E arc is the arbiter of what will be received as stimuli and how it will be coded and programmed before it emerges as output (Lawrence, 1963; Ratliff, 1962; Schoenfeld & Cumming, 1963). It is true that a language is often used that implies at least a triggering function for the ecological environment: events in the environment are said to stimulate, evoke, and instigate behavior. The fact that data are usually provided by data-generating systems that are designed by the investigator to stimulate gives support to the language used. The simple truth is, however, that to function as a stimulus, an environmental variable must be received by the organism. Thus, in most psychological thinking, nonsocial ecological occurrences at the afferent end of the E-O-E arc are assumed (a) to be indifferent to their ends via the arc and (b) to be endowed with directedness and purpose only within the intrapersonal sector. Support for this view was found even in our data: if predictions of children's behavior episodes from *social* inputs, which can at least demand that they be received, are only 50 percent accurate, predictions from nonsocial inputs will surely be much lower.

The ecological environment is conceptually incommensurate with the intrapersonal sector. The concepts that are adequate for ecological phenomena are inadequate for (incommensurate with) psychological phenomena. Because the theories and concepts of psychology are not today reducible to those of biology, physics, and sociology, it is widely assumed that only probabilistic, empirical relations can be discovered between variables of psychology and those of other sciences.

The ecological environment is seen as infinite. Another traditional reason for limiting ecological phenomena to those at the origins and terminations of E-O-E arcs is the fact that beyond these points the regress within the environment is without limit. Where does one draw the line? Where does the environment of the episode "Maud . . . watched a man serve a strawberry soda . . . to his girl" end? With the man, the soda, and the girl? With the stools on which they sit and the counter from which they eat? With the whole fountain area? The whole drugstore? The town of Midwest? Or beyond?

TEXTURE OF THE ENVIRONMENT

We had to recognize the substantial case on which these perceived barriers are based, but still our experience generated a healthy skepticism; we continually made field observations, pari passu with our systematic

effort to record the stream of behavior and its immediate ecological inputs, which called attention to the significance for behavior of the more
remote environment. We were overwhelmed with individual behavior.
The 119 children of Midwest with whom we were most concerned engaged in about 100,000 episodes of behavior each day, over 36,000,000 in
a year. We had to sample this universe, and we found that our sample was
improved if, in addition to using the usual stratification guides (age, sex,
social class, race, education), we sampled behavior in such divergent
places as drugstores, Sunday school classes, 4-H club meetings, and football games. When we recorded behavior episodes in a representative
sample of such Midwest locales, the variability of the episodes was greater
than when we recorded in restricted locales. Variety of behavior episodes
was positively related to variety of ecological sampling areas.

Related to this were three observations made during the day-long recording of children's behavior and situation. These observations fueled
our skepticism about the wisdom of psychology's traditional stand against
including the ecological environment beyond the E-O-E arc in its efforts
to account for behavior.

(1) The characteristics of the behavior of a child often changed dramatically when the subject moved from one region to another—for example,
from classroom to hall to playground; from drugstore to street; and from
baseball game to shower room.

(2) The behavior of different children within the same region was often
more similar than the behavior of any one of them in different regions.
The behavior of John and Joe was frequently more similar in a Boy Scout
meeting than the behavior of John (or Joe) in a Scout meeting and in a
Sunday school class.

(3) There was often more congruence between the whole course of a
child's behavior and the particular locale in which it occurred than between parts of the child's behavior and particular inputs from the locale.
This is shown in Maud's case. Although, as we have seen, Maud did not
conform to most of the social inputs she received in the drugstore, the
whole course of her drugstore behavior was actually harmonious with and
appropriate to the drugstore setting: Maud had her treat and enjoyed it,
she did not read the comics or handle the Christmas cards to an appreci-
able extent, she *did* sit on the stool, she did *not* have a soda, she *was*
uncoated, recoated, and shepherded from the store in a generally agreeable way. Maud's relation to her environment was quite different in the
large and in the small. If we look on this as a test of Maud's drugstore
behavior, we see that Maud failed most of the items, but she passed
the test.

All of this was evidence to us that the ecological environment beyond the distal objects of the E-O-E arc is in some way causally implicated in behavior. When we finally looked beyond immediate, discrete ecological inputs to the behavior stream of individual persons, it was not difficult to identify larger environmental units. Schoggen (1963) identified such a unit, which he called an *environmental force unit* (EFU): an action by an environmental agent toward a recognizable goal or end state for the child-subject of the observational record. The unity of an EFU comes from its constancy of direction with respect to the person on whom it bears. EFUs acting on Maud in the drugstore are represented in the third row of Fig. 8.5. Her 25 behavior episodes and the 26 social inputs she received in the drugstore are encompassed by the eight EFUs. Each EFU includes at least one social input, and the large, inclusive EFU (Maud to Have Treat at Drugstore) has 18 social inputs. Schoggen discovered many interesting facts about EFU, but for us the most interesting finding is that a person's behavior is more frequently responsive and conforming to intact EFU than to separate components of EFU. Simmons and Schoggen (1963) and Hall (1965) found that half of the EFUs whose initial inputs elicited unresponsive or unconforming behavior elicited responsive and conforming behavior at the terminal EFU input. Here was documentation of what we observed in general, namely, that conformity between the environment and behavior is more frequent over long than over short segments of the behavior stream.

Some basis for this is found in Schoggen's data, which showed that EFUs usually endure longer than episodes. This means that if behavior episodes are used as the basis for identifying parts of the environment, the resulting segments are usually not unitary parts of the environment, or multiples thereof, but random fragments. To use such fragments in an investigation of the relation between environmental input and behavioral output is, therefore, analogous to studying the relation between the slope of four-foot sectors of a roadway (the circumference of a wheel) and the speed of vehicles over them. According to these findings, the environmental component of a psychological unit—that is, the originating object or event within the E-O-E arc—is often not the environment of the unit.

These observations and fieldwork experiences led us to look again at the environment as it exists before being received within the E-O-E arc. Brunswik (1957, p. 5) wrote in this connection:

Both organism and environment will have to be seen as systems, each with properties of its own, yet both hewn from basically the same block. Each has surface and depth, or overt and covert regions . . . the interrelationship between the two systems has the essential characteristic of a "coming-to-terms." And this coming-to-terms is not merely a matter of the mutual boundary or surface areas. It concerns equally as much, or perhaps even more, the rapport between the central, covert layers of the two systems. It follows that, much as psychology must be concerned with the texture of the organism or of its nervous processes and must investigate them in depth, it also must be concerned with the texture of the environment as it extends in depth away from the common boundary.

We raised the question: What is the texture of the environment? The physical and biological sciences have amassed almost limitless information about the environment, and some of it bears directly and specifically on the issues before us. The three environmental attributes we shall discuss have been independently affirmed and reaffirmed by many observing techniques and instruments. They are far removed from the human observer; most of them are properties of the environment as revealed directly by photographic plates and recording instruments. They are elementary facts.

Order in the preperceptual environment. The environment as described by chemists, physicists, botanists, and astronomers is not a chaotic jumble of independent odds and ends, and it has more than statistical regularity. It consists of bounded and internally patterned units that are frequently arranged in precisely ordered arrays and sequences. The problem of identifying and classifying the parts of the environment—the taxonomic problem—is very great, but the problem is not, primarily, to bring order out of disorder. On the contrary, its first task is to describe and explain the surprising structures and orders that do appear in nature (within carbon atoms, DNA molecules, developing embryos, oak trees, baseball games, nations, solar systems) and to account for the occasional absence of order and organization (in atomic explosions, cancerous growths, social disorder).

It must be noted, however, that order and lawfulness are by no means spread uniformly across the nonpsychological world; not every entity is lawfully related to every other entity. The preperceptual world is not one system but many, and their boundaries and interconnections have to be discovered.

A frequent arrangement of ecological units is in nesting assemblies. Examples are everywhere: in a chick embryo, for example, with its organs, with the cells of one of the organs, the nucleus of one of the cells, the molecular aggregates of the nucleus, the molecules of an aggregate, the atoms of one of the molecules, and the subatomic particles of an atom. A unit in the middle range of a nesting structure such as this is simultaneously circumjacent (surrounding) and interjacent (surrounded), both whole and part, both entity and environment. An organ—the liver, for example—is whole in relation to its own component pattern of cells and is a part in relation to the circumjacent organism that it, with other organs, composes; it forms the environment of its cells, and is, itself, environed by the organism.

Direction and purpose in the preperceptual environment. Most units of the ecological environment are not directionless in relation to their parts. They are, rather, self-regulated entities (or the products of such entities) with control circuits that guide their components to characteristic states and that maintain these states within limited ranges of values in the face of disturbances. Some of the strongest forces in nature and some of the most ubiquitous patterns of events are found within ecological units: in atomic forces and in developmental sequences of organisms, for example. Our current understanding of cybernetic processes makes it no longer necessary to be skeptical of the reality of target-directed systems within the ecological environment.

There are mutual causal relations up and down the nesting series in which many environmental entities occur; the preperceptual environment is made up of systems within systems. An entity in such a series both constrains and is constrained by the outside unit that surrounds it and by the inside units it surrounds. This means that entities in nesting structures are parts of their own contexts; they influence themselves through the circumjacent entities that they, in part, compose. A beam determines its own strength by its contribution to the structure into which it is built; a word defines itself by its contribution to the meaning of the sentence of which it is a part.

Incommensurability in the preperceptual environment. The conceptual incommensurability of phenomena that is such an obstacle to the unification of the sciences does not appear to trouble nature's units. The topologically larger units of nesting structures have, in general, greater variety among their included parts than do smaller units: an organism encompasses a greater variety of structures and processes than a cell; a river is internally more varied than a tributary brook. Within the larger units, things and events from conceptually more and more alien sciences are incorporated and regulated. In an established pond, a great variety of physical and biological entities and processes are integrated into a stable, self-regulated unit; the component, interrelated entities range from oxygen molecules to predacious diving beetles. This suggests that within certain levels of nesting structures conceptual incommensurability of phenomena does not prevent integration and regulation. In fact, self-regulated units with widely varied component entities are, in general, more stable than units with less variety (Ashby, 1956).

In summary, the sciences that deal with the entities and events of the nonpsychological environment directly, and not propaedeutically as in psychology, do not find them to be chaotic or only probabilistic in their occurrences. It is within the physical and biological sciences that the greatest order and lawfulness have been discovered, an order and lawfulness much admired by psychologists. These sciences do not find environmental entities to be without direction with respect to their component parts, and conceptual incommensurability does not prevent the integration and lawful regulation of ecological entities.

At this point we began to take seriously the discoveries of the biophysical scientists with respect to the preperceptual environment, and we sought to identify and examine the environment of behavior as they identify and examine the environments of physical or biological entities. This was neither more nor less difficult than it is to identify and examine the habitat of an animal, the organ in which a lesion occurs, or the planetary system within which a satellite orbits. The investigator first identifies the animal, the lesion, the satellite, or, in this case, the behavior unit of interest, and then explores the surrounding area; the circumjacent unit is soon identified and examined. It was by this process that we discovered behavior settings.

BOUNDARY BETWEEN ENTITY AND ENVIRONMENT

Within any included-inclusive (nesting) series the question arises where, precisely, each entity in the series ends and its environment begins. The answer to this question has been implied in the discussion above. The operations for identifying the boundary of an entity will now be given. If one moves from a position within any phenomenon and reaches a point at which the concepts and theories that account for the phenomenon cease to apply, but beyond which there are, nevertheless, linked (interdependent) phenomena, this point marks the boundary of an entity; phenomena beyond this point that co-vary with the entity are parts of its environment.

By way of example, the movements of an automobile and towed trailer are highly interdependent, and the interdependence can be explained in terms of the concepts and theories of strength and direction of physical force. At no point in the continuum between automobile and trailer do the laws governing the movements change; automobile and trailer are, therefore, a single entity; the automobile is not a part of the trailer's environment, and vice versa. On the other hand, the movements of two unattached automobiles driven on the highway as a caravan are also interdependent; but the interdependence is mediated by psychological laws— the laws of the perceptual-cognitive-motor systems of the drivers—rather than by the physical laws that govern the interdependences within each automobile. The cars in the caravan are, therefore, separate entities; each is a part of the other's environment. It should be noted that a towed vehicle may correspond less closely to the movements of the towing vehicle than does the following car in a caravan; the distinction between entity and environment has nothing to do with closeness of coupling.

Similarly, the movements of cattle trucks on the roads of Kansas and the price of beef on the Chicago market co-vary in spite of the fact that as one goes from the truck to the cattle market the relevant concepts and theories change utterly—from miles per hour to market demand, from pressure on pistons to pressure on prices. These paired explanatory concepts are irrelated, discongruous, incommensurable; it is impossible to derive miles per hour from market demand. Yet the cattle trucks move in response to market demand, so the market constitutes a part of the environment of the cattle trucks.

Still another example may be helpful. The tenth ring of a 50-year-old tree does not form the environment of the ninth ring; the outer ring is governed by the same laws as the inner ring; they are parts of the same entity. On the other hand, some parts of a tree do form the environment of other parts; the branches and foliage on the windward side of a tree protect and are therefore coupled with those on the sheltered side, but the coupling is not by direct biological connections; it is, rather, via the meteorology of the region and the dynamics of air movement around obstacles. People form the environment of people in this way, too; they have no direct psychological links. James (1950) referred to this when he remarked that no gulf is more complete in nature than that which separates person from person. Such gulfs occur between all entities that are coupled by phenomena on disparate conceptual levels.

The relationships that define entity and environment within ecological psychology are: inside-outside (the environment is outside the entity), independent-interdependent (the environment and the entity are interdependent), and commensurate-incommensurate (the linkage between environment and entity is via incommensurate laws). This last defining relation means that the identification of an entity and its environment, and the locus of the boundary between them, is relative to the concepts in terms of which the phenomena are comprehended; what is entity and what is environment change as understanding of the governing laws changes.

ENTITY AND COMPONENT PARTS

It is unfortunate that there is no name for the inside of an entity that is equivalent to the name of its outside (that is, *environment*), for within an entity there are also interdependent phenomena on incommensurable conceptual levels. The links between an entity and its interior are in some ways more mysterious and impressive than the links with its environment. A substance, we say, is composed of its molecules, and its molecules of its atoms; the cells "make up" the organism. Yet the laws of atoms, molecules, and cells are not the laws of molecules, compounds, and organs. Nevertheless, these interior, incommensurate phenomena often seem to be more closely coupled with the state of an entity than the external phenomena that constitute its environment. The latter influence the entity, but are not often seen as required for its continuance. Phenomena within an entity, on the other hand, appear not only to be coupled with the entity but also to be essential for its occurrence. So the problem of how the essences of an entity can differ from the entity with respect to their laws has arisen as a crucial issue, even as a paradox. Yet this is so clearly true that we have an axiom for it, namely, that an entity (a whole) is different from the totality of its interior elements (its parts). It is an interesting question why the reverse relationship—namely, that the component parts are different from the whole entity they constitute—is not also considered worthy of an axiom. Interrelations between attributes of entities and attributes of their interiors, such as between the energy level and the endocrines of the same person, between an animal's learning and its brain chemistry, or between motor achievements and musculature, have been extensively explored; however, the nature of the connections are as empirical and probabilistic as those with the environment.

Within the framework of these definitions of entity, environment, and interior elements, the problem of ecological psychology is clear. In terms of the eco-behavioral circuit (Fig. 8.2), the organism sector (the person) constitutes the entity; the receptor, central, and effector systems are its interior parts; and the remainder of the circuit within the circumjacent behavior setting constitutes the ecological environment. A task of ecological psychology is to discover how the properties of the person and the properties of the ecological environment are related, in situ.

Theory of Behavior Settings

Until someone is able to present an overarching system of concepts within which such currently alien phenomena as those of perception and economics, of motivation and technology, are subsumed, it has been generally believed that we have to be content with probabilistic predictions across the person-environment boundary on the basis of empirical correlations. But the question will not down: Is it not possible that variables of the person may enter, *on their own terms* yet in a systematic and derivable way, into the structure and processes of the environment, and vice versa? Are there not theories that can account for some of the consequences of the interaction of conceptually irrelated phenomena, while these phenomena continue to operate according to their own disparate laws?

THING AND MEDIUM

We believe we can find some help here in a remarkable paper by Heider (1927/1959) written over 50 years ago. In this paper, entitled "Thing and Medium," Heider anticipates some of the concepts of cybernetics and information theory, and he applies them to certain psychological problems in ways that are still ahead of the time. We cannot do justice to this important contribution here; we can only present our interpretation of the points we consider relevant to the current discussion.

Heider considered the problem of perception at a distance within the afferent, ecological sector of Brunswik's unit (Fig. 8.1). He attempted to distinguish the attributes of objects of perception from the attributes of the phenomena that mediate between them and the perceiving organism. Heider pointed out, as is still largely true, that only processes at the receptor surface and within the organism had previously been considered. He noted that distal objects in the ecological environment at the origin of the perceptual unit have different physical properties from the particles that intervene between these objects and the receptor surface. He called the former objects *things* and the latter entities *media*. First, things are intrinsically constrained; they are relatively independent of extrinsic events for their forms and for the distribution of energy within them. A stone is an example of an object with strong thing-characteristics; its firm, strong unity seems to issue from its own intrinsic nature. Media, on the other hand, are to a high degree extrinsically constrained; they are relatively dependent on extrinsic events for the form and energy characteristics they exhibit; media are docile. The pattern of light reflected from a stone is an example of a manifold of entities with high medium-character; the pattern of the light is determined in some way by the extrinsic, alien stone.

The second differentiating feature of thing and medium is this: things are unitary; their parts are interdependent. A change in one part of a thing causes a change in the next part, which is in turn caused by a change in a previous part. The variety they can exhibit is limited by intrinsic arrangements. A medium manifold is a composite; there is no inherent internal arrangement of its elements; its parts are independent; changes in every part of a medium manifold are caused separately from the outside. The variety a perfect medium can exhibit is not limited; it is versatile.

With these characteristics, things become centers of the causal texture of the world, and their influence is carried in the form of *spurious thing-units* (to use Heider's term) by media whose forms and processes are molded by things. It is the stable, but imposed, spurious thing-units that make it possible for a medium to represent a thing at a distance.

It is important to note, however, that each *single* element of even the most docile medium has its own structure and dynamics; thus light has its own unique reflection characteristics with respect to a stone. A single quantum of light represents itself rather than the stone from which it is reflected. However, a *manifold* of light rays, each reflected independently of the next ray, but with the same index with reference to the surface of the stone, does *as a pattern* represent the stone. Other things being constant, the number of parts of a set of entities, its differentiation, is directly related to the medium-quality of the set. A single building block has poor medium-qualities, a set of 50 blocks is a better medium, and a set of 500 building blocks is much better yet: it is a medium by means of which many different structures can be built and many different things represented.

We begin here to get a glimpse of a lawful relationship between phenomena on different conceptual levels that is more than an empirical probability. The laws governing the behavior of stones and light cannot now be subsumed within the same system. But the consequences of their interaction are clearly lawful, and beyond this some of the conditions determining this lawfulness begin to appear. Perception of objects is possible because the same spurious thing-unit is imposed upon the light manifold by the object every time they meet, and this spurious unit, in turn, has an unmistakable impact on the medium of the receptor system at the periphery of the organism, which is governed by still other laws. To function in this way, light and receptor systems must have the properties of media.

The physical sciences are replete with instances in which small particles on one level provide the medium for quite different phenomena on other levels, while continuing to function according to their own laws. A jet of gas issuing under pressure from a puncture in a container has its own characteristics of velocity and diameter, yet the gas molecules within the stream continue to behave according to their own laws, of thermal agitation, for example.

Every entity, as we shall use the term, stands between phenomena on its outside and on its inside that belong to different orders of events from the entity itself and from each other. An entity forms the environment of the coupled, alien phenomena within it, and, along with other entities, it also forms the inside manifold of a superordinate alien, environing unit.

In summary, we may say the following with respect to coupled phenomena that have a thing-medium relationship: (a) The medium complies with the forces of the thing; if it is a perfect medium it does not resist, counter, or enhance them; it is docile and is receiver and transducer so far as the pattern of forces from the thing is concerned. (b) The thing imposes its pattern upon the medium via its own driving forces; if it is a perfect thing, it is unaltered by the medium; it is operator and effector so far as the pattern within the medium is concerned. (c) Although we may be unable to discover the mechanism by which thing-forces are changed into medium-patterns (such as how an idea is transformed into words), still, if the docility of the medium can be measured *on its level*, and if the driving forces of the thing can be measured *on its level*, it may be possible to account in *some* degree for the consequences that occur across unbreachable boundaries. We have tried this in connection with a particular medium-thing, entity-environment relation—namely, persons and behavior settings.

THING-CHARACTERISTICS OF BEHAVIOR SETTINGS

An essential property of a thing is a firm, strong unity and stability relative to the medium manifold with which it is coupled. One source of the stability of behavior settings is a balance between many independent forces that bear on them. Some of the forces issue from the larger community, some are intrinsic to the setting itself, and some originate within the individuals who populate the setting. Here, for example, are influences pressing a school class toward an increase and toward a decrease in functional level: toward larger and toward smaller enrollment, and toward a "better" and toward a "poorer" curriculum.

Influences from the larger community:
    Toward an increase in functional level
        There is a waiting list of applicants for enrollment.
        Parents urge a richer curriculum.

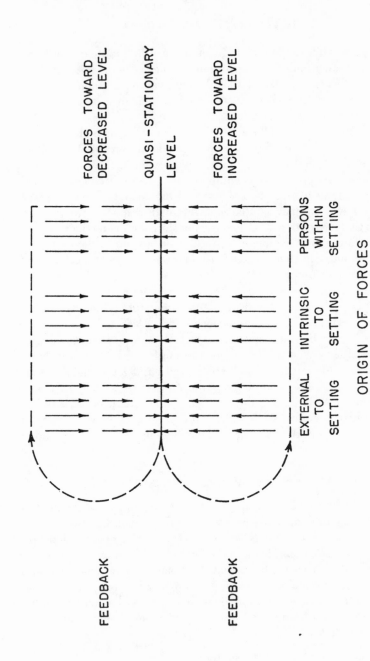

Fig. 8.6. Pattern of forces maintaining stable level of behavior settings.

Toward a decrease in functional level
  It is the policy of the school board to limit the number of students per class.
  A richer curriculum is expensive, and there is great resistance to higher taxes.
Influences intrinsic to the behavior setting:
  Toward an increase in functional level
    With a few more pupils, three suitable reading groups arranged on the basis of ability would be possible; with the enrollment as it is, the two groups have ranges of reading ability that are too great.
    The classroom is equipped with microcomputers.
  Toward a decrease in functional level
    The room is overcrowded as it is.
    The course of study is so full there is no time to teach the use of microcomputers.
Influences from individuals within settings:
  Toward an increase in functional level
    The teacher wants to extend her influence to as many children as possible.
    The girls of the class want to have a costume party.
  Toward a decrease in functional level
    The teacher is dead tired at night as it is, without any more pupils.
    The boys of the class refuse to cooperate on a costume party.

Such forces as these operate on every setting. The situation can be represented as in Fig. 8.6. The multiple, balanced forces ensure that the functional level of a behavior setting is more stable than most of its parts or conditions singly, that its standing pattern of extra-individual behavior-and-milieu is firmer than the behavior tendencies of the persons who inhabit it.

Essential to the strong unity and intrinsic integrity of behavior settings are their homeostatic regulatory systems; these are described below. Altogether it is understandable that behavior settings can have the requisite stability and permanence to operate as things relative to the people who inhabit them.

MEDIUM-PROPERTIES OF PEOPLE IN SETTINGS

People conform in a high degree to the standing patterns of the behavior settings they inhabit. Schoggen (1963) and Hall (1965) found that children comply with about 75 percent of the social inputs from environmental force units, and conformity to the total patterns of behavior setting forces is much greater than this. Although it is possible to smoke at a worship service, dance during a court session, and recite a Latin lesson in a machine shop, such matchings of behavior and behavior settings almost never actually occur; however, they would not be infrequent if these kinds of behavior were distributed among behavior settings by chance. When an individual's behavior deviates from the pattern of a setting, it is usually symptomatic of mental or physical illness, or of the normal incapacities of extreme youth and age. People, en masse, are remarkably compliant to the forces of behavior settings; in this respect the relation between people and settings is like that between medium and thing in Heider's sense.

Of all behavior setting components, the inhabitants exhibit the most varied patterns and perform the most varied functions. Rooms do not readily expand, tables do not hurry, typewriters do not make speeches. But people quickly spread out or crowd together, speed up or slow down, write or talk. People are versatile. In Midwest, for example, they produce such varied spatial-temporal structures as those involved in a band concert, a prayer service, a football game, a spelling bee, a dance, an X-ray laboratory, a horse show, a piano recital, a telephone booth, and a wedding. It is not unusual for a particular person to participate in this whole range of standing patterns. Do atoms, cells, and bricks exhibit a greater variety of patterns within molecules, organs, and buildings? The versatility of people within behavior settings is striking; in this respect, too, people and behavior settings are related as media to things.

However, no medium manifold is perfect. Two sources of inadequacy have been mentioned. First, the separate parts (components or elements) of every medium have their own structure and dynamics, and there are interdependencies between the elements of most media (p. 170). For these reasons, different media resist thing-forces to different degrees, and therefore differ in their adequacy as media. A region of sand dunes represents the pattern of wind currents much better than a field of lava; each component of the dunes (each grain of sand) is less resistant to the force of the wind and less closely tied to its neighbors than each component of a lava field (each lava cinder). Second, a source of the adequacy of a medium resides in the number of its parts, a medium-attribute that is irrelevant to the parts separately. There is an optimal number of elements in the medium manifolds of most thing-medium systems below which the adequacy of the medium declines. The inadequacy of a medium due to too few elements may be absolute; three lines will not form a hexagon no matter what the pressure (but they will easily form a triangle). The inadequacy may not be absolute, but it may be so great that a distorted pattern of the thing occurs whatever the thing-force may be; a 900-word vocabulary will produce a distorted version of *Hamlet* even with the utmost effort and care on the part of the translator. The inadequacy may not distort the pattern of the thing, but it may require unusual effort to impose the pattern upon the medium; a patient, energetic, skillful two-finger typist may be able to transcribe in ten hours a recorded interview that a skillful ten-finger typist can transcribe in 45 minutes.

We have considered behavior settings (as things) and their inhabitants (as media) in light of the second source of medium-inadequacy: too few elements. This provides one basis for making derivations from behavior settings to their inhabitants and vice versa. We have made use of this source of variation in medium-quality because the optimal number of inhabitants of a setting, and the deviations from it, can be determined with more precision than variation in medium-quality owing to differences in the personal attributes of the inhabitants. The theoretical and applied work on behavior settings with too few inhabitants—underpopulated behavior settings—is the subject of the next chapter.

Thing-medium relations between phenonema are frequently modified via feedback loops from media to things. The feedback may strengthen the forces of the thing: when my pen (medium) fails to write, feedback from the pen where it impinges on the paper via my perceptual system instigates me (thing) to press harder, and the pen writes. Or the feedback may change the pattern of the thing-forces: when my vocabulary (medium) is inadequate to express an idea (thing), feedback from my tongue-tied state modifies the idea so that I am able to express it, in less precise form perhaps. Both kinds of feedback may occur simultaneously; for example, feedback may modify the thing in ways that strengthen its forces vis-à-vis the medium. This simultaneous occurrence takes place in the case of behavior settings and their inhabitants.

Connections Between Behavior Settings as Things and Their Inhabitants as Media

The word *force* is used to indicate any kind of directed connection between thing (T) and medium (M), between behavior settings and inhabitants. In addition to force, some other terms are used to convey the same idea; for example:

M is *determined by* T	T *imposes upon* M
T *provides input to* M	T *transmits to* M
T is *the source of the causal texture of* M	there is *feedback from* M to T
	T *expends effort on* M

M is *dependent on* T   M *communicates with* T
T *influences* M   T *induces* pattern in M
M is *controlled by* T

Directed connections may convey energy, information, or order of events, and they may involve many kinds of phenomena: mechanical, physiological, electrical, perceptual, thermal, social, and so on. We use a number of terms, too, to designate particular connections between behavior settings and inhabitants, such as circuit, route, channel, action, and mechanism.

There are many phenotypic expressions of the primary behavior derivations, and secondary resultants arise from the nature of the particular circuitry that connects behavior settings as things with their inhabitants as media. Some of this circuitry is open to inspection.

CIRCUITS THAT JOIN BEHAVIOR SETTINGS AND
INHABITANTS VIA THE E-O-E ARC

Goal circuits. Within a behavior setting there are routes to goals that are satisfying to the inhabitants. A setting exists only so long as it provides its inhabitants with traversable routes to the goals their own unique natures require. In a behavior setting of the genotype Baseball Games, for example, the pitcher may achieve satisfaction by striking out batters, the umpire by earning $50, the concessionaire by selling many hot dogs, and the hometown fans by cheering the team to victory. Unless a sufficient number of the inhabitants of a baseball game are at least minimally satisfied, they will leave the setting, or will not return on another occasion, and the setting will cease.

Action along a goal route is reported in the italicized parts of the following record of the behavior of Mary Chaco, age one year, ten months, within the Midwest behavior setting Chaco Home, Mealtime (Barker & Wright, 1955, p. 376). The Chaco family was seated around the kitchen table eating the noonday meal. Mary had been eating heartily.

> 12:10 P.M. *Mary indicated that she wanted something else to eat by a string of words apparently unintelligible to her parents.*
> *She pointed toward the table, raising her voice slightly as she spoke.*
> Her father started to give her some meat.
> *She became more upset than before.* The meat definitely was not what Mary had in mind.
> *Her voice changed to a whine. She kicked her feet against the foot rest on the high chair. She was demanding and impatient.*
> By lifting each dish in turn, Mr. and Mrs. Chaco found it was jello salad that Mary wanted.

Her father immediately gave her a helping of salad.
Mary seemed pleased, but took this as a matter of course.

The essential features of this kind of connection between inhabitants and behavior settings are (a) perception by inhabitants of goals within settings and of paths to them, (b) achievement of goals, and (c) satisfaction of needs via consummatory behavior.

Program circuits. The program of a behavior setting has been defined and discussed previously (see pp. 89–92); it is the schedule of eco-behavioral occurrences that constitute a particular behavior setting. The complete program of a setting is usually stored within the inhabitants of penetration zones 6 and 5; parts of it are stored within the inhabitants of more peripheral zones, particularly zone 4, functionaries. The program is sometimes written out, as in the rules of the game of basketball (pp. 22–27), the lesson schedule of a teacher, or the agenda and operational guides (such as Robert's Rules of Order) of a business meeting.

Actions along a program circuit are reported in the italicized parts of the following record of Steven Peake, age seven years, nine months, within the Yoredale behavior setting Upper Infants Music Class (Barker et al., 1961). The class was assembled for rhythm band in the Cooking and Woodworking room of the school; it was taught by Miss Rutherford. The workbenches were pushed against the wall and the piano brought to the center of the room. The children stood in a semicircle around the piano.

> 1:52 P.M. *Miss Rutherford said, "All find your places."*
> Steven stood next to Herbert.
> Steven exchanged a playful remark with Oran.
> *Miss Rutherford started to give out the instruments, castanets, tri-angles, tambourines, drums, and cymbals.*
> Cymbals were suspended from straps by which they were held.
> 1:53. *Miss Rutherford handed a cymbal to Steven.*
> *When all the instruments had been distributed, Miss Rutherford asked that, first of all, they all stop talking.*
> Steven struck his cymbal lightly with his fist.

The essential features of this circuit are knowledge of the program by one or more inhabitants of the setting and actions by them that control the order of the occurrences that characterize the program.

Deviation-countering circuits. This is one of two types of circuits by which a behavior setting is maintained with its routes and goal-achieving possibilities intact. Deviation-countering circuits are involved within a behavior setting of the genotype Grocery Stores, for example, when the proprietor corrects a clerk's errors in pricing articles, when an employee repairs a broken shelf, or when the refrigerators operate and keep their contents cool. Inaccurate employees, broken shelving, and warm refrigerators are grocery store components that destroy and/or block routes to goals (profits, wages, groceries) that various inhabitants achieve; they are deviancies or inadequacies that must be dealt with if the program of a grocery store is to be carried out and the inhabitants are to achieve the satisfactions they seek. One way of dealing with inadequacies or deviancies of this kind is to correct or counter them. Actions on deviation-countering circuits are reported in the section of the record of Steven Peake immediately following that reported above:

> *Miss Rutherford went to the corner of the room and came back with a number of long red pencils and said, "We are short some parts of the instruments so we have to make do with these, to improvise."*
> Steven took his pencil matter-of-factly.

A few minutes later another deviation-countering action occurred.

> 1:54. *Miss Rutherford said to the class, "You never saw a real band playing all slumped over, leaning on things; now let's stand up straight."*

This circuit is characterized by (a) the sensing by inhabitants, or other components of a behavior setting, of conditions that prevent carrying out the program of the setting (achieving goals, in the case of inhabitants), and (b) actions to *counteract* the interfering (deviant, inadequate) conditions.

Vetoing circuits. These circuits are identical with deviation-countering circuits except that the behavior setting deviancy is not countered; rather, the deviant component is eliminated. Vetoing circuits are involved when an inaccurate employee is not corrected, but fired; when a broken shelf is not repaired, but discarded. Action along this circuit is exhibited in the behavior toward Oran of Miss Rutherford at a later point in the record of Steven Peake; the vetoing action is italicized.

> 2:10. Miss Rutherford commanded, "Pick up your instruments."
> Oran was acting silly.
> Miss Rutherford said, *"Evidently you do not wish to play in our band, Oran."* She took his cymbal away from him and gave it to Selna Bradley. The string holding her triangle had broken and she was without an instrument. *Miss Rutherford put Oran on the far side of the piano away from the class.*

Vetoing circuits have as essential features (a) the sensing by inhabitants, or other components of a behavior setting, of conditions that prevent the carrying out of the program of the setting (achieving goals in the case of inhabitants), and (b) actions by inhabitants to *eliminate* the interfering (deviant, inadequate) conditions.

REGULATION OF CIRCUITS THAT JOIN BEHAVIOR SETTINGS AND
INHABITANTS VIA THE E-O-E ARC

Within each of the circuits there is a control unit consisting of a behavior setting sensing mechanism (S-Mech), which senses and transmits information about behavior settings, and an executive mechanism (E-Mech), which tests information about settings against inhabitants' criteria of behavior setting adequacy and switches the circuit to the appropriate goal, program, deviation-countering, or vetoing channel. The control unit is located within the organism sector of the E-O-E arc; it is, in fact, the mechanism of the TOTE unit identified by Miller, Galanter, and Pribram (1960) as the fundamental unit of behavior. The parts of the control unit, their functions, order of functioning, and the alternative circuits they provide within the E-O-E arc are shown in Fig. 8.7; examples of control units in operation, as described or implied in the illustrative records (pp. 176–79) of the circuits, are presented in Table 8.2.

In the accompanying figures, table, and discussion, it is convenient to use abbreviations for the names of the various circuits. To help keep the meanings clear, here is a summary of these abbreviations and the full names and functions of the circuits:

S-Mech: *sensing mechanism*; senses and transmits information about
   behavior settings.
E-Mech: *executive mechanism*; tests the information against inhabitant's
   criteria of behavior setting adequacy and switches setting to O-
   Mech if setting is adequate or to M-Mech if setting is inadequate.
A-Mech: *action mechanism*; molar actions in behavior setting; includes
   all other circuits (O-Mech, M-Mech, G-Mech, P-Mech, D-Mech,
   V-Mech) except S-Mech and E-Mech.
O-Mech: *operating mechanism*; acts in accordance with standing pat-
   tern of adequate setting via goal or program circuits (G-Mech or
   P-Mech).
G-Mech: *goal mechanism*; actions that achieve goals of setting
   inhabitants.
P-Mech: *program mechanism*; actions that implement behavior
   setting program.

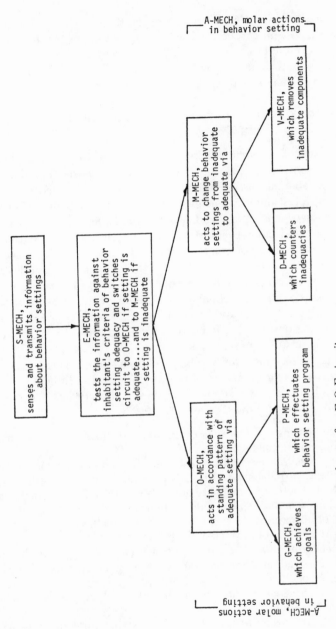

Fig. 8.7. Parts of the control unit of an E-O-E circuit.

TABLE 8.2

Examples of the Operation of Control Units in Four Eco-behavioral Circuits

Goal circuit via Mary (M)	Program circuit via teacher (T)	Deviation-countering circuit via teacher (T)	Vetoing circuit via teacher (T)
S-MECH			
M sees behavior setting (BS) component (salad)	T sees BS components (children and instruments)	T sees BS component (slumping children)	T sees BS component (silly Oran)
E-MECH			
BS component judged adequate for M's need; circuit switched to G-MECH via A-MECH and O-MECH	BS components judged adequate for intention of carrying out BS program; circuit switched to P-MECH via A-MECH and O-MECH	BS components judged inadequate for BS program; circuit switched to D-MECH via A-MECH and M-MECH	BS component judged inadequate for BS program; circuit switched to V-MECH via A-MECH and M-MECH

A-MECH			
O-MECH		M-MECH	
G-MECH	P-MECH	D-MECH	V-MECH
M's goal achieved and consumed; M satisfied	Lesson plan effectuated; intention carried out	Inadequacy of components (slump) corrected	Inadequate component (Oran) removed from setting

M-Mech: *maintenance mechanism*; actions to change behavior setting from inadequate to adequate via deviation-countering circuits or vetoing circuits (D-Mech or V-Mech).

D-Mech: *deviation-countering mechanism*; actions to correct behavior setting inadequacies.

V-Mech: *vetoing mechanism*; actions to eliminate inadequate behavior setting components.

Details of the location and connections of the parts of the control unit
within the eco-behavioral circuit (Fig. 8.2) are diagrammed in Figs. 8.8
and 8.9. The distal objects of Fig. 8.2 are the behavior setting components
of Figs. 8.8 and 8.9. Their state is sensed by S-Mech and transmitted to
E-Mech, where it is compared with the inhabitant's criteria of an adequate setting in view of that person's goal aspirations and program plans. If
the behavior setting components pass the inhabitant's test within E-
Mech, the circuit is routed via O-Mech into operating channels, becoming goal or program circuits (Fig. 8.8).

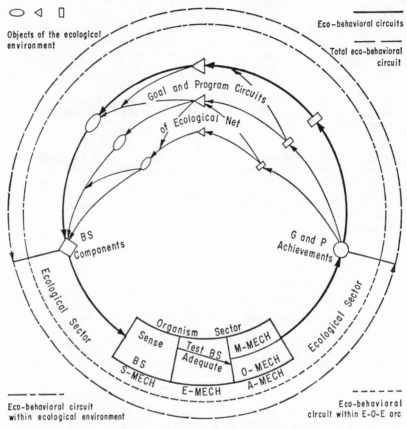

Fig. 8.8. Eco-behavioral operating circuits. The solid, directed lines represent the circuits; the broken lines are labeling guides.

But if the state of the setting does *not* pass the inhabitant's test for these actions (that is, if there is a discrepancy between the state of the setting as sensed by S-Mech and the inhabitant's standard of an adequate state for goal achievement and other plans), the eco-behavioral circuit is routed via M-Mech into maintenance channels (Fig. 8.9). The strength of the influence along the circuit from E-Mech to M-Mech is proportional to (a) the discrepancy between the sensed state of the setting and the inhabitant's standard, and (b) the importance of the setting to the inhabitant. The consequences of these changes within the setting recur as input to S-Mech; if there is still discrepancy the circuit is again channeled to M-Mech, and further alterations occur in the setting.

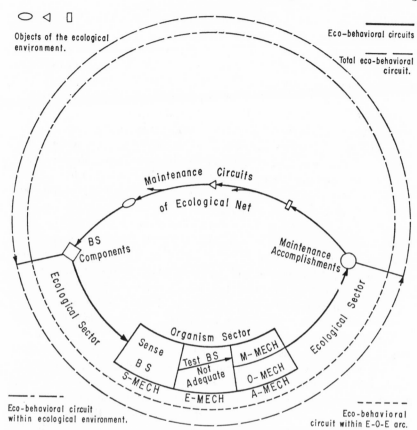

Fig. 8.9. Eco-behavioral maintenance circuits. The solid, directed lines represent the circuits; the broken lines are labeling guides.

The control units of the eco-behavioral circuits function in connection with particular behavior settings; however, they need not refer to total settings. The mechanism governing the temperature within the refrigerator of the grocery store tests and maintains no other components of this setting. Similarly, in a setting of the genotype Business Offices the testing and maintenance mechanisms of the janitor may operate with respect to a part of the setting only (the order and cleanliness of the office); the janitor may be insensitive to other components of the setting. This points to the important fact that behavior settings do not necessarily exist qua behavior settings for their inhabitants; an inhabitant need only apprehend that a particular goal is inaccessible, or that a part of a behavior setting program cannot be carried out, unless certain alterations are made in particular components of the setting. The reality and the nature of behavior settings as eco-behavioral entities do not reside in psychological processes of the inhabitants, but in the circuitry that interconnects behavior settings, inhabitants, and other behavior setting components. The components of behavior settings are richly joined (Ashby, 1956) by a complex net, which produces a self-governing entity with attributes quite different from the psychological and mechanical processes that govern its interior connections. The varied joinings that have been described suggest some of the sources of behavior setting complexity. But there are other sources.

The control unit of a maintenance circuit may be located within a single inhabitant, or its parts may be distributed among different inhabitants. When Miss Rutherford apprehended Oran's deviancy and removed its source (Oran) from the setting, all the mechanisms were within Miss Rutherford. On another occasion, Miss Rutherford noted a pupil's deviancy (a misspelled word on the chalkboard in this case); she asked another pupil what was wrong and, upon receiving a correct answer, requested him to correct the error. In this maintenance circuit the S-Mech and E-Mech of Miss Rutherford were involved, and also the S-Mech, E-Mech, and M-Mech of the second pupil. The circuit originated in Miss Rutherford, and it occurred by induction in the second pupil. Induction of maintenance forces is an important behavior setting process. It augments the maintenance forces of multi-inhabitant settings. Here is an example. The director of a play notes (S-Mech) that the behavior setting Play Practice is not going well, that it is inadequate for the program of the setting and for the director's goals within it (E-Mech): the sets are not ready, the lines are not learned. One deviation-countering course the director could take (E-Mech) would be to construct the sets and drill the cast personally (M-Mech). Another would be to bring the inadequate state of the setting to the attention of some deviant members of the cast—for example, provide input about the state of the setting to member A and member B. If A and B were to agree with the director's observations (S-Mech) and with the director's evaluation (E-Mech), actions (M-Mech) along maintenance circuits would increase, and three members would exhibit increased activity via M-Mech, rather than one. If A and B were to act, in addition, on two other setting members, seven would engage in greater activity on the maintenance circuits; if these two in turn were to act via their own M-Mech on two other members of the cast, fifteen would become more active. Such arborization of maintenance actions occurs by induction in all multi-inhabitant settings.

Another complication of behavior settings comes from the fact that not only the milieu and the other inhabitants of the behavior setting are recipients of a person's maintenance efforts; those forces are also self-directed—they apply to their originator as well as to others. If persons observe that their own attributes (physique, appearance, abilities, behavior) are below the minimal level of adequacy for the setting they inhabit, thus endangering the opportunities for satisfaction that it provides, maintenance circuits terminating in themselves as behavior setting components will be instigated. An aging member of a tennis club who observes (S-Mech) that his play is slowing down and his skill declining, thus reducing the functional level of the tennis settings in which he participates (E-Mech) and reducing his own and others' satisfactions, may take maintenance actions against himself by trying to improve his play (D-Mech) or by dropping out of the club (V-Mech).

We are particularly concerned with the maintenance mechanisms and circuits, for they are most relevant to some important applications of behavior setting theory. We shall consider some special characteristics of these circuits.

BEHAVIOR SETTING MAINTENANCE CIRCUITS

When the test of behavior setting adequacy within E-Mech finds the behavior setting to be inadequate and the circuit is switched to M-Mech, there occurs within E-Mech another decision, namely, between V-Mech and D-Mech. The behavior setting is again tested via the adequacy criterion. This time the test is of the relative adequacy of the setting if the defective component is eliminated versus its adequacy if the defective component is corrected. In some cases the result is clear: the only way to deal with such deviant behavior setting components as flies in a restaurant is to eliminate them; there is no effective way to correct or counter flies. But in the case of a silly pupil or an ineffective employee, a judgment must be made of the relative adequacy of the setting if the deviant behavior is corrected or if the deviant setting component is ejected from the setting.

Two facts are relevant to this judgment: first, it often requires less effort to veto (eject) a deviant behavior setting component than to counter its deviancy (Ashby, 1956); second, within wide ranges, reducing the number of behavior setting components reduces the medium-quality of its interior manifold and increases the effort required to maintain the setting at an adequate level. It is often easier to discard broken shelves than to repair them (but limited shelving makes it difficult to operate a store); it is often

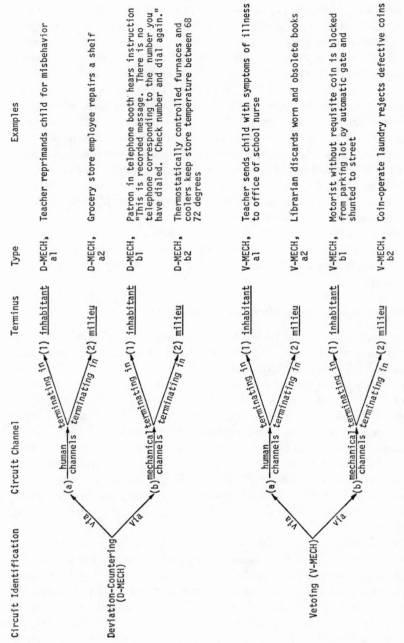

Circuit Identification	Circuit Channel	Terminus	Type	Examples
Deviation-Countering (D-MECH) via (a) human channels	terminating in (1) inhabitant		D-MECH, a1	Teacher reprimands child for misbehavior
	terminating in (2) milieu		D-MECH, a2	Grocery store employee repairs a shelf
via (b) mechanical channels terminating in (1) inhabitant			D-MECH, b1	Patron in telephone booth hears instruction "This is recorded message. There is no telephone corresponding to the number you have dialed. Check number and dial again."
terminating in (2) milieu			D-MECH, b2	Thermostatically controlled furnaces and coolers keep store temperature between 68 72 degrees
Vetoing (V-MECH) via (a) human channels terminating in (1) inhabitant			V-MECH, a1	Teacher sends child with symptoms of illness to office of school nurse
terminating in (2) milieu			V-MECH, a2	Librarian discards worn and obsolete books
via (b) mechanical channels terminating in (1) inhabitant			V-MECH, b1	Motorist without requisite coin is blocked from parking lot by automatic gate and shunted to street
terminating in (2) milieu			V-MECH, b2	Coin-operate laundry rejects defective coins

Fig. 8.10. Types of behavior setting maintenance circuits.

easier to fire an inaccurate employee than to provide training and supervision (but an understaffed store presents problems). The task of E-Mech is to balance the effort-cost of countering a deviant component against the effort-cost of maintaining the adequacy of the setting with its reduced components. Many behavior setting attributes influence this balance.

Both deviation-countering and vetoing circuits may terminate in a behavior setting inhabitant or in a milieu component; and both circuits may operate via mechanical or human channels. There are, therefore, eight types of maintenance circuits, as shown, with examples, in Fig. 8.10.

The behavior setting maintenance circuits that operate via human channels (D-Mech, a1 and a2; V-Mech, a1 and a2) have the following psychological processes within their control units:

S-Mech

(a) Perception by inhabitants of behavior setting attributes.

E-Mech

(b) Sensitivity of inhabitants to own needs and/or intentions.
(c) Identification of goals and goal-routes within behavior setting, and/or knowledge of program of setting.
(d) Judgment of minimally adequate state of setting (in view of needs and intentions, and of goals, routes, and programs).
(e) Discrimination between present state of setting (process a) and minimally adequate state (process d); judgment that setting is inadequate in view of needs and intentions; switch circuit to M-Mech in proportion to degree of inadequacy.

M-Mech

(f) Perception of maintenance routes.
(g) Molar actions along maintenance routes.

OTHER CONNECTIONS BETWEEN BEHAVIOR SETTINGS
AND INHABITANTS

The receptor, central, and effector systems of the E-O-E arc (Fig. 8.2) and the goal, program, operating, and maintenance circuits they implement (Figs. 8.8 and 8.9) are not the only channels that join behavior settings and their inhabitants. When a motorist skids into a highway guardrail and is deflected back onto the roadway, when a police officer subdues, handcuffs, and takes a rioter to prison, or when a locked vault prevents a theft, the deviant behavior setting components (the motorist, the rioter, the thief) are not dealt with via their E-O-E circuits but by the direct application of physical force in no way different from the way water is guided down a river channel, or a quarterback is sacked by a defensive tackle, or noise is kept from a room by acoustical insulation. There are direct connections, too, between behavior settings and inhabitants by way of the physiological processes of the inhabitants and, for example, the composition and temperature of the air. These connections between behavior settings and inhabitants enter behavior setting circuitry as techniques by means of which human or milieu components of behavior settings carry out program, deviation-countering, or vetoing actions with respect to inhabitants by interventions outside of their E-O-E arcs.

SUMMARY OF BEHAVIOR SETTING THEORY

This presentation of behavior setting theory raises the question of whether different ecological environments produce different behavior and of whether the differences, or lack of them, can be predicted from the environments. The answer of Brunswik (1955) and of Lewin (1951) was that behavior cannot be predicted from information or theories about the environment, that this must be determined by empirical investigation in each case, and that predictions from empirical evidence must be made probabilistically because the environment and the connections between it and people have only statistical stability.

The theory of behavior settings allows us to go somewhat further than Brunswik and Lewin thought possible. They and other psychologists have assumed that environmental variables occur without regard for the behavior of the inhabitants of the environment—that they are independent variables. According to behavior setting theory, the ecological environment of human molar behavior and its inhabitants are not independent; rather, the environment is a set of homeostatically governed eco-behaviorial entities consisting of nonhuman components, human components, and control circuits that modify the components in predictable ways to maintain the environmental entities in their characteristic states. These states are defined by schedules, or programs, or intra-entity occurrences. If one control circuit does not produce the programmed occurrence from an inhabitant or other component, other circuits are activated in accordance with feedback from the component. This means that the ecological environment varies systematically from inhabitant to inhabitant. The behavior setting Trafficways is a very different environment for a slow than for a fast motorist. It provides a motorist whose speed is slower than that programmed for the setting with recurring "speed up" inputs of varying modalities and forcefulness: *social* pressure from the succession of passing cars, from the horns of following motorists, from gesturing traffic officers, and from police summons; and *physical* force from the forward air pressure created by the passing cars and from rear-end collisions. All of these are slow-speed-countering, maintenance inputs; in case none of them corrects the motorist's deviation from the standing pattern of the setting Trafficways, vetoing inputs await: a rear-end crash destroys the offender's car or propels it out of the setting, a court order withdraws the license to drive. A motorist whose speed is faster than that programmed for the setting receives an entirely different set of "slow down" inputs: social pressure from overtaken cars, from gesturing traffic officers, and from prosecution for speeding; obstructions from the conforming traffic; and physical resistance from the curves engineered for the programmed speeds. All of these are fast-speed-countering, maintenance inputs; in case none of them corrects the motorist's deviation from the programmed speed, vetoing inputs await this motorist, too; a head-on collision destroys the car, centrifugal force propels the car out of the setting on a curve, a court order withdraws the license to drive. On the other hand, Trafficways provide inhabitants who travel in accordance with the standing pattern of the setting with *program* inputs almost entirely, such as posted speed limits. In these examples, feedback from behavior that deviates from the standing pattern of the setting produces countering or vetoing actions by the environment that are roughly proportional in strength to the degree of the deviancy.

The conceptual breach between psychological and ecological phenomena is not closed by behavior settings and their homeostatic controls. Indeed, the goal of formulating a unitary eco-behavioral theory was abandoned early in our consideration of the general problem of entity and environment. There, the environment of an entity was defined as the surrounding context with which the entity is coupled by laws that are incommensurate with those that govern the entity, and the locus of the boundary between entity and environment was identified as that point at which the concepts and theories that account for the entity cease to apply, but beyond which there are phenomena with which the entity is joined and with which it co-varies. So the conceptual breach is as great as ever. However, within behavior settings the problem is restated so that, on the one hand, the sublime but millennial goal of developing a single conceptual system incorporating psychological and ecological phenomena is detoured, and, on the other hand, the discouraging prospect of mere empiricism and probabilism is avoided. The environment in terms of behavior settings opens up the more modest and hopeful possibility of discovering general principles of eco-behavioral organization and control without a comprehensive theory of the phenomena that are regulated. It does this by means of the processes involved in the thing-medium relation.

The thing-medium relation (see pp. 169–71) refers to the transmission and maintenance of *pattern* between thing and medium, not to the transformation of thing-phenomena into medium-phenomena. The thing-medium processes involved in perception do not, for example, transform a stone into light and light into the percept of a stone. The only aspects of the phenomena at the origin and termination of a thing-medium connection that are relevant are the degrees to which they have thing-characteristics (interdependence of parts and internally determined pattern) and medium characteristics (independence of parts and externally determined pattern). Knowing that A and B are related as thing to medium makes it possible to predict some things about B from information about A, and vice versa, but only with respect to the *patterns* that are transmitted; the prediction tells us nothing about the substance behind the pattern. Nevertheless, when the thing-medium connection obtains, certain consequences with respect to pattern follow with complete certainty.

In the next chapter we turn to a consideration of such consequences in the application of behavior setting theory to an important applied problem—namely, the relation between the number of inhabitants and the operation of the behavior setting. We present a review of behavior setting theory as applied to this problem and, in the chapter thereafter, summarize a number of empirical investigations that test the theory.

9
Behavior Setting Theory Applied to Underpopulated Settings

The theory of behavior settings described in the previous chapter supports the view that the environment in terms of behavior settings is much more than a source of random inputs to its inhabitants, or of inputs arranged in fixed array and flow patterns. It argues, rather, that the environment provides inputs with controls that regulate the inputs in accordance with the systemic requirements of the environment, on the one hand, and in accordance with the behavior attributes of its human components, on the other. This means that the same environmental unit provides different inputs to different persons, and different inputs to the same person in response to that person's behavior change; furthermore, it means that the whole program of the environment's inputs changes if its own ecological properties change—if it becomes more or less populous, for example. As indicated earlier (p. 174), a change in the number of inhabitants of a setting constitutes a change in the adequacy of the medium-qualities of the components of the setting. An underpopulated setting is a setting with inadequate medium-qualities: too few elements. The relative ease with which one can assess the optimal number of inhabitants of a setting, and the deviations from it, provides a convenient basis for making derivations from behavior settings to their inhabitants and vice versa. Differences in the behavior of inhabitants of underpopulated and adequately or overpopulated settings provide one test of the theory that the ecological environment is connected with its human components and has predictable effects on them.

The differences are not only important for the testing of behavior setting theory but are of immediate practical significance as well. They provide information about the consequences for people of inhabiting underpopulated and adequately or overpopulated behavior settings. The population explosion makes this a crucial social issue. The increase in population is usually considered in connection with economic and nutritional problems, but its more direct effects on behavior deserve consideration, too. Underpopulated behavior settings are without doubt becoming less frequent, and adequately or overpopulated settings more common. This change within the United States has relevance for theories of American culture and character. The United States has been known as a "land of opportunity" and its inhabitants have been called a "people of plenty"; its environment is said to have been dominated by the "free frontier." Involved in the complex of ideas behind these aphorisms is the idea that there has been a superabundance of goals to be achieved and an excess of tasks to be done in relation to the nation's inhabitants, and that these have been important influences on the American society and people. This is, in important respects, a theory by historians of the influence of underpopulated behavior settings on a society and the characteristics of its members. A science of behavior settings should have something to say about this theory and about the consequences of the change from a society of underpopulated settings to one of adequately and overpopulated settings (cf. Barker, 1979).

On Nomenclature

The problem of terminology in discussing variations in population of behavior settings requires special comment. In the earliest writings of Barker, Wicker, Willems, and others, settings with insufficient numbers of inhabitants to comfortably carry out in sequence all the tasks required by the settings' programs were referred to as "undermanned" settings. Since then, many papers have appeared that continue this usage, giving rise to a strong tradition of work under the general heading of "manning theory." In recent years, however, as sensitivity to possible but unintended sexist implications has become general, several writers have either apologized for continuing the traditional use of the term "manning" or substituted other terms, such as "staffing theory" and "understaffed settings."

The solution adopted in the present volume is to use the term "populated" instead of "manned" when discussing the adequacy of the number of inhabitants of settings, institutions (schools, churches), and communities in general. For example, we have substituted "underpopulated settings" for "undermanned settings" and have used the more general term "behavior setting theory" instead of "manning theory." Following a sug-

gestion by Wicker (Wicker & Kirmeyer, 1977, p. 74), we have also replaced Barker's term "optimally" with "adequately" to avoid the connota-
tion of a specific, ideal level of population of a behavior setting. In the
discussion below, therefore, we use the terms "adequately populated"
rather than "optimally manned" behavior settings.

Wicker (1979a) has also correctly pointed out that behavior setting theory has included an implicit assumption that most inhabitants and potential inhabitants of behavior settings are equally eligible to penetrate the
settings to the most central zones of leadership and responsibility (the
operating zones or penetration levels 6, 5, and 4). The boundary separating the operating zones from the member, onlooker, and potential member zones (penetration levels 3, 2, 1, and 0), in other words, is assumed to
be highly permeable. Although such an assumption agrees with common
experience concerning many settings of a community, such as most settings of voluntary associations, churches, civic groups, and recreational
and sports organizations, there are obviously many important exceptions
where access to the central zones of penetration of the setting requires
special qualifications, such as the offices of professionally trained persons
and most service behavior settings.

This consideration led Wicker to propose separate assessments of adequacy of population for behavior setting operatives (zones 6, 5, and 4) and
nonoperatives (all others). He points out that a setting can be underpopulated at the level of operatives and overpopulated by nonoperatives, such
as when a restaurant has more customers than the staff can handle or
when a physician has more patients wishing to be seen than can be accom-
modated. When such behavior settings are the focus of consideration—
that is, when the assumption of permeability of the boundary between
operatives and nonoperatives is not tenable—we have used the term
"staffing" to refer to the adequacy of population at the level of operatives
and "population" for all setting inhabitants. The term "staffing" is also
used in discussions of laboratory studies in which the number of persons
and the number of setting tasks is rigidly controlled by the structure of the
experiment.

Wicker, McGrath, and Armstrong (1972) proposed a distinction between "adequate" and "over" population of a setting, and some laboratory
studies have documented differential consequences (Wicker et al., 1976)
of adequately populated versus overpopulated settings. Wicker (1979a)
also makes a strong case for taking this distinction seriously. Although this
possibility holds promise, operational application of the distinction in empirical studies appears to be difficult except in highly artificial conditions

in the laboratory. For this reason and because the emphasis in most of the relevant research has been on the consequences for behavior of setting underpopulation as opposed to either adequate or overpopulation, our discussion generally uses the phrase "adequately populated" to refer to all levels of population above "underpopulated."

Underpopulated Behavior Settings

It has been pointed out that one of the attributes of a behavior setting is its firm, strong unity and stability relative to the medium manifold with which it is coupled (p. 171). Because of this stability, a decrease in the number of inhabitants of a behavior setting below the number required for optimal medium-quality does not, within limits, change the program or the standing pattern of the setting. This has inevitable consequences for the inhabitants. Behavior setting constancy under these circumstances necessarily changes the environment of the inhabitants. We shall call behavior settings with fewer than an adequate number of inhabitants *underpopulated* behavior settings. We can make the following derivations with respect to them, in comparison with adequately populated behavior settings: (a) the number of forces acting on each inhabitant of underpopulated settings is greater because the same forces are distributed among fewer inhabitants; and (b) the range of directions of the forces on each inhabitant is greater because fewer inhabitants mediate the same field of forces. From this it follows that the inhabitants of underpopulated behavior settings, in comparison with those of adequately populated settings, (a) are more active within the settings, (b) in a greater variety of actions.

These consequences are exemplified in a baseball game played by eight-player teams on a regulation nine-player field according to the official rules. If the center fielders of the teams are missing, the left fielders are the recipients of forces normally terminating in center field in addition to the usual left-field forces; the right fielders receive some center-field forces, too; and a few marginal center-field inputs will be added to the usual quota of the second base players. In fact, in the distribution of the center fielder's environmental "load" among the remaining team members, something will be added to each player's usual share. So, with the regular nine-player number and constellation of forces distributed among fewer players, (a) the number of forces per player will be greater, and each member will play "harder"; and (b) each player will be pressed in more directions, each will engage in a greater variety of plays. This is a paradigm of most behavior settings with fewer than an adequate number of inhabitants in which the barrier between operatives and nonoperatives is relatively permeable.

It is important to note, however, that this paradigm holds only within a limited range of population decrement, for at some point in the course of population decrement a behavior setting is transformed into a different setting. Baseball, for example, may be transformed into "work-up" (taking turns at bat).

Interior Circuitry of Underpopulated Behavior Settings

According to the general theory of behavior settings, there are more forces *per inhabitant* in more directions in underpopulated behavior settings than in settings with an adequate or larger number of inhabitants, because the same field of forces is distributed among fewer inhabitants. This is accompanied by differences in the interior circuitry of underpopulated and adequately populated settings, which provide a basis for more precise predictions.

PROGRAM CIRCUITS IN UNDERPOPULATED BEHAVIOR SETTINGS

Underpopulated and adequately populated settings have, by definition, the same standing patterns and the same programs. This means that the same lists of programmed actions are implemented by fewer inhabitants in the former case and that there are, in consequence, more program actions and a greater variety of program actions per inhabitant. The program of a behavior setting is a time-ordered list of changes in the components of the setting. In the case of human components, the program describes changes in behavior without directions for the implementation of the changes. In fact, behavior settings carry out their programs via multiple channels, including such automata as the timed signal systems in schools, which terminate, for example, reading behavior and initiate arithmetic behavior. Behavior setting programs when in operation within settings are not merely permissive action guides; they are lists of orders that are enforced by input from other inhabitants and from the milieu of the setting, such as from a teacher or from objects on an assembly line moving at a fixed speed. If a programmed connection between behavior setting and inhabitant is not strong enough to instigate the programmed action, there is, in consequence, an inadequacy in the setting, and supporting maintenance forces are generated. We turn to these next.

MAINTENANCE CIRCUITS IN UNDERPOPULATED
BEHAVIOR SETTINGS

There are a greater number of stronger and more varied maintenance circuits in underpopulated than in adequately populated behavior settings. The medium manifolds of underpopulated behavior settings are, by definition, less adequate than those of adequately populated settings, and in the normal course of variation of behavior setting attributes, they are actually inadequate more frequently; their maintenance circuits are, therefore, more often activated via E-Mech. How this occurs in one case can be seen in a setting of the genotype Baseball Games when it is played by eight-player rather than by regulation nine-player teams. Three phases are discernible:

(1) Certain plays that are routine for nine-player teams are not completed by eight-player teams, because their members must cover a greater spatial area in the same time.

(2) The game notices these plays (dropped balls, overthrows) via the S-Mech of its players, coaches, and rooters.

(3) The game evaluates them as deviancies and inadequacies via the inhabitants' E-Mech, causing the circuits to be switched to M-Mech and to hum with maintenance actions (advice, encouragement, demands for greater alertness, speed, and control, and/or for the sacking of especially inadequate players). In this connection, see Fig. 9.1. This occurs more often in underpopulated behavior settings because inadequacies are more frequent.

The greater number of maintenance circuits in underpopulated behavior settings are multiplied and increased in strength by induction. Consider the net of maintenance circuits in the baseball game at the moment when a player has a precisely defined task, namely, to catch a critical fly ball when the game is in an uncertain state. The crucial ball is in the sky; the ball's image is on the player's retinas: as the ball approaches, the player moves to be under the ball (if he does not move correctly, he receives deviation-countering input from other players and from spectators); the player's arms are raised; the catching hand encounters the ball; feedback #1, via proprioceptive S-Mech, reports that the ball is not caught; feedback #2 visual S-Mech reports that the ball is not caught, that it is rolling on the ground; feedback #3, via auditory S-Mech from the umpire, reports that the ball is not caught and the batter is safe; and feedback #3a (simultaneously with #3), via auditory S-Mech from the other players and the spectators, reports that the ball is not caught, the batter is safe, and the game is in jeopardy. Feedback #3a conveys not only infor-

© United Feature Syndicate, Inc., 1967

Fig. 9.1. Vetoing circuits.

mation but counter-deviancy and/or vetoing influences as well; both of these are delivered directly and also via the team manager and other powerful persons, where the strength of the influence is increased. All of these circuits instigate maintenance actions by the inadequate player: retrieving the ball and returning it to the game as quickly as possible. If channels #1 to #3a fail to deliver the message of what happened and to instigate counter-deviancy, there is delayed feedback #4, via the coach's memory storage, his verbal mechanism, and the player's auditory channels: the coach reports ten minutes later that the ball was not caught, the batter was safe, the game lost, and all because the player was too slow. A ball game takes no chances in delivering to the player the report of and corrections for his behavior deviancy.

Objectively equivalent inadequacies are actually more injurious to underpopulated than to adequately populated behavior settings. A behavior setting is a unit; a weakness in any part weakens all parts. The more frequent and more serious inadequacies of underpopulated behavior settings mean that they require more frequent shoring up in more different parts than adequately populated settings. The more varied deficiencies require, via E-Mech, more varied maintenance circuits.

DEVIATION-COUNTERING AND VETOING CIRCUITS IN
UNDERPOPULATED BEHAVIOR SETTINGS

The interior circuitry of behavior settings produces more deviation-countering and fewer vetoing maintenance circuits within underpopulated than within adequately populated settings. This occurs because the cost in effort and time of countering deviant behavior in underpopulated behavior settings is usually less than the combined cost of vetoing the deviant inhabitants and of maintaining the settings in a state of inadequacy with their reduced numbers of inhabitants. The reverse holds in adequately populated behavior settings: the cost of vetoing deviant inhabitants is usually less than the cost of countering their deviant behavior; more adequate replacements are readily available. Some details of deviation-countering and vetoing circuits follow.

Adequately populated behavior settings differ sharply from underpopulated settings in dealing with inhabitants who bring low medium-qualities to the setting due to various limitations, such as defective physiques, low intelligence, poor motor skills, little interest, "difficult" personalities, and uncooperative attitudes. These behavior settings lose little or nothing when they discard such inhabitants, for they usually have replacements readily available, and they are saved the strong and persisting deviation-countering efforts that are usually required to obtain conformity to the patterns of the settings from such inhabitants. If there are 30 candidates for players in a softball game, a better game will result with less fuss and bother (less energy devoted to maintenance) if all four-year-olds and others who are likely to produce deviant behavior are vetoed out. The situation is different for behavior settings with fewer than the optimal number of inhabitants. These settings must make great use of deviation-countering control mechanisms because their inhabitants are functionally too important to be casually eliminated by veto. When E-Mech within the maintenance circuits of an underpopulated behavior setting balances the inadequacy of a particular inhabitant against the reduction in medium-quality of the total manifold of inhabitants if the inhabitant is eliminated, the balance often favors retaining the inhabitant and correcting or simply tolerating the deviances. Thus a four-player ball game of nine-year-olds may tolerate and nurse along via deviation-countering controls a four-year-old participant. In this case, an outfielder, even an inefficient, inept one who requires frequent help, instruction, and correction, is likely to produce a better game than with the only available alternative—no outfielder at all. There are exceptions. Some inhabitants of underpopulated settings are so resistant to deviation-countering controls that vetoing controls must be used.

In addition to underpopulated behavior settings, there are some other special settings whose programs can usually be effectuated only, or more efficiently, via deviation-countering controls. This is true of most settings that are programmed to educate their inhabitants. When this is the case, even amply inhabited settings must use deviation-countering controls such as helping, encouraging, and disciplining, however "inefficient" they may be. In a study of third grade classes, Gump (1967) found that teachers engaged in from 103 to 229 deviation-countering acts during a five-hour day but that there were very few vetoing acts. There are other types of behavior settings with special programs that are not affected by the under-populated state; Wicker (1968) has identified a number of them. But the exceptions and special programs do not threaten the generalization that deviation-countering maintenance circuits are relatively more frequent in underpopulated behavior settings and that vetoing circuits are relatively more frequent in adequately populated settings.

Internal Interdependence, Unity, and Centripetal Forces of Underpopulated Behavior Settings

One consequence of the differential occurrence of deviation-countering and vetoing circuits in underpopulated and adequately populated settings is a difference in the prevailing direction of forces within them. The prevailing forces in underpopulated behavior settings are inward; they press behavior, materials, and processes into more appropriate formats within the setting; they are centripetal, setting-unifying, and strengthening forces. Deviation-countering circuits are discriminating; they are "against" the deviant *attributes* of behavior setting components, they are "for" the deviant *components*. The direction of forces within adequately populated behavior settings is more often centrifugal; they shunt some components, both inhabitants and milieu components, out of the setting; although the final effect is to strengthen the setting, these forces are, in their immediate consequences, divisive and weakening. Vetoing forces are not discriminating; they are against the deviant attributes of behavior setting components and they are against the components, too.

Deviation-countering regulatory systems are one of the bases of an essential attribute of behavior settings, namely, interdependence of parts. The index of interdependence, K (see p. 54), was established on an empirical basis, with only general ideas about how the observed interdependence might be effected. The theories of thing and medium, of the relation of the number of parts of a manifold of elements to its medium-quality, and of the feedback loop between the adequacy of a behavior setting and the actions of inhabitants along maintenance routes, elucidate the inner working of this observable behavior setting attribute.

It should be noted, too, that the deviation-countering and vetoing maintenance circuits are evidence that a behavior setting is not only structurally bounded but dynamically bounded as well. The dynamic limits of behavior settings are usually not as definite as their structural boundaries. Deviation-countering circuits, in particular, frequently extend beyond the structural boundaries of behavior settings to bring appropriate inhabitants and potential inhabitants into the temporal-physical bounds of settings. Printed and broadcast announcements of behavior setting occurrences are parts of deviation-countering circuits that extend beyond the temporal-physical bounds of behavior settings.

We arrive at the general conclusion that behavior settings are entities that are able to compensate, within limits, for lack of components by the increased application of force. Involved in this process is a higher rate of communication via maintenance forces between underpopulated behavior settings and their components; among their components there are more deviation-countering forces, more induced forces, and more centripetal forces. Underpopulated settings are, therefore, more interdependent internally than adequately populated settings; they have stronger unity and intrinsic integrity, and they have stronger thing-characteristics than their human medium manifolds.

The theory of behavior settings has pointed to some ways that underpopulated settings differ from adequately populated settings. By way of summary, these differences and their sources in terms of the theory are charted in Fig. 9.2. The chart may be narrated as follows: underpopulated behavior settings *in comparison with adequately populated settings* have, by definition, (a) fewer inhabitants and the same standing patterns; according to the theory these produce (b) more program forces per inhabitant in a greater range of directions and (c) poorer medium manifolds, which have (d) smaller margins of adequacy, that result in (e) more frequent and more serious inadequacies, which instigate (f) more, stronger, and more varied maintenance forces; because of difference (a), the maintenance forces are (g) more frequently deviation-countering and less frequently vetoing forces, and because of difference (f) there are (h) more induced maintenance forces.

In general terms, underpopulated behavior settings in comparison with

Underpopulated behavior settings *relative to adequately populated settings* have:

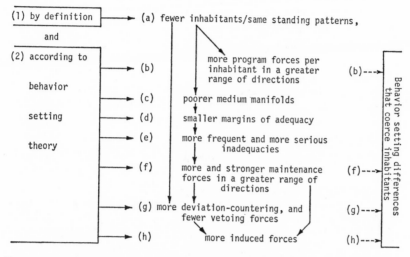

Fig. 9.2. Attributes of underpopulated behavior settings relative to those of adequately populated settings of the same genotype.

adequately populated behavior settings impose more and stronger forces on their inhabitants in more varied directions; the forces are, however, more prevailingly directed inward and toward other inhabitants. According to this, underpopulated behavior settings have stronger internal interdependence and cohesiveness; they are stronger things vis-à-vis their inhabitants than adequately populated behavior settings.

Differences in the Behavior of Inhabitants of Underpopulated and Adequately Populated Behavior Settings

PRIMARY DIFFERENCES

According to the summary of behavior setting theory (Fig. 9.2), the different medium manifolds of underpopulated and adequately populated behavior settings produce differences in the strength, direction, origin, and termination of forces that impinge on the inhabitants. In addition, according to the theory, behavior setting control systems ensure that the differences produce these predictably different actions (primary behavior) via the inhabitants' S-Mech, E-Mech, and A-Mech; in comparison with the inhabitants of adequately populated behavior settings, the inhabitants of underpopulated settings engage in

1. more program actions,
2. more varied program actions,
3. more maintenance actions,
4. more varied maintenance actions,
5. stronger maintenance actions,
6. more deviation-countering maintenance actions,
7. fewer vetoing maintenance actions, and
8. more induced actions.

These consequences for the inhabitant components of underpopulated behavior settings may be summarized as follows: the inhabitants of under-populated settings, in comparison with inhabitants of adequately populated settings, engage in *more* actions (points 1 and 3, above), *stronger* actions (5), *more varied* actions (2 and 4), *more centripetally directed* actions (6 and 7), and more actions that *originate and terminate in other inhabitants* (8). The picture that emerges is one in which the inhabitants of underpopulated behavior settings are busier, more vigorous, more versatile, more oriented vis-à-vis the settings they inhabit, and more interdependent.

It is important to note that these predictions are not made from empirical correlations between counts of the number of inhabitants within behavior settings and measures of their behavior; they are also not made from the psychological characteristics of the inhabitants, beyond the fact that all possess S-Mech to sense the state of the setting, E-Mech to test it against program requirements and their own needs, and A-Mech to act in accordance with the test. In making the predictions, the inhabitants have been considered as fixtures and paraphernalia of an extra-individual behavior-and-milieu entity, a behavior setting—that is, as instruments that sense and test the state of a setting against a standard, and as machinery that makes the indicated adjustments in the setting. According to behavior setting theory, there are sources of power and there are control mechanisms within underpopulated behavior settings to generate the greater number of more varied and more vigorous actions and the more frequent centripetal and interpersonal actions required of the inhabitants. This power and control are effective over a wide range of inhabitant motivations and ability; if they are not effective, the setting disintegrates and ceases to exist.

It is important to note, too, that the predictions refer to the actions of inhabitants as behavior setting processes, not as psychological phenomena. The prediction that the inhabitants of underpopulated behavior settings act more often and more strongly on other inhabitants carries no implications about the experiences accompanying the greater number of interpersonal acts. If the processes within a setting were completely mechanized, as sometimes happens, the machines would exhibit analogous differences between "underequipped" and "adequately or overequipped" installations.

The program of a particular behavior setting is a detailed schedule of concrete occurrences. So far as the human components are concerned, the list may refer to such simple motor movements as tapping the keys of a typewriter in a programmed order, or it may call for complicated behavior. But in every case the program includes only behavior that can be sensed and tested by the control system of the setting—by mechanical devices or by S-Mech and E-Mech of inhabitants. Within the limits of the precision of its control system, behavior within a setting can be predicted with complete accuracy from its program.

The programs of some behavior settings imply the involvement of central psychological processes such as learning (in school classes), enjoyment (in circuses), and spiritual awakening (in worship services). However, the control systems of these settings test only occurrences that are accessible to the settings' sensors, and so far as the human components are concerned, these occurrences are all objective actions (movements) emitted by A-Mech. There are continual efforts to improve methods of testing behavior setting adequacy; thermometers, photometers, hygrometers, etc., often substitute for or augment S-Mech and E-Mech in testing nonhuman components, and technically sophisticated, standardized methods are highly developed for testing human components of behavior settings. A teacher no longer has to rely on personal sensitivities and judgment in assessing the adequacy of a pupil in mathematics; the pupil's adequacy can be read in the results of a standardized test administration. Many of the tests are based on psychological theories that relate actions on the tests to presumed psychological states—for example, to intelligence, adjustment, or secretarial adequacy. Sensing and testing the adequacy of behavior settings is, in some settings, a specialized activity of professional personnel (inspectors, auditors, safety engineers, personnel psychologists, company police), and often their aim is to detect incipient inadequacies before they interfere with the program of a setting. However, even the most advanced testing and control techniques are unable to govern the full psychological content of the actions occurring within behavior settings. Although the program of a worship service may include the occurrence "silent prayer," the control system of the setting can only deal with deviations from silence.

SECONDARY DIFFERENCES

In behavior setting theory, a net of connections intervenes between inhabitants' actions via A-Mech and succeeding input from the setting via S-Mech (see Figs. 8.8 and 8.9); the net consists of shorter or longer chains of alterations in the human and nonhuman components of behavior settings. Most behavior settings are such large and richly joined systems it is impossible to trace within this net the detailed consequences of particular actions; in fact, the alterations that finally result from particular actions are indeterminate. This indeterminacy is handled within the control systems of behavior settings by sensing the state of the setting after each action via S-Mech, testing it via E-Mech, and correcting inappropriate alterations via A-Mech. But the primary behavior differences between underpopulated and adequately populated behavior settings reported above do not refer to particular actions; they refer to general attributes of actions, and these lead, singly and in combination, to certain behavior differences one or more steps removed within the net from the primary actions emitted by A-Mech. We shall consider these *secondary* differences next. They are numbered beginning with 9, to follow the eight primary behavior differences.

In comparison with the inhabitants of optimally or overpopulated behavior settings:

(9) The inhabitants of underpopulated behavior settings *enter more frequently into the central zones* of behavior settings. Obstacles to entering central zones 6, 5, and 4 (single leader, joint leader, functionary) are greater than those to entering peripheral zones 3, 2, and 1 (member, audience, visitor). The greater number of more vigorous actions (primary differences 1, 3, and 5) and their more centripetal direction (primary differences 6, 7, and 8) impel the inhabitants of underpopulated settings into central zones more frequently than the less vigorous and less inward-directed actions of inhabitants of adequately populated settings. Example: a member of a small high school class who is without special aptitude for dramatics is under greater pressure from the setting to take part in the class play than a similar member of a large class, and the small-class member takes more vigorous action toward the setting; these primary differences carry the person through obstacles surrounding the central zones of the setting (such as long hours of practice) into the central zone of cast member, a zone that a similar member of a large class does not penetrate.

(10) The inhabitants of underpopulated behavior settings *engage in difficult actions more frequently*. Inhabitants of behavior settings engage

in actions that vary in difficulty, where difficulty is defined in terms of abilities, the more difficult actions being nearer the top of the inhabitants' ability ranges. The greater number of more vigorous actions by the inhabitants of underpopulated behavior settings (primary differences 1, 3, and 5) overcome ability difficulties more frequently. Example: the untalented member of the small class after long hours of practice engages in more actions that are difficult for him or her personally (such as speaking loudly and clearly, projecting one's voice) than a counterpart member of a large class.

(11) The inhabitants of underpopulated behavior settings *engage in important actions more frequently*. The inhabitants of behavior settings engage in actions that vary in importance where importance is defined as the amount of impairment suffered by a setting when an inhabitant is inadequate or absent. The more varied program and maintenance actions of inhabitants of underpopulated settings (primary differences 2 and 4) and their entrance into more central zones of settings (secondary difference 9) make their actions more important than those of inhabitants of adequately populated behavior settings. Example: consider (a) a member of a small high school class who because of shortage of members has two positions within zone 4 (functionary) of the setting Class Play, namely, a part in the play and electrician in charge of the lighting and sound equipment, and (b) two members of a large class with ample membership, one of whom has a part in the play, and the other of whom is the electrician. Because the actions of the player-electrician implement the same eco-behavioral circuits as the actions of the player *and* of the electrician in the large class, the inadequacy or absence of the double-duty small-class person is more damaging to the setting than the inadequacy or absence of either of the large-class members; the player-electrician is a more important person.

(12) The inhabitants of underpopulated behavior settings *behave in response to important actions more frequently*. The greater frequency of induced actions (primary difference 8) in underpopulated behavior settings has dual significance: the inhabitants induce actions in others more frequently and actions are induced in them more frequently. The greater number of inducing actions that inhabitants of underpopulated settings give and receive differ from those given and received by inhabitants of adequately populated settings on all the characteristics listed—that is, they give and receive more, stronger, more varied, and more important actions. Not only do inhabitants of underpopulated behavior settings engage in important actions more frequently (secondary difference 11), but they also behave in response to important actions more frequently.

The Nature of Predictions from
Behavior Settings to Behavior

The 12 predictions of primary and secondary behavior differences can be made univocally within the limits prescribed by behavior setting theory. These limits will now be reviewed.

First, only attributes of overt actions can be predicted from the programs and medium manifolds of behavior settings; the motives and experiences of inhabitants cannot be predicted. This is the case because the control systems of behavior settings sense only ecological events (objective, spatial-temporal movements) pertaining to behavior setting functioning.

Second, only total medium manifolds are regulated by the control systems of behavior settings; individual inhabitants as unique entities are not regulated. As components of the medium manifolds of behavior settings, only those limited attributes of inhabitants are discriminated that implement or interfere with behavior setting programs; persons who possess the same implementing or interfering attributes are equivalent, that is, interchangeable within behavior settings. This interchangeability is limited, however, by the structure of the settings in many cases. As Wicker (1979a) has pointed out, in many kinds of settings (such as service behavior settings and offices of professional or licensed workers) the structure of the setting provides strong resistance against movement of setting inhabitants across the boundary separating nonoperative zones (3, 2, 1, and 0) from operative zones (6, 5, and 4). The problem of a dentist's office that is overpopulated with waiting patients cannot be solved internally—patients cannot become dentists as an ordinary high school class member can assume a part in the class play.

Third, behavior settings impose their standing patterns upon inhabitants in two ways: by coercing inhabitants to behave appropriately via deviation-countering influences, and by eliminating deviant inhabitants. Behavior settings are self-validating entities, and statements of the following kind are true: If individual X *inhabits* behavior setting A, then that person's behavior is congruent with some part of the behavior pattern of A. But statements of the following kind are not true: If individual X *enters* behavior setting A then that person's behavior is congruent with some part of the behavior pattern of A. The latter is not true because after entering behavior setting A, the behavior of X may prove to be so incompatible with every part of the behavior pattern of A that the person is eliminated.

Fourth, the dual control system of behavior settings ensures that the behavior of all inhabitants of a behavior setting is within the limits set by the program that defines its standing pattern. Because the standing pattern of most behavior settings is not homogeneous, inhabitants can act appropriately while engaging in very different kinds of actions. Consider, for example, the wide differences in kinds of actions included in the standing behavior pattern of a basketball game. Nevertheless, the behavior of individual inhabitants can be predicted within the bounds of the standing pattern of a setting. All inhabitants of a setting of the genotype Drugstores behave drugstore and all inhabitants of a Tavern behave tavern. Despite the heterogeneity of the standing patterns within drugstores and taverns, there are clear, meaningful differences between them, well recognized by people who know their programs. Behavior settings require conformity in the behavior of their inhabitants, but they do not require uniformity.

Fifth, the control systems of behavior settings are unprecise in varying degrees; there is noise in the systems. This allows for some behavior deviancy that is not corrected or eliminated.

The kind of prediction that can be made from behavior setting theory is not the kind Lewin (1951) considered to be adequate for a scientific psychology; only univocal derivations of individual behavior from the contemporaneous situation of the subject were acceptable to him. To accomplish this he created the concept of the life-space, a psychological concept. Although it is true that predictions of the sort he demanded cannot be made on the basis of behavior setting theory, the theory does advance beyond the empiricism and probabilism that Lewin thought were the only possibility for an eco-behavioral science and that Brunswik (1955) accepted as the basic model for the science of psychology.

Psychological Differences Between Underpopulated and Adequately Populated Behavior Settings

The motives and experiences of inhabitants of behavior settings issue from interactions between the motivational and cognitive processes that inhabitants bring to settings and the input that settings provide inhabitants. Because the resulting motives and experiences are not sensed, tested, and selected by behavior setting control systems, they cannot be univocally predicted from behavior settings as overt actions can.

However, some probabilistic predictions can be made. Some motivational and cognitive processes have a basic similarity across most people, and some input from a behavior setting is similar across all of its inhabitants. To the degree that these conditions hold, the motives and experiences of the different inhabitants of a setting are similar, and they are

different from the motives and experiences of the inhabitants of other settings with different input. Here is a simple example: most inhabitants of a
behavior setting illuminated with light of wave length 512 microns (an attribute of the radiant input of the setting) see the setting as emerald
green, and they see behavior settings that are illuminated with light of all
other wave lengths differently. There are exceptions to this generality;
about 8 percent of male inhabitants and 0.5 percent of female inhabitants
do not have a green experience from wave length 512 microns. If one
knows (a) the percentage of the inhabitants of a setting who have common
motivational and cognitive processes, (b) the percentage who receive
common input from the setting, and (c) the motivational and cognitive resultants of the interaction of the common processes and inputs, one can
make a probabilistic prediction of the motives and experiences of the inhabitants. To the degree that different behavior settings have different inputs to all of their inhabitants, and to the degree that the inhabitants of all
settings have common motivational and cognitive processes, the motives
and experiences of the inhabitants of different behavior settings differ in
predictable ways. This basic mechanism tends to homogenize the motives
and experiences of inhabitants of a behavior setting. Two other processes
have the same tendency. First, behavior settings that veto inhabitants and
potential inhabitants because of their inadequate actions reduce some of
the diversity of motives that would otherwise obtain within them. This
occurs because there are positive correlations between some actions and
some motives. When the behavior setting Football Practice vetoes inhabitants who do not engage in the fast and strong physical actions that the
program of the setting requires, it also eliminates negative motivation for
football, because one source of slow speed and low vigor in football is low
motivation. Second, people select behavior settings that satisfy their motives and harmonize with their cognitive styles; they inhabit behavior settings (except those they are required to inhabit, such as school and court
settings) only so long as they gain some personal satisfaction. But behavior
settings are limited in the goals and cognitive possibilities they provide;
hence the inhabitants of most settings are self-selected for a limited range
of motives and experiences.

For these reasons, the inhabitants of settings of the genotype Parties
are, in general, psychologically happy: these settings provide "happy" inputs (inputs that are known on the basis of long experience to generate
happiness in most inhabitants), potential "wet blankets" are not invited
(they are vetoed in anticipation), and the despondent and depressed eliminate themselves. The happy behavior at Parties is for most inhabitants
more than a behavior emission of A-Mech triggered by E-Mech. Simi-

larly, the inhabitants of behavior settings of the genotype Attorneys' Offices are usually serious, psychologically: the inputs are "serious," inhabitants who regularly engage in frivolous actions are eliminated, and blithe spirits seeking gaiety pass by Attorneys' Offices.

On the basis of empirical associations between psychological states and a number of the ecological conditions that differentiate underpopulated and adequately populated behavior settings, differences in the motives and experiences of their inhabitants can be predicted. Probabilistic predictions of these kinds, in addition to the univocal derivations of actions as described above, can be made concerning the experiences of inhabitants of underpopulated settings wherever they are found, in small towns, small schools, or other institutions. The predicted psychological differences are numbered, beginning with 13, to follow the list of primary and secondary behavior differences.

In comparison with inhabitants of adequately populated behavior settings:

(13) The inhabitants of underpopulated settings have *less sensitivity to and are less evaluative of individual differences in behavior*; they are more tolerant of their associates. This is a consequence of the greater variety in the direction of the forces within underpopulated settings; under their influence inhabitants and their associates engage in a variety of activities, for some of which they are not well fitted. Nevertheless, an inhabitant must accept him/herself and others as suitable for a number or roles despite wide differences among occupants of the same roles. It is a consequence, too, of the greater strength of maintenance forces; recalcitrant media (the self and others) are relatively docile, and an inhabitant accepts as right the diverse behavior in which he or she and others are coerced to engage. And it is a consequence of the greater number of deviation-countering forces; when essential personnel are in short supply, it is necessary to "accept" those persons who are available and can do the job. Because the continuation of the setting is at stake, ability to carry out essential tasks within the setting takes priority over individual differences.

(14) The inhabitants of underpopulated settings see themselves as having *greater functional importance* within the settings; the relative scarcity of inhabitants makes them more important people. It sometimes happens that everyone in an underpopulated setting is a key person, and knows it.

(15) The inhabitants of underpopulated settings have *more responsibility*. In striving to maintain a setting for his or her own personal reasons, the key inhabitant inevitably contributes something essential to the other inhabitants. Responsibility is experienced by a person when a behavior setting and what others gain from it depend on his or her actions. A set-

ting that is adequately populated does not entrust its program to indispensable personnel; people are too unreliable, so substitutes, understudies, vice-presidents, a second team are regular features of adequately populated settings.

(16) The inhabitants of underpopulated settings have *greater functional identity*. When the population of a behavior setting is below the optimum for the setting, the questions "What has to be done?" and "Who can do this job?" are crucial, and the inhabitants are seen in terms of the varied and important functions they can perform. A person with an essential function is seen as more than a person, as a person-in-context. There is less possibility of judging a person-in-context with respect to the kind of person he or she is; the concern is, rather, "Is the job coming off?" If it is an important job, and it is being done, the person takes on some of the value of this achievement no matter what "kind of person" he or she may be. When a behavior setting has an optimal or larger number of inhabitants so that the operations are fully staffed by functionally adequate persons, the question "What kind of a person am I (is she/he)?" and the interpersonal relations of being liked or not liked are important, individual differences are salient, and personality analysis (by self and others) regularly occurs.

(17) The inhabitants of underpopulated settings *experience greater insecurity*. Under the pressure of engaging in more difficult and more varied actions, a person in an underpopulated setting is in greater jeopardy of failing to carry through assigned tasks. To the person's own uncertainty is added that which arises from lack of reserves in the behavior setting as a whole. The latter amounts to increased dependence on all other persons carrying through their assignments.

We have made eight derivations of differences in primary behavior (A-Mech emissions), four derivations of difference in the secondary behavior consequences of A-Mech emissions, and five probabilistic predictions of psychological differences for inhabitants of underpopulated and adequately populated behavior settings. We turn, next, to data bearing on the correctness of the derivations and predictions. It will become apparent that available data are relevant to only some of the derivations and predictions and that some of them have more empirical support than others. Much research remains to be done before an adequate assessment of behavior setting theory as applied to underpopulated environments is achieved.

10

Evidence from Empirical Studies of Underpopulated Behavior Settings

We have made predictions from differences in the number of inhabitants of behavior settings (as media) to differences in the attributes of behavior settings (as things); these predictions were listed in Fig. 9.2. Some of the predicted differences in behavior setting attributes, in turn, require different behavior from the inhabitants of the settings. We have called them primary behavior differences; they are open to observation, and so provide a test of the theory of the environment that has been presented.

The situation in this respect may be clarified by an analogy. In the process of remodeling a house, (a) a number of structural components are removed, such as walls and foundation stones (analogous to fewer inhabitants of a behavior setting); this action (b) does not change the house in essential respects (analogous to same standing pattern), but it (c) does change the pattern of forces that maintain the house (analogous to greater range of direction of forces); this, in turn, (d) changes the pressures and strains on the remaining components, such as cross beams and corner posts (analogous to differences in effort exerted by inhabitants). In the absence of instrumented measures of the changes in the pattern of forces within the house, the changes in the shape of the remaining components provide alternative, cruder measures. Differences in the behavior of inhabitants of underpopulated and adequately populated settings provide analogous data; they are one test of the theory that the ecological environment is connected with its human components and has predictable effects on them.

The review of the evidence presented below is neither comprehensive nor thorough. It is intended, rather, as an indication of the main trends in research findings relevant to the theory. The original papers cited should be consulted for more complete information. Other reviews of research relevant to behavior setting theory are also available (Barker & Gump, 1964; Bechtel, 1977, 1982; Greenberg, 1979; Price, 1976; Schoggen, 1983; Stokols, 1978; Wicker, 1973, 1979a, 1979b; Wicker & Kirmeyer, 1977).

Evidence from Studies of School Size

Studies of voluntary, extracurricular behavior settings in small and large high schools carried out at the Midwest Psychological Field Station, University of Kansas (Barker & Hall, 1964; Gump & Friesen, 1964; Wicker, 1967, 1968, 1969a; Willems, 1963, 1964b, 1965, 1967), constitute the most extensive program of research on underpopulated versus adequately populated settings yet available in the research literature.

The first question to consider in connection with these studies concerns the extent to which the small schools are characterized by settings that are, relative to those in large schools, underpopulated, because this is the attribute of the settings from which the behavior differences are derived. Careful tabulation of the occupancy of individual behavior settings in the Kansas studies showed that the settings of the large school had about three times the median number of students as the settings in small schools (Barker & Barker, 1964, pp. 49–50; Gump & Friesen, 1964, pp. 82–83). Wicker (1968) found a similar pattern of underpopulation in small-school settings analyzed separately by kind of setting, such as Games, Meetings, Plays, Dances. These studies demonstrate that, although underpopulated and adequately populated settings occurred in both kinds of schools, the settings in the small schools were generally underpopulated relative to large-school settings. Thus students in small schools, more often than their large-school counterparts, found themselves in settings with relatively few associates.

Turning now to behavior differences, the Kansas studies yielded the following findings about students in small schools in comparison with students of large schools:

(1) They reported twice as many pressures on them to take part in the programs of the settings. In their own words, small-school students reported more frequently: "I had to march in the band"; "My family urged me to take part"; "Everyone else was going." These pressures were neither uniformly nor randomly distributed among the students; they occurred selectively, and the basis of the selection differed in the two types of schools. In the small schools, marginal students (students without the abilities and backgrounds that facilitate school success) reported almost as many pressures to participate as did regular students (those with the abili-

ties and backgrounds for school achievement). But within large schools, the marginal students reported about one-fourth as many pressures to participate as did the regular students. Not even one of the marginal students in the small schools reported *no* pressures to participate in the voluntary, extracurricular settings of the school, whereas about one-third of the marginal students in large schools reported no pressures. The small behavior settings with modest activity programs generated more forces toward participation than the large settings with ambitious programs. These results were supported in a later replication of this study with twice as many students in the sample (Willems, 1967).

(2) They performed in 2.5 times as many responsible positions, on the average; for crucial, central positions, such as team members or chairpersons of meetings, they performed in six times as many positions. Two percent of the small-school students filled no important and responsible positions, whereas 29 percent of their counterparts in the large school were nonperformers. Furthermore, the students in the small school filled important and responsible positions in twice as many behavior setting genotypes as their counterparts. The schools with the smaller and less varied settings were, for their students, functionally larger and more varied than the schools with the more populous and more varied settings.

Wicker's (1968) study is especially important because he measured, setting by setting, the number of performers in relation to the total population of the setting. His data showed that the frequency with which a student occupied important and responsible positions in behavior settings decreased with increases in setting population *regardless of school size*. His data also confirm the expectation that underpopulated settings are more common in small schools. Thus small-school students, because they live more often in underpopulated settings, occupy positions of importance and responsibility in settings more often than do their counterparts in large schools.

(3) They reported having *more* satisfactions related (a) to the development of competence, (b) to being challenged, (c) to engaging in important actions, (d) to being involved in group activities, (e) to being valued, and (f) to gaining moral and cultural values. In their own words, students reported having more experiences of these kinds in the small schools: "It gave me confidence"; "It gave me a chance to see how good I am"; "I got the speakers for all of these meetings"; "The class worked together"; "It also gave me recognition"; "I feel it makes a better man of me." The same students reported some other satisfactions *less* frequently than their counterparts in the large school. They reported fewer satisfactions referring (a) to vicarious enjoyment, (b) to affiliation with a large entity, (c) to learn-

ing about the school's persons and affairs, and (d) to gaining "points" via participation. In the students' own words, again, fewer experiences of these kinds came from the small-school students: "I enjoyed watching the game"; "I like the companionship of mingling with the rest of the crowd"; "I enjoyed this because I learned who was on the team"; "You get to build up points for honors." Students in the schools with the less consequential behavior settings had more frequent satisfactions relating to themselves as persons of consequence—as competent, important, valued, and good— than students in the school with more consequential behavior settings.

Again Wicker's (1968) study adds an important measure of understanding to these findings about student experiences in underpopulated and adequately populated settings. His analyses showed that differences in student experience were more often related to whether the student occupied a position of importance and responsibility in the setting than to the size of the school. With performance level in the setting controlled, school size differences disappeared in seven of the twelve experience scale ratings. Wicker concludes, "In short, when they had a job, students from small and large schools were alike in feeling involved and concerned. When they did not have any responsibility, they were alike in having relatively little involvement or concern" (1979a, p. 102). But because students in small schools more often occupy positions of importance and responsibility in settings, they do feel involved and concerned more often than large-school students.

These findings of the Kansas studies are in general agreement with the results of an early study (Larsen, 1949) which found that students in large high schools reported taking part in either no activities or only one while in high school more often than students in small schools. The large-school students also reported difficulty in getting into activities.

Baird (1969) subjected the central hypothesis of the *Big School, Small School* report to critical examination and obtained relevant new data from a large national sample of 21,371 students drawn randomly from the 712,000 who took the American College Test (ACT) and Student Profile for college admission. High school size was studied in relation to number of high school nonacademic achievements and activities reported by each student. A checklist of extracurricular accomplishments yielded scores in the following six areas: leadership, music, drama and speech, art, writing, and science. Students with high scores presumably had attained a high level of accomplishment that required complex skills, long-term persistence, or originality. "These scales represent achievements which are generally set at a high level of 'participation.' They require a student to be a central figure performing a difficult task which generally involves public recognition when successfully completed" (Baird, 1969, p. 254). High school size was also based on students' reports of size of graduating class grouped into four size categories: less than 25, 25–99, 100–399, and more than 400. The results showed that students from small high schools, presumably characterized by underpopulated behavior settings, reported significantly higher levels of nonacademic achievement in four of the six areas: drama and speech, leadership, writing, and music. No difference by school size was found in the other two areas, science and art. Total scores on all nonacademic achievements were also significantly different in favor of small-school students. Students from large high schools also reported *no* achievements more often than small-school students in the same four areas. In terms of percentages of students with low and high numbers of nonacademic achievements, the same pattern in the results was found: more of the small-school students reported high numbers; more of the large-school students reported low numbers.

Although it is clear that Baird's findings of greater participation in extra-curricular activities by students in smaller high schools are consistent with expectations based on behavior setting theory, these results say more about the relation between high school size and participation than about the consequences of underpopulated behavior settings. Baird did not demonstrate that the settings in the small schools were, in fact, under-populated relative to the comparable settings in large high schools. How-ever, in view of the careful demonstration in the Kansas studies that small-school settings actually contained only about one-third as many stu-dents as similar settings in the large high school (Barker & Gump, 1964, pp. 49–50, 82–83; Wicker, 1968, p. 257), it may be reasonable to assume that the same pattern would be found if it were possible to obtain a careful count of students in the individual settings of the schools in Baird's study. In most of the studies reviewed here, some measure of school enrollment has been accepted as proxy for the behavior setting population variable.

Kleinert (1969) reported a similar pattern of results in a study of student participation in the schools' extracurricular activities in a random sample of 63 high schools in southern Michigan ranging in size from less than 100 to over 3,000 in the upper three grades.

Baird's findings were virtually duplicated in a study by Downey (1978) using a sample of entering freshmen at Kansas State University in 1974–75. Again, size of high school (as indicated by number in the graduating class in seven size groups from less than 25 to over 900) was negatively related to participation in four of the six kinds of nonacademic activities included on the ACT Student Profile (leadership, music, drama and speech, and writing) and no difference was found on the other two (art and science). Similar findings came from analysis of data from a separate sample of all Kansas high school graduates who took the ACT during the 1973–74 school year. Additionally, Downey found greater participation in high school athletics among small-school that large-school students.

Pence and Taylor (1978) found evidence supporting the expectation from behavior setting theory that the use of vetoing circuits would be more common in adequately populated settings. Using archival data from a sample of 27 Virginia high schools, they found that the drop-out rate, which they took as an index of vetoing behavior, was positively correlated with school size (r = .58).

Congruent results were obtained in one of the more sophisticated studies of high school size and student participation in extracurricular activities by Morgan and Alwin (1980), who "were quite successful in predicting the gross amount of activity in schools from school size using a simple linear function" (p. 246). Here school size was measured by the number of juniors and seniors in the school; the size range was from 17 to 1,205 across 55 randomly selected high schools in Washington state. Participation was measured by self-reports of students on their involvement in the voluntary, nonacademic activities of the school in nine activity categories.

In a more recent study, Grabe (1981) obtained self-report measures of participation in voluntary, extracurricular activities by almost 1,600 students in 20 high schools in Iowa classified as large (N = 5 with enrollment in upper three grades more than 580 students) and small (all others). Students from smaller schools were involved in more activities and in more diverse kinds of activities in all five areas of out-of-class activities measured: academic (such as National Honor Society), athletics, social, art/music/drama, and clubs.

Lindsay (1982, 1984) reported two important studies relevant to the issue of high school size and student participation, both using data from the National Longitudinal Study of the High School Class of 1972 (NLS), sponsored by the National Center for Educational Statistics. "The NLS is a representative sample of seniors enrolled in public and private high schools in the 50 states and the district of Columbia in spring 1972" (Lindsay, 1982, p. 59). Schools were grouped into three size ranges according to the number of students in the senior class: small (100 or fewer), medium (101–400), and large (more than 400). Participation was measured by questionnaire responses concerning the students' level of involvement in four kinds of school activities: athletics, drama/music/debate, journalism, and student government. Controls were utilized for three variables: urban or rural location of the school, students' socioeconomic status (SES), and students' academic ability. School rates of student attendance were also recorded. The results indicate that "school size affects student participation and satisfaction, independent of the effects of SES and academic ability. This study adds new findings that the effects of school size are independent of urban or rural location and that school size also has independent effects on student attendance" (Lindsay, 1982, pp. 63–64).

The second study (Lindsay, 1984) evaluated a model of school size effects on participation in extracurricular high school activities and the effects of this participation on social participation in young adulthood, using the data from repeated surveys of the NLS in 1973, 1974, 1976, and 1979. Controlling for a number of other variables and using path analysis, this study found that "high school activity participation is determined more by high school size than by each of the other variables in the model: family SES, academic ability, gender, sociability, curriculum track, and rank in class" (p. 81). The most important new finding, says Lindsay, "is that students who participate in extracurricular activities during high school are more likely to participate in a broad range of social activities as young adults, controlling for other known influences" (ibid.). It is also worth noting that Lindsay's results indicate that community size has a small negative effect on young adult participation.

Further evidence on this relationship comes from a recent study of 10,412 students in 27 high schools in central New York state ranging fairly evenly across senior classes of about 20 to over 600 students (Schoggen & Schoggen, 1988). Tabulation of the numbers of students pictured and listed by each activity in the school yearbook as participants in the voluntary, extracurricular activities of the school showed that the average number of students per activity was larger in the large schools than in the small schools by a factor of four. These data further support the reasonableness of the assumption that underpopulation of settings is more common in small schools than in large schools. As in the other studies, students in smaller schools participated in many more of the schools' extracurricular activities than did students in larger schools. Especially striking was the large proportion of seniors—three-fifths—in larger schools who participated in *none* of the activities as compared with only about one-fourth of the small-school seniors.

It is perhaps worth noting that this is the only study we have seen that did not rely on self-reports by students as the measure of participation in school activities. That the findings are congruent with those of the other studies gives new confidence in the robustness of the relationship.

All of the studies mentioned above examined participation of high school students. Campbell et al. (1981), however, report an investigation of participation by 786 Australian seventh-year (the last year before high school in Australia) students in the out-of-class behavior settings of 14 primary schools located mainly within the Brisbane metropolitan region. The number of settings available to the seventh-year primary school students was much smaller than the number typically available to high school students; the median number of settings identified in their 14 schools (p. 210) was about half the median number of settings identified in the 13 high schools in the *Big School, Small School* report (Barker & Gump, 1964, p. 49). Moreover, the difference between the large and small schools in mean number of behavior settings in the Campbell et al. study was not great. Despite this limitation, they report greater participation, in terms of both amount and variety of kinds of activities, among students in small schools.

We have discovered only two studies of schools that obtained results apparently not consistent with the findings in all the studies mentioned above. Rutter et al. (1979), in their important study of 12 secondary schools in inner-city London, England, found that school size was not related to their outcome measures: attendance, staying in school, examination success, and delinquency rates. However, the range of school sizes included in this study is not reported clearly; it appears to have been so restricted as to give the findings little relevance to the size question.

So far available only in a preliminary technical report, the other study (Gottfredson, 1985) was primarily concerned with the relation between school size and school disorder. Participation was measured on a checklist of ten kinds of out-of-class school activities and two kinds of community activities (youth organizations and church groups) completed by each student. The findings indicated no difference in the amounts or variety of participation reported by students in schools of different size when other background factors were controlled. Marginal students, however, were found to participate more frequently and in a wider variety of activities in small than in large schools. At least in this respect, Gottfredson's findings agree with those of other studies (Willems, 1964b, 1967).

For several reasons, however, we are not sure how much confidence can be placed in these findings. The sample of students included all grade levels from 6th through 12th. However, the availability of extracurricular school activities for students in grades 6 through 9 is probably much less than for high school students, as the data from the Campbell et al. (1981) study indicated. Thus the range of choices and the opportunities to engage in voluntary activities are more restricted for students in grades 6 through 9, which would dilute the usual relationship between size and participation of students at the high school level. Even so, the usual negative relation between school size and participation was found, but it was not statistically significant when several background variables were controlled.

The report indicates also that the schools studied were located predominantly in major metropolitan areas—Chicago, the South Bronx, Harlem, Houston, Miami, St. Paul, and Pasadena—whereas most of the other studies have included schools located predominantly outside large population centers. For several of the analyses most directly relevant to the size/participation relationship, the schools were grouped into three categories, each covering a wide range of school size—small (388–625 enrolled students), medium (644–1,089), and large (1,104–3,100)—but with no indication of how many grades of the school these figures include (K through 12, 6 through 12, or 9 through 12). The sample also included "all students who were part of an experimental manipulation within each school (about 10% of the total sample)" (Gottfredson, 1985, p. 12).

DIFFERENCES IN THE REGULATORY SYSTEMS OF UNDERPOPULATED AND ADEQUATELY POPULATED BEHAVIOR SETTINGS

The school data provide evidence on how regulation of behavior settings is accomplished. In the small schools, with meagerly populated settings, regulation occurs by means of deviation-countering feedback (D-Mech) to all students—that is, pressures against deviation from the programs of the settings. Here, for example, are reports by students of small schools of D-Mech actions toward them: "My teacher talked me into it"; "They needed girls in the cast"; "Everyone was supposed to be there"; "I was assigned to work there." Such deviation-countering inputs occur twice as frequently in the small schools as in the large schools, and virtually all students of the small schools, even marginal ones, receive them. This control system contributes to the harmony between the behavior of the individual inhabitants and the programs of the settings by regulating the behavior of all the students.

In large schools, on the other hand, regulation is in two stages: (a) discriminating between students with more and less promising behavior, and (b) providing deviation-countering feedback to the more promising (regular) students and no feedback at all or vetoing feedback to most of the less promising (marginal) students. In the large school most of the pressures to participate at the performance level of behavior settings are applied to regular students; many marginal students receive no pressures against failure to perform; others are excluded from performing. This control system contributes to the harmony between individual behavior and behavior-setting programs by selecting the students who will require the least regulation and by allowing the others to veto themselves or by actively vetoing them to onlooker or visitor positions.

The behavior settings of the small and large schools do not differ greatly in the number of satisfactions students report, but they do differ greatly in the content of the satisfactions. The students of the small schools report more frequently that they achieve satisfactions by being competent, by accepting challenges, by doing important things, by engaging in group activities, and by engaging in valued actions, all of which can be gained only by serious performance in the programs of the settings. The students of the large schools report more frequently that they achieve satisfactions by watching others participate, by mingling with the crowd, by learning about the school, and by gaining points, none of which require serious performance in the schools' settings. Performance satisfactions undoubtedly elicit stronger goal actions than visitor and spectator satisfactions, and the former are available to almost all students of the small schools but only to those students of the large schools who have not been vetoed or allowed to veto themselves from the performance zones of the settings. This is one source of the differential behavior of the inhabitants of the underpopulated and adequately populated behavior settings, but it is a psychological resultant of ecological differences that cannot be derived from a theory of behavior settings. Although it is likely that a behavior setting inhabitant who has an important role in the setting will experience gratification, it is not certain.

The differential control systems of behavior settings have wide significance for inhabitants. Behavior settings with deviation-countering feedback and central satisfactions to almost all inhabitants for appropriate, responsible performances provide quite a different environment from settings where control is achieved by restricting feedback and central satisfactions to promising inhabitants, and where marginal inhabitants are allowed to, or required to, withdraw from the performance zones.

EVIDENCE OF LONG-TERM SIGNIFICANCE OF PARTICIPATION IN HIGH SCHOOL ACTIVITIES

There is evidence that the greater amount of participation and involvement in high school voluntary, extracurricular activities is related to personal, social, and cognitive development, continuing through college age and into adult living. Spady (1970), in a longitudinal study of 297 boys as seniors and again four years later, holding constant family SES, IQ, and grades, found that those with high levels of participation in high school service and leadership (but not sports) activities had a higher survival rate in college. Otto's (1975) findings confirm Spady's; involvement in high school activities including sports "plays a significant role in the educational attainment process [for males], independent of the influence of background socioeconomic statuses, academic ability, and academic performance" (p. 171). His study covered an even longer period of time, 15 years. He also reported (Otto, 1976) that involvement in high school activities was a strong predictor of involvement in adult voluntary activities, such as civic groups, church and lodge groups, sports teams, and charity and welfare organizations. As discussed above, Lindsay (1984) found similar results but over a shorter time span. Hanks and Eckland (1976), also using a longitudinal design over a span of 15 years with a large national sample, reported that involvement in high school and college activities other than sports had "relatively strong direct and total salutary effects on academic performance and achievement in both [high] school and college for both sexes" (p. 271). Barthell and Holmes (1968), using high school yearbook senior summaries as the measure of participation, found that high school graduates who were later diagnosed as schizophrenic had, while in high school, participated in significantly fewer social activities—such as student council, language or other special-interest clubs, or school paper staff—than normal comparison subjects from the same class.

Halsall's (1973) extensive and careful review of the research relating to size of school led her to conclude that small schools provide a more favorable environment for personal development of students. "The pressures which small schools are shown to exert more successfully than the large ones help to contribute to a sense of competence, since whether weak, strong, inept, skillful, young or experienced, each pupil really is important. Many activities cannot continue without his participation, and the increased sense of responsibility which this situation generates is likely to produce greater and earlier maturity, as well as greater capacity for leadership" (p. 95).

Elder (1974) employs a similar rationale to account for the rather surprising finding that children in deprived families during the great depression actually benefitted from the experience:

The labor-intensive economy of deprived households in the 30s often brought older children into the world of adults. . . . These children had productive roles to perform. But in a more general sense they were needed, and, in being needed, they had the chance and responsibility to make a real contribution to the welfare of others. Being needed gives rise to a sense of belonging and place, of being committed to something larger than the self. However onerous the task may be, there is gratification and even personal growth to be gained in being challenged by a real undertaking if it is not excessive or exploitative. . . .

Since the Depression and especially World War II various developments have conspired to isolate the young from challenging situations in which they could make valuable contributions to family and community welfare. Prosperity, population concentration, industrial growth with its capital-intensive formula, and educational upgrading have led to an extension of the dependency years and increasing segregation of the young from the routine experiences of adults. In this consumption-oriented society, urban middle-class families have little use for the productive hands of offspring, and the same applies to community institutions . . . most contemporary schools are organized around the educational contributions of adults; little is formally expected of children in educating their peers. . . .

This society of abundance can and even must support "a large quota of nonproductive members," as it is presently organized, but should it tolerate the costs, especially among the young; the costs of not feeling needed, of being denied the challenge and rewards which come from meaningful contributions to a common endeavor? [pp. 291–93].

Baird (1969) reports that the higher levels of participation by students in small high schools did not carry over to similarly high levels of participation in activities in college, but that level of participation in college was related to size of college: smaller colleges were associated with higher levels of participation, as in smaller high schools. Although Baird's measure of participation in college activities was taken during the students' sophomore year, rather early in one's college career to obtain a complete measure of college activity participation, similar results were obtained in a recent study (Berk & Goebel, 1987) that measured participation of college seniors rather than sophomores. In view of the other evidence reviewed above showing clear relationships between high school participation and later involvement in both college and community activities, the findings of these two studies on college participation levels should be viewed with caution.

There is substantial agreement in the findings of most of these studies: small schools with underpopulated settings encourage participation by students in school activities, and this participation is associated with subsequent educational attainment, personal development, and involvement in community activities in young adulthood. Together they suggest that the well-rounded development of the individual student in small schools— those graduating 150–200 students per year—may have been sacrificed in the effort to achieve economies of scale and academic excellence that are assumed to require large high schools.

SUMMARY OF EVIDENCE FROM THE SCHOOL STUDIES

The evidence provided by these studies appears to support two main conclusions about the relation between underpopulated and adequately populated behavior settings and student participation and experience in the voluntary, extracurricular behavior settings of high schools. First, at the level of particular behavior settings where the number of participants was directly measured in each setting, it was found that underpopulated settings, more than adequately populated settings: (a) encourage nonparticipants to enter and become involved in the setting; (b) engage participants in the central or leadership zones in the operation of the setting; (c) exert pressure to retain participants in the setting; and (d) apply all these pressures almost equally to marginal and regular students.

Second, at the level of the institution, where school size must be taken as a proxy variable for underpopulated versus adequately populated behavior settings because direct measurement of the population on the individual behavior settings is not feasible, there are consistent if not universal findings that (a) greater participation, (b) more frequent involvement in positions of responsibility within settings, (c) satisfactions related to personal achievement, and (d) longer-term beneficial consequences in college achievement and involvement in organized social and community activities as young adults are all associated with participation in the voluntary, extracurricular activities of small schools. The preponderance of evidence at both levels, therefore, is consistent with the expectations based on behavior setting theory.

Evidence from Studies of Church Size

A number of studies have sought to determine whether the relationship between participation and behavior setting underpopulation that emerged so consistently in the studies of high schools would also be found in churches. Participation in church behavior settings, as in the extracurricular activities studied in high schools, is, for almost all inhabitants, entirely voluntary. But as Wicker (1979a) pointed out, churches are populated by the full age spectrum, not just by adolescents as in high schools. Also, churches often maintain good records on membership and attendance so that adequate data on some important variables can be obtained quite unobtrusively.

Wicker (1979a) provides an excellent review of several studies carried out by him and his associates (Wicker, 1969a; Wicker & Mehler, 1971;

Wicker, McGrath, & Armstrong, 1972; Wicker & Kauma, 1974), ranging from an intensive study of two churches, one small and one large (Wicker, 1969b), to a study using a national sample of 320 churches from all 37,000 churches in one denomination (Wicker, McGrath, & Armstrong, 1972). The 320 churches in the sample were spread evenly across the size range from less than 100 to 3,200 members.

Wicker's first finding is that, based on detailed inventories of all behavior settings occurring during a one-year period in five churches ranging in size from 127 to 1,599 members, the data show that church behavior settings are increasingly overpopulated as church size increases. "Consistent with findings in schools, the number of behavior settings increased with church size, but at a slower rate than the increase in number of members. The largest church had 12.6 times as many members as the smallest church, but only 2.4 times as many behavior settings. The ratio of members to settings increased progressively with increases in church membership, from 1.51 in the smallest church to 7.80 in the largest church" (1969b, p. 281).

Interview data from samples of members in small and large churches on their participation in church behavior settings showed remarkable similarities to the data from the high school studies. Wicker interprets these data in terms of behavior setting theory: "When there are many settings operating in an organization and relatively few people to staff them, members experience more and stronger demands on their time than is the case when people are abundant. These pressures led the members of the small church to take on more positions of responsibility and leadership, to participate more in a variety of different settings, and to feel that such higher levels of support were appropriate for themselves and others" (Wicker, 1979a, p. 116).

Subsequent studies of member behavior in churches varying in size obtained findings generally consistent with behavior setting theory. Small churches draw new members into active participation more readily than do large churches (Wicker & Mehler, 1971). After a small and a large church merged through a joint agreement, the level of participation of all members in the behavior settings of the new church declined from previous levels but the decline was much larger for the former members of the small church (Wicker & Kauma, 1974).

Wicker, McGrath, and Armstrong (1972), in their study using archival data on a large national sample of churches, were limited to records of average attendance at Sunday worship service, average attendance at church school, and the number of church-school officers and teachers. No data were available in the archives on the many other behavior settings in the churches or on the important and responsible positions occupied by members. The findings indicated that participation, as measured by attendance at Sunday worship service and church school, was not proportionately higher in the small churches than in the large churches, as would be predicted on the basis of behavior setting theory. Wicker concludes, however, that these data should not be taken as seriously challenging behavior setting theory because the worship service and the church school settings were probably not underpopulated in any of the churches, regardless of size, "at least not to the extent that their continued existence was in jeopardy due to the limited numbers of people" (Wicker, 1979a, p. 126). In small churches, underpopulation is more likely to occur in settings other than Sunday worship service and church school—for example, in committees, social clubs, and work groups. This is consistent with Barker's own view as described by Wicker (1979a) that some kinds of settings are not adequate for testing behavior setting theory; such settings include church worship services and church school classes, in which there are relatively few positions of responsibility and most of the occupants are only members of the audience or spectators (p. 128).

This conclusion is supported by the findings of a study by Wilken (1971), part of the extensive literature in sociology and organizational behavior concerned with organizational size and member behavior. Focusing directly on church size, and making no reference at all to behavior settings, Wilken's data nonetheless are relevant to behavior setting theory in the same way that the school size literature is—namely, it is necessary to assume on the basis of admittedly limited evidence that large schools and churches are made up predominantly of relatively overpopulated behavior settings. Using 157 Lutheran congregations in South Dakota ranging in size from 34 to 1,899 members, with a mean of 414, Wilken found a strong negative relation between size of congregation and six of seven measures of member participation in church activities: Sunday worship, Holy communion, men's/women's/youth organizations, and financial contributions to the church. The one exception, Sunday school participation, was slightly positive.

Although Wilken appears to have been unaware of behavior setting theory, the reasons he suggests to account for the negative relation between church size and amount of participation are congruent with the rationale presented above on the differences between underpopulated and adequately populated behavior settings. He says, for example, that large size "makes it very difficult for a member to communicate with a significant number of other members, which leads to a predominance of secondary relationships. Fewer demands are made on a member because there is a larger pool of members from which to draw" (p. 176). He also asserts that the number of important and responsible positions in church activities, such as teaching Sunday school and holding office in church organizations, does not keep pace with the increase in membership.

One other study from the organizational size literature focused on churches. Houghland and Wood (1980) reported data on a sample of 58 Protestant churches in Indianapolis, Indiana. Based on study of church documents and interviews with ministers, lay officers, and members, this study found that "church size is the best single predictor of identification and involvement" (pp. 94–95).

Studies of Community Size

According to behavior setting theory, small communities—like small schools and small churches—should be predominantly characterized by behavior settings that are underpopulated relative to their large community—large school, large church—counterparts. The experience of living in communities of different size provides strong impressions consistent with this expectation about settings in the public arena in general; more people are usually found in the stores, meetings, schools, churches, offices, etc., in large cities than in small towns. Systematic, empirical documentation of such impressions, however, has not often been provided.

THE MIDWEST-YOREDALE STUDIES

Some direct evidence is found in the Midwest-Yoredale comparisons reported by Barker and Schoggen (1973). Before considering the evidence on the population of behavior settings in Midwest and Yoredale, however, it is pertinent to review the Midwest-Yoredale comparison in terms of habitat size as measured in centiurbs (number of behavior settings with number per year, per day, and per hour weighted equally, see pp. 81–82) and in terms of habitat claims for operatives (the number of positions of importance and responsibility in the operation of the towns' behavior settings—positions in behavior setting penetration zones 6, 5, and 4, see pp. 127–29).

Habitat size or extent in terms of behavior settings and centiurbs shows that the towns were remarkably similar. Although Midwest had more behavior settings than Yoredale during the year (884 versus 758), Yoredale had more settings in an average day and in an average hour, producing extent in centiurbs of 107 and 113 for Midwest and Yoredale, respectively.

Thus Midwest's habitat for molar behavior was smaller than Yoredale's, amounting to 95 percent as much (Barker & Schoggen, 1973, pp. 56–57).

In 1963–64, Midwest and Yoredale had 10,220 and 7,764 habitat-claims for operatives, respectively. These are the numbers of important and responsible positions within the towns' behavior settings, the slots that require human components to make the towns' public habitats operational in terms of their prescribed programs (chairpersons, hostesses, entertainers, cooks, speakers, team-members, clerks, secretaries, etc.). Thus Midwest had more claims for operatives than Yoredale—2,456 more claims, amounting to 132 percent as many in all, 138 percent as many per centiurb of habitat, and 208 percent as many per town inhabitant (ibid., pp. 59–60).

Although both towns were small in terms of population, Midwest, (MW) was substantially smaller; it had only 63 percent as many town inhabitants as Yoredale (YD) in the 1963–64 data (830 for MW versus 1,310 for YD). Midwest also had fewer inhabitants than Yoredale in relation to the size of the community as measured by centiurbs of habitat; Midwest had only 67 percent as many inhabitants per centiurb as Yoredale (7.8 for MW, 11.6 for YD). In relation to the number of habitat claims for operatives, Midwest's population was even more deficient than Yoredale's; Midwest had only 47 percent as many inhabitants per habitat claim for operatives as Yoredale (0.08 for MW, 0.17 for YD). Moreover, Midwest's population inferiority to Yoredale was still greater in the districts and regions surrounding the towns (6,000 for MW, 17,000 for YD) (ibid., pp. 60–61).

Wicker (1979a, pp. 126–27) has pointed out that we need to go beyond comparisons based on crude ratios such as these—for example, total town population divided by number of centiurbs (settings)—as measures of degree of setting under/overpopulation. It is preferable to count, on a setting-by-setting basis, the number of persons actually occupying each setting and the number of important and responsible positions (habitat claims) in the setting. We have, therefore, gone back to the data files on which the Barker and Schoggen (1973) report is based and made some additional tabulations and analyses of all the behavior settings in both towns (884 in MW, 758 in YD, for the 1963–64 survey year).

Looking first at the total population of each setting on a setting-by-setting basis—that is, the total number of different persons (including both town residents and nonresidents) who entered the setting one or more times during the year—Midwest settings involved on the average about half the number of persons entering Yoredale settings (means, medians, and modes were 151, 43, and 15 for MW; 318, 75, and 38 for YD). The same tabulation counting only town residents yields similar but somewhat smaller differences (means, medians, and modes were 58, 20, and 2 for MW; 101, 28, and 2 for YD).

Bearing in mind that many settings occur more than once during a given year (some as often as every day), we also examined each setting in both towns to determine the average population on a typical occurrence of the setting in relation to the number of persons who were *operatives*— those who occupied positions of importance and responsibility in the operation of the setting (penetration zones 6, 5, or 4)—during a typical occurrence of the setting. This is expressed as the *operative/population ratio* for a typical occurrence of the setting. For example, the Midwest setting Boy Scout Troop Meeting met once a month throughout the year with two Scout leaders, two patrol leaders, and 17 Scouts present on a typical occurrence of this setting. The operative/population ratio for this setting, therefore, is 4/21 or 0.19.

The tabulation of operative/population ratios for each of the several hundred settings in both towns showed that, on the average, the ratio was twice as high in Midwest as in Yoredale: means, medians, and modes were 0.24, 0.15, and 0.01 for MW; 0.14, 0.07, and 0.01 for YD. These data indicate that, in general, the settings of Midwest, in comparison with those in Yoredale, had smaller populations relative to the number of operatives.

These detailed, setting-by-setting tabulations provide essentially the same picture of the towns in terms of behavior setting under/overpopulation as did the crude ratios. They show that Midwest had fewer inhabitants than Yoredale to implement a greater number of habitat-claims for operatives. Midwest's habitat called for more proprietors, secretaries, choir members, teachers, court reporters, chairpersons, janitors, team members, bandmembers, organists, waitresses, speakers, election officials, bus drivers, bookkeepers, umpires, salespersons, mechanics, librarians, and so on, yet it had a smaller pool of inhabitants from which to draw them.

To summarize these habitat and population differences between Midwest and Yoredale, the data show that Midwest, relative to Yoredale, had (a) a somewhat smaller habitat as measured by centiurbs, (b) more claims for behavior setting operatives, (c) fewer inhabitants both in the town and in the surrounding region, (d) about half as many different persons entering each setting during the year, and (e) settings with smaller populations relative to the number of operatives in each during a typical occurrence of the setting.

Barker and Schoggen (1973, pp. 248–58) present a detailed explication of behavior setting theory as applied to the Midwest-Yoredale comparison. Here there is only space to abstract some of the most important features and findings from their presentation. They describe the main thesis of behavior setting theory as follows:

> The basic idea of behavior setting theory is that the inhabitants of behavior settings are one class of components, among other classes (nonhuman behavior objects), that make up the internal media of behavior settings. The number of available inhabitants of a behavior setting, relative to its optimal number, affects its operation—including, via sensors and feedback circuits, the strengths and directions of the forces acting upon its human components. One critical relationship is between number of inhabitants and the strength and range of directions of the forces acting upon them; *forces upon a town's inhabitants toward participation in . . . its behavior settings vary in mean strength per inhabitant . . . inversely with the number of available inhabitants.* This relation holds when the number of inhabitants varies between the minimum number required to operate and maintain the setting at its lowest operating level and the optimal number required to operate and maintain it at its most effective level. To the degree therefore that Midwest and Yoredale differ within these limits in number of human components, there are predictable differences for their inhabitants [pp. 250–51; emphasis in original].

According to behavior setting theory, the habitat differences summarized above should produce certain differences in the behavior output of Midwest as compared with Yoredale behavior setting inhabitants. On the basis of the theory, we would expect that inhabitants of Midwest settings, as compared with those of Yoredale settings, would (a) enter more of the town's public behavior settings, (b) spend more time in them, and (c) occupy positions of importance and responsibility in the operation of more settings.

The data show that, in general, all these predictions were more or less strongly confirmed. As measured by inhabitant-setting intersections (see above, pp. 141–43, for definitions of measures of behavior output), Midwest residents entered only somewhat more of the public settings of the town than did the residents of Yoredale: 4 percent more. Midwest residents, relative to Yoredale residents, spent more time (person-hours, or occupancy time) in the public settings of their town; the average Midwesterner spent 3 hours 44 minutes (224 minutes) per day as compared with 2 hours 58 minutes (178 minutes) per day for the average Yoredale resident—thus the average Midwest resident spent 126 percent as much time in the town's behavior settings as the average resident of Yoredale. On the average, therefore, the residents of Midwest in comparison with those of Yoredale engaged in appreciably more behavior in the public areas of the town.

Each of Midwest's inhabitants, on the average, undertook responsibilities (claim-operations) in eight different settings (as teacher, secretary, choir member, umpire, etc.), and each of Yoredale's inhabitants assumed similar responsibilities in 3.2 settings, amounting to 250 percent more in Midwest. Thus, on the average, Midwesterners, in comparison with their Yoredale counterparts, carried out many more responsible tasks in the operation of the town's behavior settings; they worked harder.

In the occupancy of the highest levels of difficult, important, and responsible positions in settings (leader acts; see Barker & Schoggen, 1973, p. 48), the average town inhabitant in Midwest occupied 1.8 such positions during the year, compared with only 0.7 for the average resident of Yoredale, amounting to 257 percent as many.

The percentage of a town's inhabitants who are leaders of one or more settings (town leaders; see ibid.) is a measure of the breadth of distribution of highest public responsibility among its inhabitants. In Midwest, 339 of its 830 town residents were leaders in one or more settings during the year; in Yoredale, the comparable number was 262 of its 1,310 town residents. Thus Midwest distributed its positions of behavior setting leadership much more widely across town inhabitants than did Yoredale; 41 percent for MW, only 20 percent for YD.

In summary, the data show that Midwesterners were, on the average, busier in the public settings of the town than were residents of Yoredale, especially in the difficult, important, and responsible undertakings of behavior setting operatives (functionaries and leaders), where they were more than twice as active as their Yoredale counterparts. The data are in accord with behavior setting theory, which asserts that the observed behavior differences result from differences in the towns' habitats, of which the residents of Midwest and Yoredale are the essential human components.

WRIGHT'S LARGETOWN-SMALLTOWN STUDY

Wright (1971) describes a study that is focused explicitly on size of community and its impact on child residents. Largetown had a population of 33,000, whereas Smalltown was a composite of three small towns with populations each less than 1,000. A sampling procedure yielded data indicating that Smalltown settings, relative to those in Largetown, were underpopulated; Largetown settings had more persons per setting by a factor of 4.4 (p. 491).

Wright compared the activities and experiences of children in the 6-to-11-years-old range in their home communities outside the home and exclusive of school activities. For each measure, matched samples of at least 24 children from each community were included.

The behavior settings in the lives of these children were studied by several different procedures, none of which, however, involved direct measurement by the researchers of the settings themselves. In the first procedure, the child was supplied with miniature objects and materials to stand for behavior settings, people, and other parts (houses, stores, schools, churches) and asked to construct on a wide open floor space a replica of the child's community. While doing so, the child also responded to the researcher's requests for detailed information about the behavior settings included in the construction. In a second procedure, the child was accompanied by the researcher on a walk past the 50 homes nearest the child's own while responding to the researcher's questions from a prepared interview schedule. A third procedure extended the coverage to the rest of the town by a structured interview during an automobile trip around the town.

From these sources of information, the researchers constructed various measures of the child's *acquaintance range* in the town. Comparisons of the results in Largetown and Smalltown revealed substantial and consistent differences, the most important of which Wright describes as follows:

> This prominent difference is paradoxical even if not surprising. It is simply that, despite the greater number of knowable parts in the larger town, the smaller one had per child the larger number of known parts and attributes: more known—and remembered—whole behavior settings, subsettings, and various elements per setting; more known persons in general, yet only adults in particular (adults who were not relatives of the child); more known acts and traits of persons; more known surrounding homes at the core, environing towns around the rim, and miscellaneous qualities of settings, persons, and things. . . . [A]s measured by the ratio of knowns to unknowns, the space in Smalltown had in greater degree per child a special cognitive quality . . . namely, the quality of clearness or familiarity [p. 487].

This greater familiarity of the Smalltown child with the community led Wright to investigate the movements and depth of penetration of the children as inhabitants of behavior settings. The main procedure in this phase of the study involved the child's mother as a paid research assistant. She recorded and described briefly as to place, time, and the "main thing done" for every setting entered by the child other than home and school settings through 56 consecutive days. Here the results showed that the Largetown child visited a larger number and a wider variety of settings but that the Smalltown child entered the same settings more often and spent more time in each. "The Smalltown child, in other words, kept revisiting the same settings and amassing time in them, one by one, more than his Largetown counterpart" (p. 489).

Consistent with expectations based on behavior setting theory, Wright also found that the Smalltown child, relative to the Largetown child, occupied positions of importance and responsibility (penetration zones 5 and 4) in more of the behavior settings entered and was in the position of a bystander or member of the audience only (zones 3, 2, and 1) in fewer behavior settings. In describing later reanalyses of these data, however, Wright (in a personal communication, January 4, 1987) indicates that this difference was not confirmed, but he describes newer data that are consistent with expectations based on behavior setting theory. The conclusion reported in the original paper, therefore, is still largely correct:

> What we come to from these findings on the community in use by its children is that the space of the smaller town is larger in a sense (more differentiated) and clearer on balance as the child sees and knows it partly because his participations in its behavior settings are more repetitive per settings, less dispersed per variety [genotype], and deeper per visit [p. 490].

ADELBERG'S AND WRIGHT'S URBANTOWN STUDY

Although no evidence concerning behavior setting under/overpopulation is given, a study by Adelberg (1977, working with Wright; summarized briefly in Gump & Adelberg, 1978) is relevant in the present context because it was concerned with the behavior and experiences of urban children living in a section of a major population center in comparison with those of the Largetown and Smalltown children studied in the other investigation by Wright described above. The urban residential area was a community of around 6,000 persons separated from the surrounding metropolitan area by a river bluff, major highways, and a railroad. It included the kinds of settings usually found in self-sufficient communities: churches, stores, schools, a park, recreation center, and so forth. Called Urbantown by the researchers, one major contrast with the other towns Wright studied was that Urbantown was part of a city of 700,000, surrounded by a metropolitan area of some 2,000,000.

Again using matched samples of children in the different communities, the Activity Range was determined for each child. Although Urbantown appeared to have sufficient community resources to be self-sufficient in terms of behavior settings, the study found that Urbantown children left their community more often than did their counterparts in either Largetown or Smalltown. These forays outside their own community usually involved being escorted by an adult member of the family.

Within their community, Urbantown children entered settings designed and supervised by adults for children (such as Little League) proportionately more often than the Smalltown children. They also entered adult or community settings (such as Rotary Club) considerably less often than either Smalltown or Largetown children. Urbantown children more frequently re-entered commercial settings (candy store, variety store, cafe) but not organized group activity settings that usually involve an hour or so at a time (Boy Scout meetings, church functions). Perhaps a consequence of this difference was that the Urbantown children spent less time per setting than Smalltown children. "If setting knowledge is built upon extensive exposure, the knowledge of the urban child would tend to be less, and somewhat limited to commercial settings" (Gump & Adelberg, 1978, p. 1184).

Like Largetown children, Urbantown children differed from their Smalltown counterparts in less frequent occupancy of the central zones of penetration of adult noncommercial settings, at least in part because they rarely entered such settings at all. To check on the possibility that Urbantown children left their community in order to gain access to kinds of settings not available near home, the study examined the settings visited outside the community. The results showed that they were the same kinds of settings that the children entered most frequently within their home community—that is, commercial and recreational settings. Gump and Adelberg conclude: "Overall, the material on the setting activity of the white, urban child does not encourage the idea that a city neighborhood will generate a way of life for children similar to that found in a small town" (p. 184).

Evidence from Studies in the Workplace

We have identified a few studies of the relation between setting underpopulation and individual behavior in commercial and professional places of work. Wicker and Kirmeyer, in several reports (Wicker, 1974, 1979a; Kirmeyer, 1978; Wicker & Kirmeyer, 1976, 1977), describe their interesting and innovative study of the reactions of National Park rangers to natural variations in workload induced by variations in the numbers of visitors to Yosemite National Park in the summer. The rangers studied all had jobs that brought them into direct contact with park visitors: collecting fees at entrance stations and campgrounds, patrolling roads and campgrounds, providing information at the visitor center, or presenting naturalist programs. Wicker and Kirmeyer present a valuable conceptual model that distinguishes between ordinary behavior settings and service behavior settings—that is, settings in which the program requires employees (or owners) to provide some kind of service to consumers, users, or visitors. In such settings, the boundary between operatives (park rangers) and other setting occupants (park visitors) is impermeable. They point out that such settings may be understaffed for operatives and at the same time overpopulated with other occupants (nonoperatives), and they discuss strategies for dealing with such departures from a good balance between staffing and population levels.

On the basis of park rangers' responses to a composite of questionnaire items concerning their felt involvement with their work on a given day, the study found that "this measure generally had a weak, positive relationship with the number of visitors entering the park and a somewhat stronger positive relationship with rangers' perceived work loads. In other words, feelings of involvement of the kind dealt with by . . . [behavior setting] theory were greater on days when rangers felt their job demands were also heavier. Among the rangers in our study, expectations based on . . . [behavior setting] theory were confirmed" (Wicker, 1979a, p. 174).

Oxley and Barrera (1984, p. 211) describe a "model of causal relationships among the number of employees in a setting, setting claim, and several attitudinal and behavioral outcome variables" using path analysis. Research participants in this study were 188 randomly selected employees at all levels in 22 branch offices of one bank in a metropolitan area of the Southwest. The branch banks ranged in size from 7 to 40 employees, with a mean of 22.14 (standard deviation = 7.94). Setting claim was measured using a questionnaire designed to reflect the respondent's felt obligation to help keep the setting operating satisfactorily. This instrument, a modification of one developed by Wicker et al. (1976), included items derived from behavior setting theory, such as the extent to which the participant felt that he or she worked hard, was needed, had an important role, and was involved with the group task. Stronger behavior setting claim is associated with smaller numbers of persons to carry out the tasks necessary for the operation of the setting. Although the bank branches varied substantially in size, each of them operated as an integral unit; even the largest branch offices were not organized into subunits.

The results of this investigation suggest that "size of work settings affects the amount of claim felt by their occupants in the same way that the size of churches and schools has been shown to influence claim" (Oxley & Barrera, 1984, p. 230). The authors caution, however, that because none of the branches in the study were very large, the findings may not be applicable to organizations with a much wider range of unit sizes.

Vecchio and Sussman (1981) studied the relations of "staffing sufficiency" (number of workers relative to the number needed) to a variety of job enrichment constructs, following the suggestion of Greenberg (1979) that there is a curvilinear relation between worker motivation and staffing sufficiency. In this model, both extreme understaffing and extreme overstaffing produce low motivation on the part of workers to maintain the setting functions, whereas moderate understaffing produces the highest motivation by the workers to carry out the tasks necessary for successful setting operation.

These investigators obtained questionnaire responses from 83 low-level supervisors in a variety of primarily manufacturing organizations concerning job satisfaction, job dimensions (variety, task identity, task significance, etc.), psychological states (experienced meaningfulness, responsibility, and knowledge of results), and outcome variables (intrinsic motivation and growth satisfaction), taken from the Hackman-Oldham (1975) model. The respondents also provided information on their perception of staffing sufficiency in their immediate work groups. The authors conclude from their study:

> Our analyses indicate that the intuitively anticipated curvilinear relations between staffing sufficiency and various job enrichment indices are indeed demonstrable. However, the present evidence suggests that the assessments of core job dimensions are relatively independent of degree of staffing while the critical psychological states and the outcome variables are related in the hypothesized manner. This suggests that Greenberg's original proposal (i.e., staffing is proximally related to perceptions of core job dimensions) be modified. Apparently, the perceptions of core job dimensions are relatively immune to degree of staffing while the psychological states and outcome variables are susceptible. . . . Furthermore, sufficient support was yielded by the present evidence for Greenberg's proposal that a moderate degree of understaffing is optimal for "enrichment" purposes. Once again, the support was comparatively strongest for the psychological states and the outcome variables [Vecchio & Sussman, 1981, p. 184].

Evidence from Laboratory Studies

The relationship between the number of persons available in a setting and the number and sequence of tasks requiring performance in the program of the setting has also been the subject of investigations under the controlled conditions of the laboratory. Again Wicker and his students and colleagues have reported an important series of studies (Hanson & Wicker, 1973; Petty, 1974; Petty & Wicker, 1974; Wicker et al., 1976). Because Wicker has summarized these studies in his readily available text (Wicker, 1979a), only a brief review is needed here.

All of these studies used, with minor variations, a slot-car game first reported in Petty's (1971) unpublished master's thesis. In the most extensive of these studies (Wicker et al., 1976), male college students were recruited to participate in groups of four members each. The structure of the slot-car activity made possible experimental variations so that two, four, or six persons were needed to operate the game. Thus three different staffing conditions were created: understaffed (four persons available but six needed); adequately staffed (four persons available and four needed); and overstaffed (four persons available but only two needed). Measures of behavior included records of game performance (speed and errors), direct observations of players, tape recordings of player verbal interchanges, and responses to questionnaire items based on behavior setting theory: the extent to which the player felt he worked hard, was needed, had an important role, was involved with the group task, was concerned with the group's performance, contributed to the group, demonstrated his skill, and coordinated his efforts with those of others. The results showed that

> Members of . . . [understaffed] groups typically gave uniformly high ratings on the above dimensions, indicating that they had similar, intense feelings of involvement. In contrast, members of . . . [overstaffed] groups tended to report less intense and more variable feelings: typically, some members of a group would indicate high levels of involvement and other members lower levels. And members of adequately . . . [staffed] groups were generally intermediate in intensity and variability of reported feelings. These results suggest that the different . . . [staffing] conditions can, in fact, lead to differential experiences among people who are exposed to them [Wicker, 1979a, p. 153].

Arnold and Greenberg (1980) used a similar slot-car game in a study focusing specifically on Barker's hypothesized vetoing mechanism in overstaffed settings. Three conditions of staffing were experimentally established, as in the Wicker et al. (1976) study described above. Arnold and Greenberg's study used female college students in groups of four: three naive subjects and one confederate in each group. In half the groups, the confederate took a model role—that is, she adhered closely to the group's prediction of their performance in the discussion session prior to each trial. In the other groups, the confederate took a deviant role by disagreeing with other group members and informing them that she felt the group could achieve one-third more laps than the highest estimate given by any of the three naive subjects. Measures of subjective experience were obtained from each subject on six questionnaire items: importance, expended effort, worked hard, responsibility, anticipation level, and needed. In addition, subjects evaluated the confederate and the other group members on several dimensions, such as conforming versus deviating, like versus dislike, and not helpful versus helpful. Post-discussion questionnaires also provided a ballot whereby subjects could nominate each of the other group members for one of three positions in subsequent trials: driver, crewmember, or observer. The latter nomination was interpreted as a vetoing mechanism because the role of observer was essentially that of a nonparticipant.

The analyses showed that members of relatively understaffed groups perceived themselves as more important and expending greater effort in group activities than members of groups more adequately staffed. In brief, these data are consistent with those of previous laboratory studies regarding the effects of staffing levels on participants' self perceptions. Concerning the rejection of deviates, the authors conclude:

> The hypotheses concerning vetoing mechanisms are strongly supported. A vote for the confederate as an observer was interpreted as a rejection of the person from future group activities. The more votes a person received for the observer position, the greater the degree of rejection the group was demonstrating. The results indicate that the . . . [overstaffed] groups with a deviate rejected that deviate more often than all other groups. Thus, as expected, the deviate was incorporated into most of the groups except in the . . . [overstaffed] condition. In this condition, she was ostracized to a nonparticipating position as a consequence of deviating from the group norm. In contrast, modes [conforming confederates] were almost always accepted and voted into an active participating role in all . . . [staffing] conditions. Even though all groups disliked deviates more than modes, under- and adequately . . . [staffed] groups seem to have ignored this dislike when assigning the deviate a role in future group activities [p. 423].

Perkins (1982) has recently reported an important and sophisticated laboratory study designed to test behavior setting theory while examining the mediating influences of individual differences among research participants and structure of the experimental task. To create the perception of individual differences, one subject in half of the groups was openly labeled as less competent than the others on the basis of test performance. The instructions to the groups were varied to create different task structures, using Steiner's (1972) distinction between *additive* group tasks (tasks on which the outcome is determined by sum of the individual efforts of group members, such as rope-pulling) and *conjunctive* tasks (tasks in which group productivity is dependent on the single poorest individual performance, such as on a manufacturing assembly line). Perkins makes the interesting observation that most of the field research on underpopulated or understaffed behavior settings has been carried out in communities and institutions in which the behavior settings probably include a large proportion of additive tasks. Wicker's laboratory studies, however, used a group task that was more nearly conjunctive, the slot-car race. This difference may account for the finding of few effects of staffing on task performance in the laboratory studies.

In addition to the usual kinds of predictions based on behavior setting theory (occupants of understaffed settings relative to those of overstaffed settings would show more task-related behavior, participation in more challenging and important activities and in a greater variety of different behaviors, harder work, etc.), Perkins predicted that perceived individual competence and task structure would interact with the staffing condition, producing enhancement of these predictions for incompetent relative to competent occupants and a similar enhancement of the usual setting effects under additive relative to conjunctive task structure conditions.

Perkins' study involved 255 college students in 56 groups, half understaffed (two or three persons) and half overstaffed (six or seven persons). The experimental task was the construction of a set of bookshelves using bricks and shelf boards following detailed instructions. Behavior was recorded through direct observation from behind a one-way mirror and through tape-recordings of verbal interactions. A post-task questionnaire was developed and used to measure via self-report three dimensions of group feeling: cohesiveness, involvement, and incongruence. The main findings of this study showed that members of understaffed groups, relative to members of overstaffed groups, (a) performed much higher proportions of task behaviors, (b) performed more difficult and more important tasks, (c) performed more different task behaviors, but (d) correctly laid fewer bricks (lower productivity).

With regard to this last finding, the report states that there was a significant staffing X task interaction, indicating that overstaffed groups performed significantly better only under additive conditions and that, when group size was factored out as a co-variate, understaffed groups performed significantly better than overstaffed groups. Thus understaffing elicits better performance or harder work *per occupant* than does overstaffing. Analysis of the post-task questionnaire data found no group differences in cohesiveness, involvement, or incongruence.

One interesting finding that is opposite to what behavior setting theory would predict is that in overstaffed settings, the subjects identified as *incompetent* performed a higher proportion of task behavior than did competent subjects. Perkins comments on this finding:

> [T]he finding that subjects labeled incompetent performed more task behaviors than competent subjects in . . . [overstaffed] settings, while contrary to the prediction, still argues that individual factors can compete with and override . . . [staffing] influences under some conditions (e.g., the desire to repudiate a label of "incompetence" by assuming greater-than-expected task involvement) [p. 632].

Perkins concludes with a caution that some of the dependent variables, particularly the measures of cohesiveness, involvement, and incongruence, may have been restricted by certain of the experimental features. He recommends that future work should examine settings of longer duration where occupants know each other and where they actually differ in important personal characteristics.

Relevance to Other Theories on the Effects of Community or Organization Size

The research summarized above was inspired by behavior setting theory, and the results obtained are generally consistent with expectations derived from that theory. But these data are relevant to other theories as well. In sociology, for example, Wirth's classic paper (1938) proposed that human relations among persons living in large population centers are segmentalized:

> Characteristically, urbanites meet one another in highly segmental roles. They are, to be sure, dependent upon more people for the satisfactions of their life-needs than are rural people . . . but they are less dependent upon particular persons, and their dependence upon others is confined to a highly fractionalized aspect of the other's round of ac-

tivity. . . . The contacts in the city may indeed be face to face, but they are nevertheless impersonal, superficial, transitory, and segmental. . . . The individual . . . loses . . . the spontaneous self-expression, the morale, and the sense of participation that comes with living in an integrated society. This constitutes essentially the state of *anomie* or the social void to which Durkheim alludes [pp. 12–13].

In contrast, Gans (1962a, 1962b) sees the city as made up of numbers of village-like communities in which persons belong to societies of people with shared values and characteristics, resulting in rich and satisfying social relationships. Similarly, Fischer (1973, 1976) claims that the greater structural differentiation of the city produces more numerous and more specialized settings. The city dweller is therefore provided with a wealth of opportunities to affiliate with others whose interests and characteristics are similar to his/her own, thus facilitating the development of close and supportive social relationships.

In general, the findings reviewed above from the research on behavior setting participation, and especially those from Wright's Largetown-Smalltown and Urbantown studies, appear to be more congruent with the views of Wirth than with the positions of Gans and Fischer, bearing in mind that these data concern the behavior and experiences of children, whereas the theories of Wirth, Gans, and Fischer concern persons presumably of all ages, not just children. Specifically, the findings that Smalltown children, relative to Largetown and Urbantown children, had greater clearness or familiarity with their behavior settings, with other persons, and with various qualities of their environments are consistent with Wirth's view. He says of urban residents, "[I]n relation to the number of people whom they see and with whom they rub elbows in the course of daily life, they know a smaller proportion, and of these they have less intensive knowledge" (Wirth, 1938, p. 12).

On the other hand, Wright's finding that Largetown and Urbantown children entered more and a wider variety of behavior settings could be seen as consistent with the views of Fischer and Gans. But the further data showing that the Urbantown children, in their forays beyond their home territory into the wider realm of the large metropolitan center, entered not different but the same kinds of settings as those nearer home, does not support Fischer's contention that urbanites seek out more highly specialized activities.

These studies of behavior in relation to population size are at least indirectly related to a substantial literature in organizational and industrial psychology, organizational sociology, and the environment-behavior field. Although this literature is too extensive for consideration here, we can identify a number of other papers that review the empirical evidence from several different points of view. The paper in which Barker (1960) presented the first published statement of behavior setting theory also contains references to field studies and studies in industrial psychology on attendance and absenteeism in organizations differing in size, such as Rotary Clubs, factories, coal pits, air bases, churches, and schools. Willems (1964a, p. 28) reviews studies of size effects "upon individual members within organizations, their range and depth of participation in group activities, their feelings, their experienced pressures, and so on." His paper includes both laboratory and field studies, many of which postulate a negative relation between size and attraction toward participation in organizational activities. Indik (1963) provides a careful review of many of the earlier studies on the effects of organization size on member attitudes and behavior (such as absence, accidents, morale, and output). The studies described by Barker, Willems, and Indik produced findings that appear to be generally consistent with expectations based on behavior setting theory—that is, a negative correlation between size of group and participation in group activities.

Warner and Hilander (1964) identify a number of empirical studies, primarily in sociology, that are relevant to their empirical research on voluntary organizations. They conclude that "the findings of this study support previous research in documenting a negative relationship between organizational size and membership participation" (p. 38). They report that some of their measures of participation are much more closely related to size than others.

Kimberly (1976) presents an extensive review and critique of the role of size as a variable in studies of organizational structure on the basis of an analysis of 80 empirical studies within the organizational sociology paradigm. This work is only tangentially related to our present concerns because of its emphasis on the consequences of variations in size on structural aspects of the organization—communication, levels of administration, and patterns of control and affiliation—rather than the significance of size for the behavior of members.

Of greater direct relevance here is the review by Sadalla (1978) entitled "Population Size, Structural Differentiation, and Human Behavior." He points out that social psychology has more often been concerned with density than size of community but that "a body of evidence is accumulating which indicates that population size may be a more critical variable" (p. 271). Sadalla sketches the theoretical views of Wirth and Durkheim and then summarizes empirical research evidence suggesting that there is a reliable statistical relationship between social role differentiation (oc-

cupational specialization) and city size and that city size and differentiation influence the social behavior of individuals. He then discusses major
hypotheses regarding the psychological consequences of size and structural differentiation under the headings *anonymity* (Gans, 1962a, 1962b;
Goffman, 1959; Latané & Darley, 1969; Milgram, 1970; Wirth, 1938; Zimbardo, 1969); *deindividuation* (Baron, 1971; Gergen, Gergen, & Barton,
1973; Jorgenson & Dukes, 1976; Singer, Brush, & Lubin, 1965; Zimbardo, 1969; and others); *deviance* (Clinard, 1968; Fischer, 1975); and
personality development (Madsen, 1971; Madsen & Shapira, 1970; Weisner, 1974; Whiting & Whiting, 1975). Sadalla (1978) summarizes his findings as follows:

> The principal theme which pervades this literature is that large aggre-
> gations of individuals allow for the formation of alliances between indi-
> viduals with special interests, and that these alliances in turn increase
> the opportunity to engage in those special interests. The city may thus
> be seen as a milieu which leads to the genesis of new opportunities,
> both prosocial and antisocial.
>
> Certain styles of social interaction such as competitiveness, domi-
> nance, and dependence appear at an early age among urban residents,
> and appear to be related to the degree of social role differentiation in
> the milieu. . . . [A]vailable data suggest that urban settings, by their
> task structures and their personnel, tend to model and reinforce indi-
> vidually oriented, competitive behavior. Rural contexts, on the other
> hand, tend to reinforce conflict avoidance, group orientation, and co-
> operative behaviors [p. 288].

Greenberg (1979) reviews research on the effects of organization size
and subunit size on participants' attitudes and behavior from the perspectives of industrial psychology and behavior setting theory. He points out
that "it has been well documented in the industrial psychology literature
that the size of an organization or its subunits affects the attitudes and behaviors of workers" (p. 228; see, for example, Payne & Pugh, 1976; Porter
& Lawler, 1965; Porter & Steers, 1973). Most of the studies reviewed involved correlating unit size with organizational indexes such as job satisfaction, turnover, absenteeism, and productivity. Although these studies
yielded varying results—depending on whether subunits or whole organizations were studied, the kind of industrial population studied, and the
particular measures used of attitudes and behavior—most of the studies
indicated that larger work groups promote more dysfunctional attitudes
and behavior in their workers (pp. 229–30). Greenberg also suggests an
interesting approach to integrating job redesign theory and behavior setting theory.

In an intriguing and freshly original recent paper, Latané, Williams, and Harkins (1979) describe two experiments on the tendency of individual effort to decrease as the number of persons in the situation increases, a phenomenon they call "social loafing." This work was inspired in part by several published discussions and replications of a never-published study done by a German psychologist named Ringelmann in the 1920's. Ringelmann reportedly asked German workers to pull as hard as they could on a rope, alone or with one, two, or seven other people, and then, using a strain gauge, measured in kilograms of pressure how hard they pulled. As a maximizing, unitary, and additive kind of task (Steiner, 1972), rope pulling would be expected to generate pressure in direct proportion to the number of people pulling on the rope. In contrast, however, Ringelmann found that with increasing group size, the collective group performance (total amount of pulling pressure) increased substantially less than the sum of the individual efforts, with dyads pulling at 93 percent of the sum of their individual efforts, trios at 85 percent, and groups of eight at only 49 percent.

Latané found the Ringelmann phenomenon of interest partly because it provides a different arena for testing his theory of social impact (Latané, 1973), an idea strongly reminiscent of Barker's behavior setting theory of underpopulated or understaffed settings. Latané et al. (1979) summarize the theory of social impact as follows:

> Social impact theory holds that when a person stands as a target of social forces coming from other persons, the amount of social pressure on the target person should increase as a multiplicative function of the strength, immediacy, and number of these other persons. However, if a person is a member of a group that is the target of social forces from outside the group, the impact of these forces on any given member should diminish in inverse proportion to the strength, immediacy, and number of group members. Impact is divided up among the group members, in much the same way that responsibility for helping seems to be divided among witnesses to an emergency (Latané & Darley, 1970). . . . Ringelmann's asking his workers to pull on a rope can be considered social pressure. The more people who are the target of this pressure, the less pressure should be felt by any one person. Since people are likely to work hard in proportion to the pressure they feel to do so, we should expect increased group size to result in reduced efforts on the part of individual group members. These reduced efforts can be called "social loafing"—a decrease in individual effort due to the social presence of other persons [p. 823].

Latané et al. replicated the Ringelmann study but used an entirely different yet physically and psychologically demanding kind of task: making as much noise as possible by shouting (Rah!) and clapping hands. "The making of noise is a useful task for the study of group processes from the standpoint both of production and of measurement—people are practiced and skilled at making noise . . . and acoustics and audio engineering are sufficiently advanced to permit sophisticated data collection" (p. 828). Groups of six undergraduate male college students performed this task alone, in pairs, or with four or six other members. In the first experiment, subjects could see and hear the other participants during the trials. The more people clapping or cheering together, the more intense the noise and the more sound pressure produced. But it did not grow in proportion to the number of people: two-person groups generated only 71 percent of the sum of their individual capacities, four-person groups were at 51 percent, and six-person groups were at 40 percent; the sound of 12 hands clapping is not even three times as intense as the sound of 2.

The second experiment by Latané et al. was patterned after a study of Ingham et al. (1974), which replicated the Ringelmann study but eliminated the possibility of output loss due to lack of synchronization or coordination of effort among the subjects, leaving only "social loafing" to account for any obtained differences in output. Subjects were blindfolded and led to believe that others were pulling with them, but in fact they were always pulling alone. Ingham et al. still found a substantial drop in output with increases in perceived group size. When Latané et al. instituted similar controls in their second experiment (with subjects blindfolded and wearing earphones making loud sounds so that subjects were unable to hear or see each other), the results were still similar to those obtained in the first experiment. The report states:

> In addition to shouting in actual groups, individuals also performed in pseudogroups in which they believed that others shouted with them but in which they actually shouted alone, thus preventing coordination loss from affecting output. . . . [P]eople shouted with less intensity in pseudogroups than when alone, $F (2, 10) = 37.0$, $p < .0001$. Thus, group size made a significant difference even in pseudogroups in which coordination loss is not a factor and only social loafing can operate [p. 828].

The authors discuss their findings in relation to social impact theory and note the similarity of their findings and those of various other studies, including Wicker's (1969b) study in which he found, as we have seen, that the proportion of church members taking part in church activities is lower in large churches, presumably because the responsibility for taking part is more diffuse.

Conclusions

Most of the evidence reviewed above is consistent with behavior setting theory. Field studies of underpopulated and understaffed behavior settings in schools, churches, workplaces, and communities as well as laboratory studies provide an impressive array of evidence that the behavior of persons in small, underpopulated settings differs from the behavior of inhabitants of adequately and overpopulated settings in ways consistent with expectations derived from behavior setting theory. An examination of the available evidence specific to each of the 17 predictions and derivations from behavior setting theory shows that (a) most of them are supported by evidence in several of the relevant studies; (b) there is supporting evidence from at least one study for each of the predictions and derivations; (c) there are a few studies that report findings apparently inconsistent with behavior setting theory but in each case there are sufficient questions about methodology to render the findings less than convincing; and (d) much of the supporting evidence, especially that from field studies, is less direct and specific to particular predictions and derivations than would be ideal.

On the basis of the available evidence, therefore, we conclude that there is substantial support for the main features of behavior setting theory as applied to underpopulated and understaffed behavior settings. Further tests of the theory, especially through careful studies of intra-setting processes using direct observation (Wicker, 1973), are needed.

11

Overview of Selected Empirical Applications

In this chapter we identify and summarize briefly a number of empirical investigations that utilize behavior settings either as the basic unit of analysis or in some other way central to the purpose of the study. Unlike those reviewed in the previous chapter, the studies considered here are not derived from any single theoretical problem but are concerned with a wide variety of issues, often without explicitly developed theoretical significance. For convenience, the studies are grouped according to common features. It will be apparent that, in the space available, it is possible to do little more than give a general idea of what these studies have tried to do and how the behavior setting unit has been utilized in each case. Of course, full appreciation of the strengths and limitations of these studies requires direct consultation of each original report.

Describing Community Environments

QUALITIES OF LIFE IN MIDWEST AND YOREDALE

The most extensive study of whole communities in terms of behavior settings involved surveys of the two small towns mentioned earlier—Midwest, Kansas, in the United States, and Yoredale, Yorkshire, in England—on two different occasions separated by a decade, 1954–55 and 1963–64 (Barker & Schoggen, 1973). Of the many ways in which behavior settings were used in this study to describe various characteristics of the two towns as environments for behavior and human development, only a few can be summarized here in order to illustrate the fruitfulness of the method.

Habitat variety within Midwest and Yoredale. Although the towns were both in the small size range, Yoredale's population of 1,310 was somewhat larger than Midwest's 830. This difference might lead to an expectation that Yoredale would provide a wider range of different kinds of behavior settings than Midwest. To measure variety, the settings of the towns were grouped into *genotypes* of similar settings, following procedures described above (Chap. 5). Settings are similar to the extent that major components of the settings could be exchanged with little functional disruption. In Midwest, the genotype Barbershops includes two behavior settings, Keith Barbershop and Riffle Barbershop. They belong to the same genotype because major components (staff, equipment) could be exchanged without appreciably disturbing the functioning of either setting. However, such an exchange of major components between Keith Barbershop and Gwyn Cafe would not be possible; they therefore belong to different genotypes. The interested reader will find a complete catalogue and description of all the genotypes in both Midwest and Yoredale, including the names of the behavior settings in each genotype, in the appendixes of Barker and Schoggen (1973).

In the 1963–64 survey, the 884 behavior settings of Midwest constituted 198 genotypes, whereas Yoredale's 758 settings fell into 213 genotypes. These genotypes are the numbers of standing behavior patterns whose programs are not interchangeable. Although Midwest's population amounted to only 63 percent of Yoredale's, Midwest had 93 percent as many behavior setting genotypes. Although Midwest was smaller in size, it provided only slightly less variety in habitat than Yoredale. Midwesterners had a total range of habitat and behavior opportunities and obligations that was nearly as extensive as that available to Yoredale residents. Moreover, a comparison of the genotypes of the two towns showed that one-third of all the genotypes were common to both towns and that these common genotypes included half of all the behavior settings in the towns. The importance of common genotypes is that they identify the common ground of the towns. Visitors from one of the towns to the other would feel quite "at home" in behavior settings belonging to common genotypes, such as Auction Sales, Dances, Elementary School Classes, Libraries, Parades, Plays and Programs, Scout Meetings, and Worship Services.

A number of completely unique behavior setting genotypes were found in each town. Eight percent (16) of the 198 genotypes that occurred in Midwest in 1963–64 did not occur in Yoredale: for example, Baseball Games, Chiropractor's Office, Ice Cream Socials, and Piano Recitals. In Yoredale, 10 percent (22) of its genotypes had no counterpart in Midwest: for example, Commission (betting) Agents, Cricket Games, Fish and Chips Shops, Military Training Classes, and Taxis. On the basis of the numbers of settings in these unique genotypes, it appears that visitors to

Midwest from Yoredale would find the town less "foreign" than would visitors to Yoredale from Midwest: about 1 in 16 of the behavior settings of Midwest would be completely new to visitors from Yoredale; this would be true of about 1 in 10 of Yoredale's settings for visitors from Midwest.

Change in habitat variety. A genotype is lost to a town when all behavior settings of the genotype cease to exist; a new genotype appears when one or more behavior settings of a previously nonexistent genotype occur. Differential rates of genotype erosion and accretion are processes by which the nature of a town's habitat changes; this may result in renewal, adaptation, and increased vigor, or it may result in deterioration.

Between the two survey years, Midwest lost 12 percent (21) of its 1954–55 genotypes. Some of these are probably permanent losses due to basic changes in the economy, technology, or culture; for example, the loss of the genotype Ice Depots reflects the growth of electric refrigeration; Telephone Exchanges yielded to dial telephones; Book Exchange Services (where used school books were bought and sold) ceased when a statewide policy of renting textbooks was introduced. Other genotype losses appear to be the result of temporary conditions in 1963–64: Horse Shows, Lotteries, Shoe Repair Shops, and Veterinary Services seem likely to return in the future.

In Yoredale, similarly, 10 percent (17) of the 1954–55 genotypes were gone by 1963–64: Slaughter Houses disappeared because central meat processing became more economical than local plants, and Bicycle Runs succumbed to the more crowded highways and the greater affluence. Beauty Culture Classes, Dinners with Business Meetings, and Sewing Service are examples of Yoredale setting genotypes that, though absent in 1963–64, are likely to reappear.

The later survey found a number of genotypes that had not been present in 1954–55. In Midwest, 24 percent (48) of the 1963–64 genotypes were new, such as Bowling Games, Ten Pins; Kennels; Kindergarten Classes; Optometrist's Services; Retarded Children's Classes; and Tractor Pulling Contests. In Yoredale, 29 percent (62) of the genotypes were new in 1963–64, such as China-Painting Classes; Cross-Country Running Competition; Egg Packing Plant; Motor Vehicle Operator's Classes; Dog Shows; and Typing Classes. These genotype additions represent crucial growing points in the two towns. Many broad categories of habitat variety are added, such as new habitat resources for education (Typing Classes), for personal services (Kennels), for health (Optometrist's Services), for recreation (Bowling Games, Ten Pins), and for business (Egg Packing Plant). In Yoredale many of the new genotypes are associated with the schools, whereas in Midwest the main source of habitat innovation is the private enterprise system.

Local autonomy of behavior settings. The quality of life for those who live in a community is influenced by the extent to which those people control the settings of the town (see Chap. 6 above). Events within Keith Barbershop are controlled largely by barber Keith. He determines the hours of operation, what services to offer, what prices to charge, whether to hire a second barber, and what grooming aids to sell. Influences on this setting from beyond the town are quite limited, such as state or federal regulations on sanitation or union membership policies. Keith Barbershop is an example of a setting with *high local autonomy.* In Yoredale, by contrast, the setting British Railways Freight Office and Delivery is controlled largely in centers far from Yoredale. Those persons who operate the setting are appointed and its program is determined by authorities located outside Yoredale and its surrounding region. Residents of Yoredale have very little influence on the operation of this setting; it is an example of a setting with *low local autonomy.*

Rating all the behavior settings in both towns in 1963–64 showed the towns to be very different on this dimension. Almost 50 percent of Midwest's behavior settings but only 20 percent of Yoredale's were judged to have high local autonomy, whereas only 9 percent of Midwest's but 37 percent of Yoredale's settings showed the characteristics of low local autonomy. The remaining settings were intermediate on local autonomy. These data mean that Midwest is more of a local town than is Yoredale. Important behavior setting genotypes that were largely organized, programmed, and financed within Midwest but were organized, programmed, and financed at a distance from Yoredale were Elementary School Basic Classes, Fire Stations, Hotels, Libraries, Nursing Homes, and Trafficways. To the extent that having real power to control one's environment is a desirable quality of community life, the residents of Midwest enjoy a better quality of life than do those of Yoredale.

Freedom of movement of children. Freedom to move about one's environment, to enter and leave behavior settings, is a highly prized and widely valued liberty; it is normally an indication of power. Prohibited and coerced movements are widely deplored; they usually signify weakness. Because the investigators were especially interested in describing Midwest and Yoredale as habitats for child development, settings were grouped according to whether children were allowed some freedom of choice about entering, on the one hand, or were coerced, on the other—

either required to attend, as in many school settings, or prohibited from attending, as in Hooker's Tavern (see pp. 133–38). Behavior settings in the first category constitute regions of relative free movement for children; large parts of them impose no restrictions or coercions, and where restrictions are imposed, they are not absolute and can be breached by determined children. Within these regions, the needs of children are dominant in determining the settings they inhabit. The second category consists of settings that require or prohibit the attendance of children. These settings constitute reserved areas of the town. The attendance-required settings are reserved for children (under the control of older persons), and the attendance-prohibited settings are reserved for older persons, free from intruding children.

Here again, the towns differed. Midwest's region of free movement for children included 78 percent of all the town's behavior settings, whereas in Yoredale the comparable figure was 68 percent. Put the other way, regions of coerced movement—settings requiring or prohibiting child attendance—amounted to only 22 percent of Midwest's but 32 percent of Yoredale's behavior settings in 1963–64 (Barker & Schoggen, 1973, p. 413). Thus children in Midwest, relative to children in Yoredale, were growing up in an environment in which they enjoyed greater freedom of movement.

Price and Blashfield (1975) reanalyzed data from the 1968–69 behavior setting survey of one of the small midwestern towns conducted by the staff of the Midwest Psychological Field Station. In an effort to discover the underlying dimensions along which behavior settings vary, they prepared a correlation matrix using all 43 variables of the original behavior setting survey on all 455 behavior settings in the town. Subjecting this correlation matrix to factor analysis produced nine interpretable factors (such as adult members and targets, religion versus government, and young performers) that accounted for 62 percent of the total variance. A second study reported in the same paper sought to discover what types of settings existed in the town and the similarities and differences among them. Cluster analysis produced 12 clusters (such as youth performance settings, religious settings, women's organizational settings, and family-oriented settings). These clusters each included between 7 and 90 different behavior settings. These data are discussed from the standpoint of the problem of person-environment congruence and the theory of social or community settings.

BECHTEL'S REMOTE REGIONS HABITABILITY STUDIES

In a series of reports, Bechtel and his associates (1976, 1980; summarized in Bechtel, 1977, 1982) describe their use of behavior setting sur-

veys to study the habitability requirements of communities whose inhabitants are confined indoors most of the time due to temperature extremes
or who live in isolation and have limited contact with the outside world for
prolonged periods of time. These studies, completed under special research contracts (for example, from the U.S. Army Cold Regions Research
and Engineering Laboratory), have aided in the development of design and community-planning guidelines used by the military, government, and private business to produce more cost-effective solutions to the
special problems of maintaining quality of life in remote habitation, such
as in Federal Aviation Administration (FAA) and U.S. Air Force stations in
Alaska, or in mining communities in the Australian desert and the Arctic.
Using a shortened form of the behavior setting survey for economy, these
small, remote communities were compared with each other and with a
larger military installation. Among many other findings, the investigators
reported that the levels of participation and occupancy of leadership positions in behavior settings were higher in the small, remote stations. Not
surprisingly, the FAA sites showed greater local autonomy of their behavior settings than was true of the military installations regardless of size.
The remote mining communities, however, exerted local control over even
more of their settings than did any of the other communities studied.

These and other studies by Bechtel and his associates have utilized
modifications of the standard behavior setting survey procedures in order
to reduce costs. These include reducing the total time period covered by
the survey, simplifying several of the rating procedures, and relying on
interview and other self-report measures for certain kinds of data. These
changes are described in Bechtel (1977, 1982).

COMMUNITY IMPACT OF MAJOR ENVIRONMENTAL CHANGE

Harloff, Gump, and Campbell (1981) describe their use of behavior setting surveys to measure changes in the public life of six small communities
in northeastern Kansas resulting from the construction of a large flood
control, conservation, and recreational reservoir nearby. Behavior setting
surveys of the six towns were made by the staff of the Midwest Psychological Field Station in 1959, well before construction of the dam began in
1964. Then, in 1969, about one year after the dam was completed and the
lake filled, the Field Station staff carried out another behavior setting survey in each of the six towns, making possible the before and after comparisons reported in the Harloff et al. (1981) paper.

Prior to the construction of the dam, strong local controversy centered
on the anticipated consequences of the project for the region. The report
states:

Pro and anti groups were active. Established farmers generally opposed the project, land speculators favored it. Many town merchants thought the development would be good for business, numerous town residents were concerned about traffic problems, increased crime, higher taxes. Stories of both dire and beneficial consequences for towns near other Corps of Engineers projects were told and retold [p. 687].

The most general finding from the surveys was that the changes in public life in the six towns turned out to be appreciably less than anticipated, given the environmental change incident to the opening of such a large lake: 20 miles long, covering 12,200 acres with another 25,000 acres converted to a flood plain. The two towns closest to the lake lost population but the other four towns gained. Similarly, the size of town habitat as measured by centiurbs decreased substantially in the two towns nearest the lake, but the others all gained appreciably in habitat extent. Analyzing change in terms of the authority systems (see Chap. 6 above) to which the behavior settings of the towns belonged indicated that the School authority system showed the most extensive changes; however, these were apparently related not to the new lake but rather to major changes in school policy adopted during the period by the state of Kansas, which mandated the closing of many small schools and redrawing of school district boundaries.

The Private Enterprise authority system showed only minor changes except for the one town that was relocated to a new site; its extent of Private Enterprise behavior settings was reduced by 62 percent. Two of the towns showed small increases but none increased as much as some of the lake boosters had expected. The predicted prosperity for the towns as measured by changes in the extent of the private enterprise habitat did not occur.

Behavior settings in the Government authority system increased in extent in five of the six towns but most substantially in the county seat town, where the increased burden of heavy activity was reflected in the work of the sheriff's office, the Register of Deeds, the county clerk, and the county treasurer. Similar changes were reflected in the numbers of person-hours spent in the operating zones of the behavior settings in the several authority systems.

The investigators concluded that, except for the one town that was physically relocated by the creation of the lake, the effects of the reservoir on the nearby communities were not nearly as substantial as had been anticipated. They report that "the behavior setting description of the communities yielded a comprehensive and intuitively realistic picture of the behavioral opportunities available to community inhabitants" (p. 705).

STUDIES BY GERMAN ECOLOGICAL PSYCHOLOGISTS

A recently published volume in German edited by Kaminski (1986) presents papers prepared originally for a 1981 conference, the "Fourth Annual German Colloquium on Ecological Psychology," held at Schloss Reisenburg, near the city of Ulm, West Germany. In Germany, the term "ecological psychology" (or ecopsychology) is roughly equivalent to what North Americans refer to as "environmental psychology" (Kruse, 1987; cf. Barker, 1987). Under sponsorship of the German equivalent of the National Science Foundation, the theme of this colloquium was the behavior setting concept. Some 25 German psychologists, anthropologists, sociologists, and geographers reviewed the conceptual background and methodological features of the behavior setting approach, presented constructively critical evaluations of the behavior setting approach from the standpoint of several social science disciplines, offered attempts to integrate the behavior setting concept with other conceptions and theories of environment-behavior relations, and described attempts to apply the behavior setting approach to a variety of problems. An English translation of this volume is not yet available, but the editor kindly arranged to have several of the papers sent to us. Subsequently, Fuhrer provided us with a copy of his review (1986) in English of the Kaminski volume and encouraged us to draw from it for this summary, to which we now turn.

Kaminski's introduction to the volume claims that the most specific contribution of the behavior setting concept is its recognition of the highly structured nature of the ecological environment, but he criticizes the approach for neglecting transitions between settings and failure to provide adequately for behavior in settings that does not conform to the standing patterns of behavior.

The next section offers papers by J. Koch and W. Saup, who describe the classical behavior setting approach and its recent elaborations, especially the concept of overpopulation ("manning theory"). They are critical of the conception of settings as regulated by homeostatic mechanisms and point out the failure of the setting approach to deal with setting inhabitants as psychological beings. Fuhrer, however, suggests that these weaknesses are addressed in recent work by Wicker and his associates (Wicker, 1987; Wicker & King, 1988) in their efforts to focus on the life cycles of behavior settings.

The third section of the Kaminski volume includes reports of three empirical studies that attempted to use the behavior setting to address specific problems: one dealt with problem-solving behavior and the second with aggressive interactions, but neither found the behavior setting concept to be sufficiently sensitive or specific for the task. In the third study, however, W. Molt found the behavior setting concept with appropriate adaptations and elaborations to be quite useful for his empirical studies of the influence of streets as behavior settings on the behavior of inhabitants.

The fourth section contains three papers, all of which in different ways propose to "psychologize" behavior settings by integrating the behavior setting concept more closely with concepts, methods, and lines of inquiry from other psychological subdisciplines. These efforts are reminiscent of the recent transactional conceptualizations of settings by Stokols (1981), Stokols and Shumaker (1981), and the life-cycle perspective on settings by Wicker (1987). E. Boesch demonstrates how behavior settings are embedded in certain "action-fields"—comprehensive and temporally enduring goal structures such as the family or a friendship. L. Kruse is concerned with the cognitions of setting occupants that are neglected by behavior setting theory and finds a relationship between behavior settings and the script concept of Schank and Abelson (1977; cf. Chap. 13 below). Kaminski's paper is concerned with the heavy investment of time and other resources required by the traditional behavior setting survey and the resulting coarseness of the setting approach to everyday behavior. He favors a more psychologically oriented naturalistic analysis of behavior settings.

Several other papers discuss behavior settings from different points of view. I. Greverus, a cultural anthropologist, stresses the cultural embeddedness of behavior settings. B. Hamm compares the Barker approach with the social-ecological approach within modern sociology and calls for greater recognition of the importance of behavior settings as vehicles of functional and social meanings and of symbolic meanings of historical experiences. Stokols and Jacobi (1984) have recently made a similar case. P. Weber discusses the value of behavior settings in relation to several recent theoretical approaches from behavioral geography.

J. Zimmerman, speaking as a planner and architect who works with a team planning new towns to serve the metropolitan area of Cairo, Egypt, discusses the usefulness of behavior settings in this work. He finds three aspects of the behavior setting concept to have special importance in approaching these problems: the focus on the relation between behavior and the physical milieu; the regularity (permanence, durability); and the extra-individuality. He is attempting to use behavior setting analysis to investigate the behavior patterns of users in order to have something better than common sense and personal experience in seeking solutions to the complex problems of designing new towns that will work.

In the final section, the editor reviews the main points of the volume and discusses possible reasons for the relative isolation of the behavior setting concept from mainstream psychology and its lack of penetration into other social sciences. He considers the behavior setting concept to be not a genuine psychological concept but a "pre-psychological" construct, hence its lack of appeal to many psychologists. He notes also that the traditional behavior setting work has not stressed intersetting linkages, the socio-physical and cultural surroundings of settings, and the value systems of encompassing communities or societies. There is also the broad focus of the setting approach in its concern with environment-behavior phenomena, a perspective that contrasts with that of mainstream psychology, which is largely an experimentally oriented, "small range" science.

Fuhrer concludes his review by noting that "the book represents the first intensive and interdisciplinary-oriented examination of Barker's behavior setting concept. In that respect, it represents an excellent source of promising ideas that challenge and offer vitality to the behavior setting concept." He also presents a brief summary of his proposal (Fuhrer, in press) to bridge the conceptual breach between the objective, ecological environment of the behavior setting and the subjective, psychological world of the individual setting inhabitant.

Community Status of Population Subgroups

Behavior setting surveys of whole communities are especially well suited to the task of describing the position occupied by members of particular population subgroups within the public arena of the town. Many such results were included in the Midwest-Yoredale comparison (Barker & Schoggen, 1973, chaps. 11, 12). Children in Midwest, for example, occupied positions of leadership and responsibility in the behavior settings of the town twice as often as their Yoredale counterparts. "This means . . . that Midwest children play in City Band Concerts, assist in Household Auction Sales, collect tickets at the Parent-Teacher Association Carnival, run a lawn mower at the City Park Volunteer Work Group, carry the Capitol City Paper Route, recite at the Mother-Daughter Banquet, act as secretary of Jolly Juniors 4-H Club Meetings, and so forth, twice as often as Yoredale children" (p. 410).

This pattern of more frequent responsible participation in the town's behavior settings was found to obtain not only for the children but also for the adolescents and for people aged 65 and older in Midwest as compared to Yoredale. These findings are congruent with the underpopulated condition of Midwest more generally as discussed in the previous chapter: in Midwest, relative to Yoredale, the number of persons available to fill the positions required to operate the town's behavior settings was small; this shortage of personnel meant that the Midwest system required the responsible participation of children, adolescents, and old people; Yoredale, by contrast, with no such personnel shortage, was not dependent on nonadults to assume these important responsibilities. These data suggest that the quality of life for all residents but particularly for children, adolescents, and old people was very different in the two towns.

Eddy and Sinnett (1973) describe an interesting study of the utilization of behavior settings by emotionally disturbed college students. Using a self-report measure of behavior setting participation (Sachson, Rapoport, & Sinnett, 1970), clinical judgments by mental health professionals, and Minnesota Multiphasic Personality Inventory (MMPI) scores, the results via factor analysis supported the predictions of relationships between clinical judgments, MMPI scores, and behavior setting utilization.

Evaluation of Program Impact

Behavior settings have proven to be useful to measure the impact of particular programs in the community in which they are located. Ragle, Barker, and Johnson (1978), for example, describe the impact of the Agricultural Extension Service (AES) in the town of Midwest, including how the town would be different if the AES program were to be eliminated: the town's size in terms of number of behavior settings would be reduced by 5 percent; Midwest's environmental variety in terms of number of genotypes would be reduced by 4 percent; eight genotypes (containing 17 settings) would be completely lost to the town; there would be almost eight fewer behavior setting occurrences per week, lasting 45.5 hours; and 14 percent of Midwest's inhabitants not professionally connected with the AES would have about 34 hours per year each to spend in other (non-AES) behavior settings. Also reported were changes in the AES over the decade between 1954–1955 and 1963–1964, one of which was a decrease in the participation by adolescents in AES settings. When this was noted by AES officials, a special effort was mounted to create new AES settings with special appeal to adolescents. The previous underoccupation of AES settings by adolescents was soon remedied.

A similar analysis of the impact of churches on small towns is reported by Barker, Barker, and Ragle (1967), comparing the churches of Midwest and Yoredale in terms of behavior settings and their utilization by town residents. They found, for example, that the churches of Midwest contributed 22 percent of the town's behavior settings in 1963–64; the compa-

rable figure in Yoredale was 13 percent. The church-related behavior settings of eight other small towns in England, Canada, Norway, and the
United States constituted from 18 to 29 percent of their towns' behavior
settings. Looking at the changes in church-related behavior settings over
the decade from 1954–55 to 1963–64, Midwest showed an increase from
13 to 22 percent of the town's settings, whereas Yoredale experienced a
decrease from 15 to 13 percent. It appears, therefore, that Yoredale
churches were the source of fewer of the town's behavior resources than
was true of Midwest.

Data on behavior setting utilization by town residents show a similar
pattern. As measured by number of person-hours per year, Midwest residents in 1963–64 spent 1,361 hours per person in all community behavior
settings, 25 percent more than Yoredale residents. In church-related settings the difference was greater: Midwest residents spent 40 hours per
person per year in them, 54 percent more than Yoredale residents.

Analysis of leadership in one of the two major churches in Midwest
showed that church leadership was widely distributed among all the
church's inhabitants, that most of the church leaders were also active leaders in behavior settings of the wider community, and that leadership in
the church was shared almost equally by men and women. Overall, 87
percent of the women who were active in the church were more than attenders; they held positions of power and responsibility. On their reliability and competence depended the effectiveness of important religious,
social, and recreational programs of the church.

The authors conclude with suggestions about the practical significance
of their findings:

> It is not surprising, in view of two of the findings, that small commu-
> nities frequently cling to their "inefficient," "outdated" churches with
> what may appear to outsiders to be unreasonable stubbornness. These
> findings are (a) that churches usually provide a substantial proportion of
> the total behavior resources of small towns; and (b) that in the behavior
> settings of small churches many inhabitants have responsibility and
> power, and are important and valued people. The residents of small
> communities know that the removal of their churches, for example, by
> amalgamation with "strong" churches in larger towns, destroys perhaps
> one-quarter of the behavior resources of the town. . . . Those who do
> inhabit small churches know that consolidation with a larger church re-
> duces for them the likelihood of having an important, responsible part
> in church activities. Most of the deacons, elders, board members, and
> presidents of small churches can look forward in the larger church to
> the role of faithful member [p. 187].

Gump (1969, 1975b, 1982, 1987) has found the behavior setting concept useful in analyzing elementary school classroom environments. For this purpose, he used the term *segment* to refer to a behavior setting–like unit of the preperceptual environment within the classroom. "The use of segments has made it possible to describe classrooms in a manner that respects their structure and internal differentiation" (Gump, 1969, p. 206). Examples of classroom segments include "Seatwork," "Word Usage Drill," "Story Discussion," and "Gym Preparation." Such segments were reliably identified and their characteristics and attributes were described, such as their *concern* (academic content, classroom activity maintenance), *activity pattern* (nature of teacher participation, grouping of pupils), and *site* (physical location within the classroom). The data showed that differences between segments were related to variation in pupil behavior: pupils behave differently in different segments. Thus "segments in which pacing of pupil action came from the outside (for example, recitation and tests) showed greater involvement than segments in which pupil initiative provided the immediate push to activity (study sessions)" (Gump, 1969, p. 214).

Gump and Ross (1977) report an unusual application of the basic property of behavior settings—milieu/behavior program synomorphy—to the study of open classroom schools. Analysis of three public schools with open design that had been in operation for varying periods of time revealed that modifications had been made in both the physical milieu and in instructional programs in order to improve the synomorphic relation. Cabinets, bookcases, and other items of moveable furniture were appropriately substituted for the missing walls to restore some degree of the privacy formerly enjoyed in traditional separate classrooms. Modifications in instructional programs included careful scheduling of activities that generate noise (such as playing phonograph recordings) and combining classes for dramatic presentations or guest speakers. The openness of the milieu generated greater mobility among the students and faculty; students and teachers entered a larger number of synomorphs per unit of time in the open schools. The report concludes:

> The open milieu puts children and teachers in a state of objective and unavoidable interdependence. As one teacher expressed it, "What I do can affect 100 children, not just 30." This interdependence at the first level is not at all psychological—it is physical and it requires that steps be taken. In School C, at the early grade level, these steps were to reduce, even oppose, the intrinsic interdependence by shielding. Schools A and B, over time, developed programmes which utilized interdepen-

dence; for example, they took joint responsibility for large groups of children and they worked out various forms of team teaching [p. 87].

A recent contribution to the literature on person, setting, and interaction (Bem & Allen, 1974; Bowers, 1973; Ekehammar, 1974; Endler & Magnusson, 1974; Raush, Dittman, & Taylor, 1959) is reported by Schuster, Murrell, and Cook (1980). In this study, children were observed in six preschool settings: Discovery Time, Table Time, Free Play, Group Time, Lunch Time, and Transition Time. In total, 8,930 brief time samples of the behavior of 17 children in these settings were grouped by trained raters into behavior categories such as Positive-Active Interaction, Positive-Passive Interaction, and Nonsocial Behavior. Both aggregate and individual level analyses are reported using relatively sophisticated statistical techniques—for example, goodness of fit tests via maximum likelihood estimators, minimum chi square, and logit analysis. The aggregate analysis found significant main effects for both person and setting and found that the interaction of person and setting was also significant. However, relative to the person effect, the setting effect was shown to be significantly larger. Analysis at the individual level showed that the six settings differed in their coerciveness; Lunch Time exerted strong pressure on the different children to conform to the setting pattern, but Discovery Time and Transition Time exerted much less pressure. Schuster et al. conclude:

> The finding from the aggregate analysis that each of the three components, person, setting, and interaction, made a significant contribution to predicting behavior is consistent with those of earlier cited studies. The cumulative effect of these studies, . . . is to clearly establish the untenability of either a strict personality trait, a strict situation-deterministic, or an exclusively interactionist position for the prediction of social behavior. The finding in this study that the setting predicted behavior significantly better than person should not be taken as evidence for the universally superior predictive power of situation but in the more situationally specific sense suggested by Argyle and Little's (1972) work, i.e., as a suggestion that perhaps settings will have stronger predictive power for general social behaviors by children in natural nursery school–type environments [pp. 34–35].

Comparisons of Behavior in Different Behavior Settings

Although in many ways quite similar to the work summarized in the preceding section, the studies next identified place major emphasis on the behavior of persons in different, usually contrasting, behavior setting environments. In an early example of such investigations, Gump, Schoggen, and Redl (1963) used a team of observers to record via the specimen-record procedures (Wright, 1967) a single nine-year-old boy's behavior for an entire waking day on two separate days, one while the boy was attending summer camp and the other ten days later in the boy's own home and neighborhood. Careful, quantitative analysis of the record revealed some differences between the two days in the boy's behavior and in the treatment he received from others; such differences, however, were less extensive than might have been anticipated given the obvious differences between the behavior settings comprising the camp and the home environments. The report also attempts to relate behavioral differences to differences in environmental supports and coercions characteristic of the behavior settings entered on the two days.

Using much the same observational and analytical procedures as Gump et al., Tars and Appleby (1973) observed one eleven-year-old boy at home and in a children's hospital where the boy was admitted for in-patient treatment for emotional problems. Adult behavior and interactions between the boy and his adult associates were similar at home and in the hospital, but interactions with child associates were markedly different: there was less assertiveness and more appeasement in the boy's behavior toward other children in the hospital than was true at home. Among the interesting findings in this study is the suggestion that the highly programmed environment of the hospital, with its many environmental supports, may "represent a form of homogeneity that can curtail the expression of creativity and initiative" (p. 25) rather than facilitate exploration and variety in experience among the patients. Consistent with the findings of studies using other methods, Tars and Appleby documented in rich detail the lack of privacy in the settings of the hospital and some of its likely consequences.

Grannis (1983) reports an intriguing and innovative use of behavior settings in an observational study of high school students who were enrolled in a special program for educationally disadvantaged inner city seniors interested in a career in the health field. Observations were made of the setting and the subject's behavior in two types of setting: academic and skills training classrooms and in field placement sites—such as physical therapy or nutrition laboratory—where the students were placed for experiential learning. All settings were located on the premises of Mt. Sinai Medical Center in New York. A special observational guide, called the Setting and Behavior Instrument (SBI), was developed and used over a three-year period. Elements of the SBI were based on the U.S. Employment Service's *Dictionary of Occupational Titles* to analyze levels of functioning of the subject and other persons in the setting in terms of their dealings with people, data, and things. The SBI coding form provides for recording various attributes of the setting: the setting concern; the interaction format; an inventory of data sources, people, and things involved in the setting; both the modal and the highest level of functioning of each category of setting occupants in each of the three areas (people, data, things); and who initiated activity by the student subject. These ratings were made by trained observers during 20-minute on-site visits to the settings (after prior arrangements with the person in charge of the setting). The observer held interviews with each subject shortly after the observations were completed in order to clarify the nature of the performances observed. These procedures were carried out in two different years, 1978 and 1979.

Illustrative findings from this study include the following: (a) the two kinds of settings (classrooms versus field placements) differed more from each other than either did with itself across the two years on most of the variables studied; (b) the kinds of people, data, and things observed did correspond to the program rationale for the two kinds of settings; (c) students in placements, relative to those in classrooms, were less involved in discussion, more involved in independent activities, and initiated more of their own activities; and (d) the SBI proved to be sensitive to changes in the program between the two time periods. Grannis concludes that the SBI worked well and that it could be adapted for a variety of studies where there is need for an objective profile of setting characteristics.

An early study (Shure, 1963) compared the behavior of nursery school children in five settings for indoor activities, art, books, dolls, games, and blocks. Direct observations of the children's behavior yielded measures of participation, affect, constructiveness, and social participation following Parten (1932). Results are reported for population density within and mobility between these areas and for behavior differences across areas. Significant differences were found between the five areas on all four of the behavior dimensions measured. No evidence is presented, however, that the five activity areas would satisfy the criteria for behavior settings.

Another early study comparing settings of four nursery schools was reported by Berk (1971). Two of the schools (Montessori and University) served primarily middle-class families, while the other two (Head Start 1 and 2) provided programs for children from lower-class backgrounds. The programs of the Montessori and the University nursery schools differed in that the Montessori program was more highly structured—that is, most activities were preplanned and sequenced. The two Head Start programs differed primarily in size of classroom and teacher-children ratio. Observers used short time samples to record conflict environmental force units, or EFU (Schoggen, 1963), defined as actions by associates directed toward the child subject of the observation that are not congruent with the child's own wishes at the time. The EFUs were later classified according to the kind of conflict situation involved, such as a conflict of desires between the subject and another child, a subject's desire to do something being blocked by her/his own lack of ability, or a conflict between the teacher's expectations and the child's desires. The classification scheme was originated by Jackson and Wolfson (1968). The child subject's mode of response to each conflict EFU was categorized using 14 specific response categories in four broad classes of adaptation: unresponsive-withdrawing, dependent-compliant, thoughtful-persistent, and offensive-combative.

The study sought evidence concerning, among other things, the effects of specific characteristics of the preschool environment on the incidence of different kinds of conflict EFU and children's adaptations to them. The results of the analyses revealed some important differences; for example, children in the Montessori school encountered significantly more conflict EFU than did children in the University program, a difference due primarily to a much higher incidence of conflict between the expectations of the teacher and the wishes of the child subject. Adaptations of the children to conflict EFU also showed a striking difference in favor of several types of compliant behavior in the Montessori school. These differences were attributed to differences in the classroom environments, such as the highly structured materials and ritualized expectations for their use in the Montessori program. Berk concludes about the differences between these two nursery school environments and their impact on child behavior as follows:

> In general, the differences found between the two nursery schools substantiate Barker's (1965) notion that environmental inputs to individuals, in this case conflict EFU which lead to behavioral consequences, are themselves embedded in environments, or behavior settings, and that these settings interact with and regulate the inputs in accordance with the requirements of the environment. The results of this study illustrate both sides of the coupling of environmental and behavioral phenomena: (*a*) the relationship of characteristics of the environment to critical inputs and (*b*) the relationship of critical inputs to behavioral responses [p. 866].

Kounin and Gump (1974) conceptualized formal lessons for nursery school children as behavior setting–like environments with coercive properties characteristic of all synomorphs. Videotapes were made of 596 lessons given singly by 36 different teachers in separate rooms to small groups (3–9) of age-matched children over a span of two years. A total of 87 different children were the unrehearsed participants in lessons designed by the teachers on subjects of their own choosing without direction or instruction from the researchers. The dependent variable was the amount of involvement in the lesson shown in the behavior of the child-subject. The child's behavior was coded from the videotape every six seconds from the time the lesson started until it was over, usually less than 20 minutes.

These authors suggest that formal lessons contain external provisions called "signal systems" because they signal to the children the kinds of behavior that are appropriate to the setting. "These provisions include the communications of the teacher ('Let's see what sticks and what doesn't stick to a magnet') and the props that go with the lesson (magnet, paper clips, pieces of paper and cloth, nails). A lesson also includes the standing pattern that goes with the lesson (making piles of objects that stick or don't stick to the magnet, listening to a story being read)" (p. 556).

Different lessons are characterized, however, by signal systems of differing strength. For instance, the teacher reading or playing records to the attendant children constitutes a single, continuous source of signal emission; it should generate high child involvement or at least very little off-task behavior. In contrast, group discussions, group projects, or unrehearsed role play sessions rely on multiple, shifting signal sources staffed by other children. Such a format is subject to lags and faltering continuity, making low involvement and frequent off-task behavior likely. In all, six different lesson types were identified in terms of their different signal systems.

Type 1 produced significantly less off-task behavior than the others; it consisted of individual-construction lessons that contained continuous signals from the results of the child's own behavior, such as making a collage of photographs cut from a magazine. This signal system also appeared to be well insulated from external intrusions. Other types, particularly lessons involving recitations, role play, group construction, and music and movement, were found to generate high frequencies of off-task behavior, presumably attributable to lack of continuous sequencing, dependence on faltering inputs from other children, or the intrusiveness of intense props and behavior (in music and movement). The report concludes:

The model presented here, then, suggests that the pattern and quality of the signal system is a crucial area in predicting child involvement in prescribed lessons in preschool. Three dimensions related to signal input which are suggested by the present research include (*a*) *continuity* of signal input, (*b*) *insulation* of participants from potentially distracting stimuli, and (*c*) *intrusiveness* of respondent action [p. 559].

In an exploratory study, Scott (1977) compared the behavior of nursery school teachers in two typical nursery school behavior settings, Morning Greeting and Large Group Activity, using specimen record observations and analysis (Barker & Wright, 1955; Wright, 1967). Unlike the earlier work, however, Scott's observers recorded and analyzed teacher behavior, one of the few studies to apply the specimen record observational methodology to the behavior of adults rather than to children.

Two findings are of particular relevance here: (1) the two settings differed in their coerciveness on the teachers, that is, Morning Greeting tolerated greater individual variation among teachers than did the more structured, relatively more formal Large Group Activity; and (2) differences in teacher behavior were greater between the two settings than between any two teachers in the same setting. Scott concludes that the behavior setting is a coercive force on behavior. She also suggests that the study demonstrates the usefulness of the specimen record observational and analytical procedures and the behavior setting concept in the study of teacher behavior.

Focusing more directly on the physical environment, Moore (1986) studied the effects of spatial definition of "activity pockets" or behavior settings on children's behavior in child-care centers. Systematic naturalistic observations were made of the behavior of children in 14 child-care centers matched in three groups according to three degrees of the spatial definition of the activity pockets within the center. Significantly more exploratory behavior, social interaction, and cooperation occurred in centers with spatially well defined behavior settings. The authors conclude that "the effects of the physical environmental variables can only be understood when studied in interaction with social environmental variables" (p. 205). Although Moore uses the term behavior settings, there is no discussion of program or standing patterns of behavior associated with the physical environmental areas with which the study is concerned. It is not clear from the report given whether the "activity pockets" would meet the definition of behavior settings.

Studies of Institutions

Willems and Halstead (1978) and LeCompte (1972b) describe their use of the behavior setting survey and ecological observational methods in an extended program of research on the behavior of patients and the environment provided by a large rehabilitation hospital for persons with spinal cord injuries, the Texas Institute for Rehabilitation and Research (TIRR) in Houston. This program of research documented, through extensive specimen-record-type observations, the behavior of patients in the settings of the hospital over the full course of their hospital stay, thus permitting the researchers to present charts showing behavioral changes on important dimensions in the various behavior settings during several months of a patient's rehabilitation process.

The research showed clearly that profiles of patient behavior varied dramatically from one setting to another, a finding congruent with those from other studies indicating that behavior is strongly determined by the particular setting in which it occurs (Raush, Dittman, & Taylor, 1959, 1960). For example, behavioral measures of independence—the proportion of patient actions initiated and executed without assistance—showed that such independence varied dramatically as patients moved from one behavior setting to another within the hospital. Much more independence was found in the settings Cafeteria, Hallways, and Ward than in the treatment settings of Occupational Therapy, Physical Therapy, and Recreational Therapy. Such findings run counter to the expectations based on traditional, person-centered theories of human behavior and their assumption that a person's degree of independence is largely a function of individual personality and therefore likely to be relatively constant across situations.

Finally, a recent report by Perkins and Perry (1985) describes their use of the behavior setting survey supplemented with interviews to identify and describe the characteristics of a large community residence for mentally ill women. The study has obvious practical significance in view of the trend in recent years toward deinstitutionalization of psychiatric patients. The primary goal of the research was to identify the dimensions of the behavioral demands placed on the residents by settings of the residence home.

The behavior setting survey of the residence identified 93 settings, such as Cooking Class, Breakfast, and TV Room. Information about setting attributes—average attendance, duration of occurrence, level of required interpersonal interaction, and so on—was obtained through structured interviews, usually with the staff members who led the settings. Factor analyses of the descriptive variables were used in an empirical solution to the theoretical problem of dimensionalizing behavior setting demands. An overall index of "demandingness" was generated for each setting using the results of the factor analysis, permitting comparisons of the various settings on this dimension. The authors conclude from these data:

"Although the specific values presented here for overall demandingness are arbitrary, relative differences among these scores provide a meaningful basis for distinguishing among settings as to the overall level of behavioral demands they place on participants" (p. 358). Substantively, the report shows that the settings of the residence emphasized functional skills basic to social behavior: how to dress acceptably, how to cooperate, how to get along in group settings. These findings are said to be congruent with those frequently reported in the literature suggesting low functional levels for chronic clients.

In the next chapter, we turn to a very different kind of application of the behavior setting unit. Professor Karl Fox, an economist, describes his own work and that of several of his colleagues in developing an approach to social system accounting using the behavior setting as the basic unit of analysis.

12

Behavior Settings and Social Systems Accounting

Karl A. Fox

In an article first published in 1969, Barker (1978a, pp. 43–44) expressed the need for "an eco-behavioral science independent of psychology" that would answer the many pressing questions facing society. This science would require concepts and theories appropriate to the phenomena involved. The concepts and theories would be grounded on empirical data concerning the patterns of events within the psychologist-free settings where people live their lives.

Barker goes on to say that if psychologists were to create this new science, they would have to learn how to collect ecological data (which are "phenomena centered and atheoretical"); how to accumulate and preserve these data in archives and to make them generally accessible; how to analyze the data; and how to establish and operate field stations within particular bounded communities and institutions. This would be a logical extension of the program pioneered by Barker and his associates at the Midwest Psychological Field Station. If several universities were to establish similar programs and arrange for the sharing of data and the maintenance of central archives, eco-behavioral science as conceived by Barker could be developed rapidly and cumulatively over the next decade or two.

This chapter is intended as a bridge between eco-behavioral science and the public data systems used by economists, demographers, sociologists, and others. I believe the behavior setting concept can be enormously useful to these scientists. Their attempts to measure and to under-

Much of the research underlying this chapter was supported by the National Science Foundation under research grants SOC 74-13996 and SOC 76-20084; this support is gratefully acknowledged.

stand social phenomena have led them from fragmentary bodies of data through economic and social indicators to economic, demographic, and social accounts. In my judgment, behavior settings hold the key to the next major advance in social accounting at all levels, from small communities to nations.

In reviewing a paper by Fox and Ghosh (1981), the economist Richard Ruggles (1981, p. 465) said:

> The concept of the space-time behavior setting can provide a comprehensive basis for classifying and analyzing human behavior. There is considerable validity in the proposition that accounts drawn up on this basis do delineate the human activity of a society, and that differences observed over time and space can reveal how a given society changes with the passage of time or how the pattern of life in different countries varies. Certainly this vision of social accounting is on a grand scale worthy of Darwin, Marx, and Veblen.

Ruggles went on to say that such a system would be quite difficult to implement on a large scale and that many operational features of it remained to be worked out. This was certainly true in March 1980 when his comments were written. However, two new data systems published in 1981 and the Organization for Economic Cooperation and Development (OECD) list of social indicators published in 1982 have greatly improved prospects for implementing the proposed accounts. I have made further conceptual advances and have drawn back from the more speculative suggestions in the Fox-Ghosh paper. These developments have been reported by Fox (1983, 1984a, 1984b, 1985, 1986). My economist colleagues Prescott (1985, 1987), Sengupta (1986, 1987), and van Moeseke (1985, 1986, 1987) have made related advances in dynamic and mathematical models with behavior settings as basic units.

During 1985–87, I worked on a research project entitled "Development of Time-Allocation Matrices to Describe and Measure Changes in Patterns of Living in Communities and Urban-Centered Regions and for Impact and Policy Analyses" (NSF research grant SES-84 11958 to Iowa State University). I believe I can show that time-allocation matrices (TAMs) based on behavior settings can be estimated roughly by combining published data of various sorts using regression and other techniques. The estimated TAM for any specific community in a given year would be based on published data for certain characteristics of many different communities in a given region and over a certain size range. The estimated TAM would be analogous to a factory-made suit; a good fit might require local alterations, but these should be less expensive and less time-consuming than doing the entire job locally.

The exploratory efforts I propose could certainly be extended by others. The existence of approximate TAMs based on behavior setting genotypes for (in principle) all U.S. communities should greatly enhance the value of research results in eco-behavioral science as such. It should also facilitate communication between ecological psychologists, eco-behavioral scientists, and all producers and users of public economic, demographic, and social data systems.

The next three sections will review the development of public data systems up to 1980. The fourth through tenth sections will discuss methods of linking public data systems to the concepts and measures used in behavior setting surveys. The eleventh through fourteenth sections deal with the estimation of TAMs at all levels from small towns and their trade areas to the United States as a whole. The fifteenth section considers sources of initiative and support for the development of social accounts based on behavior settings, and the concluding section comments on some broader implications of behavior settings for the social sciences.

The Development of Public Data Systems up to 1932

Mitchell (1975, p. vii) says that most statistics published in European countries prior to 1900 were by-products of taxation or military preparedness. The collection of data as part of a systematic effort to measure social phenomena is almost wholly a development of the twentieth century.

In the United States, the Constitution required a population census every ten years to reapportion seats in the House of Representatives. State legislatures created counties, chartered municipalities, and in some cases adopted constitutions calling for periodic reapportionment of one or both of their chambers on the basis of population. From 1790 to 1900, the census organization was a temporary one; the Census Bureau was established as a permanent federal agency only in 1902.

To finance their expenditures, all governmental units needed revenues; these had to be justified and accounted for. Import duties required data on quantities and/or values of the dutiable commodities; excise taxes on alcoholic beverages required data on their domestic production and sales. Taxes on property, retail sales, and incomes required data on them. License fees required data on the things licensed, such as taverns, restaurants, and vehicles.

Other data systems were developed in response to problems that became major political issues. The Interstate Commerce Commission was created in 1887 to regulate railroads, and good data on railroad transportation began in that year. The Federal Reserve System was established in 1914 to remedy weaknesses in the banking system; banking data were thenceforth greatly improved. A wholesale price index was initiated in 1890 partly to measure changes in the relative positions of debtors (largely farmers) and creditors in a period of declining farm prices. A consumer price index was authorized and household expenditure data were collected in 1917–19 partly to show that rising money wage rates during World War I were needed to offset increases in the cost of living.

The 1920's brought increased professionalism in the major federal statistical agencies: the Bureau of Agricultural Economics, the Bureau of Labor Statistics, the Bureau of Foreign and Domestic Commerce, and the Census Bureau. The National Bureau of Economic Research, founded in 1920 as a private, nonprofit organization, also developed extensive data archives as a basis for its long-term research program on business cycles, economic growth, and national income measurement. Problems of comprehensiveness and internal consistency of data systems received increasing attention; leading economists debated the logic and techniques of constructing price and production indexes and of separating economic time series into trend, seasonal, cyclical, and erratic components. Establishment of a new journal by Harvard University in 1919, the *Review of Economic Statistics*, was symptomatic of the growing professional interest in economic measurement.

The Development of Economic Data Systems After 1933

The Great Depression, which began in the latter part of 1929, quickly demonstrated that no person was independent of the market economy. From 1929 to 1933, the gross national product (GNP) of the United States fell by 46 percent in money terms and 30 percent in real terms. Unemployment rose from 3 percent of the civilian labor force in 1929 to 25 percent in 1933.

The economy gave no indication of righting itself, and the New Deal administration inaugurated in 1933 undertook many new programs and interventions. It became clear, particularly to younger economists, that the fragmentary data systems then existing were inadequate to monitor changes in economic conditions; it would be necessary to develop a set of national income and product (NIP) accounts covering *all* economic activity. Data on employment, prices, and production should also be coextensive with the whole of economic activity as defined in the NIP accounts.

The British economist Keynes (1936) published a prescription for economic recovery in which current data on the national income and its components played a crucial role. Starting from an accounting equation or identity $Y = C + I + G$, where Y is the gross national product in billions of dollars, C is consumer expenditures, I is business expenditures on new plant and equipment, and G is government spending, Keynes showed that the GNP and associated total employment could be increased directly by raising government expenditures (for example, on highways and other construction projects) or indirectly by stimulating increased spending by consumers and business firms.

Kuznets (1937) published annual estimates of the U.S. national income and its components from 1919 through 1932. A Dutch economist, Jan Tinbergen (1939), used Kuznets' data and Keynes' theory to construct a dynamic model of the U.S. economy during 1919–32; the model included some 45 equations and as many dependent or "endogenous" variables. The model was dynamic in the sense that some relationships operated with time lags (for example, an increase in wage rates from Year t to Year t+1 might be associated with an increase in prices from Year t+1 to Year t+2). Accounting identities such as Keynes' $Y = C + I + G$ for the GNP and its components were built into Tinbergen's model.

Leontief (1936) published a square "interindustry relations matrix" for the U.S. economy with approximately 40 rows and 40 columns. With some subsequent refinements, this matrix could be viewed as a set of interrelated accounts for each of 40 industries whose "deliveries to final demand" add up to the GNP. The matrix also features "interindustry transactions," such as purchases by the automobile industry of "inputs" from the steel industry, the rubber industry, the electrical machinery industry, and others. The total gross *output* of the automobile industry consists of its sales to other industries plus its deliveries to final demand. The total gross *input* of the automobile industry consists of its purchases from other industries plus its payments for "primary factors of production"—workers, plant, and equipment employed in the automobile industry itself.

Lewin (1951) attached great importance to the concept of interdependence between regions within a life-space or other field. Barker uses a cutting point of 21 on his index of interdependence, *K*, to partition Midwest's ecological environment into behavior settings. Leontief's matrices dramatize the extreme interdependence among industries in the U.S. economy; in some respects the entire economy must be regarded as a single field.

From the 1950's through the 1970's, economic data systems in the United States were substantially expanded and improved. Censuses of manufactures, trade, services, and agriculture were taken at approximately five-year intervals; these were used in part as the bases for new interindustry relations matrices, and they in turn were used to provide new benchmarks for the annual and quarterly NIP accounts. In the 1970's, annual data on wage and salary income and employment at the level of 11 industries or sectors were developed for each of the 3,000 or more U.S. counties, and somewhat more detailed data were developed for urban-centered regions (Standard Metropolitan Statistical Areas [SMSA] and Bureau of Economic Analysis [BEA] Economic Areas) delineated as clusters of contiguous counties centered on cities of 50,000 or more people.

The extreme interdependence among regions and sectors of the U.S. economy results primarily from flows of goods and money. A decision made in Detroit to reduce automobile production for a few months may affect production in several other industries and in many states within days or weeks, as auto producers curtail new orders to their many suppliers. If a behavior setting survey were under way in a community containing such a supplier, some adults would suddenly be ejected from work-related settings and would spend offsetting amounts of time in other community (including household) settings. The sudden rearrangement of occupancy times would show up in certain rows and columns of the community's TAM, but it could only be explained by means of the Detroit-based decision and the resulting flows of messages, goods, and money between automakers and their suppliers.

The Development of Social and Demographic Data Systems After 1933

Demography has a long history but, until about 1900, a rather sporadic one. In the United States, the collection of death statistics on an annual basis began in 1900 with ten registration states and the District of Columbia; the collection of birth statistics began in 1915, also with ten states and the District of Columbia. From 1933 on, the birth and death registration areas have comprised the entire United States. Even into the 1980's, U.S. data on immigration and emigration were collected only as administrative records and were not viewed by the collecting agency as part of a complete system of demographic statistics.

The concept of national income and the associated concepts of employment and production provided criteria for judging the comprehensiveness and internal consistency of economic data systems. The Employment Act of 1946 committed the U.S. government to promoting "maximum employment, production, and income." This commitment was subject to important qualifications, but it certainly made the accurate *measurement* of employment, production, and income a matter of high public priority. The act also created a Council of Economic Advisers to the president and a Joint (House and Senate) Economic Committee of Congress and required the president to submit to that committee an annual economic report. An appendix of "Statistical Tables Relating to Income, Employment, and Production," occupying some 130 pages, became an established feature of that report (see, for example, *Economic Report of the President*, 1987, pp. 239–368).

Public support for economic data systems was further strengthened by developments within the economics profession. "Macroeconomics" became a major new field of specialization at the graduate level during the 1940's; from 1948 on, an increasing number of undergraduate texts included several chapters on macroeconomics—the analysis of fluctuations in national income, employment, and production and of policies designed to moderate those fluctuations. As students familiar with these concepts moved out into businesses, banks, and public agencies, they constituted a large and influential community of users of data pertaining to national economic conditions. In general, they supported the efforts of federal statistical agencies to improve economic data systems and to obtain the appropriations necessary to do so.

In contrast, public data systems of primary interest to sociologists received little support during the 1940's and 1950's. But this situation changed dramatically in the 1960's as the U.S. government assumed broader responsibilities for health, medical care, education, the rights of minorities, urban renewal, community development, and the attempted elimination of poverty—in brief, for a "Great Society." The founders of the *social-indicators* movement were quick to see the implications of these commitments for official data systems. They were interested in social measurement partly for pure science and partly as a basis for social policy. Bauer (1966) expressed these two interests succinctly: "For many of the important topics on which social critics blithely pass judgment, and on which policies are made, there are no yardsticks by which to know if things are getting better or worse" (p. 20). In the same volume, Gross's (1966) article, "The State of the Nation: Social Systems Accounting," expressed the long-term interest of the movement in comprehensive social system accounts—as distinct from a collection of indicators, each separately designed to track a particular problem.

The bill drafted by leaders of the movement and introduced by Senator Walter Mondale in 1967 was entitled "The Full Opportunity and Social Accounting Act of 1967." It directly paralleled the Employment Act of 1946, providing for a Council of Social Advisers, an annual social report by the president, and a Joint Committee of Congress on the president's social report. The proposed act was not passed, but government agencies and foundations provided greatly increased support for exploratory research on social indicators.

A great deal of the published work done in the name of "social indicators" during the late 1960's and early 1970's was undisciplined and eclectic—sometimes wildly so. Sophisticated social scientists and government statisticians avoided publicity during these years and concentrated on the development of data systems that would address the new social concerns while maintaining high standards of statistical quality. In particular, the OECD sponsored a social-indicators program that began in 1970 and published the *List of Social Concerns Common to Most OECD Countries* in 1973. Several years of complex developmental work ensued on designing indicators to measure these concerns. *The OECD List of Social Indicators* (1982) is the result, and we will discuss it below (pp. 275–78).

Stone (1971, 1975) made major advances in social and demographic accounts, as distinct from indicators. In his 1971 report, *Demographic Accounting and Model-Building*, prepared for the OECD, Stone sought to provide "a comprehensive and consistent basis for education and manpower research, policy, and planning" (p. 13). The system of demographic, educational, and occupational statistics he proposed should make it possible "to integrate information on human stocks and flows just as a system of national accounts [NIP] statistics makes it possible to integrate information on economic and financial stocks and flows" (ibid.).

Stone's accounting system is designed initially to classify people among an exhaustive set of categories covering the entire population of, say, a nation during a particular year. The population would be classified by age and sex. Within any age and sex class, a person would be counted in (1) a specific category of formal educational activities, (2) a specific category of earning activities, or (3) a specific category of what Stone calls the "passive sequence." The "active sequence" includes people engaged in full-time formal education or as members of the labor force; the "passive sequence" includes the rest of the population.

Stone emphasizes "transition matrices," which allocate persons occupying a particular status (cell) in Year t among the various statuses (cells) such persons occupy in Year t+1 when they are a year older. Some leave the system through death or emigration; new persons enter the system through birth or immigration.

Stone revised and extended his transition matrix model and made other contributions in his 1975 report, *Toward a System of Social and Demographic Statistics*, prepared for the United Nations.

Translating Public Data Systems into Social
Accounts Based on Behavior Settings

Public data systems are most highly developed at the national level. If we can show that categories used in these systems (for example, industries) correspond to categories used by Barker (in this case, genotypes), then eco-behavioral data relating to genotypes can be combined with economic data relating to industries. Barker's genotype titles in many cases correspond to the occupations of their zone 6 leaders, and Barker's genotype programs include the common occupational titles of all paid participants, such as teachers, plumbers, salespersons, and waitresses. A 1981 report by the Bureau of Labor Statistics (BLS) contains a cross-tabulation of total U.S. employment by 260 industries and 425 occupations.

A 1981 publication by the BEA presents data on stocks of buildings, other structures, machinery and equipment, and consumer durable goods at the national level. In Barker's system, these data refer to the *circumjacent milieus* of behavior settings and their durable *behavior objects*. Buildings are categorized according to their purposes (commercial, religious, educational) and these purposes often correspond to the prominent *action patterns* of genotypes concerned with business, religion, and education. Barker's *behavior mechanisms* have affinities with data on worker functions in the Standard Occupational Classification, the *Dictionary of Occupational Titles*, and the *Handbook for Analyzing Jobs*.

The OECD List of Social Indicators (1982) will be taken to reflect many of the "pressing social questions" to which an eco-behavioral science might address itself. After discussing this list, we will consider the U.S. data systems mentioned in some detail.

Relating Behavior Setting Concepts to the OECD
List of Social Indicators

Publication of the OECD list marked a new level of maturity and consensus in the social-indicators movement; the list is reproduced in Table 12.1. It includes 33 specific indicators grouped under eight major headings: health; education and learning; employment and quality of working life; time and leisure; command over goods and services; physical environment; social environment; and personal safety. We believe all the objective indicators in the OECD list can be related to social accounts based on behavior settings.

The 1982 OECD report recommends that five standard disaggregations

TABLE 12.1
The OECD List of Social Indicators

Social concern	Indicator
Health	
Length of life	Life expectancy
	Perinatal mortality rate
Healthfulness of life	Short-term disability
	Long-term disability
Education and learning	
Use of educational facilities	Regular education experience
	Adult education
Learning	Literacy rate
Employment and quality of working life	
Availability of employment	Unemployment rate
	Involuntary part-time work
	Discouraged workers
Quality of working life	Average working hours
	Travel time to work
	Paid annual leave
	Atypical work schedule
	Distribution of earnings
	Fatal occupational injuries
	Work environment nuisances
Time and leisure	
Use of time	Free time
	Free-time activities
Command over goods and services	
Income	Distribution of income
	Low income
	Material deprivation
Wealth	Distribution of wealth
Physical environment	
Housing conditions	Indoor dwelling space
	Access to outdoor space
	Basic amenities
Accessibility to services	Proximity of selected services
Environmental nuisances	Exposure to air pollutants
	Exposure to noise
Social environment	
Social attachment	Suicide rate
Personal safety	
Exposure to risk	Fatal injuries
	Serious injuries
Perceived threat	Fear for personal safety

SOURCE: Organization for Economic Cooperation and Development, 1982, p. 13.

be used in presenting nearly all indicators: age, sex, household type, socioeconomic status, and community size. It suggests optional "standard" disaggregations by ethnic group and citizenship in countries where these distinctions are relevant and also by region (that is, by geographical location within a country) according to the classifications customary in each country.

The OECD report lists other disaggregations applicable to several indicators: branch of economic activity, occupation, type of activity, working hours, level of education, tenure status (home owner versus tenant), and age of dwelling. It states that the breakdown of branch of economic activity should be based on the International Standard Industrial Classification codes at the two-digit level; the breakdown of occupation should follow the International Standard Classification of Occupations at the two-digit level, with three digits used where possible in coding occupational groups with a wide range of occupations such as managers; and the breakdown of levels of education should follow the International Standard Classification of Education, which defines seven levels of education plus a residual category. The corresponding classifications used in the United States are closely comparable to the international ones cited.

All but one or two of the OECD indicators are objective and based on data systems of high (or potentially high) quality. Behavior settings are also directly observable, objectively defined entities; as such, it should be possible to relate them to the OECD list.

The OECD indicators "are designed to measure trends in individual well-being, as reflected in common Social Concerns" (OECD, 1982, p. 9). Thus the OECD concept of the physical environment corresponds quite closely to the physical aspects of behavior settings. Three of the six indicators of quality of the physical environment relate to housing conditions: indoor dwelling space; access to outdoor space adjacent, or very close, to one's dwelling unit; and basic indoor amenities. Two other environmental indicators are exposure to air pollutants and exposure to noise; in principle, they should be measured in residential neighborhoods. The sixth indicator is the proximity of residences to selected services (such as shopping facilities, emergency health care, schools, day-care centers, recreational centers, and public transportation).

In addition to these six indicators pertaining to the residential environment, a seventh relates to work environment nuisances and an eighth— travel time to work—reflects physical aspects such as traffic congestion, efficiency of public transportation systems, and distances of residential areas from commercial and industrial districts.

Several indicators measure attributes of individuals or probabilities of undesirable events befalling individuals: life expectancy, perinatal mortality rate, short-term disability, long-term disability, regular education experience, literacy rate, fatal occupational injuries, suicide rate, fatal injuries, and serious injuries. A subjective indicator, fear for personal safety, is associated with levels of stress and probably also with actual rates of street crimes.

Two other indicators refer explicitly to the use of time: free time, and free-time activities. Several more indicators relate to levels and distributions of earnings, income, and wealth and to the availability of employment (unemployment rate, involuntary part-time work, and discouraged workers).

If we assumed a hypothetical community with no in- or out-migration, we might say that the quality of life in the community could be improved in three ways: by improving the attributes of individuals, by improving the attributes of behavior settings, and by improving the allocations of time to individuals among behavior setting-and-role combinations. If the community were closed to imports and exports of goods and services as well as to in- and out-migration, improvements in the health, skills, and educational levels of its residents would require higher levels of activity and/or greater efficiency in the behavior settings concerned with these "human capital" enhancements; improvements in air quality, noise levels, and housing conditions would require more or better-organized activity in settings that produced air-scrubbers, mufflers, and built or remodeled houses.

If the community could implement its own full employment policy, it would enable many residents to improve their allocations of time and increase their command over goods and services. Hence, the OECD indicators would be useful in conceptualizing how the behavior settings of a community could contribute to improvements in the quality of life of its residents.

Relating the Physical Aspects of Behavior Settings to BEA Data

The walls, counters, furniture, equipment, machinery, and other relatively fixed physical features of a behavior setting are referred to by Barker as its circumjacent milieu; the milieu is designed to contain, facilitate, and channel the behavior called for by the setting's program. In most if not all cases, the program of a setting also calls for behavior objects: chalk, pencils, and paper in a school class, musical instruments in a band concert, various hand tools on a construction job, and so on. The behavior objects are not all durable, but some of the most important ones are; their durability implies an expectation that the program of the setting, or at least the program of its genotype, will persist for several or many years.

These physical aspects of behavior settings (their circumjacent milieus and their durable behavior objects) are reflected, though at a high level of aggregation, in the time series data published in 1981 by the BEA: estimates of stocks of fixed nonresidential private and residential capital, government-owned fixed capital, and durable goods owned by consumers.

The basic data underlying Table 12.2 are time series of annual estimates running from 1925 through 1979. The original series were published by the BEA in the form of U.S. totals; we have expressed them *per 1,000 persons* as though they referred to a small, closed community with a constant population of 1,000 but reflecting all the changes in stocks of build-

TABLE 12.2

Microcosm, U.S.A.: Constant-Dollar Gross Values of Residential Structures and Consumer Durable Goods per 1,000 Persons, 1929, 1954, and 1979

(thousands of 1972 dollars)

	Gross values per 1,000 persons		
Category	1929	1954	1979
1. Residential structures	4,448	4,790	7,301
2. Furniture, tableware, and other durable house furnishings	678	733	1,237
3. Kitchen and other household appliances	57	155	450
4. Jewelry, watches, opthalmic products, books, maps	140	214	479
5. Radio, TV, records, musical instruments	27	83	538
6. Wheel goods, durable toys, sports equipment, boats, and pleasure aircraft	27	70	353
7. Other motor vehicles (excludes automobiles)	6	31	296
8. Total consumer durables, except automobiles	935	1,286	3,353
9. Automobiles owned by consumers	424	667	1,732
10. Total, residential structures and consumer durables including automobiles owned by consumers	5,807	6,743	12,386

SOURCE: Special aggregations and computations by Karl A. Fox and Shu Y. Huang from detailed data published by the U.S. Department of Commerce, Bureau of Economic Analysis (1981).

ings, equipment, and consumer goods per capita in the United States as a whole. Types of physical capital not shown in Table 12.2 (such as factories; commercial, educational, religious, and government buildings; public utilities, streets, and highways; and all types of machinery and equipment) amounted to about $14,000,000 per 1,000 persons in 1979 (measured in 1972 dollars).

The changes over time in several categories of consumer durable goods are dramatic. Item 3, kitchen and other household appliances, reflects great changes in the technology of household production; Item 5 reflects great changes in patterns of passive leisure associated (since 1954) primarily with television; Items 6 and 7 reflect major changes in active leisure and outdoor recreation; and Item 9 reflects the role of consumer-owned automobiles in transforming the spatial distribution of homes and nonhousehold behavior settings and the size distributions of shopping centers and cities.

Table 12.3 shows similar estimates of gross stocks of selected types of "central-place" buildings, which are usually located within a few miles, and sometimes within a few blocks, of the homes of the people who use them. Most of the genotypes found in Midwest occur in buildings of these resident-oriented or central-place kinds.

Finally, Table 12.4 shows the distribution of gross stocks of all types of physical capital (except military) and consumer durable goods. The central-place category (Item B) contains all buildings shown in Table 12.3 plus their associated equipment and additional types of structures. The export base category (Item C) consists mainly of manufacturing, mining, and agriculture; the public utility and highway transportation categories

TABLE 12.3

Microcosm, U.S.A.: Constant-Dollar Gross Values of Selected Types of Central Place Buildings per 1,000 Persons, 1929, 1954, and 1979

(thousands of 1972 dollars)

Type of building	Gross values per 1,000 persons		
	1929	1954	1979
Commercial	690	515	1,174
Educational	365	462	919
Hospital and institutional	99	158	366
State and local government (except schools and hospitals)	68	128	308
Religious	85	105	181
Total	1,307	1,368	2,948

SOURCE: Same as for Table 12.2.

TABLE 12.4

Microcosm, U.S.A.: Constant-Dollar Gross Values of Stocks of Physical Capital and Consumer Durable Goods per 1,000 Persons, Total and Five Major Categories, 1929, 1954, and 1979

(thousands of 1972 dollars)

Category of structures and equipment (including consumer durable goods)	Gross values per 1,000 persons		
	1929	1954	1979
A. Residential structures and consumer durables (except automobiles)	5,384	6,075	10,654
B. Central-place structures and equipment	1,755	2,232	5,274
C. Export base structures and equipment	3,409	3,260	4,459
D. Public utility structures and equipment	768	994	1,819
E. Highway transportation structures and equipment	1,117	2,871	3,908
F. Total, civilian structures, equipment, and consumer durables	12,433	15,432	26,114
Addendum:			
G. Gross community product (GCP)	2,592	3,780	6,572
Ratio, total stocks to GCP	4.80	4.08	3.97

SOURCE: Same as for Table 12.2.

are self-explanatory. The expansion of central-place structures and equipment since 1954 is consistent with the great expansion of employment in all kinds of services in retail trade. The modest growth of the export base category is consistent with the slow growth of employment in manufacturing and declining employment in agriculture; most of the capital expansion since 1954 has been in equipment, not structures.

People not only behave in behavior settings—they *learn* to behave in behavior settings. The equivalent of four years of the community's gross economic product is embedded in the buildings (the "built environment") and equipment in which and with which people live and work. The houses last an average of perhaps 70 years, various other structures 30–50 years, and various types of equipment and consumer durables perhaps 8–15 years. Their persistence imposes a gyroscopic stability and continuity upon most of the activities of daily life over periods of one or a few years.

Nevertheless, human life expectancy is such that the entire stock of factory and office equipment and consumer durables is replaced several times during a typical person's life span, the stock of commercial and industrial buildings twice, and the stock of residential structures once. In the short run, physical capital enforces stability; in the long run, it enforces change. The immediate physical environment of our behavior changes in size, shape, and technology and in its distribution over space. Our physical environment and our behavior are integrated in and through behavior settings.

The estimates in Tables 12.2–12.4 are available on an annual basis from 1929 through 1979. As applied to Microcosm, with its constant population of 1,000 persons, in each successive year 8,760,000 person-hours are spent in and/or in association with these structures and objects. In each successive year, behavior settings are associated with the structures, and their programs make use of the objects; the living-time of the population is allocated exhaustively among these behavior settings.

Relating Behavior Setting Genotypes to Industries in the Standard Industrial Classification

Public data systems make extensive use of the Standard Industrial Classification (SIC: U.S. Executive Office of the President, 1978). The SIC is intended to cover the entire field of economic activities; its scope is coextensive with that of the national income, employment, and production statistics. The basic unit in an SIC industry is an *establishment*. An establishment is an economic unit, generally at a single physical location, where business is conducted or where services or industrial operations are performed. In nearly all cases it occupies a definite space containing one or more gainfully employed persons who usually operate on a regular time schedule. In brief, an establishment is typically a unit of the ecological environment and consists of one or more behavior settings belonging to the same formal organization.

An establishment is not necessarily identical with a firm (company or enterprise), because a firm may operate two or more establishments at different locations. An SIC industry is an aggregate or collection of similar establishments.

Most of Barker's Private Enterprise genotypes in Midwest correspond to SIC industries. Examples of such industries include attorneys' offices, banks, beauty shops, clothing stores, drugstores, dry cleaners, garages, grocery stores, and lumber yards. In Midwest, each of the establishments in these industries consists of a single behavior setting. The great majority of retail and service establishments even in Des Moines, Iowa (SMSA population about 330,000) have fewer than ten workers and probably consist of single behavior settings.

A one-to-one correspondence between a genotype and an industry would mean that the program and other attributes of the genotype could be safely ascribed to the industry. However, if typical establishments in an industry contain two or more behavior settings, the settings may belong to different genotypes. For example, a small window-and-door establishment in Midwest consisted of an assembly shop and a front office. The assembly shop belonged to genotype 64 (Factory Assembly Shops; see Barker & Schoggen, 1973, appendix A) and the front office to genotype 38 (Commercial Company Offices): total occupancy time (OT) in the shop during 1963–64 was 18,288 person-hours and in the office 7,200. The shop was occupied by a foreman and several workers assembling glass and aluminum into windows and doors. The office was occupied by the two joint proprietors, a secretary, a bookkeeper, and customers. The programs and staffing patterns of the two settings were quite different.

In an SIC establishment report, data for the two settings would be lumped together. However, if the SIC report contained a tabulation of the number of workers in each occupation, a person with some knowledge of the industry could readily infer that the white-collar workers were grouped in the company office and the blue-collar workers in the shop. If customers were excluded from the shop, the hours worked by the blue-collar personnel would be the total OT of the shop (genotype 64). The hours worked by the white-collar personnel, plus the hours spent in the establishment by customers, would constitute the total OT of the office (genotype 38).

The 1972 SIC would credit Midwest's School authority system with two establishments—the elementary school and the high school—whereas Barker credits Midwest's School authority system with 233 behavior settings belonging to some 68 genotypes. The bulk of the OT in the elementary school is spent in 13 settings of genotype 58 (Elementary School Basic Classes), but there are lunch rooms, playgrounds, hallways, music classes, physical education classes, and some extracurricular activities. The high school's academic subjects belong to several different genotypes: commercial classes, English classes, Latin classes, mathematics classes, and others. There are also some minor subjects and many extracurricular activities.

The SIC would recognize four establishments—that is, churches of four different religious denominations—in Midwest's Church authority system; Barker found 193 behavior settings in 31 genotypes. Over 70 percent of the OT was spent in five genotypes that accounted for 107 of the settings, but there were also weddings, funerals, board and committee meetings, pastors' studies, and various social, cultural, and recreational activities.

The SIC includes religious organizations under the broad category of "membership organizations"; Barker refers to membership organizations *other than churches* as "voluntary associations." Barker found 212 behavior settings in Midwest's Voluntary Association authority system, belonging to 48 different genotypes. I have not tried to tabulate the number of different associations in the Barker and Schoggen (1973, appendix A) catalogue of Midwest's behavior settings, but most of the six "industries" recognized by the SIC were represented. It is not clear how many establishments of these types in Midwest would be included in the economic censuses, because most of Midwest's voluntary associations had no paid officers or employees and some had no real estate and no fixed address.

In Midwest's Government authority system, Barker found 114 behavior settings during 1963–64 belonging to 52 genotypes. Many of these genotypes reflected Midwest's status as the county seat of a county of 11,000 people; in addition to county government offices as such, several federal and state agencies had offices in Midwest. The SIC industries concerned with justice, public order, and safety include courts, police protection, correctional institutions, and fire protection (all of which are represented in Midwest) plus two others not found in Midwest County because of its small population. Four additional SIC industries are listed under "executive, legislative, and general government, except finance"; at least three of these are represented in Midwest. The SIC includes 17 other industries under the broad category of public administration. To the extent that their performers (zones 6, 5, and 4) are paid, Barker's government genotypes can probably be related to SIC industries about as readily as can his private enterprises.

Relating the Roles in Behavior Setting Genotype Programs to Occupations in Standard Data Systems

For present purposes, the Standard Occupational Classification (SOC; U.S. Department of Commerce, 1977) and the classification used in the *Dictionary of Occupational Titles* (*DOT*; U.S. Department of Labor, 1977) are equivalent. Among other correspondences, the code numbers in the SOC and *DOT* include the same three digits describing the complexity of a worker's relations to data, people, and things, respectively, in the relevant occupation.

Every *paid* role in Midwest's genotype programs can be identified with an SOC-*DOT* occupation; this is equally true in the Private Enterprise, School, Government, Church, and Voluntary Association authority systems. All paid roles are found in zones 6, 5, and 4 of behavior settings; these are "performing roles" needed to implement their genotype programs.

Unpaid performing roles (by definition in zones 6, 5, and 4 of settings) can in most cases be identified as amateur versions of standard occupations: actors, musicians (instrumental and vocal), athletes, stage managers, athletic team managers, and many others involved in activities sponsored by the schools, churches, and voluntary associations of Midwest. Barker and Gump (1964, p. 187) found that 86 percent of the different kinds of performing roles filled by Midwest high school students in a given year were "described in the *Dictionary of Occupational Titles* as standard occupations in American culture." Moreover, these standard occupations absorbed at least 99 percent of the person-hours involved; the nonstandard performing roles included such brief and infrequent ones as witnesses at a district court session or attendant at a wedding.

Roles in zones 3 and 2 of behavior settings are almost always less demanding than those in zones 6, 5, and 4. To account for the total OT in school classes, we need one or more "quasi-occupations" for students; in retail and personal service enterprises, we need one or more quasi-occupations for customers. We need similar categories for clients in law offices, for patients in health care establishments, and for spectators and audience members at sporting events, movies, and musical or dramatic performances. The number of such quasi-occupations should be rather small. In a time-allocation matrix with industries for columns and occupations for rows, it should be obvious that the zone 3 occupants of attorneys' offices are clients and those of doctors' offices are patients.

One possibility is to rate roles in zones 3 and 2 using the *DOT* scales for job complexity in relation to data, people, and things. For example, the program for Midwest's drugstore with its pharmacy, fountain (lunch counter), and variety department calls for a pharmacist, a manager, sales persons, food service workers, and customers. The complexity ratings for the paid roles, taken primarily from the *DOT*, are shown in Table 12.5.

The most demanding rating on each scale is 0; the least demanding is 6 for data, 8 for people, and 7 for things. The roles of pharmacist and manager involve a high level of complexity with respect to data (information of all sorts); that of pharmacist also involves a high level of precision with respect to things (the meticulous weighing, selecting, and combining of ingredients). Sales persons function at an intermediate level and food service workers and customers at a low level of complexity with respect to data; all roles other than that of pharmacist involve a low level of complexity with respect to things (merely handling them). The pharmacist, manager, and customers operate at a moderately low level of complexity with

TABLE 12.5
Complexity of Roles

Job or role	Complexity of worker's (incumbent's) function with respect to:		
	Data	People	Things
Pharmacist	1	6	1
Manager	1	6	7
Sales persons	4	7	7
Food service workers	6	7	7
Addendum: customers (rated by Fox)	6	6	7

respect to people (speaking and signaling), whereas sales persons and food service workers operate at a still lower level (serving).

In this example, the quasi-occupation of "drugstore customer" could be given a quasi-*DOT* code that would include the three complexity digits 667.

The BLS National Industry-Occupation Employment Matrix

In 1981 the BLS published a national industry-occupation employment matrix, with 260 industries as columns and 425 occupations as rows, for each of the years 1970, 1978, and projected 1990. The 1970 matrix allocates total U.S. employment in that year exhaustively (a) among 260 industry columns, (b) among 425 occupation rows, and (c) among the elements of the matrix.

Table 1, which takes up 385 pages in Volume I of that report, presents for each industry the percentages of its total employment accounted for by each of the 425 occupations. Thus for the industry "grocery stores" we find managers, officials, and proprietors constituting 20.0 percent of the total, cashiers 22.5 percent, meat cutters and butchers 8.1 percent, and stock handlers 22.2 percent. These four occupations account for 72.8 percent of the industry's total employment. The fact that one worker in five is classified as a manager or administrator suggests that many grocery stores are still small establishments and that the departments in most supermarkets involve only a few workers each.

In the industry "drugstores," 21.1 percent of total employment is accounted for by pharmacists, 6.0 percent by managers and proprietors,

34.2 percent by sales workers, and 11.3 percent by cashiers; here again some 72.6 percent is contributed by four occupations. Another 8.3 percent consists of food service workers.

In the industry "offices of dentists," the percentages of total employment include dentists 34.5, dental hygienists 5.4, receptionists 8.5, and dental assistants 36.0, or 84.4 percent for the four occupations combined. It should be noted that "private households" is also one of the 260 industries; it employed child-care workers (31.3 percent), cooks (2.2 percent), housekeepers (6.5 percent), cleaners and servants (42.2 percent), and gardeners and groundkeepers (10.1 percent), or 92.3 percent in the occupations listed.

Many of the retail trade and service industries (as Barker found in Midwest) bear the names of the occupations of their zone 6 leaders. For such industries we could visualize a diagonal submatrix with (for example) offices of dentists occupying column 1 and dentists row 1, drugstores occupying column 2 and pharmacists row 2, and so on. Within this submatrix, the taxonomy of industries would correspond to the taxonomy of occupations. Most of their establishments would be small, consisting of single behavior settings, so that (apart from some large and/or anomalous establishments) the industries would correspond to genotypes.

In principle, every paid role in the behavior settings of the United States in 1970 is included in Table 1 of the BLS publication. On the basis of data on hours worked per person per year by occupation and industry, Table 1 could be transformed into a matrix in which the unit would be, say, millions of person-hours. Because the industries include private households, the entire living-time of the U.S. population in 1970 was allocated de facto among the industries of the transformed matrix.

All paid roles occur in zones 6, 5, and 4 of the relevant settings. As a first approximation, we might assume that all settings in certain industries contain only paid workers. (This assumption would be subject to empirical verification or modification later.) All of the OT in such settings would be accounted for in the 425 occupation-rows of the transformed Table 1. Manufacturing, mining, agriculture, wholesale trade, and some other industry categories whose establishments do not ordinarily deal directly with members of the general public could be treated initially in this fashion.

For the retail trade and service industries, which depend on customers, patients, students, spectators, and other occupants of zones 3 and 2 of their settings, we would have to add rows for the corresponding quasi-occupations: for example, customers (row 426), patients (row 427), and students (row 428). Just how detailed such quasi-occupations should be is a matter for research. An enormous amount of living-time would at the outset be entered in, say, row 429, household members, in the private-households "industry."

In the fuller development of such a matrix, the private-household industry would have to be subdivided into more detailed activities. Within the duration of our 1985–88 research project, we will be emphasizing the applications of Barker's approach to non-household industries whose behavior settings require zone 3 and zone 2 participation by members of the general public. Some of these industries (schools, churches, voluntary associations) sponsor a great many settings in which even the zone 6, 5, and 4 performers are unpaid and which are therefore missed completely by our economic data systems. The manufacturing and other industries whose settings contain only gainful workers are extensively covered by standard industry-and-occupation data systems.

Translating Time Allocations Among Industries into Time Allocations Among Behavior Setting Genotypes

Given an estimated allocation of the living-time of the U.S. population among industries in a certain year (as just described above), we would face the problem of translating it into an allocation of time among behavior setting genotypes.

In the Private Enterprise authority system, the establishments in each industry could be classified by size (number of employees), and a sample of establishments could be chosen from each size class for site visits, enumeration of settings, their classification into genotypes, and proration of their total occupancy times among genotypes. Pretests might disclose that establishments with fewer than, say, ten workers could be assumed to consist of single behavior settings. The prevalence of national chains and franchise operations and the replication of similar clusters of establishments in hundreds of shopping centers suggest that the number of establishments sampled in each industry need not be large.

A similar sampling approach should be suitable for establishments in the Government authority system; most information about such establishments is in the public domain. A great deal of information about schools is collected and published by the U.S. Department of Education; behavior setting surveys of a sample of schools of different sizes at each level of instruction should permit estimates of time allocation among genotypes. Samples of churches, voluntary associations, and households would also be required to translate published establishment-type data about them into estimates of time allocations among genotypes.

Suppose we found 400 different genotypes. At this stage we would have, in Barker and Schoggen's terminology, the gross behavior product of the U.S. population, in billions of person-hours, allocated exhaustively among these genotypes. Because our allocation procedure would have made use of employment data in all SIC industries, it should be possible to relate all public economic data systems directly or indirectly to this vector of time allocations among genotypes.

Each genotype would have its set of ratings on action patterns and other attributes. It should be possible to allocate stocks of physical capital (which are estimated by the BEA in considerable industry detail) exhaustively among the genotypes. These stocks constitute the circumjacent milieus and durable behavior objects associated with the person-hours of behavior and experience embodied in the standing behavior patterns of the genotypes.

Suppose the genotypes were grouped according to their prominent action patterns: Aesthetics, Business, Education, Government, Nutrition, Personal Appearance, Physical Health, Professional Involvement, Recreation, Religion, and Social Contact. These prominent action patterns are goal-directed or output-oriented; they answer the question, "What is the setting *for*?" We could then use the 33 OECD social indicators as a checklist of possible ways in which each genotype might contribute to improvements in individual well-being. Presumably genotypes in which the Physical Health action pattern is prominent make some contribution to the health indicators; likewise, prominent Education action patterns contribute to the education indicators, and so on. The checklist approach could serve as a starting point for attempts to quantify some of the relationships between particular genotypes and particular indicators.

Time-Allocation Matrices for the United States

In the previous section, we lumped together the person-hours of all population subgroups. We could regard the assumed 400 genotypes as columns of a matrix, each row of which would allocate the total person-hours of a specified population subgroup among genotypes. The U.S. population could be classified in many different ways, such as by age, sex, education, or occupation separately or by combinations of two or more such attributes. Thus we could envisage a whole family of time-allocation matrices with the same 400 genotypes as columns but with rows based on various classification principles.

The row for any population subgroup, converted into hours per year *per subgroup member*, would summarize the life style of the subgroup in a given year. Various sets of published data could be used to distribute the total OT of each genotype among population subgroups, and the sample surveys mentioned earlier might also be designed to yield information on subgroup occupancy times.

If U.S. time-allocation matrices were estimated at intervals of five years, they should reveal changes in the life styles or per capita *time allocation vectors* of the various population subgroups. It should also be possible to develop annual estimates of time-allocation vectors at a somewhat lower level of reliability than the five-year benchmarks, because data on employment, school enrollments, retail sales, and other series helpful in estimating time allocations are available on annual or even shorter-term bases.

All public data systems relating to population numbers and characteristics would be used directly or indirectly in arriving at the estimated time-allocation matrices. Hence, it should be possible to link demographic accounts and models of the types developed by Stone (1971, 1975) for the OECD and the United Nations to time-allocation matrices based on behavior setting genotypes at the national level.

Time-Allocation Matrices for BEA Economic Areas and Other Large Urban-Centered Regions

As of 1977, the BEA had clustered the 3,000 or more counties of the United States into an exhaustive set of 183 BEA Economic Areas. These areas are delineated in such a way that very few persons residing in one area commute to work in any other. Because trips to schools, churches, and shopping centers are, on average, considerably shorter than the journey to work, people who reside in a BEA Area during a given year spend nearly all their living-time within its boundaries. Nearly all the OT of the area's behavior settings is contributed by the area's own residents; hence, time-allocation matrices based on behavior setting data should quite accurately describe the life styles of those residents.

The establishments included in public data systems for the United States as a whole can be allocated exhaustively among the BEA Areas. The procedures used for translating industry data into genotype estimates at the U.S. level would have to be replicated for each BEA Area. These areas range in population from 100,000 to 10,000,000 or more, but at least two-thirds of the areas have populations of less than 1,000,000.

It may be that no single BEA Area contains settings from all of the assumed 400 U.S.-level genotypes. In general, the more populous areas will include larger numbers of genotypes, but the progression of genotype numbers with population size will be quite moderate. Recall that Midwest, with its town-and-trade area population of about 1,600, had 198 genotypes in 1963–64.

Some BEA Economic Areas contain two or more home-to-work commuting fields, or *functional economic areas* (Fox & Kumar, 1965). Thus, the Des Moines BEA Area (as delineated in 1969) contained 26 counties and a total population of nearly 800,000. Eight of these counties, with a combined population of 500,000, constituted the Des Moines commuting field, centered on the city of Des Moines (SMSA population about 330,000). Ten other counties constituted the Ottumwa commuting field, with a total population of 150,000, centered on Ottumwa with its 30,000 residents. The remaining eight counties formed two separate clusters with populations of 50,000–80,000 and more limited arrays of wholesale functions and occupations than are found in complete commuting fields.

Because most economic data are available on a county basis, it should be technically possible to translate establishment data into estimates for behavior setting genotypes in individual counties and in any cluster or aggregate of two or more counties. However, the individual counties within a commuting field are "wide-open systems"; for example, more than half of the employed residents of Warren County, Iowa, are employed in adjacent Polk County, which contains the city of Des Moines. Warren County residents also spend much time in the shopping, recreational, community college, and other facilities of Des Moines. Thus, Warren County is not a "natural human-ecological unit"; it is an arbitrary political one.

Similarly, the mere facts that a town has a name, a budget, and jurisdiction over certain activities within the town limits do not make it a complete ecological unit for social accounting purposes. For those purposes, the "natural" ecological unit is the town *plus* its retail trade, school and church attendance, and voluntary association membership areas. We can illustrate the importance of this consideration with some Barker and Schoggen (1973) data for Midwest, from which we have compiled Tables 12.6–12.8.

Table 12.6 shows that nonresidents contributed slightly more than half of the total OT of Midwest's behavior settings in the School and Church authority systems, slightly less than half in the Voluntary Association authority system, and about 39 and 28 percent respectively in the Government and Private Enterprise authority systems; the weighted average over all five systems was 40 percent.

Table 12.7 shows that about half of the claim-operations by number in the Church and Voluntary Association systems were performed by non-

TABLE 12.6

Person-Hours of Occupancy Time in Behavior Settings,
by Authority System, in Midwest, Kansas, 1963–64

Authority system	Number of settings	Total OT	By town residents	By non-residents	OT by town residents as % of total
		OCCUPANCY TIME (in person-hours)			
Private Enterprise	132	734,183	531,555	202,628	72.4
Government	114	308,075	186,896	121,179	60.7
School	233	650,124	310,516	339,608	47.8
Church	193	69,753	33,173	36,580	47.6
Voluntary Association	212	118,595	62,994	55,601	53.1
Total	884	1,880,730	1,125,134	755,596	59.8
		PERCENTAGES			
Private Enterprise	14.9	39.0	47.2	26.8	
Government	12.9	16.4	16.6	16.0	
School	26.4	34.6	27.6	45.0	
Church	21.8	3.7	3.0	4.8	
Voluntary Association	24.0	6.3	5.6	7.4	
Total	100.0	100.0	100.0	100.0	

TABLE 12.7

Habitat-Claims and Claim-Operations in Behavior
Settings, by Authority System, in Midwest, Kansas, 1963–64

Authority system	Habitat claims for operatives	Claim-operations			
		Total	By town residents	By non-residents	Town residents as % of total
Private Enterprise	450	694	439	255	63.3
Government	740	1,306	453	853	34.7
School	3,999	5,316	2,149	3,167	40.4
Church	1,682	2,581	1,289	1,292	49.9
Voluntary association	3,349	4,352	2,312	2,040	53.1
Total	10,220	14,249	6,642	7,607	46.6

residents, very much in line with their shares of OT. Claim-operations in the School authority system included performances by high school athletes and officials from several other school districts; performers in court cases and hearings came from all parts of Midwest County; and there was evidently a higher rate of turnover among nonresident workers in the Private Enterprise settings than among workers residing in the town itself.

TABLE 12.8
Inhabitant-Setting Intersections, by Zones Within
Behavior Settings, in Midwest, Kansas, 1963–64

	Numbers			% of total performed by town residents
Measure	Total	By town residents	By non-residents	
Leader acts (zones 6 and 5)	2,104	1,482	622	70.4
Other claim-operations (zone 4)	12,145	5,160	6,985	42.5
Total claim-operations (zones 6, 5, and 4)	14,249	6,642	7,607	46.6
Other inhabitant-setting intersections (zones 3, 2, and 1)	115,831	44,167	71,664	38.1
Total inhabitant-setting intersections, all zones	130,080	50,809	79,271	39.1

Over the five authority systems combined, nonresidents accounted for 53 percent of all claim-operations.

Table 12.8 partitions three categories of inhabitant-setting intersections (ISI) between town residents and nonresidents. Town residents were responsible for 70 percent of the leader acts (performances in zones 6 and 5). However, nonresidents provided 58 percent of the performances in zone 4 (other claim-operations) and 62 percent of the ISIs in zones 3, 2, and 1 of Midwest's behavior settings.

We note again that nonresidents contributed slightly more than half of the total OT of Schools and Churches in Midwest and only slightly less than half of the total OT of Voluntary Associations. Apparently, the attendance and membership areas of these three authority systems were virtually coextensive and contained about the same number of residents in the open country as in the town. These same open-country residents most likely accounted as customers for about half of the retail sales and personal services of Midwest's private enterprises; a large part of the OT of private enterprises attributed to town residents reflected their roles as proprietors and employees.

As a full-convenience trade center with an elementary school, a high school, three or four churches, and a number of voluntary associations (not to mention the county courthouse), Midwest and about 50 square miles of the countryside surrounding it formed a relatively complete and self-contained community. If each ISI is viewed as a line on a large map connecting a particular individual to one of the town's behavior settings, the array of settings connected to an open-country resident would probably be nearly identical with the array connected to a town resident of the same age and sex. Beyond a certain radius, very few country residents would be connected with Midwest's behavior settings; rather, they would be connected with similar arrays of settings in other towns ten miles or so from Midwest.

A community with this degree of completeness and closure is the smallest territorial unit for which a complete set of social accounts might be justified. If Midwest lost its high school, over 20 percent of the total OT contributed by nonresidents would be diverted to another location; if it also lost its elementary school, another 20–25 percent of nonresident OT would be diverted. The resulting travel patterns of open-country residents to new consolidated schools might also encourage shopping and recreation at centers other than Midwest.

Extending Time-Allocation Matrices from Small Communities to Successively Larger Urban-Centered Regions

Nearly all the genotypes Barker found in Midwest also existed in hundreds of other U.S. towns with town-and-trade area populations of 1,500 to 2,500. About 25 of Midwest's genotypes in the Government authority system were associated with its status as a county seat; most of them were replicated in every other U.S. town that also served as a county seat, though they would have been most easily identified in county-seat towns of 5,000 population or less.

It has been amply documented that, within a given society, nearly all "residentiary" or consumer-oriented functions found at one level in a central-place hierarchy are also found at every higher level. Borchert and Adams (1963) classified central places in a five-state area just north of Kansas according to the presence or absence of selected retail and wholesale functions. According to their criteria, Midwest in 1963–64 would have been classified as a *full-convenience* retail trade center. Six additional types of retail stores (usually found in U.S. towns of 2,500–5,000 people) would have qualified it as a *partial* shopping center; a further increment of five additional types of retail stores (usually found in towns of 5,000–15,000) would have qualified it as a *complete* shopping center. The next higher level, a *secondary wholesale-retail* center, included several more types of retail stores and at least 10 of 14 specified types of wholesale suppliers. The highest level included all 14 wholesale functions; these *primary wholesale-retail* centers served city-and-wholesale trade area populations of 250,000 or more.

Analogous progressions exist in some other divisions of the Private Enterprise authority system, in the School and Government systems, in some Church and Voluntary Association systems, and in the Health and Medical Care system (which Barker did not have to consider separately within the town of Midwest).

The main point is that additional genotypes would have to be added to the list of 198 found in Midwest at each successive level in the central-place hierarchy. The numbers of genotypes added at each stage would not be large; 15 additional genotypes in retail trade (a florist, a photo studio, a music store, a shoe store, and a few others) plus 14 in wholesale trade would satisfy the Borchert-Adams criteria for a primary wholesale-retail center. We have conjectured that the number of genotypes in the United States as a whole may be about 400.

In nearly all cases, the Borchert-Adams primary wholesale-retail trade centers are also the central cities of commuting fields and the largest cities in the corresponding BEA Economic Areas. This is also true of some cities in the Borchert-Adams *secondary* wholesale-retail trade center class.

Each trade center has a corresponding trade area. In Iowa, some individual counties are virtually coextensive with the trade areas of their county-seat towns; the towns would qualify as partial or complete shopping centers. Such counties would be suitable units for time-allocation matrices if the volume of out-commuting is fairly small.

Moving from Small Community Up

Eco-behavioral scientists in Barker's sense may be more comfortable with an approach that starts with Midwest and its trade area and moves up the Borchert-Adams hierarchy step by step. At each step, settings of additional genotypes would be identified, their programs spelled out, and their ratings on action patterns and other attributes estimated. A clear understanding of "what goes on here" might be retained for several steps—perhaps up to central cities of 300,000 and total commuting field populations of 500,000. Insights concerning shortcuts, data sources, and sampling techniques might be gained at each step. The last level hypothesized is equivalent to Des Moines and its eight-county commuting field. The other components of the Des Moines BEA Economic Area would be much simpler and easier to comprehend.

Within this area, many different procedures for estimating consistent time-allocation matrices for counties, towns and trade areas, and even Census tracts could be explored. The step from BEA Areas to U.S. totals is a rather short one and can probably be taken without seriously disturbing our estimates of time allocations among the various subareas of, say, the Des Moines BEA Area.

The Development of Social Accounts
Based on Behavior Settings

In the third section of this chapter, we pointed out that the development of economic accounts and data systems after 1933 received strong support from the U.S. government. As an outgrowth of experience during the New Deal period and World War II, it became clear that only the federal government had the fiscal capacity and the monetary instruments to cause deliberate massive changes in the level and direction of national economic activity.

The Employment Act of 1946 assigned substantial responsibility to the president and to Congress for using these powers to promote high, stable levels of employment, income, and production. The proper exercise of these powers required relevant, accurate, and timely economic data. The economy was recognized to be a highly interdependent system, rather quickly responsive to major policy changes. A few widely known indicators—the unemployment rate, the consumer price index, and the prime interest rate—were taken as summary measures of the state of the economy as a whole.

Support for social indicators was much more difficult to muster, and this situation may continue, at least for a time, despite publication of the OECD list. We tend to compartmentalize the social concerns listed in Table 12.1 into a health problem, an education problem, a housing problem, a crime problem, an air pollution problem, a noise problem, and so on. The indicators are not widely publicized or understood. We recognize intuitively that measureable improvements at the national level will come slowly, because they depend on motivating students, teachers, health-care workers, employers, police officers, state and local government officials, and others in thousands of communities, millions of establishments, and a hundred million behavior settings.

Although the policies are slow-acting and the real costs of implementation are high, the values assignable to improvements in these indicators are majestically large. The value of an increase of one year of healthful life for the U.S. population should be at least as great as that of a year's GNP (4.2 *trillion* dollars in 1986), and probably some small multiple of that amount. Improvements in all aspects of the physical environment listed in Table 12.1 involve rearranging and upgrading major components of our total stock of physical capital (gross value about four years' GNP if built new).

We could perhaps dramatize the implications of Table 12.1 by following up on a suggestion made on page 289 above. Suppose changes in the 33 indicators from their values in some base year were treated as outputs of changes in the numbers of person-hours allocated to the various behavior setting genotypes, changes in the values of physical capital assigned to each, and improvements in the productivities of genotypes per person-hour and per dollar of physical capital. As of July 1, 1986, the U.S. population was estimated at 241.5 million. At 8,760 hours a year, the total living-time of the population during 1986 was 2.12 trillion person-hours. At the 1979 ratio of physical capital to GNP, the gross value of physical capital and consumer durables used in conjunction with these person-hours was about 16.8 trillion dollars. About 10 percent of the person-hours and perhaps 40 percent of the value of physical capital plus consumer durables were used in, or in support of, settings that produced the GNP of 4.2 trillion dollars. It would be useful to include GNP as a social system output along with the OECD indicators.

Perhaps 35 percent of total person-hours and 15 percent of physical capital plus durables are used in the "activity" of sleeping and resting. The remaining resources, perhaps 55 percent of all person-hours and 45 percent of physical capital plus durables, are used in waking activities other than gainful employment. It is hard to avoid the judgment that the value of these activities to the participants is equivalent to at least twice the GNP, and that the value of all social outputs, economic and non-economic combined, is equivalent to at least three times the GNP.

In this hypothetical table, all living-time, behavioral inputs, and physical capital available to the society in a given year would be represented as used in, or in support of, the standing behavior patterns of its behavior setting genotypes. If changes in the various OECD indicators and GNP could be accurately attributed to changes in the amounts and qualities of resources used in specified genotypes, then the *resource costs* of accomplishing unit improvements in the various indicators could be estimated and compared. The *values* of unit improvements could be estimated in various ways; in some cases the "value judgments" might vary over a wide range.

Terleckyj (1975), in a path-breaking study, developed a table similar in some respects to the one suggested here. His output variables were the maximum improvements in each of 22 indicators (such as life expectancy) that were judged to be technically possible within a ten-year period in the absence of resource constraints. He identified some 31 programs that, if operated simultaneously over the decade at specified levels of GNP cost, should collectively produce the estimated maximum improvements in all 22 indicators.

The overriding constraint on the total cost of all 31 programs was the projected GNP *minus* the cost of continuing other GNP expenditure patterns at their base-year levels. Terleckyj concluded that the GNP cost of achieving the 22 maximum improvements would be two or three times the amount available for the 31 programs. He then estimated the program costs of less ambitious goals, such as achieving one-third or half of the maximum improvements in all indicators. The relationships of indicator improvements to program expenditures were not necesarily proportional or linear.

Terleckyj did not prescribe what *should* be done; he estimated the costs of what *could* be done. His table captured the interdependence of the social system by showing that (for example) a program directly aimed at reducing highway fatalities and injuries would also increase life expectancy, reduce short-term and long-term disabilities, increase GNP, reduce the number of persons living in poverty, and so on. Similarly, several different programs might affect the same indicator. Terleckyj made no use of behavior setting concepts. He did not use data on stocks of physical capital and consumer durables, and he did not attempt a complete allocation of time.

Federal statistical agencies are currently collecting most of the basic data required for the individual OECD indicators. This is expensive and time-consuming, and it requires sizable professional, clerical, and data processing staffs on a continuing basis. For the next few years, research on integrating these and other data into more elaborate frameworks—including social system accounts and models—should perhaps be left to scientists in universities and private research organizations until consensus is reached on a few well-defined alternative accounting systems. Financial support for much of this research could, of course, come from federal agencies.

A single research team could perhaps carry out the pilot attempts described in this chapter to develop methods for translating existing public data systems into time-allocation matrices and social accounts based on behavior settings at all levels, from small communities and counties to the United States as a whole. The effort should continue for several years and its archives should go to some permanent institution or agency that would make them generally accessible to other research workers.

Published data from the U.S. censuses of population and housing could be used to extend some elements of a social accounting system from the national level through BEA Economic Areas, commuting fields, and counties down to townships, villages, and towns in rural areas and to census tracts, enumeration districts, and blocks within SMSAs and urbanized areas. These same data are used by local governments currently, in conjunction with primary data needed for their various functions (such as street, water, and sewer system maintenance; planning and zoning; traffic control; public health; police and fire protection; public school administration; parks and playgrounds; and abatement of excessive noise levels and air pollution). Local governments could, if they chose, adapt behavior setting accounts to the analysis of alternative policies in their own departments. Within a comprehensive behavior setting and time-allocation framework, they should be better able to distinguish between policies that merely shift a problem between neighborhoods or departmental jurisdictions and policies that are likely to solve a problem in situ and/or with minimal adverse effects on other neighborhoods and programs.

Experimentation with social accounts and models based on behavior settings could proceed at several levels and on many independent initiatives. Official data systems are most fully developed at the national level. Comparability among the official data systems of many countries has been promoted by international organizations (such as the United Nations and OECD) since the late 1940's, so that experimental accounts for one country should demonstrate potentials and problems that would be relevant to many others.

At some stage, international organizations might undertake the task of promoting a consensus as to those aspects of the accounts that were ready for widespread implementation at a given time. A U.N. publication, prepared by Stone (1975) and reflecting the suggestions of statisticians from many countries, makes concrete proposals for accounts and data systems covering 19 areas of economic and social concern; pilot efforts should be made to reformulate these as (or in) a comprehensive eco-behavioral system.

Local governments could experiment with accounts based on behavior settings to see if they clarify some of their planning and administrative decision problems. We hope that unintended consequences of proposed changes in the physical, economic, or social environments of the community could then be recognized and demonstrated within a behavior setting and time-allocation framework for the community as a whole or for any subdivision of it that was nearly self-contained with respect to a proposed change and its more obvious impacts.

An independent line of experimentation and research, which might be called *microsocial accounting*, could be carried on within organizations.

It would involve attempts to identify and measure the inputs and outputs of each type of setting in an organization using Barker's rating scales, SOC-*DOT* measures of job complexity and worker traits, and the organization's financial and other accounts and output measures. Some components of existing simulation models of organizations could be reformulated in terms of categories of behavior settings.

Barker and associates (1978) made extensive applications of behavior setting concepts to schools, hospitals, churches, and other kinds of organizations. However, they have not yet tried to link these concepts with the economic accounts of organizations or with the organizational counterparts of comprehensive social accounts. Organizations would be justified in implementing and maintaining such accounts and related models if they were sufficiently helpful in planning and decisionmaking and in explaining themselves to employees, members, and other constituencies.

Some Broader Implications of Behavior Settings for the Social Sciences

In my judgment, the implications of behavior settings for the social sciences are far-reaching and profound. I believe that the behavior setting concept may come to play as important a role in the social sciences as the cell concept does in biology. It seems to me that the interests of several disciplines converge in behavior settings. All roles are played in them; all organizations are composed of them. Felson (1979) asserts that all sociologically interesting phenomena involving direct physical contact between persons occur in behavior settings, and that they appear to be ideal units for describing and modeling social processes. Behavior settings in nonmarket organizations seem to be empirically valid analogues of the economist's markets. Small group phenomena occur in behavior settings; they can be viewed from the standpoints of group dynamics, transactional analysis, game theory, and the theory of teams. Lewin's (1951) concept of an individual's life-space remains intact as the means by which a behavior setting secures the behavior appropriate to it.

Public data systems are not discipline oriented. Barker's (1968; Barker & Associates, 1978) description of human activities and communities in terms of behavior settings is singularly free of borrowings from sociology, anthropology, economics, or any traditional field of psychology. He started from a base in experimental psychology under Calvin Stone and Kurt Lewin and psychological measurement under Lewis Terman, but he turned his skills in a direction entirely his own—to the systematic observation of naturally occurring human behavior in complete communities. He continued in this direction from 1947 to 1972 with substantial research support. Until 1968, he described his research as ecological psychology—that is, as a distinctive field within psychology. Since 1969 he has recognized the need for "an eco-behavioral science independent of psychology" but certainly not coextensive with any other established science (see Chap. 14 of this volume).

Barker's research program has been one of the most original in the recent history of the social and behavioral sciences. Its legacy is an eco-behavioral view of human societies that is comprehensive in scope yet concrete and operational in detail.

13

Behavior Settings in Relation to Other Concepts

We turn next to a consideration of behavior settings in relation to a number of concepts from social science and the field of environment and behavior. It appears that workers in several related fields have more or less independently developed concepts that have much in common with behavior settings. There are some points of obvious similarity between behavior settings and, for example, the well-established concepts of status and role as found in sociology, anthropology, and social psychology. In addition, however, we want to identify briefly a number of other concepts, perhaps less familiar than role and status to many social scientists, that indicate concern with phenomena related to behavior settings. Here our main purpose is to consider such concepts in relation to behavior settings and to suggest where they and behavior settings may fit within the broad structure of social science.

It seems to us that behavior settings anchor one end of a continuum of such concepts because they are concerned strictly with the nonpsychological, objective, preperceptual, or ecological environment of molar human behavior. Most closely related to behavior settings on such a dimension are Gibson's affordances, Hagerstrand's domain, and Melbin's spant. Although Chapin's activity patterns appear to be concerned with objective behavior sequences, the method of study relies heavily on self-report by individuals rather than on independent observation of behavior patterns. The concepts of status, role, and customs as used in sociology, anthropology, and social psychology focus on social structure, but the writings of most role theorists display a strongly person-centered orientation. The other concepts reviewed here—Forgas' social episodes, Goffman's frame analysis, and Schank and Abelson's scripts—target aspects of psychological reality of particular persons, and the concern is with describing and understanding the behavior and cognitions of individuals rather than the concrete, ecological environment of molar behavior.

Gibson's Affordances

In James Gibson's 1979 book, *The Ecological Approach to Visual Perception*, he defines affordances as what the environment *"offers* the animal, what it *provides* or *furnishes*, either for good or ill. The verb *to afford* is found in the dictionary, but the noun *affordance* is not. I have made it up. I mean by it something that refers to both the environment and the animal in a way that no existing term does. It implies the complementarity of the animal and the environment" (p. 127; emphasis in original). As an illustration of an affordance, Gibson, with characteristic candor and directness, says:

If a terrestrial surface is nearly horizontal (instead of slanted), nearly flat (instead of convex or concave), and sufficiently extended (relative to the size of the animal) and if its substance is rigid (relative to the weight of the animal), then the surface *affords support*. It is a surface of support, and we call it a substratum, ground, or floor. It is stand-on-able, permitting an upright posture for quadrupeds and bipeds. It is therefore walk-on-able and run-over-able. It is not sink-into-able like a surface of water or a swamp, that is, not for heavy terrestrial animals. Support for water bugs is different. . . . Terrestrial surfaces, of course, are also climb-on-able or fall-off-able or get-under-neath-able relative to the animal. Different layouts afford different behaviors for different animals, and different mechanical encounters. The human species in some cultures has the habit of sitting as distinguished from kneeling or squatting. If a surface of support with the four properties is also knee-high above the ground, it affords sitting on. We call it a *seat* in general, or a stool, bench, chair, and so on, in particular. It may be natural like a ledge or artificial like a couch. It may have various shapes, as long as its functional layout is that of a seat. The color and texture of the surface are irrelevant. Knee-high for a child is not the same as knee-high for an adult, so the affordance is relative to the size of the individual. But if a surface is horizontal, flat, extended, rigid, and knee-high relative to the perceiver, it can in fact be sat upon. If it can be discriminated as having just these properties, it should *look* sit-on-able. If it does, the affordance is perceived visually. If the surface properties are seen relative to the body surfaces, the self, they constitute a seat and have meaning [pp. 127–28; emphasis in original].

The concept of affordance is not limited to the physical environment, however; other living beings also provide the individual with crucially important environmental affordances:

The other animals afford, above all, a rich and complex set of interactions, sexual, predatory, nurturing, fighting, playing, cooperating, and communicating. What other persons afford, comprises the whole realm of social significance for human beings. We pay closest attention to the optical and acoustic information that specifies what the other person is, invites, threatens, and does [p. 128].

Gibson's view of where environmental affordances lie on the psychological or subjective versus the nonpsychological or objective dimension is expressed as follows:

An important fact about the affordances of the environment is that they are in a sense objective, real, and physical, unlike values and meanings, which are often supposed to be subjective, phenomenal, and mental. But actually, an affordance is neither an objective property nor a subjective property; or it is both if you like. An affordance cuts across the dichotomy of subjective-objective and helps us to understand its inadequacy. It is equally a fact of the environment and a fact of behavior. It is both physical and psychical, yet neither. An affordance points both ways, to the environment and to the observer.

The niche [a set of affordances] for a certain species should not be confused with what some animal psychologists have called the *phenomenal environment* of the species. This can be taken erroneously to be the "private world" in which the species is supposed to live, the "subjective world," or the world of "consciousness." The behavior of observers depends on their perception of the environment, surely enough, but this does not mean that their behavior depends on a so-called private or subjective or conscious environment. The organism depends on its environment for its life, but the environment does not depend on the organism for its existence [p. 129].

These excerpts make clear that the views of Gibson about the environment in relation to the behavior of any given inhabitant are very similar to those of Barker: both are concerned with the objective, preperceptual environment that exists out there independent of the psychological processes of any particular observer or actor. We know of no evidence that Barker, in writing *Ecological Psychology*, was aware of Gibson's work, and Gibson's 1979 book makes only a passing reference to Barker:

Environmentalism is a powerful movement nowadays, but in psychology it has generated more enthusiasm than discipline. There is no central core of theoretical concepts on which to base it. The right conceptual level has not yet been found. This book makes an effort to find the right level. A few psychologists, such as E. Brunswik (1956) and R. G. Barker (1968), have moved in this direction, but none has ended with the sort of theory being put forward here [pp. 2–3].

Gibson's insistence on beginning with this concept of the environment as independent of any perceiver is all the more impressive in view of his primary interest in the field of visual perception. That Gibson and Barker, working independently in fields as different as perception and the development of social behavior and personality in children, should develop systems based on virtually the same conception of the environment suggests that the ecological environment deserves serious consideration by other behavioral scientists.

Hagerstrand's Domain

Torsten Hagerstrand, the pioneer geographer of the Lund school, has introduced the concept of *domain* into his work in what is known as "time geography" as part of a broader effort to develop a kind of space-time ecology. He says:

We need a geography today which helps us to see ourselves, our fellow passengers and our total environment in a more coherent way than we are presently capable of doing. To me, the answer seems to lie in the study of the interwoven distribution of states and events in coherent blocks of space-time [Hagerstrand, 1978, p. 123].

Although this approach has not been fully developed nor extensively applied, Hagerstrand offers some illustrative analyses. He describes the concept of domain as central:

It refers to a specific kind of social construct brought into being in order to secure a certain amount of order and predictability in human affairs. The concept . . . refers to the intricate lattice of *earthbound spatial units* in which specified individuals or groups have socially recognized rights to exert control. In this sense the domain appears in all scales from informal divisions *inside a home, over work-rooms, real-estate units and municipal territories up to states and confederations. . . .* But . . . the concept *also stands for "position" ("office")* that is to say for a derived "space" which by contrast gives its holder certain rights as well as duties [ibid., p. 124; emphasis added].

Hagerstrand suggests that a complete record be made in sequence of all the transactions of a person with each other person and object in each domain throughout the person's entire lifetime. The actual analyses that he reports, however, are much less ambitious—for example, a study of all the occupants of a single farm in Sweden from 1840 to 1940. Though still in an early stage of development, Hagerstrand's approach with its central concept of domain appears to offer a promising way of studying the environment as encountered in everyday life. It shares with the behavior settings approach a clear focus on the ecological, as opposed to the psychological, environment of behavior.

Melbin's Spant

The importance of time in imposing both order and constraints upon human activities has been recognized by a number of investigators, not so prominently in psychology as in related social science fields, especially sociology and geography. Studies of time use appeared as early as Bevans' 1913 book, *How Working Men Spend Their Time*. Sorokin and Berger's 1939 book, *Time-Budgets of Human Behavior*, includes data from self-reports of 100 subjects on their activities 24 hours per day, every day for four weeks. Under the editorship of Szalai and several associates, a monumental report on time-use studies in several nations was published in 1972. One of the clearest statements on the importance of the time dimension in environment-behavior research appears in a book, *Man, Time, and Society*, by an economist, W. E. Moore (1963):

> Much of social behavior depends for its orderly qualities on common definitions, assumptions, and actions with regard to the location of events in time. Certain activities, for example, require simultaneous actions by a number of persons, or at least their presence at a particular time—the starting of a work shift at a factory, the departure of a fishing boat from a wharf or beach, or the calling of an association meeting to order. Thus one element of temporal ordering is *synchronization*. Other activities require that actions follow one another in a prescribed order; thus *sequence* is a part of the temporal order. For still other activities, the frequency of events during a period of time is critical; thus *rate* also is one of the ways that time impinges on social behavior. For all these elements of social coordination the term *timing* is useful . . . timing is an intrinsic quality of personal and collective behavior. If activities have no temporal order, they have no order at all [pp. 8–9; emphasis in original].

There is lively interest in time in the field of geography as well. Under the arresting title *Timing Space and Spacing Time*, Carlstein, Parkes, and

Thrift have edited a three-volume series that appeared in 1978. The second volume in this series, *Human Activity and Time Geography*, is a treasure trove of papers that say a lot about the state of current thinking in the area by geographers, although the book does include some papers by psychologists and sociologists. One of these was written by Murray Melbin, a sociologist at Boston University. His primary focus is on temporal ecology, and he suggests the term *spant*, an acronym for *sp*ace *an*d *t*ime unit, to help us think about the problem:

> The size could be noted as appropriately needed by subscripts referring precisely to longitudes, latitudes, dates and hours of the day. Several diverse understandings suggest themselves for this label. History is the study of spants. A treatise on Elizabethan England refers to a certain place during a certain era. When a parent tells a youngster "this is not the time or place to behave like that," the childrearing effort has been focused on a spant. The idea of human destiny is improved by thinking of *people-per* spant. . . .
>
> To chart a city in spants, one would have to set the sizes of the space and time boundaries per unit . . . the spants for day-time in the central business district will be very dense. Those for night-time in the same place will be extremely sparse. . . .
>
> We can trace the movements of individuals along series of spants. Two people may not encounter one another merely by having been in the same place. Nor are there good odds that they will meet just because they are up and outside their dwellings at the same time. They probably will meet if they are in the same spant [Melbin, 1978a, pp. 101–2; emphasis in original].

Although the spant has not been utilized extensively in empirical studies, the concept seems significant nonetheless because it, like the behavior setting, is one of the few unit concepts proposed in social science that include both space and time as integral parts of the unit definition. Melbin's interest in temporal ecology is demonstrated in another fascinating paper (1978b) concerning the opening up of "the frontier of the night"—the worldwide trend toward 24-hour operation of many organized activities, including retail businesses, industrial establishments, and entertainment facilities.

Chapin's Activity Patterns

F. Stuart Chapin, a sociologist at the University of North Carolina at Chapel Hill, has described an approach that centers on the concept of *ac-*

tivity patterns. His 1974 work develops the underlying rationale for the
study of activity patterns, translates this approach into an analytical strat-
egy, and examines field techniques used in making it operational. He also
reports empirical results from a large city and a national sample. He describes an activity as "a classificatory term for a variety of acts grouped
together under a more generic category":

> The nature and the extent of the grouping . . . are dictated by the uses
> to which activity data are put. For example, an activity class might be
> simply "shopping," but it might be (1) driving from home to the shop-
> ping center, (2) buying groceries, and (3) driving home again. It might
> also consist of (1) driving from home to the shopping center; (2) hunting
> for a parking space; (3) parking the car; (4) walking from the parking lot
> to the supermarket; (5) picking up a cart, walking the aisles, and select-
> ing grocery items; (6) going through the check-out line, paying the
> checker, and waiting for the groceries to be packed in bags; (7) carrying
> the groceries to the parking lot and loading them into the car; (8) driv-
> ing home; (9) carrying the grocery bags into the kitchen; and (10) put-
> ting the groceries away. If the concern is simply with shopping as a phe-
> nomenon of our culture and the gross time allocation involved, then the
> first definition is adequate; if the concern is with public transportation
> planning, the second breakdown may be a more logical one. If the con-
> cern has to do with studying the supermarket chain's merchandising en-
> vironment with a view to attracting a larger share of the market, the
> third breakdown may be the most appropriate. . . .
>
> An activity has . . . *a duration, a position in time, a place in the se-
> quence of events, and a fixed location or path in space.*
>
> "Activity pattern" refers to a tendency for people in a given popula-
> tion to behave in a similar way. More precisely, . . . existence of a "pat-
> tern" means that some criterion for the minimum number of persons in
> a population engaging in the activity has been established. . . . Activity
> patterns are measured primarily in mean hours of duration and mean
> locus of an activity [pp. 36–37; emphasis added].

Chapin and colleagues have studied activity patterns using both eth-
nographic and survey research methods, including structured interviews
in which subjects are asked to list things they actually did the previous
day and when and where they did them. Activities so reported are listed
in a sort of dictionary of 225 specific activity codes (categories)—such as
picnics and outings, carpentry, and visiting library, which were later col-
lapsed into 40 activity classes for some purposes—but most of the data are
reported in terms of 12 broader groupings, such as main job, eating, shopping, and homemaking. The book reports many interesting findings on activity patterns so measured, including data on how many subjects en-

gaged in each of the 12 main activities during each of the 24 hours of the day. Chapin's work provides some important data on behavior in the real-world contexts of everyday life. Although the concern in this approach is with activity patterns of individual behavior rather than with the environment, and although the method relies heavily on self-report, the resulting descriptions of activities bear resemblance to behavior settings.

Status and Role

In considering where behavior settings may fit into the range of social science concepts such as culture, society, status, and role, it seems necessary to begin with a review of how such terms have been used in the field. We cannot, of course, do justice to the voluminous literature dealing with these and related concepts, but some discussion of the relation between the concepts of role and status and behavior settings is needed. Although there is considerable variation among definitions of these terms given by different writers, it may suffice for our purposes here to take the views of the eminent anthropologist Ralph Linton as our starting point.

In his pioneering formulation, Linton (1936) describes culture as the social heredity of human beings, the mechanism that "serves to adapt the individual to his place in society as well as to his natural environment" (p. 85). Involved is "the capacity of human beings to learn, to communicate with each other, and to transmit learned behavior from generation to generation" (p. 78). Central to this process is the training of new individuals for particular positions in society. "The new members must be divided into various categories, and those of each category taught to do different things. The society must also develop more or less conscious patterns of what the behavior of individuals in certain positions should be so that it will have guides to the training of these individuals" (p. 99). Such patterns are thought to originate in remembered and rationalized behavior and are subject to a process of continual modification as required by changing objective environmental conditions. Linton makes clear that such ideal patterns exist in people's minds and that they rarely coincide closely with actual behavior:

> In spite of their origin in behavior and their susceptibility to modification through changing behavior, ideal patterns are something quite distinct from behavior. As systems of ideas they become a part of the culture of the group and are transmitted from generation to generation by conscious instruction as well as imitation. While they guide society in its attempts to shape the individual, they are also guides to the individ-

ual in situations for which he has not been specifically trained. The fact that such patterns are conscious makes it possible for them to survive the interruption of their expression in overt behavior for a considerable period [p. 100].

Although the ideal patterns are carried in the minds of individuals and can find overt expression only through the medium of individuals, the fact that they are shared by many members of the society gives them a super-individual character. They persist, while those who share them come and go [p. 102].

We note parenthetically here the striking similarity of Linton's ideal patterns, with their super-individual character, and Barker's standing patterns of behavior in behavior settings, with their extra-individual character.

The combination of all these ideal patterns collectively constitutes the social system of the society. For smooth functioning of the society, different things have to be done by different individuals. "Consequently, the patterns which control the activities of individuals must be adjusted in such a way that these activities can be carried on without mutual interference" (p. 105).

According to Linton, these ideal patterns are implemented through the operation of statuses and roles. The following statements from Linton (1936) summarize the view of status and role identified in the sociological literature as *functional role theory* as espoused, for example, by Linton, Parsons (1951), Bates and Harvey (1975), and Nye (1976).

A status, as distinct from the individual who may occupy it, is simply a collection of rights and duties [p. 113].

A *role* represents the dynamic aspect of a status. The individual is socially assigned to a status and occupies it with relation to other statuses. When he puts the rights and duties which constitute the status into effect, he is performing a role. Role and status are quite inseparable, and the distinction between them is of only academic interest. There are no roles without statuses or statuses without roles. Just as in the case of *status*, the term *role* is used with a double significance. Every individual has a series of roles deriving from the various patterns in which he participates and at the same time *a role*, general, which represents the sum total of these roles and determines what he does for his society and what he can expect from it.

Although all statuses and roles derive from social patterns and are integral parts of patterns, they have an independent function with relation to the individuals who occupy particular statuses and exercise their roles. To such individuals the combined status and role represent the minimum of attitudes and behavior which he must assume if he is to participate in the overt expression of the pattern. Status and role serve to reduce the ideal patterns for social life to individual terms. They become models for organizing the attitudes and behavior of the individual so that these will be congruous with those of the other individuals participating in the expression of the pattern [p. 114; emphasis in original].

Following World War II, writings on roles appeared with increasing frequency, and many prominent figures of sociology and social psychology published both theoretical and empirical papers concerned with various aspects of roles (see, for example, Merton, 1957; Newcomb, 1950; Parsons, 1951; Rommetveit, 1968). In their well-documented review and discussion of the history of role theory, Biddle and Thomas (1966) point out, however, that this literature contains a wide diversity of definitions of the role concept, a problem also discussed by Sarbin and Allen (1968) and more recently by Burr et al. (1979) and Biddle (1986). This diversity is summarized by Biddle and Thomas:

The idea of role has been used to denote prescription, description, evaluation, and action; it has referred to covert and overt processes, to the behavior of the self and others, to the behavior an individual initiates versus that which is directed to him. Perhaps the most common definition is that role is the set of prescriptions defining what the behavior of a position member should be. But this much agreement is at best but an oasis in a desert of diverging opinion. A careful review of the definitions reveals, however, that there is one nearly universal common denominator, namely, that the concept pertains to the behaviors of particular persons [p. 29].

Rommetveit (1968) expresses the same emphasis on the behavior of the individual:

Role behavior, we argue, is social interaction brought about by stereotyped expectations referring to the individual who plays the role and the latter's internalization of these expectations and resultant felt obligations. We do not assume that such expectations must be clearly recognized by the individual who plays the role to the extent that he can verbalize them as a list of "musts" and "must nots." He may be rather sensitive toward them even though they are never verbally expressed [p. 35].

It appears, therefore, that functional role theory's concern for ideal patterns of behavior is tied closely to the behavior of individual persons. The standing patterns of behavior in the behavior settings approach, by contrast, are tied not to persons but to specific physical-geographical-temporal loci.

In his recent review of developments in role theory, Biddle (1986) describes four other perspectives on roles as found in the literature of sociology and social psychology in addition to functional role theory: symbolic interactionism, structural role theory, organizational role theory, and cognitive role theory.

Symbolic interactionism dates back to Mead (1934) and emphasizes "the roles of individual actors, the evolution of roles through social interactions, and various cognitive concepts through which social actors understand and interpret their own and others' conduct" (Biddle, 1986, p. 71). Recent work in this tradition includes papers by Gordon (1976) on the development of role identities, by Stryker and Macke (1978) on similarities between status inconsistency and role conflict, and by Turner and Shosid (1976) on the effect of others' responses on interpretation of role behavior. The concept of roles appears to be about as closely tied to the behavior and experience of the individual in symbolic interactionism as it is in functional role theory.

Structural role theory gives "little attention to norms or other expectations for conduct. Instead, attention is focused on 'social structures,' conceived as stable organizations of sets of persons (called 'social positions' or 'statuses') who share the same, patterned behaviors ('roles') that are directed towards other sets of persons in the structure" (Biddle, 1986, p. 73). In this approach, popular problems include social networks, kinships, role sets, and exchange relationships. Recent work includes mathematically expressed, axiomatic theory concerning structured role relationships (Burt, 1976, 1982; Mandel, 1983).

Here the focus is more on the social environment and less on the individual. There is virtually no concern with a person's phenomenal experience. In this respect, structural role theory may be more similar than any other role theory perspective to the behavior setting approach.

Organizational role theory focuses on "social systems that are preplanned, task-oriented, and hierarchical. Roles in such organizations are assumed to be associated with identified social positions and to be generated by normative expectations, but norms may vary among individuals and may reflect both the official demands of the organizations and the pressures of informal groups" (Biddle, 1986, p. 73). Research within this conception of roles has addressed problems such as role conflict (Van Sell, Brief & Schuler, 1981; Fisher & Gitelson, 1983), role transition, and how an actor copes with changes in social position or expectations for the actor's position (Allen & van de Vliert, 1984).

The concern of organizational role theory for social positions in formal organizations parallels behavior setting research rather well, but the problems addressed by these role theorists appear to be more person-centered than environment-centered.

Cognitive role theory, which is closely linked with cognitive social psychology, has "focused on relationships between role expectations and behavior. Attention has been given to social conditions that give rise to expectations, to techniques for measuring expectations, and to the impact of expectations on social conduct" (Biddle, 1986, p. 74). Work in cognitive role theory includes the early paper by Moreno (1934) and more recent studies (such as McNamara & Blumer, 1982) on role playing; in addition see Sherif's (1936) pioneer work and later papers on group norms (Moreland & Levine, 1982; Hollander, 1985), theories of anticipatory role expectations (Brewer, Dull, & Lui, 1981; Duckro, Beal, & George, 1979), and role-taking (Enright & Lapsley, 1980; Underwood & Moore, 1982).

In cognitive role theory, the focus again is on the individual with considerable emphasis on expectations and their influence on behavior. The ecological environment of behavior setting work seems rather remote from this perspective on role theory.

In all of these perspectives in role theory, there is concern for the positions that persons occupy within the social structure. In these theories, the environment is represented in the roles and statuses that are elements of the social structure; they are examples of what Durkheim (1938) called social facts. In this sense, it is correct to say that the study of roles, like the study of behavior settings, is concerned with the environment of behavior.

The chief difference in the approaches to the environment as seen in the study of roles and in the study of behavior settings is this: Whereas behavior settings are based on patterns of behavior identified with particular physical-geographical-temporal contexts, roles refer to patterns of behavior that are associated with positions in the social structure of society.

This consistent linking of roles and statuses to positions in society is readily seen in work on many problems. *Ascribed statuses* are assigned to individuals on the basis of their enduring personal characteristics that show their position in the social structure (such as sex, age, family characteristics); *achieved statuses* are based on the accomplishments of an individual through effort and hence show the person's position based on "merit" (high school graduate, computer programmer). *Role performance* or *role enactment* (Sarbin & Allen, 1968) refers to the behavior of particular persons, given their position within society. Individuals are said to have multiple identities (Thoits, 1983) based on involvement in different roles (mother, wife, attorney-at-law, PTA president, Democratic party canvasser). *Role set* (Merton, 1957) identifies the complement of role relationships a person has by virtue of occupying a particular status. *Role conflict* (Stryker & Macke, 1978) and *role strain* (Goode, 1960; Sieber, 1974) concern incongruencies among the multiple roles a person carries out (such as being a good father versus spending more time and energy on one's career). *Role transitions* (George, 1980) occur when an individual gains or loses roles associated with changes in status (the student role is lost when the person graduates). *Role expectations* or *role prescriptions* refer to widely held ideas concerning appropriate behavior for an individual in carrying out a particular role.

It is of interest to note that roles associated with achieved status (violinist, president, teacher, pharmacist, chairperson) are closer to the behavior setting concept than are roles associated with ascribed status (mother, teenager, brother, man) because they are more closely tied to certain kinds of environmental contexts (a recital, a company or other organization, a classroom, a drugstore, a committee meeting). The ascribed roles, by contrast, are more trans-situational, going with the person from place to place.

Thus it seems that the study of roles and the study of behavior settings have much in common, representing different yet complementary contributions to the ecology of human behavior. Both roles and settings are centrally concerned with behavior patterns that remain largely unchanged when the occupants of either roles or settings change. Both roles and settings can be classified and described along similar dimensions, such as artistic, business, and educational. Both roles and settings vary in the degree of coerciveness that they impose upon their occupants. Roles are obviously related to settings in that settings constitute the environments of roles: the role of pharmacist is implemented in the drugstore setting; the role of music pupil occurs in the music lesson setting; the role of chairperson occurs in the business meeting setting. The study of behavior settings focuses on the properties, attributes, and characteristics of settings as environmental entities in which the standing patterns of behavior are prominent. The study of roles focuses on patterns of behavior associated with position in the social structure. One prominent writer on roles and role theory says of Barker and associates in their work with behavior settings that they "developed methods for studying community roles and a host of facets for expressing role content" (Biddle, 1979, p. 238).

Customs

The relation between behavior settings and customs has hardly been considered in the published literature, so far as we know, but it has been suggested to us that settings involve little more than customs. However, it seems to us that customs are really quite independent of behavior settings—that is, within behavior settings there is ample room for the operation of customs in the usual way.

Take, for example, the regular meetings of Rotary Clubs in small towns in eastern Kansas and in North Yorkshire. By the criteria for the definition of behavior settings, Rotary Club Meeting qualifies as a behavior setting in towns in both countries. They belong to the same genotype because their programs are largely interchangeable without important disruption. But the customs of the two cultures require some significant differences in the ways their programs are implemented, and these customs derive from significant differences in the climate and the economy, among other things.

Although the Rotary Club meetings in eastern Kansas and North Yorkshire have almost identical programs, the properties of the behavior objects, both the built milieu and the setting inhabitants, differ in important respects: the setting inhabitants differ physically (taller versus shorter, tanned versus florid) and behaviorally (Midwest twang versus Yorkshire dialect, fork manipulated by the right hand versus fork manipulated by the left hand, business conducted formally versus business conducted informally). Such differences are often referred to as customs. There are many reasons for such uniformities within the national regions and for the differences between them.

For example, most Yorkshire Rotary Club meals have potatoes in three forms: baked, roasted, and creamed. Kansas Rotary meals usually have potatoes in but one form, French fried. Why the difference? Yorkshiremen like potatoes because their physiology calls for warm, nourishing food, because the climate and the rooms are cold, because potatoes are good, because potatoes are cheap (it is a potato-growing region), and because the technology is at hand in the kitchen to bake, roast, and cream the potatoes. The regress goes on and on. In Kansas, all of these conditions are different (potatoes are "too filling," the rooms too warm, potatoes are expensive, frying technology is available, etc.). It is perhaps the physiology of Yorkshire men (based on the climate) and technology of Yorkshire (based on agriculture) that transforms them as human components of the behavior setting Rotary Club Meeting (ecological environment) into potato-liking persons (psychological environment). So the customs within the Rotary Club meetings of the two cultures are different, but the settings are nonetheless equivalent. There is room within equivalent settings for such cultural differences.

Forgas' Social Episodes

With the concept of *social episodes* as discussed by Joseph Forgas (1979), we turn to several concepts that deal with the environment primarily as perceived by individual persons. The book by Forgas is especially interesting because it includes extensive reviews of both historical and current usages related to social episodes or social situations, terms that Forgas uses interchangeably. His coverage includes the work of both psychologists and sociologists, and he notes that the long-standing mutual ignorance of workers in these two disciplines is at last beginning to erode. Forgas gives the following definition of social episodes:

> Social episodes will be defined here as cognitive representations of stereotypical interaction sequences, which are representative of a given cultural environment. Such interaction sequences constitute natural units in the stream of behaviour (Dickman, 1963; Harré & Secord, 1972), distinguishable on the basis of symbolic, temporal, and often physical boundaries. More importantly, however, there is a shared, consensual representation in the given culture about what constitutes an episode, and which are the norms, rules and expectations that apply. This definition of episodes as cultural objects implies that individual members of a specified culture should have an implicit cognitive knowledge and understanding of the episodes practiced in their environment. The major task of the proposed study of social episodes is thus to empirically represent at least some aspects of this implicit knowledge [p. 15].

In discussing one of his own empirical studies of social episodes, Forgas explains that a major purpose of the work was to quantify differences in episode perception between members of different subcultural groups. Subjects were asked to give detailed accounts of their social interactions during the previous 24 hours, such as "Having morning coffee with the people in the department," "Discussing an essay during a tutorial," "Going out for a walk with a friend." Analysis using multiple dimensional scaling showed that "a two-dimensional representation of social episodes was optimal for housewives, while a slightly more complex three-dimensional episode space best represented the episode domain of students" (p. 176).

Forgas considers social episodes and behavior settings as closely related concepts (see, for example, his p. 115). He discusses the behavior setting approach in considerable detail as one of four basic strategies for studying social episodes that he reviews appreciatively in terms of both methodology and findings (see his chap. 5). Forgas also recognizes important differences between behavior settings and social episodes:

Barker's understanding of the behaviour setting and its "standing patterns" of behaviour, and our approach to social episodes are remarkably similar. Both refer to stereotypical, culture-specific sequences of behaviour with a consensually understood rule-structure. The differences are mainly in emphasis: Barker regards the behaviour setting as the most important and accessible subject for analysis, while the present definition focuses more on the global characteristics of an episode as cognitively represented by individuals. His definition includes nonsocial, that is, solitary episodes, whereas we are mainly interested in interactive episodes. This distinction is a subtle one, since even nonsocial episodes are governed by social conventions. Finally, behaviour patterns must be uniquely anchored to particular space-time loci. The same requirement does not apply to social episodes, which may occur in different locations, at different times, as long as such episodes are perceived and interpreted as globally equivalent [pp. 149–50].

Although we are in general agreement with this statement, it fails to recognize the fact that the behavior setting is a unit for the study of environments, not individual behavior, whereas social episodes are concerned with the behavior of individuals. Nor does Forgas' statement recognize the synomorphic relationship between the standing patterns of behavior and the space-time locus that is an essential feature of the definition of a behavior setting.

Forgas is quite explicit in recognizing another important difference when he concludes: "Perhaps the most important difference between a social psychological approach and Barker's ecological psychology is that social psychologists would be interested in the subjective interpretations, meanings and perceptions that individuals attach to behaviour settings, whereas for Barker, only the external, observable similarities in behaviour are of interest" (p. 151).

Goffman's Frame Analysis

Unlike Forgas, Erving Goffman apparently sees little relationship between his frame analysis and the behavior settings approach. His 1974 book mentions Barker only in a footnote reference to chap. 7 of Barker and Wright (1955), *Midwest and Its Children*, for its discussion of dividing the behavior stream (the analysis of observational records of the behavior of individual children), but there is no mention of behavior settings. This may seem surprising, but closer study of Goffman's work shows that there is less in common between the two approaches than appears at first. Goffman (1974) states his purpose as follows:

My aim is to try to isolate some of the basic frameworks of understanding available in our society for making sense out of events and to analyze the special vulnerabilities to which these frames of reference are
subject. I start with the fact that from an individual's particular point of
view, while one thing may momentarily appear to be what is really
going on, in fact what is actually happening is plainly a joke, or a dream,
or an accident, or a mistake, or a misunderstanding, or a deception, or a
theatrical performance, and so forth. And attention will be directed to
what it is about our sense of what is going on that makes it so vulnerable
to the need for these various rereadings [p. 10].

Goffman credits Gregory Bateson with introducing the term "frame" in
the sense that Goffman means it in frame analysis:

[M]uch use will be made of Bateson's use of the term "frame." I assume
that definitions of a situation are built up in accordance with principles
of organization which govern events—at least social ones—and our
subjective involvement in them; frame is the word I use to refer to such
of these basic elements as I am able to identify. That is my definition of
frame. My phrase "frame analysis" is a slogan to refer to the examination in these terms of the organization of experience [pp. 10–11].

This book is fascinating in large part because of his reliance on profusely
reported anecdotes from real life, the press, literature, cartoons, the
stage, and the arts. As in his other books, he deals here with phenomena
of captivating and intrinsic human interest—such as fraud, deceit, con
games, and drama.

Throughout Goffman's work, his concern is with social interactions as
perceived by the persons involved, not with the structure of society as
studied by other sociologists or with the nature of the ecological environment that Barker and other students of environment and behavior wish to
examine:

This book is about the organization of experience—something that an
individual actor can take into his mind—and not the organization of society. I make no claim whatsoever to be talking about the core matters
of sociology—social organization and social structure. Those matters
have been and can continue to be quite nicely studied without reference to frame at all. I am not addressing the structure of social life but
the structure of experience individuals have at any moment of their social lives [p. 13].

In other places, however, Goffman appears to stray a bit from this narrow concern with individual perceptions. Particularly his chap. 8, "The
Anchoring of Activity," reaches beyond psychological reality for the per-

son and asks about the relation of the frame to the environing world in which the framing occurs:

> It has been argued that these frameworks are not merely a matter of mind but correspond in some sense to the way in which an aspect of the activity itself is organized—especially activity directly involving social agents. Organizational premises are involved, and these are something cognition somehow arrives at, not something cognition creates or generates. Given their understanding of what it is that is going on, individuals fit their actions to this understanding and ordinarily find that the ongoing world supports this fitting. These organizational premises—sustained both in the mind and in activity—I call the frame of the activity [p. 247].

What follows, then, is an interesting discussion of the relation between a particular framed activity, such as two persons playing checkers, and the surrounding environment. One focus is on the issue of how the boundaries of the framed activity are identified—that is, brackets or markers indicating the temporal and spatial "edges" of the frame:

> These markers, like the wooden frame of a picture, are presumably neither part of the content of activity proper nor part of the world outside the activity but rather both inside and outside, a paradoxical condition already alluded to and not to be avoided just because it cannot easily be thought about clearly. One may speak, then, of opening and closing temporal brackets and bounding spatial brackets. The standard example is the set of devices that has come to be employed in Western dramaturgy: at the beginning, the lights dim, the bell rings, and the curtain rises; at the other end, the curtain falls and the lights go on. . . . And in the interim, the acted world is restricted to the physical arena bracketed by the boundaries of the stage [p. 252].

It is in this passage that Goffman approaches a concern with environmental entities that bear obvious similarity to behavior settings. This interest is further explored in the subsequent discussion of roles and their coerciveness on actors, the limitations in casting, and the shaping of a part by the enduring characteristics of the actor. The dramaturgical terms used here should be understood only as models for myriad activities of everyday life, not just the theater. Nevertheless, it seems clear that Goffman's interest remains on the psychological level, with the subjective experience of persons. The relatively limited attention he gives to the environment both within and surrounding framed activity appears to be of interest primarily in terms of its significance for understanding personal experience.

Schank and Abelson's Script Analysis

One intriguing effort to deal conceptually and methodologically with the analysis of behavior in context has been described recently by Roger Schank and Robert Abelson (1977; Abelson, 1981; Schank, 1982). Their papers present, among other things, a new method of analyzing sequences of behavior in situations of everyday life. For this purpose, they introduced the concept of *scripts*, defined as follows:

> A script is a structure that describes appropriate sequences of events *in a particular context*. A script is made up of slots and requirements about what can fill those slots. The structure is an interconnected whole, and what is in one slot affects what can be in another. Scripts handle stylized, everyday situations. They are not subject to much change, nor do they provide apparatus for handling totally novel situations. Thus, a script is a predetermined, stereotyped sequence of actions that defines *a well-known situation* (Schank & Abelson, 1977, p. 41; emphasis added).

Scripts differ according to the role of a particular participant. Thus, in a restaurant, a customer's script differs from that of either a cook or a waitress. Many such scripts could be combined to form the "whole view" of the restaurant, which might well correspond to the concept Restaurant. In his 1982 book, Schank offers some substantial revisions in the script concept and places it within a hierarchy of more general knowledge structures, such as scenes, Memory Organization Packets (MOPs), and Thematic Organization Points (TOPs). Detailed analysis of stories about behavior in restaurants, airplanes, labor negotiations, automobile accidents, and diplomatic trips, for example, are presented as illustrations of script analysis. A number of empirical studies using scripts have recently appeared (for example, Bower, Black, & Turner, 1979; Kaminska-Feldman, 1982; Graesser et al., 1980; McCartney & Nelson, 1981).

Although there appear to be points of similarity between concepts in this approach and behavior settings, particularly in the discussion of the distinctions between physical, societal, and personal scenes and MOPs, what most clearly differentiates the two approaches is that all of the concepts in script analysis represent cognitive structures in the head of a particular perceiver or actor; script analysis deals only with the entities used by the memory of a particular person. Schank's interest is in developing a theory of the human memory system:

> Recall that we are interested in more than just good understanding systems. We want systems that *learn* as well. Further, and perhaps most

important, we want to understand how the human mind processes experiences. We want to know how it copes with new information and derives new knowledge from that information. To do all this we need a coherent theory of adaptable memory structures—in other words, a dynamic memory [Schank, 1982, p. 4].

Schank recognizes only tangentially the importance of the objective, non-psychological, preperceptual world that is the province of behavior setting analysis:

No two people are likely to have identical structures except where those structures reflect the physical nature of the world or when those two people must function in identical societal arrangements. Even there, our experiences alter an individual's view of the world to such an extent that we can expect major differences. From a far enough distance away, any two members of the same physical or social world are likely to have similar mental structures. But viewed up close, these structures will contain distinct personal experiences [ibid., p. 127].

Script analysis lies at the junction of cognitive psychology, social psychology, and linguistics. Although Schank and Abelson rely almost entirely on self-reports about processes that occur inside people's heads, it seems to us that script analysis would be greatly strengthened by including a more systematic representation of the objective physical and social world, such as that provided by the study of behavior settings. Behavior setting research has shown that the setting accounts for much of the variance in individual behavior. The structured and organized nature of the objective environmental situation is an essential prerequisite to the learning of scripts, MOPs, and TOPs. If the ecological environment were not so organized, if it were as unstructured and unstable as alleged by Brunswik (1955), Leeper (1963), and other psychologists, script analysis would be impossible.

Conclusion

In this chapter, we have reviewed a selection of social science concepts that appear to bear some more-or-less close relation to behavior settings. We make no claim of comprehensiveness in our coverage; indeed, we know that it is incomplete and that a number of other concepts in the literature might well have been included, such as "culture space" (Voegelin & Voegelin, 1972; Yamamoto, 1979). We hope, however, that this review will help to show where behavior settings fit within the total spectrum of social science concepts. It should be clear that this comparative review should not be read as an evaluation of such approaches. We are not suggesting that some are better than others but rather that they are different approaches, designed to address different questions. In the current relatively undeveloped state of research and theory in social science, there is clearly not only room but also a need for a variety of theoretical and methodological approaches to central problems. Our primary interest is in showing that research on behavior settings has earned a place alongside other concepts—those reviewed here and many others—in the total armamentarium of social science.

The next chapter is a reprint of an article by Barker that appeared originally in the *Journal of Personality and Social Psychology*. It demonstrates some of the ways that behavior settings and the behavior of individuals are linked. It is included here at the suggestion of Irwin Altman, who was series editor of a special series in that journal on historical aspects of social-psychological research.

14

Settings of a Professional Lifetime

Roger G. Barker

I was Professor of Psychology and Department Chairman at the University of Kansas in Lawrence in 1948. On a particular day of that year, I worked on a research report in my Study at Home, answered correspondence, and made some calls at my desk in the Chairman's Office, met my Graduate Class in Experimental Social Psychology for two hours, conferred with the Dean of the College of Arts and Sciences in the Dean's Office, chaired a meeting of the Department Faculty, and attended a Departmental Colloquium; these six behavior settings made up my professional environment. During my life in psychology, which began, I shall presume, when I entered upon graduate study at Stanford University in 1928, and has continued to this day, the stream of my behavior as a psychologist has meandered through thousands of behavior settings. These settings have constituted the environment of my professional life, and in this article I shall describe some of their features and consequences for me.

The settings of my environment have had widely varying attributes; I have entered some of them by my own choice and have been coerced in varying degrees to inhabit others; in some settings I have had considerable influence, in others little power. The Chairman's Office differed greatly in these respects from the Experimental Social Psychology Class: in the Office there was great diversity of both human and nonhuman components (secretaries, faculty, students, typewriters, telephones, files, people conversing, dictating, typewriting, and more), and all of these were incorporated into a relatively stable, multiform pattern of Office ac-

This paper was originally published in 1979 by the *Journal of Personality and Social Psychology*, 37, 2137–57. Reprinted by permission of the American Psychological Association, Inc.

tivities. In the Class there was less diversity (no secretaries, telephones, typewriters, files, people conversing or dictating) and a radically different, less complex standing pattern of lecturing, listening, and note taking. I entered the Chairman's Office by my own choice, but I was under strong compulsion to turn up for the Class at the scheduled time. I was powerless to change the program of activities of the Dean's Office, but I was able to alter the program of the Class, although my power was by no means unlimited. This setting had been a part of the College and the University before I joined the faculty, and they imposed certain features upon it that I was powerless to alter: I had to teach experimental social psychology, the setting's raison d'être (not ecology, a great interest of mine at the time), and I had to give grades (objectionable to me, but a policy of the University). Still, within these and other limits, I was in command of the program of activities.

When I have inhabited a behavior setting—whatever its attributes, the conditions of my entrance, and my power—I have become one of its component parts, and my behavior and experience have been formed by its ongoing program; these, therefore, have changed appropriately as I have moved from setting to setting. I did not pick up my mail or dictate letters in the Experimental Social Psychology Class or give lectures or quizzes in the Chairman's Office. The impress of some settings upon me has not extended beyond their boundaries; the stamp of others has been long-lasting. The influence of the Chairman's Office ceased abruptly at the door, whereas some attributes of my behavior and experience first occurring in response to forces within the Class have remained with me. In this account, I shall pay special attention to behavior settings that had long-continuing consequences for me.

Unfortunately the data I have to work with are poor. Few contemporaneous accounts of any setting are available, and still fewer are by independent observers. Most of what I am able to report is the fallible memory of how settings appeared to one inhabitant. In an attempt to mitigate the faults of the data, I shall confine my account to those settings for which there are contemporary data or very clear memories and that appear to have been crucial to my scientific activity. Fifteen behavior settings or clusters of settings most adequately meet these requirements. Here they are listed in temporal order of their occurrence and with their institutional connections: Stanford University, 1929–1935 (Terman's Seminar, Miles' Later Maturity Facility, Stone's Animal Laboratory); University of Iowa, 1935–1937 (Lewin's Offices, Nursery School Laboratory, Topology Meetings); Harvard University, 1937–1938 (Murray's Clinic, Child Psychology Class, Boring's Sack Lunch); University of Illinois, 1938–1942

(Study at Home, Extension Classes); Stanford University, 1942–1945 (Office of Disability Survey); Clark University, 1946–1947 (Office at the University); University of Kansas, 1947–1972 (Office of Department Chairman, Field Station in Oskaloosa).

I shall introduce each of these settings with its specifications under six rubrics: program, physical attributes, temporal characteristics, human components, powers of human components, and boundary properties. Then I shall report the forces and circumstances that brought me into them, the actions and experiences they elicited from me when I inhabited them and after I left them, and my power within them.

But first I must describe the 1928 person who was to make the trip through these behavior settings.

The 1928 Person

He was unsound physically, his intellectual powers were unknown, his financial resources were meager, his motivation was strong but unfocused.

An osteomyelitis infection of the left hip and right knee had had many acute phases since its beginning 12 years before. In 1928 the disease was quiescent, but acute episodes were a threat; a flare-up kept him out of school during 1929–1930. In its quiescent periods the disease was mildly debilitative, and its destruction of joints caused some locomotor impairment.

The 1928 person was 25 years old and three years behind academically. He attributed this to missing school because of illness, but he did not know what it signified for a career in science. Perhaps his isolation in sickrooms and his six instead of eight years of secondary and college education handicapped him for advanced study; he was poorly grounded in mathematics and languages; he had studied no physics and had had only elementary courses in chemistry and biology. He remembered many evidences of intellectual marginality and inadequacy. There was his experience in the fourth grade, when the teacher could not decide if he belonged with the A group or the B group, so she had him sit alone between the elect and the scrubs. And he could not forget failing the first course in high school algebra, having to repeat it, and edging through the second go by memorizing the answers to likely problems, ending with the unanswered question: "How can it be possible to add, subtract, multiply, and divide letters, and why do it in any case?" Years later, too late to be of any comfort to him, he discovered that George Bernard Shaw had also had trouble with algebra, "mistaking the a, b, n and x for goods" such as eggs and cheese "with the result that I rejected algebra as nonsense" (Shaw, 1949, p. 41). Shaw blamed the instruction; "I had been made a fool of"; the 1928 person blamed himself. And there was his mother's aunt, an intelligent and insightful person, who was devoted to him during his adolescence and greatly worried about his future; she summed up her impressions of his assets and liabilities with the advice that he should prepare himself to be a short-order cook in a country restaurant. There was some evidence on the other side. There was the occasional, ambiguous remark about him by partisan adults: Still water runs deep. But this was less convincing than his great aunt's explicit evaluation. There was the thrilling time in the eighth grade when he was called upon to stand before the class and explain how to point off decimals in the quotient of a long division problem, and the teacher praised him. Having graduated from Stanford University with sufficient promise for the Psychology Department to accept him for graduate study would have been reassuring had there been entrance requirements; at least he was not discouraged by Professor Terman, the chairman. By far the most persuasive evidence, which tipped the scale in his self-evaluation, was the engagement between him and Louise Dawes Shedd. Louise Shedd knew him well, she herself had high scholarly credentials and bright goals for a life in the classroom and laboratory, and she was not about to link her life with that of a short-order cook. He was willing, in fact, relieved, to accept her evaluation, and he hoped to justify it.

His financial resources were less than zero, for during his undergraduate years he had accumulated hundreds of dollars in tuition loans that became due to the University in years immediately ahead.

Psychology for him was a means, not an end. His undergraduate introduction to the subject matter and methods of the science had no special appeal to him, but he believed it to be the least onerous route to his goal of "doing good" for mankind. He was a thoroughgoing, naive idealist and ardent reformer. He considered medicine but was sure he would not be accepted as a student, and his long, discouraging experience as a consumer of medical services had alienated him from the profession. He found economics too remote from particular people, and sociology too speculative and wordy. He tried to get a handle on demography but could discover no people or publications to inform him sufficiently about it. He did not consider literature, art, or the physical and biological sciences of any relevance to his goals. Psychology seemed to be a promising route, but even as he began graduate study he did not foreclose other routes, and within psychology's varied and vast domain, he had no preference.

Although the zeal of the 1928 person was great, there were clouds on the horizon. He anticipated that the psychology route to good works would have difficult and unpleasant stretches, and he was keenly aware of the likelihood of recurring acute phases of his illness. His prescience in the latter respect was verified by the flare-up in 1929–1930, and he hesitated about persisting, but for reasons impossible for him to comprehend to this day, his fiancée stood fast, encouraged him, and even married him in the summer of 1930. So in the autumn of 1930 he made a second start and became an anxious, vigilant, expectant psychologist in the making.

Stanford University, 1929–1935

I was a graduate and postgraduate student at Stanford University for six years. For four years I attended classes, did research under supervision, led "quiz sections" of elementary psychology, did various departmental chores (mimeographed class notes and exams, scored Strong Vocational Interest Tests, and cared for the animal colony), passed examinations, and received the MA degree (1930) and the PhD degree (1934). Being unable to find a regular position in the depression year of 1934, I was fortunate in being kept on as a research associate for two more years. The work was rewarding and the salary of $100 a month was satisfactory; with Louise's $1,800 a year as high school biology teacher we were able to pay my tuition loan debts to the University and save some money. Three behavior settings were crucial to me during these Stanford years.

TERMAN'S SEMINAR

Program: Report by seminar member, usually a student, with interruptions by others discussing or questioning points made. *Physical attributes*: Locus, Terman's home on the Stanford University campus, in an attractive living room of sufficient size for a single-row circle of 25 persons. *Temporal characteristics*: Weekly meetings (with occasional skips) for about two hours during most autumn, winter, and spring terms; approximately 20 meetings most years. *Human components*: Dr. Lewis M. Terman, one or two other faculty members, occasional guests, 10–20 graduate psychology students. *Powers of human components*: Program determined at three levels of power. Terman's power extended over the entire setting (he selected the speaker, approved the topic, opened and closed the meeting); the speaker's power was supreme over the content and method of his report; the power of the other inhabitants was limited to supplementing, correcting, criticizing, and approving the speaker's presentation. *Boundary properties*: Admission at the invitation or urging (in the case of students) of Dr. Terman.

Reports usually described completed research or plans for research; occasionally books or monographs were reviewed. Almost all reports were concerned with research, emphasizing methods; theories or general issues were very rarely seminar topics. Interchanges between reporters and other members were usually for more information about procedures. The Seminar was eminently civilized and controlled, the occasional disagreements and arguments being muted. Terman set the tone, being quietly attentive, making few contributions himself other than introducing the speaker and ending the session with general remarks. Despite its appearance of tranquility, many students reported, outside the Seminar, that it was a tense, even traumatic experience for them. Many of the controlled interactions were undoubtedly reactions to the Seminar as a dangerous place for students; they were on trial before powerful present and future evaluators.

When Terman opened the Seminar to me, I eagerly attended. The name of the game for me was to learn as much as possible, to discover if I was likely to make the grade in scientific work, and to improve my chances of doing so by demonstrating what strength I had to Terman, the other faculty members, and my peers. The first and last intentions were not congruent. Optimal learning requires acknowledgment of ignorance, whereas putting one's best foot forward requires masking ignorance. And to walk on thin ice, as I did in the Seminar, always on the brink of both disaster and improved footing, is not conducive to a wide perspective and clear thinking; it is inhibiting. Still, one must act; to remain motionless on the ice, or dumb in the Seminar, is a sure way to disaster. Alert caution is essential. Under these circumstances motives and abilities and disabilities are not openly revealed, and valid judgments of persons are not possible, though reputations are made. I never knew my reputation among the members of the Seminar, but I did know my self-estimate. I placed myself near the median of the student seminarians, I was uncertain of passing the examinations, and I was quite sure my destiny was at best to become a journeyman psychologist, perhaps in a junior college where, after all, there was plenty of scope for good works. Considering the people against whom I was judging myself, this self-estimation is not surprising; during the years of my attendance they included six who became president of the American Psychological Association and a number of others who were honored by the Association for their scientific contributions.

My immediate reaction after the Seminar was frequently one of great dismay: at my ignorance of what seemed to be common knowledge, at my failure to contribute what afterward appeared to me to be a valuable input, and at my espousal of weak, foolish, or irrelevant ideas. Louise came to dread the late-night aftermath of the Seminar.

I cannot now remember what I learned; I am quite sure that I encountered no mountain peaks of new understanding. But the Seminar provided a regular update of what was happening in psychology, especially with respect to methods of investigation. More than this, I became acculturated into the language, the mores, the ethos of the psychology tribe. And I made acquaintances who have continued to be valued personal friends and influential connections within the profession. On the negative side, I first encountered an aspect of academic life that has continued to be distasteful to me: the ubiquity of judging others (passing and failing students, approving and not approving candidates, promoting and not promoting colleagues, accepting and not accepting research proposals, and so forth) and of being judged by others. The fact that most interpersonal relations within Terman's Seminar involved, explicitly or implicitly, judgments of personal worth reduced its attraction as a social occasion and eroded its educational benefits.

MILES' LATER MATURITY FACILITY

Program: To study change in abilities from middle to later years of life. *Physical Attributes*: Located near the central business district of Palo Alto in a one-time residence. The former reception hall, parlor, living room, dining room, and bedrooms were modified for use as offices and for administering tests and experiments; office furnishings and equipment for tests and experiments. *Temporal characteristics*: Operated weekdays for several months during academic year 1931–1932 from 9:00 A.M. to 5:00 P.M. *Human components*: Walter R. Miles, graduate student research assistants, secretary, subjects. *Powers of human components*: The power of Miles extended over the entire setting and program; he planned the research, secured the financing, selected the staff, recruited the subjects, approved the methods of testing and experimentation. The power of each research assistant was dominant within his laboratory room. The only power of subjects was to refuse to participate in a particular procedure; to my knowledge this did not occur. *Boundary properties*: Free access by staff; subjects admitted by appointment.

I had completed my master's degree work under Miles with a thesis on finger maze learning, and it was now time to undertake research for the

PhD degree. So when Miles returned from a trip East, bringing the news of a grant for the magnificent sum of $10,000 to support a study of old age, I eagerly embraced the opportunity to participate. For reasons I cannot recall, I chose to study muscular fatigue. Miles gave me complete freedom to devise a muscle fatigue test suitable for both robust 50-year-olds and frail centenarians, and I took considerable satisfaction in adapting a spirometer to determine hand and arm fatigue quickly. Other graduate students investigated changes in intelligence, learning, memory, motor skills, and sensory acuity. Subjects were recruited from clubs, churches, and living groups by paying the organization for each member who became a subject. They were brought to our experimental rooms by the secretary. At the time, I did not appreciate the luxury of having subjects provided to me with no effort on my part; many times since, I have appreciated Miles' efficient logistics.

I greatly enjoyed working with the Later Maturity Facility; the freedom within my own domain and the straightforward problem were agreeable. I went home most nights feeling I was making progress toward providing some potentially useful new knowledge.

The more enduring consequences of this setting for me were, first, increased confidence in my ability to engage in research on my own; after approving the area of my contribution, Miles took no part in my project; it became my own. Second, I learned something about the possibilities and difficulties of a kind of field study; I observed the extensive public relations activities required to secure subjects, and I was especially impressed with the effectiveness of approaching citizens by way of the organizations to which they were devoted. I also noted that the demands of public relations, at which Miles was very effective, divorced him from the details of the research. Because of this experience, I believe it was easier for me, when I later engaged in field studies myself, to realize that they require staffing different from that of laboratory investigations with captive or hired subjects and that community experts are as essential as observers, interviewers, testers, and so forth.

STONE'S ANIMAL LABORATORY

Program: To investigate motivation in animals, chiefly rats, with emphasis on sexual behavior. *Physical attributes*: Locus, third-floor attic of the building housing the psychology department in an area partitioned into a sky-lighted animal room for about 100 animal cages, perhaps ten small rooms for assistants and equipment, and Stone's large office. The equipment was primitive by present standards: student-made mazes, jumping apparatus, activity drums, Monroe hand calculators, simple shop equipment. *Temporal characteristics*: Functioned at some time every day. *Human components*: Calvin P. Stone, one or two postdoctoral fellows, two graduate assistants, several thesis students, a few students doing class projects, visitors. *Powers of human components*: Stone's power extended over the entire laboratory; he approved the fellows, selected the assistants, admitted the students and approved their research, set rules and standards. Fellows had complete power over their own research; assistants controlled their particular segment of the total program of the laboratory after consultation with Stone. Visitors' power was limited to viewing approved areas and asking questions. *Boundary properties*: Fellows, assistants, and students admitted by Stone personally; visitors were tolerated, but except for professionals, they were not welcomed.

As in 1931 (the opportunity to participate in the Later Maturity Facility came at a crucial time), I was fortunate in 1933 to be able to work in Stone's Animal Laboratory when I could not find a regular job. I did not choose to spend two years in this setting, but neither did I object; it was inevitable.

I found work in the setting even more satisfying than in the Later Maturity Facility. I had passed all examinations and written my thesis; that tension was gone. The intellectual camaraderie was congenial; postdoctoral fellows brought news and innovations from other laboratories; the pace of activities was not determined by tightly scheduled subject appointments. But there was a vigorous, steady program of activities; almost all the animal work required regular cleaning, feeding, observing, testing, and examining; Stone was a hard, regular worker himself, and everyone knew that he valued industriousness right along with honesty and intelligence. He was known to disapprove strongly of the policy of another university that reportedly provided technicians to do such detail work for graduate students as sectioning and preparing tissues for examination and running rats in mazes. In Stone's Laboratory, students cared for their own animals and spent the boring hours putting them through the necessary procedures. Inasmuch as Stone was in and out of the laboratory many times most days, beginning at 7:30 A.M., his power and reputation were sufficient to maintain a fairly tight ship without many definite rules and regulations.

Special emphasis during this period was on variation in the age of sexual maturity of rats, its genetic basis, and its relation to other behavior and somatic characteristics. Parallel investigations were conducted of the age of maturity of human females and its relation to their size and their interests and attitudes. I came to find much of the work interesting, and some of it had a permanent influence on me. Even the evening after evening of testing young male rats for age of first copulation became enjoyable when Louise came along and read aloud from a high stool in the center of the animal room. (Conrad, Tolstoy, and Galsworthy in no way diverted the rat subjects from their putative activities.)

It was here that I first became aware of the potential value of archival data for psychological science. Stone was interested in the intellectual level of children of abnormally early sexual maturity, and he had previously reviewed and summarized the literature. He set me to updating the survey, and I was impressed to find that although most evidence was in the form of reports of single or a very few cases, and none were adequate methodologically in terms of number and selection of cases and methods of testing, still, en masse, these data, reported by many independent investigators at widely varying times, in diverse situations and cultures, provided overwhelming evidence that early intellectual maturation does not accompany abnormally early sexual maturation. I noted that almost no cases were reported in the psychological literature, whereas medical journals served as valuable archives for these rare cases. I began to see that the insistence of academic psychology that every publication conform to all current canons of scientific adequacy was depriving the science of data on important issues. Years later I discovered a pair of identical adolescent twins, one of whom had been seriously crippled since childhood, and I saw this as an exceptional opportunity to obtain data from a very rare natural experiment on the effects of physique on personality; I studied them extensively. But I was advised not to attempt to get the material published because "one case means nothing." I wondered: Would a paleontological journal reject a study of one dinosaur egg because the investigator did not present data on 50 eggs? The lesson I began to learn in Stone's Laboratory has stayed with me, and I and my colleagues have not hesitated to collect "inadequate" data under certain circumstances, namely, when the problem to which the data refer is important, when fully acceptable data cannot be obtained due to their temporal or physical dispersion or their rarity, and when the data are such that investigators at other times and in other places can add to them.

It was in Stone's Laboratory that I first encountered a set of problems that have occupied me ever since, namely, environmental influences on behavior. At the time, however, I did not see the particular problem in this context. It arose from our studies of relations between age at menarche and physical and social development in girls. We discovered that in the early adolescent years, early maturing girls are more similar to older females in measurements of physique than are late maturing girls of the same chronological ages, and when we asked if this same relation holds for social interests and attitudes, we found that it does: Postmenarcheal girls 12, 13, and 14 years of age are more similar to older females in their responses to interest and attitude test items than are premenarcheal girls of the same ages. So we faced this question: To what degree are the differences in attitudes and interests due to direct hormone influences, and to what degree to the fact that the physiques of the early and late maturing girls provide the girls and their associates with stimuli with different social significances, thereby imposing different social environments upon them? We could not answer this question with the data at hand. Five years later, at the University of Illinois, I returned to this problem and found evidence that powerful adults (parents, teachers) bring greater pressure on physically mature girls to engage in mature behavior than on physically immature girls. And ten years later, when I was back at Stanford, I returned to the problem in connection with studies with my students of the psychological consequences of physical crippling.

In addition to initiating this particular continuing interest, Stone's Animal Laboratory further strengthened an attitude I carried with me from other Stanford settings, namely, that strong and persisting but rather narrow programs of activities are productive. There were no brilliant performances at Stanford. The research of Terman on the gifted, of Stone on animal motivation, and of E. K. Strong on interests yielded no remarkable breakthroughs, but they were and have continued to be recognized as substantial achievements. This was not an "Aha!" experience for me; but as I look back I can see that it became a deeply rooted conviction that this was to be my way of doing science. Along with this vaguely developing insight there was increased self-assurance. At the end of my six years at Stanford, I was more sure that my aspirations for a productive career in science were not hopeless. However, I did not have a strong commitment to any problem. I had worked on a rather wide range of problems via a considerable number of methodologies, but I had become devoted to none. I was still unfocused, at the beck and call of almost any opening that would allow me to earn a living as a psychologist. In the spring of 1935 an opening came that radically altered my intellectual lifestyle and threw me again into uncertainty about myself.

I took part in many behavior settings at Stanford other than the three I have described: classes, lectures, seminars, laboratories, projects, examinations. They enriched my intellectual life and widened my perspective, but only one of them had particular, identifiable consequences for me. This setting channeled the stream of my behavior as a psychologist into its first great bend. Kurt Lewin came as a visiting professor for the year 1932–1933. I was very busy during this year finishing my doctoral thesis so I was able to attend Lewin's class only as a visitor. He attracted me greatly as a person, but his psychology confused me or, perhaps more correctly, it was incomprehensible to me. Fairies and ectoplasm would have been more comprehensible than life space, valence, psychological force, inner-personal regions, substitute value, psychological satiation, and so forth. Stanford students knew something about Gestalt psychology experiments and theories of perception from the writings of Wertheimer and Köhler, and of development from the works of Koffka, but Lewin's so-called Gestalt psychology seemed to have nothing to do with these, as we expected. And equally disconcerting, Lewin seriously reported experiments with seven subjects, and instead of replicating the experiments, he changed the conditions; even worse, if the results from the altered conditions were in accord with his predictions on the basis of theory, he took this as a verification of the findings and the theory. I suppose Stanford University in those days was among the least auspicious places in the United States for an understanding of Lewin; theory was almost a non-word in the psychology department, although we did use it in connection with Spearman's interpretation of intelligence test intercorrelations (theory of general intelligence) and we read about psychoanalytic theory. But most of us had no background in the philosophy of science, and the place of theory in science. So Lewin's *Dynamic Theory of Personality*, which I reviewed (with Terman) and which he taught in his course, was a transient foreign body, a UFO, to most of us. I cannot recall that any of the students who attended his class took and retained a serious interest in his viewpoint unless they had later association with him. The gulf was too wide to be bridged quickly, and the dissonance was so great that some rejected his ideas out of hand. I was not negative; I was tolerantly baffled.

So when the opportunity arose to join Lewin as a General Education Board Fellow at the University of Iowa for the year 1935–1936 I was intrigued; here was a chance to learn a different kind of psychology, to earn a full living for Louise and me for the first time, and to have the prestige of the fellowship. Indeed, I had no choice; circumstances beyond my knowledge and control were turning the stream of my professional behavior, indeed my whole life, in a new direction. I have no idea to this day how my nomination to this fellowship came about, but I am sure that an important factor on the Stanford side must have been: It is really time for Barker to push off the home place. I thought so, too.

University of Iowa, 1935–1937

Kurt Lewin went to the Iowa Child Welfare Station in the autumn of 1935 on a grant from the General Education Board, with provision for three research assistants. The first assistants were Tamara Dembo (who had been a student of Lewin's in Berlin), Herbert F. Wright (who had been a student of Donald K. Adams' at Duke University; Adams had studied with Lewin in Berlin), and me. My fellowship was extended in the spring of 1936 for one more year. Three behavior settings were of primary importance to me at Iowa.

LEWIN'S OFFICES

Program: To plan the research project we would undertake, and to discuss and make decisions about procedures and problems when it was underway; to analyze data from the project and write up reports; to read the writing Lewin was doing, to listen to his proposals for reformulations and additions, and to criticize and make suggestions. *Physical attributes:* Located in four adjacent office rooms on an upper floor of East Hall, University of Iowa campus; the building had been a hospital and the rooms were former single-patient rooms; they were a little crowded with a desk, a bookshelf, a blackboard (in Lewin's office), and four chairs when we were all present in a single office. *Temporal characteristics:* In operation at some time almost every day, with one or more participants; sessions with Lewin occurred whenever the project needed his attention and whenever he had something to discuss. *Human components:* Lewin, the three assistants, frequent visitors. *Powers of human components:* Lewin established the program of the setting; he decided that the research would be on frustration, but the details of procedure were worked out in group consultation, where he was first among equals; he was, of course, in total control of his own writing, the assistants serving more as persons upon whom he could try out his ideas than as consultants or collaborators, although he took seriously all criticisms and suggestions. *Boundary properties:* Assistants selected and admitted by Lewin; free entrance for visitors.

It is difficult to imagine more different climates for scientific work than those obtaining at Stanford and at Iowa. At Stanford, science gathered facts about behavior via experiments and tests, determined their central tendencies, and analyzed their interrelations; in Lewin's setup, science explored ideas about behavior via experiments and observations. At Stanford, conclusions were in terms of the means, dispersions, and correlations of samples of *facts* about behavior; my own work discovered that the rate at which 80-year-olds pump air into a spirometer declines faster during a work period than the rate at which 50-year-olds pump air. At Iowa, conclusions were in terms of verified or altered *ideas* about behavior; in our work there we found (in accordance with a theory) that in psychological frustration, inner-personal systems can be considered to be in a state of blocked tension that amounts to functional dedifferentiation, one expression of which is lowered level of intellectual activity, that is, intellectual regression.

In the beginning, the sessions in Lewin's office were an ordeal for me; they were bewildering and tiring. The ideas we were to explore and clarify in connection with the frustration study were too unfamiliar for me to make many contributions; as for the monograph Lewin was working on, *The Conceptual Representation and Measurement of Psychological Forces*, the ideas were utterly baffling. Lewin's eagerness and the energy to back it up seemed boundless. Whereas the tension and alertness of the two-hour sessions of Terman's Seminar had left me dog-tired, after meeting with Lewin, Dembo, and Wright from 2:00 to 7:00 in the afternoon (with Lewin reading aloud what he had dictated the day before, interlining new sentences, rearranging the order, violently objecting to a criticism by Dembo, turning to Wright—"Herbert, is she right?"—accepting Dembo's criticism, diagramming a relation on the blackboard, crossing the whole page out, dictating a new version to Dembo, and so forth), I was ready to drop. After 5:00 I would hope beyond hope that my dear, pregnant wife, lonesome at home, would telephone that I was urgently needed. Sometimes she did. A frequent concluding remark by Lewin was "We must think about this," and that after three, four, five hours of nothing else. Did this add up, perhaps, to a kind of brainwashing? In any case, as the months went by, I began to understand Lewin, and his ideas have remained at the center of all my subsequent work. But equally important to me has been the new, higher level of intellectual effort to which I became adapted. I could never come close to Lewin's intensity; I had to take it much slower, but his refrain, "We must think about this," has stayed with me. Although no one could have been more subordinate to Lewin in terms of knowledge, I was always treated as a colleague, never as a pupil. My contributions, however naive, were always taken seriously, Lewin often seeing in them more than I had intended.

NURSERY SCHOOL LABORATORY

Program: To carry out the research on frustration we planned in the offices in East Hall. *Physical attributes*: Two ground-floor rooms in a remodeled residence across the street from the station's nursery school equipped with a one-way observation booth, child-sized chairs and tables, toys, and a movable barrier in accordance with the research design. *Temporal characteristics*: Setting occurred intermittently during winter and spring of 1936–1937, according to a schedule of appointments. *Human components*: Tamara Dembo and myself, alternating as observer and experimenter, and a single child from the nursery school at each occurrence. *Powers of human components*: Dembo and I had joint authority over the entire setting, although, according to the experimental design, we did not intrude into regions designated for free play; child subjects had no power except in designated free play regions. *Boundary properties*: Free access to Dembo and me; child subjects, a different one on each occasion, selected and required to attend in accordance with decisions made by us and nursery school staff.

Basic to much of the early research Lewin initiated is the theory that psychological tension systems correspond to intentions to engage in molar actions. The studies of interrupted and substitute tasks issued from this theory. Lewin came to Iowa with the intention of investigating this idea further; he thought that the undischarged tensions that occur in frustration result, via increased rigidity and spread of tension to adjacent regions of the person, in functional dedifferentiation, and that one manifestation of this is intellectual regression to a state normal for an earlier age. The problems for the assistants were to devise a frustrating situation and methods of assessing intellectual level inside and outside this situation. The nursery school setting in which we worked on these problems elicited from me two insights that have remained with me. I discovered the value, for studies of molar actions, of situations where the investigator intrudes not at all or very little, and the value of detailed narrative records of behavior. The frustration study involved, for the most part, a continuation of the child's usual nursery school day, and in his free situation, we were able by means of nonintrusive narrative records to assess intellectual level as accurately as formal intelligence tests do. In later work, my colleagues and I have come to depend very extensively on narrative records of behavior in situations that are completely free of our influence, and we continue to be impressed with the value of ordinary language as a coding system for the subtleties and complexities of behavior. The Nursery School Laboratory was a welcome refuge for me from the conferences in Lewin's Office. Here I found a kind of therapy in applying my Stanford expertise to the gathering and analyzing of masses of data.

TOPOLOGY MEETINGS

Program: To discuss Lewinian theory and research findings. *Physical attributes*: Occurred in academic conference rooms of various universities. *Temporal characteristics*: Took place during Christmas vacation for two or three full-day and evening sessions. *Human components*: Lewin and invited guests; the latter were former and present students and colleagues, and a few others interested in Lewin's ideas. *Powers of human components*: Designated persons at host institution controlled local arrangements, Lewin arranged program of papers; free discussion. *Boundary properties*: Invitations issued by Lewin and by people at host school.

The Topology Meetings were as much a part of my Iowa experience as were Lewin's Office and the Nursery School Laboratory, even though the meetings were held at Cornell University and Bryn Mawr College in those years. They agitated me somewhat as Terman's Seminar had, although the testing aspect was less pervasive and the learning aspect more pervasive; still these settings were new and strange, and I was alert and cautious. In them my world expanded greatly, to encompass many new friends and acquaintances, many new concepts applied to new problems, and many new locales and institutions (I had not previously been east of the Mississippi).

The adjustments I made to the three crucial behavior settings at Iowa were only part of the intellectual turmoil I experienced. There were other upsetting settings. In some of them Herbert Feigl expounded physicalism and the views of the Vienna Circle; in others, Spence's kind of Hullian behaviorism was expounded. Iowa, for that brief time, at least, was a bubbling cauldron of antagonistic ideas. With my nontheoretical background, I was severely buffeted by the strongly asserted convictions of these sophisticated advocates. Lewin's handling of these disturbances impressed me and has been a model for me since. Although he defended his viewpoints strongly, he was not rigidly partisan. An early remark he made to a student objector at Stanford, when his English was poor, expressed his position: "Con be, but I sink absolute uzzer." He did not think current controversy would settle basic issues, that only empirical evidence would in the long run sift the true from the false, and that the business of science was to get ahead with empirical tests. He strongly deplored the disruptive partisanship within German psychology.

Before the end of my second fellowship year a new opportunity arose that I could not decline: an instructorship at Harvard University to teach a course in child psychology. As with the General Education Board Fellowship, I have no knowledge of the forces that brought this opportunity to me. But again, after nine years, the stream of my professional behavior was to flow in a ready-made channel. Previously, the Later Maturity Facility, the Animal Laboratory, and the General Education Board Fellowship had taken charge of my life in psychology, and now the Harvard Psychology Department took over with no effort by me. But there was a difference: Whereas previously I had been in the role of pupil (to Terman, to Miles, to Stone, to Lewin), now I was to be on my own in my teaching and in my research.

Harvard University, 1937–1938

I arrived at Harvard under the cloud of an illness, not my old familiar trouble, but suspected appendicitis. I presume now, more than I admitted then, that the symptoms were of psychosomatic origin. And why not? I was confronted with the task of teaching a subject new both to me and to the Harvard Psychology Department (Child Psychology had not been in its curriculum before) to hypercritical Harvard students (Boring warned me of them in a letter in which he also expressed the concern of the Department about its reputation among undergraduates for good teaching) before the eyes of some of psychology's top brass (Boring, Allport, Murray, Lashley) and its brightest lieutenant colonels (S. S. Stevens, B. F. Skinner, Robert W. White).

MURRAY'S CLINIC

Program: To carry out studies of personality; the program was minimal this year, however, as Murray was on sabbatical leave. *Physical attributes*: Located in a converted residence on Plimpton Street, a block and a half from Emerson Hall, headquarters for the Department; clinic office, staff offices, library, experimental rooms, shop, kitchen; the library and several offices were elegantly furnished with fine rugs and period furniture. *Temporal characteristics*: In regular operation weekdays and at any time for particular staff members. *Human components*: Acting director, three or four staff and/or psychology department members, a postdoctoral fellow, several students, clients and subjects, secretary, shop man. *Powers of human components*: The acting director was Robert W. White, who had final control of the entire setting, although staff members and the fellow were quite independent; the secretary and shop man were semiautonomous within their areas; powers of clients and students were limited by the staff members with whom they were associated. *Boundary properties*: Free access to official personnel, clients and subjects by appointment.

Murray's Clinic was my salvation: It was leisurely and quiet; my office was large, with comfortable chairs and a couch; after the hectic pace at Iowa, it was a refuge. Here I could sit and think about where I had been and where I was going, emerging only at intervals to grapple with my one class. Part of where I had been was with me in the form of a partially completed manuscript about the Iowa frustration experiment; sitting on my desk in a big box, it was a continual irritant, but it did not claim or oppress me. I tested where I was going by doing an experiment on conflict resolution: it was a Lewinian experiment and it was congenial to me, but I did not see it as a channel to a lifetime of research; I did only one other study of conflict. I believe I became dimly aware, then, that further investigation of conflict resolution would lead to finer grained and more complex theories and more detailed and precise experimental procedures that did not suit me. This may have been the beginning of my aversion to the reduction of theoretical explanations of molar events to theories of their more molecular components, with the implication that the latter are the more fundamental. Murray's Clinic was my first experience of a behavior setting without a coercive program. Whereas the settings at Stanford and Iowa took me in hand and put me through their paces, Murray's Clinic protected me from impositions. Settings of this kind have fortunately occurred at regular intervals in my career.

CHILD PSYCHOLOGY CLASS

Program: To teach child psychology to undergraduate students. *Physical attributes*: Classroom for about 40 students in the basement of the Clinic; chairs, podium, blackboard; furnishings and decorations somewhat shabby. *Temporal characteristics*: One hour's duration, three times weekly for one semester. *Human components*: Instructor and 35 students. *Powers of human components*: Program under complete control of instructor; powers of students limited to expressing approval or disapproval. *Boundary properties*: Access only for instructor and registered students.

The sensitivity of the Psychology Department to the students' regard for the teaching it provided caused me to approach this, my first teaching, with more than my usual trepidation. I worked hard welding my Stanford and Lewinian background into what I am sure was a unique course of study.

There were a few rough places in this setting, marked by some foot shuffling, but it ended with an acceptable round of applause. So I emerged with some confidence in my teaching ability and with a course outline that was a long-time asset.

BORING'S SACK LUNCH

Program: To combine an economical lunch with friendly conversation among colleagues. *Physical attributes*: Locus, Boring's office in Emerson Hall; table around which eight people could sit comfortably; sack lunches; in the background a desk and shelves filled with books. *Temporal characteristics*: 1:00 to 2:00 P.M. most weekdays. *Human components*: Boring and, usually, five or six staff members and visitors. *Powers of human components*: Boring's benign influence pervaded the setting. *Boundary properties*: Access at Boring's invitation.

I was flattered to be invited. I expected stimulating conversation of the kind I had heard took place at the high tables in the English colleges, but in this I was disappointed. Despite the high caliber and great achievements of a number of the attenders (B. F. Skinner, S. S. Stevens, Boring, occasionally Lashley and Beebe-Center), small shoptalk about equipment, library resources, particular research results, publishing problems, together with bantering but restrained gossip about current university, community, and national affairs prevailed. I emerged from this setting with some impressions of eminent and soon-to-be eminent people, but nothing of professional value to me. It did strengthen my belief, originating at Stanford and strengthened at Iowa, that the effective men in the science were blue-collar, hard-hat workers, not gentlemen scholars. Here was Boring, well past middle age, the Mr. Psychology of the profession in America, eating his cold egg sandwich with the boys and discussing the nuts and bolts of research and writing, not lunching gracefully in the Harvard Faculty Club with his professional and administrative peers on the Club's famous horsemeat steaks.

My time at Harvard was one of greatly expanded perspective, not of psychology as a field of study, but of the people, institutions, and cultural milieu of the science. Other settings that contributed to this expansion were conferences sponsored by the Macy Foundation, where I encountered the eastern wing of the child development movement and for the first time directly heard psychoanalysts expound their views.

Although I was no longer in the role of a student, I was still a probationer. As I understood the Harvard policy, it was: three years at most as an instructor and then up or out. As I saw no possibility of my moving up, I determined before the end of the year to seek another position. Behind this decision there were a number of considerations: uncertainty if I would be appointed for a second year and apprehension about finding a place in two or three years, when I would need one; the belief that nine years as apprentice (six years at Stanford, two at Iowa, one at Harvard) with the continual strain of being tested was enough; and the realization that I was veering sharply away from my goal of using psychology for the direct benefit of people. So when I heard that a position as Assistant Professor of Educational Psychology was open in the College of Education at the University of Illinois, I applied for it and was appointed. As it turned out, another year at Harvard was offered to me, and some surprise was expressed that I chose Illinois. But Louise and I went with few regrets; we were at last taking a hand in the direction of my professional career, our economic future did not come to a dead end in one or two years, and education was surely a promising place to apply what I had learned at Stanford and Iowa.

University of Illinois, 1938–1942

We arrived in Urbana, Illinois, in July 1938 with our two-month-old and two-year-old children. We rented a house while looking for one to buy; we were ready to settle down.

STUDY AT HOME

Program: To get on at last with my own version of psychology. *Physical attributes*: We soon purchased an old house from a retired academic who had made himself a study to match, on a small scale, the library on Plimpton Street: paneled walls, a fireplace that worked, many shelves, stained glass windows, space for a large desk and work table. *Temporal characteristics*: Occurred at my discretion during the Illinois years. *Human components*: Myself, my students, Louise, and our children. *Powers of human components*: I was in overall charge, but in these years Louise began to participate in the research, a partnership that has continued, with some breaks when she has had outside jobs. *Boundary properties*: Penetrable to me, Louise, and children at any time; to students on invitation.

What I had prepared for the Harvard students of child psychology seemed good enough also for the Illinois students of educational psychology, so I turned early from preparations for my class to other undertakings. Two of these were rooted in Stone's Laboratory, two in Lewin's Offices, and one was a "do good" effort.

The question of whether differences in the attitudes and interests of premenarcheal and postmenarcheal girls have a basis in the social significance of their different physiques was left unanswered five years earlier, so I returned to it now and found evidence that, indeed, the adult associates of mature adolescent girls provide a different (more "mature") social environment for them than they do for immature girls. And I expanded my concern for the environmental significance of physique to physically disabled people and asked if they also live in a different environment from that of physically normal people by reason of their physiques. I began a long involvement with this question with two case studies. Although the roots of my interest in the environmental significance of physique were in Stone's Laboratory, my interpretations and theories came from Lewin's Office, and undoubtedly my expansion of this interest to physical disability was influenced by my personal experience with the problem.

The unfinished manuscript of the frustration research still occupied a prominent place on my desk, and I continued to wrest time from more immediately interesting new tasks to inch along toward its completion. And the conflict resolution study had become such an uncompleted task for me that I was impelled to replicate (and verify) the findings by an entirely different method.

My "do good" effort was carried out in collaboration with Herbert F. Wright, my fellow Fellow at Iowa, and Jacob S. Kounin, my new colleague at Illinois. This was a collection of reports of psychological research in the field of child development. It was intended to provide a "bookshelf" of primary research for students of child development and thereby promote scientific child study as a field for both practitioners and scientists. It is my impression that this was the first "reader," as they are now called, in child psychology, and perhaps in psychology as well (Barker, Kounin, & Wright, 1943).

My Study at Home was not only a place to get on with my version of psychology as a science; it became a place to teach my version, as well. In the early autumn of 1940 an acute phase of the bone infection occurred, and I was completely incapacitated for the term. Jack Kounin came to my rescue, taking over my classes, presumably for a short time. But as it turned out, I was out of commission for four months. Due to Jack's heroic efforts and the tolerance of the College and University, my pay continued. In the second semester, although still in a full body cast, I was able, again with the kind indulgence and special arrangements of the College, University, and students, to meet small classes in my Study at Home. Perched on a high tavern-type chair within a specially built surrounding pulpit, I was able to expound the word to a score of students at a time.

Again, as with Murray's Clinic, my Study at Home saved me from possible disaster. This one nourished projects I brought to it from Stanford and Iowa, and in it new, long-continued undertakings originated.

EXTENSION CLASSES

Program: To teach educational psychology at the graduate level to primary and secondary school teachers. *Physical attributes*: Located in classrooms of state teachers' colleges, which did not at that time offer graduate-level instruction. *Temporal characteristics*: Occurred on Saturday mornings for two hours during each semester. *Human components*: Instructor and 20–40 students from the schools of the area. *Powers of human components*: Program controlled by instructor. *Boundary properties*: Only students satisfying registration requirements of the University were admitted.

The Saturday trips from Urbana to outlying teachers' colleges, usually by automobile but in some cases by train, were enjoyable and satisfying. The mature, practicing teachers brought me into contact with real teaching problems in the towns where they taught; they educated me perhaps as much as I educated them. And the trips revealed to me something about the rural midwest. I was intrigued with the small towns, and elsewhere I have related how the general problem that dominated the last 25 years of my professional life occurred to me as I was rushed through them by the train on the trip from Urbana in the center of Illinois to Carbondale in the south (Barker & Associates, 1978). In short, I had an overwhelming *negative* "Aha!" experience: Here I was, a native of the culture and an expert on child behavior (and especially on frustration) who knew no more about the everyday behaviors and environments of the children of the towns than laymen know. I was aware, too, that other child psychologists knew no more than I did, and furthermore, that we had no means of discovering more; no methods of determining the extent and conditions of frustration, joy, anger, success, conflict, problem solving, fear, and so forth among the towns' children. I thought how different the position of an agronomist would be. He would know or could determine the kinds, yields, and qualities of the crops we were passing, the properties of the soils in which they were growing, and the relations between soil conditions and output. This was the beginning of a growing conviction that a science that knows no more about the distribution in nature of the phenomena with which it is concerned than laymen do is a defective science, and it was the beginning of my impression that small towns of the kind I observed in Illinois and learned about from the teachers are favorable places to begin to remedy the defect. It was seven years before the seed planted in the Extension Classes and on my trips across the plains of Illinois began to sprout.

It was not long after we went to Illinois to "settle down" that irritants began to appear. There were the disagreeable administrative impositions upon my teaching that finally became intolerable to me. And I was soon to discover that my flight from a marginal position vis-à-vis the upper uppers of the profession at Harvard had landed me squarely with the lower lowers. I attempted to establish collegial relations with psychologists in the Psychology Department but without success. Part of the difficulty was structural: I was separated from them spacially, temporally, and administratively; I was in a different building, their seminars and other gatherings often conflicted with my staff meetings and other duties, and administrative messages were on different communication networks. And in addition, I found that a psychologist in a college of education is distinctly lower-class. This so impressed me and it was so important to me personally that I used my experience as evidence for an analysis of the values and dynamics involved. Finally, I became discouraged about my ability to combine scientific work with applications. I began to see that it required more than clear lectures to alter the practices of teachers. My own experience, namely, that because of impositions from the encompassing system I could not practice in my own teaching at the University the principles that my science showed me to be true, should have made this immediately clear to me, but it took time. I struggled on with increasing dissatisfaction. Finally, in the spring of 1942, these multiple environmental stresses became so great that I wrote to Terman telling him of my disenchantment. To the surprise and delight of both Louise (who, surprisingly, did not thrive with a troubled mate) and me, Terman answered immediately with the offer of a place at Stanford for the duration of the war.

At Illinois I learned some important things about myself and about my profession; I closed out some unfinished tasks and initiated some new ones. I look back on the time there as a rough but beneficial passage.

Stanford University, 1942–1945

The Stanford appointment was as Acting Associate Professor. I understood clearly that this was an emergency appointment to bolster a war-depleted staff. At the time its temporary nature did not trouble me or

Louise; the advantages were many: I was free to teach as I pleased (the motto for Stanford of its first President, David Starr Jordan, "The winds of freedom are blowing," was fully realized in the classrooms of the Psychology Department); I was again a member of psychology's upper class; we were home among friends; Louise was welcomed back on a part-time teaching basis to her old school; my health was on the upgrade and promised to improve more in the California sunshine. We were in such good shape, in fact, that our third child was born in the spring of 1943. Furthermore, it turned out that I was able to make an important immediate application of my psychological knowledge.

But not all was rosy. The war was ever present on the West Coast, with blackouts, shortages, relatives and friends embarking for Asian combat, and casualties disembarking. The teaching load was heavy; in addition to the regular offerings, short cram courses were given for officers in training. I taught a number of subjects new to me, so I had to do much homework to keep ahead of the classes. Most of these three and a half years at Stanford were a steady grind. Only one setting stands out as of special significance for my career. It came about through a fortunate conjunction of (a) my desire to make a contribution to the war effort; (b) the national need for rehabilitation service for war casualties; (c) my interest in, my exploratory research on, and my personal experience with, physical disability; and (d) resources that the Social Science Research Council (SSRC) made available. A crucial person in tying together these separate strands was my colleague Quinn McNemar, who was a member of the relevant SSRC committee; it was at his instigation that the Council funded the preparation of a survey of what was known about the psychological aspects of the rehabilitation of the physically disabled (Barker et al., 1953). I set up a special study at home for this project.

OFFICE OF DISABILITY SURVEY

Program: Preparation of monograph *Adjustment to Physical Handicap and Illness*. *Physical attributes*: We were living in a house built by Walter Miles, my former professor and thesis adviser, which had a fine, spacious, isolated study; it became headquarters for the monograph project. *Temporal characteristics*: Occurred whenever I had time during the years 1943–1945. *Human components*: When the magnitude of the project became clear, I was fortunate in obtaining contributions from Beatrice A. Wright, Lee Meyerson, and Molly Gonick. *Powers of human components*: Overall control was in my hands; others had complete autonomy for their own contributions. *Boundary properties*: Ready access by the four participants.

In this setting I experienced some of the great satisfactions of my professional life, and they have continued to this day. In the first place, I felt competent; I believed I was as able as anyone to do the job at that time. Second, I saw this as my first opportunity to bring my skills to bear on an urgent practical problem. As it turned out, the time was ripe for this; beginning with World War II, concern and services for the disabled have increased greatly, so any firm foundations laid in 1943 have had continuing consequences. And third, I believed at the time that I was able to contribute to this firm foundation by pointing out that some psychological problems of the disabled are not unique to them, that adolescents and ethnic minorities, for example, face the same problems; I was able to do this in terms of Lewin's concepts of marginal men and overlapping situations. I have not followed the course of rehabilitation psychology in recent years, so I have no firsthand knowledge of the permanence of this contribution, but I am told that the monograph is still in demand. Clearer evidence of the enduring consequences of the Disability Office is the fact that both Beatrice Wright and Lee Meyerson have become leaders of this field of psychological study.

In 1945 I wore the child psychology label, primarily, and there was not much demand for this branch of the science at Stanford. Members of the Department had ambitions to develop a program of studies in child psychology, but money was scarce and progress slow; their principle efforts went to accommodating regular staff members returning from war service and to filling vacant, established slots. So in October 1945 I was told that there was no hope for me beyond the next spring semester. As of June 1946 I would be through at Stanford. The likelihood of this subsidence of the stream of my professional life had long been within my time perspective, but the reality was more vivid than the distant prospect. It gave a new urgency to the somewhat relaxed inquiries I had initiated before reality descended. I had communicated about possible jobs with a number of schools, including Clark University, and in the summer I had an interview with President Atwood about the vacant G. Stanley Hall Professorship in Child Psychology. I did not take this possibility seriously. So, when a definite offer came from Clark in November, Louise and I were almost overwhelmed by the drastic alteration in our prospects. But we were able to make the transfer; we arrived in Worcester, Massachusetts, for the second semester in January 1946.

Two firsts of some importance occurred during the three and a half years at Stanford. One was advising graduate students on their thesis research. In line with my interest in the disability problem and my work on the survey, three students undertook theses on attitudes toward the disabled. The other first was the establishment of the Disability Survey Office as a major behavior setting with a program after my own specifications; until this time, apart from minor side excursions, I had operated in behavior settings with programs arranged by others. At Stanford I was born as a psychologist, and on my return 15 years later I gained these two evidences that I had at last reached my majority.

Louise and I left Stanford older and with more experience of the stream of university life. We had drifted through the dangerous, white waters of Harvard, portaged to the slow Illinois channel with its sandbars and driftwood, portaged again to the steady, full flow at Stanford, on whose banks we were briefly stranded until an unexpected flash flood carried us to Clark. One more portage was to come.

Clark University, 1946–1947

Clark turned out to be a bayou for us. The top administrators changed six months after we arrived, the Psychology Department had been understaffed for some time and had an acting chairman, and I was uncertain of the direction of my next efforts, having completed the disability monograph. With so much in the process of change, all of us—the University, the Department, and I—marked time. It was now that the seed planted in my mind on the plains of Illinois began to grow, and I seriously considered a project to discover and describe the living condition and behavior of the children of a small town. I took two actions. I explored the towns around Worcester, and I discussed the project with Kurt Lewin, who was then at the Massachusetts Institute of Technology and was living only 30 miles away. The exploration was discouraging. The small settlements of the region were not self-contained towns as in the Midwest; they were spacially dispersed and often specialized fragments of political units (towns) often straggling many miles along streams or across forested ridges. The children of these fragments did not have a common community environment as did the children of the towns I had seen in Illinois. But the discussions were encouraging, and in fact Lewin was enthusiastic. He, himself, was moving from laboratory experimental research to "action research" in communities and institutions to study the consequences for the inhabitants of induced changes in their structures and programs. So he was supportive of efforts to establish baselines in unaltered communities against which to assess the effects of changes. With his encouragement, I worked on an application for funds for a community study with the intention of doing the research at a distance from Worcester if necessary.

And now luck was with us. The United States Public Health Service was expanding its support of basic research, particularly on children. The advisory committees included persons familiar with my work whom I had met at Stanford, Iowa, Illinois, and the Macy Foundation and Topology Meetings. The project was approved, and the research was funded early in 1947. And then Dean Lawson of the University of Kansas turned up in Worcester. He was looking for candidates for the chairmanship of their Psychology Department. The department was at a low ebb, and the administration was ready to make a new beginning and provide the support required to bring psychology at Kansas to its former vigorous state.

Why should I be interested? I had just come to Clark, to an endowed professorship with some status and to a department that also was set to make new beginnings. One could interpret my career as exhibiting clear signs of instability; a solid and frank New Englander, on hearing from Louise of the towns in which we had lived, remarked, "I see your husband is something of a floater." Surely it was time to settle in and stay on course. But there was the research and the dispersed Massachusetts towns. I told Dean Lawson of the project and the kind of town it required. Did he know of such a town in the Lawrence area? "Yes," he said without any hesitation, "I know the place. I've spoken there several times. Its name is Oskaloosa." I made two trips to Lawrence that spring; on the second trip I asked my former fellowship colleague at Iowa, Herbert Wright, to come along and consider joining in the department and the research. We visited Oskaloosa. He came and he joined. So Louise and I made one more portage.

University of Kansas, 1947–1972

We arrived in Lawrence in late August 1947 in a 115-degree heat wave. But, no matter, important things were underway. Fritz and Grace Heider were joining us, along with Herbert and Lorene Wright. There were houses to rent, a new department office to establish, instructors, teaching assistants to hire, and the University's rules and regulations to master.

I learned slowly why I had been chosen for this job over some other strong candidates. G. E. Coghill, a stellar name in biology in those days, had recently retired, and psychologists Raymond Wheeler, F. T. Perkins, and J. F. Brown had lately left the University. All of these men were well known for their "organismic" viewpoints. It was the wish of the two regular staff members who remained, Beulah Morrison and Anthony J. Smith, and of the administration, that this tradition be continued. Without making this explicit, Dean Lawson apparently saw that I would do this naturally and with enthusiasm. And in fact he had two immediate signs of the correctness of his insight when I recruited Herbert Wright and Fritz Heider within a couple of months. In the next three years we added Martin Scheerer, Alfred Baldwin, and Erik and Beatrice Wright. The new senior staff members were all from the center or the fringes of the Gestalt psychology movement.

Two behavior settings dominated my professional activities over the next 25 years; one of them was of my own creation, and I had considerable power over the other.

OFFICE OF DEPARTMENT CHAIRMAN

Program: To invigorate and expand the psychology department and to establish and administer settings subordinate to it according to University and Staff policies. *Physical attributes*: Suite of four rooms in Strong Hall with office furnishings and equipment. *Temporal characteristics*: My occupancy continued for three years; open for regular business weekdays 8:00 A.M. to 5:00 P.M., and for special business at any time. *Human components*: Myself, other staff members, students, secretaries. *Powers of human components*: The basic policies of the Department were determined by external settings: those of the University administration and the setting Department Staff Meeting. Within the constraints imposed by these settings, the chairman had complete control of the Office. *Boundary properties*: Open access.

In my 19 years of academic life the extent of my administrative experience was limited to registering and advising students at Illinois and Stanford and to voting on minor issues in the College Staff Meeting at Illinois. My former colleagues at Stanford expressed anxious surprise that I would or could become an administrator. Their surprise was not justified. They did not know the strength of my commitment to certain academic and educational principles and my eagerness to have more of a hand in promoting them than hitherto; and they did not know that administration was part of the package that included Oskaloosa, the crucial component. There were grounds for their anxiety, though not the ones they probably had in mind. They would know of my deficiencies in keeping appointments, answering correspondence, arranging schedules, making and keeping to budgets, gregariousness, and so forth. But they would underestimate, I think, the power of the behavior setting Office of Department Chairman to take me in hand in these respects. However, their anxiety (and mine, too) would have been justified had they known of the probable conflict between the duties of the Office of Department Chairman and those of the research setting Field Station in Oskaloosa. I lasted three years as chairman.

The usual conflict between administration and research was exacerbated in this case by a geographical factor; we found it impossible to do the research in Oskaloosa, 20 miles from Lawrence, without living there and having full-time headquarters there, and the urgencies that occurred in both places could not be scheduled. However, if I had found administration congenial and rewarding, I might have remained longer as chairman. But I did not. For one thing, I did not have easy relations with my superiors. Some sort of a personal status and power problem was involved. I saw myself as being too submissive to policy directives I opposed, and thereafter I felt guilty of betraying my principles. I did not stand up to authority in the way I thought I should. This was partly a matter of my divided commitment; I did not have the time to prepare for hassles with top administrators; but there was also inability to confront superior power. Another problem for me as chairman was the discovery that persons with whom I agreed and had harmonious relations were not always in agreement and harmony among themselves. My ambition was for a unified, amicable department, and with incredible naiveté I supposed that those with whom I was congenial would be congenial inter se. There were no great conflicts within the department, but not the unity I had hoped for. An added circumstance that interfered with maintaining a department with a common point of view on psychological matters was the rapid increase in the staff to serve the great increase in university enrollment after 1947. Inevitably those added were of a variety of psychological persuasions. In my three years in the chairman's slot, the Department was invigorated with staff members who received wide recognition as scientific scholars in the next two decades.

These were tremendously busy years for me, with increasing conflict between the demands of the chairmanship and the research, with increasing dissatisfaction with my relations with University administrators, and with some disappointment that my goal of a small, excellent, unified group of scholars was not more completely achieved. So, my occupancy of the chairman's position in the Office of the Department of Psychology brought me both satisfactions and regrets.

Classroom teaching was not clear sailing either. I had decamped when there was administrative interference with the way I wished to function as instructor at the University of Illinois. Now, it was discouraging to me to discover that there were other, more pervasive institutional obstacles to my teaching. The Kansas University administration intruded very little in class operations, but a generally prevailing program of classroom instruction made it difficult for me to establish the kinds of programs I desired. This was my first experience with the fact that the settings of an institution may be so interdependent that deviant settings cannot function. My classes were arranged to foster students' skill in formulation of questions, finding and using the most relevant evidence, and writing reports on the basis of the evidence. Learning facts had no place in my classes; today's facts are obsolete tomorrow, and the current ones are always available if one knows where to find them and how to use them. My classes could operate best if the students had some unscheduled time: to think of interesting and answerable questions, to search for relevant evidence, and to analyze, organize, and present the findings. But who can think, search, analyze, and write when confronted with two quizzes a week in one class, 500 pages of reading in another, and nine hours of laboratory attendance in another? As so-called standards went up and competitive grading became more severe, the students lost their freedom to act as inquirers, problem solvers, and expositors to the imposed demands of fact-, page-, and hour-oriented classes.

In addition to trouble with the teaching system within the University, I found that classroom settings and research settings do not mix—that the activities required by classroom teaching and by research are so conflicting as to be mutually injurious. I have observed this to be true for others, too. Both Terman and Lewin were excellent classroom teachers when they devoted themselves to it, but when they were deep in research, as they usually were, their teaching declined precipitately.

From the intrusions of the Illinois Dean I escaped to Stanford; from the interference of the prevailing teaching system and the conflicts with research I escaped to Oskaloosa. Fortunately a Research Career Award from the National Institute of Health made this possible.

FIELD STATION IN OSKALOOSA

Program: In the beginning, the program was to describe the living conditions and behavior of all the children of the town; later, all inhabitants were included. *Physical attributes:* Suite of offices in Oskaloosa, Kansas, with office furnishings and calculators; at intervals a satellite Station was established in Leyburn, Yorkshire, England. *Temporal characteristics:* Operated during regular office hours, and often into the evening for particular staff members, from the fall of 1947 through the spring of 1972. *Human components:* Three to seven staff members, one to four graduate students, and occasional town residents. *Powers of human components:*

During the first seven years, the Station was administered by the codirectors Herbert F. Wright and me; we had power over the entire setting; when Herbert left the Station, I was in charge. Next in power were professional scientists (field workers, data analysts) who had complete control of their special operations; after them came the graduate students with power over their projects in consultation with their advisers, and finally the secretaries, who were masters of their own desks and secretarial facilities. Townspeople and other visitors had no power. *Boundary properties*: Staff and graduate students selected and admitted by Station directors; they thereafter had free access; townspeople also had free access.

Here, at last, in the Midwest Psychological Field Station, the stream of my professional behavior entered a setting constructed to my own design: I initiated it, and its program was arranged cooperatively with Herbert Wright. Most other major settings I had inhabited had ongoing operations into which I was incorporated, with limited power to make alterations. I soon discovered, however, that in the Station I was not a free spirit but was captive of the setting I had established—a setting that embodied a past I could not escape and a future I could not control. Herbert and I had programmed the Midwest Field Station to describe the behavior and psychological habitat of the children of the town individually. With the setting underway (procedures developed and tested, staff trained, computer programs set up, citizens alerted and cooperative), it was not a simple matter when our insights and intentions changed to alter the program to one of describing extra-individual behavior within behavior settings. We had to struggle against our own creation. It makes one wonder how much of the stability of individual behavior has its source in the stability of the behavior settings people create and inhabit, a stability that is sustained by the fact that people establish new settings according to designs they carry with them from previous settings.

The origins of some features we built into the Midwest Field Station are fairly clear: The aim to describe the living conditions and behavior of all of the children originated in the Extension Classes in Illinois; concern with the naturally occurring environment was brought from Stone's Animal Laboratory and the Iowa Nursery School Laboratory; disciplined, persisting concentration on a rather narrow program of activities, the policy that "dogged does it," came aboard in the Stanford settings; the dual importance of precise data and precise theories welded together characteristics of both the Stanford and the Iowa settings; the particular theories that undergirded the program of the Midwest research came from Lewin's Offices in Iowa; the importance attached to archives of atheoretical data originated in Stone's Animal Laboratory; the first data collecting system we installed, the narrative record, dated back to the Iowa Nursery School Laboratory; the importance given to community relations was first met in Miles' Later Maturity Facility.

These problems, emphases, methods, and theories with which we endowed the Field Station were imported from earlier settings. We installed the past in the present. But the inheritances were assembled in new relationships, and new elements were added, including staff members, methods, ideas, and data; the Station developed a dynamic of its own with unforeseen consequences for its inhabitants. For me these were far-reaching. In this latest stretch of the stream of my professional behavior, I entered the Field Station as a psychologist aiming to study the naturally occurring behavior and environments of the people of the town as individuals. For a long time I clung to the view that this was the way to observe and explain their everyday activities. But the Field Station finally turned me around and showed me that more than people and the stimuli that impinge upon them individually are required, that an eco-behavioral science of extra-individual behavior and its nonbehavioral context is needed. The course of this change has been presented in a number of publications (Barker, 1960, 1963a, 1963b, 1965, 1968; Barker & Associates, 1978; Barker & Gump, 1964; Barker & Schoggen, 1973; Barker & Wright, 1951a, 1955).

Other Places, Other People

I have had to omit many rewarding and pleasant reaches of my behavior stream and most of the people who shared parts of it with me and gave me tows and directions. Space is a factor here, but more important is absence of records of the early days. And there were important hidden settings (committees, administrative offices, and so forth), whose inhabitants I do not know, that gave me free time (Research Career Award; Fellowship, Center for Advanced Study in the Behavioral Sciences), research grants (U.S. Public Health Service, Society for the Aid of Crippled Children, Commonwealth Fund, Ford Foundation, Carnegie Foundation of New York, University of Kansas, Kansas University Endowment Association), honors (Kurt Lewin Award, Society for the Psychological Study of Social Issues; Research Contribution Award, American Psychological Association; G. Stanley Hall Award, Division on Developmental Psychology, American Psychological Association), and summer appointments (Columbia, Oregon, Colorado, California). I regret especially not being able to name the graduate students who studied with me at Stanford University, Clark University, and the University of Kansas, some of whom have become valued colleagues, and many of whom contributed greatly and still contribute to my intellectual development.

My story would be too incomplete, however, without four prime influences on the odyssey. Louise Shedd Barker was an eager spectator, a frequent adviser, and an occasional stand-in in all the early settings. But when we discovered that the Station could not be operated from Lawrence, that it required us to live in Oskaloosa, Louise became an essential operative as chief field worker and our main line of communication with the community. She was well prepared. In her own professions she had experience as a field ecologist, first as biologist at the Stanford Marine Station and on the University campus, and then as high school "home visitor," searching out the homes of absent children and investigating the causes of their absence. Fritz Heider's ideas about media and things provided the link between people and behavior settings that prompted me to see the latter as more than convenient areas for sampling behavior but rather as entities (things) that impose patterns upon their components, including their human inhabitants (media). It was this insight that raised behavior settings for me from a technological convenience to the basic unit of an eco-behavioral science. Herbert F. Wright was co-equal developer of the Field Station's program during its first years, making unique contributions to the study of individual behavior; and Paul V. Gump was equally important in the latter years by bringing the Station's ideas and methods to bear on school and community operation.

Conclusion

I began this trip with the desire to benefit humanity. I have not, myself, been able to satisfy this desire, for I have found that, as with teaching, the time and skills required to make and disseminate applications have so conflicted with those required by the research as to make the former impossible for me. So the zeal and success of a small number of former staff members, students, and others to bring our methods and findings to earth in connection with hospitals, schools, architecture, town planning, child development, and even the movement "small is beautiful" have given me keen satisfaction. I began the journey, too, with reservations about my ability to make it in the scientific world. When I report that the self-doubt has not been dispelled, the response may well be: How greedy can he be? What does he want in brownie points? The answer: The stream of my professional life has skirted the areas of psychology that are currently richly cultivated and harvested, and in fact, it has finally landed me outside the turf of the psychology tribe. Being something of a maverick has its rewards from those (and there are many) who value what they hope will prove to be worthwhile innovations. The innovator hopes so, too, but in the meantime he is at a disadvantage vis-à-vis his mainstream associates, since he cannot keep up with them in the main channel. So, how can he be sure where he stands?

15

The Need for an Eco-Behavioral Science

Ecological problems and methods of science can be differentiated with precision from experimental problems and methods. Ecological phenomena occur without input from the investigator; they consist of things and events unchanged by the techniques used to observe them or by conditions imposed by the investigator; they answer the question "What goes on here?" Experimental phenomena involve input from the investigator; they answer the question "What goes on here under these conditions that I impose?"

Ecological approaches to scientific problems are not incomplete or defective experimental approaches. On the contrary, they provide knowledge that the best experimentation cannot provide, because experimentation by arranging conditions according to the concerns of the experimenter destroys the very thing an ecological investigation seeks to determine. The importance to science of experimental methods is everywhere recognized, but it is perhaps less widely realized that the ecological side of science is also essential. From a purely scientific viewpoint, it is important to determine how nature is arranged and how it is distributed on every level without alteration of any kind, and this can only be accomplished by ecological methods. And, for the applied sciences, information about the unaltered world is necessary before applications can be made. An engineer cannot build a bridge without detailed information about the bridge site, and this information can be secured only by methods that do not destroy the site in the process of surveying it. Such knowledge is equally important for the behavioral sciences; a teacher making an assignment or a judge passing a sentence should know the psychological terrain on which the assignment or the sentence is to be placed. But this information is seldom available, because the ecological side of the behavioral sciences is poorly developed.

Questions about the effects of the environment on human behavior and development are being put with increasing frequency and urgency. What are the consequences for human behavior of poverty? of controlled climate in factories, offices, and homes? of congested cities? of transient populations? of high population density? of computer technology? of ghettos? of large schools? of "bedroom" communities? Behavior scientists often respond hopefully to these questions with the promise that, given time and resources, answers will be provided by the tried and true methods, concepts, and theories of the psychological sciences that have answered so many questions about human behavior: about perception, about learning, about intellectual processes, and about motivation. The view presented here is, on the contrary, that the methods, concepts, and theories of the psychological sciences cannot answer the new questions; a new science is required to deal with them.

Scientific psychology knows and can know nothing about the real-life settings in which people live in ghettos and suburbs, in large and small schools, in regions of poverty and affluence. One might think that in the course of its necessary concern with stimuli, psychology would have become informed about the human environment. But this is not the case. Psychology has necessarily attended to those elements of the environment that are useful in probing its focal phenomena, namely, the behavior-relevant circuitry within the skins of its subjects, within psychology's black box. Psychology knows much about the physical properties of the environmental probes it uses: of distal objects of perception, for example, and of energy changes at receptor surfaces. But it has excised these environmental elements from the contexts in which they normally occur: from mealtimes, from offices, from airplanes, from arithmetic classes, from streets and sidewalks.

In view of psychology's concern with dismantled fragments of the environment, it is not surprising that general concepts of the environment have a minor place in the science and that they provide a distorted view of intact settings in which behavior occurs. The most common notion, which can hardly be called a theory, is that the nonbehavioral, ecological environment of human beings is an unstructured, probabilistic, and largely passive arena in which humans behave according to the programming they carry about within themselves. Brunswik (1955, p. 686), for example, speaks of "the behaving organism living in a semichaotic environmental medium"; Leeper (1963, p. 388) notes "the kaleidoscopically changing stimulation" organisms receive; and Lewin (1951, pp. 58–59) writes that "psychology should be interested . . . in those areas of the physical and social world which are not part of the life-space . . . [but this] has to be based partly on statistical considerations about nonpsychological [events]." Although these assertions are true within the limited environmental perspective of the science of psychology, they are not true within a wider perspective. It is the universal testimony of the physical and biological sciences that the ecological environment circumjacent to human beings is organized and patterned in stable and surprising ways; it is, in fact, one task of these sciences to explore, describe, and account for the patternings.

Psychology has fallen into a self-validating roundabout here; its prevailing methods of research shatter whatever pattern and organization may exist within the natural environment, and the conclusion is reached, on the basis of the resulting evidence, that the environment is not a source of the order and organization observed in behavior. This leads to further study of the mysterious mechanism of the black box that appears to bring order out of chaos, and this is done via ever more theory-determined and ever less setting-determined environmental variables. Psychology fell into this error when it became, so early in its history, for whatever reason, a science of the laboratory and the clinic, when it installed psychologists as environment surrogates, and when it thereafter neglected the psychologist-free environment. For 100 years now, psychology has largely directed inputs to its subjects in accordance with theoretical games evolved from input-output relations previously observed in laboratories and clinics. It has inevitably become more and more removed from settings that are not arranged by scientists, and it has become more and more impressed with the black box as the determinant of behavior.

Here is an example of what we have come to. The problem of Citizen Sam is presented in a standard work on personality. The following characterization is given of the days of Citizen Sam.

> He moves and has his being in the great activity wheel of New York City. . . . He spends his hours . . . in the badlands of the Bronx. He wakens to grab the morning's milk left at the door by an agent of a vast dairy and distributing system, whose corporate maneuvers, so vital to his health, never consciously concern him. After paying hasty respects to his landlady, he dashes into the transportation system, whose mechanical and civic mysteries he does not comprehend. At the factory, he becomes a cog for the day in a set of systems far beyond his ken. . . . [T]hough he doesn't know it, his furious activity at his machine is regulated by the "law of supply and demand." . . . A union official collects dues; just why he doesn't know. At noon-time that corporate mon-

strosity, Horn and Hardart, swallows him up, much as he swallows one after another of its automatic pies. After more activity in the afternoon, he seeks out a standardized daydream produced in Hollywood [Allport, 1964, p. 284].

In this account, it would appear that we are at least getting down to psychologist-free situations within an urban environment, to their nature and their consequences for behavior and personality. The author reports that Citizen Sam is confronted by the vast, anonymous dairy; that he is incorporated into the incomprehensible subway; that he is driven and regulated by the overwhelming factory; that he is swallowed by the mechanical cafeteria; and that he relaxes in a ready-made movie daydream. Citizen Sam is mightily busy, but he is not involved. According to the author, this, unfortunately, is characteristic of an important segment of our population, and so we are confronted with an important social question. What is this question? In Allport's words, it is: "What precisely is wrong with Sam?" (p. 284). The question is not "How do the city's settings (with its vast dairy, complex subway, coercive factory, mechanical cafeteria, prefabricated movie) and Citizen Sam (with his motives and cognitions) interact to produce the grabbing, hasty, dashing, uncomprehending, furious, standardized, uninvolved behavior he displays?" So far is the science of psychology removed from real-life settings.

However, writing as a psychologist, Allport is correct in asserting that what goes on within the black box labeled Sam is the only question psychology can answer, even though it is not the question society is asking in this case. The black box is the legitimate focus for psychology. It makes psychology a prospectively unified science explicated by a single set of interrelated concepts, and it makes psychology a practically important science, for the answers to many human problems (although not the problem of cities as human habitats) are to be found in the internal programming people carry from setting to setting. The wonder is that psychology has ever been expected to have the answer where such nonpsychological variables as poverty and wealth, segregation and nonsegregation, overpopulation and underpopulation prevail. Our only errors, as psychologists, have been to ignore the limits of our competence or to allow others to do so.

The phenomena of psychology and the environments in which they occur are interrelated; they are interdependent. They are interdependent in the way a part of a system and a whole system are interdependent: as the electrical generator of an engine and the functioning engine, or as the bats and balls and game of baseball. Predictions from electrical generators to engines and vice versa, and from bats and balls to ball games and vice versa, require complete accounts of the superordinate phenomenon (of the engine, the ball game) and of the place of the part system within the whole. This is true, too, for naturally occurring situations and behavior. The theory of electrical generators cannot account for the behavior of internal combustion engines, nor can engines explain generators; similarly, psychology cannot explain the functioning of taverns, school classes, or other real-life settings, and theories of settings cannot account for the behavior of the inhabitants. Generators and the environing engines within which they function and people and the settings that constitute their environments are different phenomena and require for their explanation different concepts and theories.

The distinction between the phenomena to which the urgent questions about such things as poverty, technology, and population refer and the phenomena with which psychological science deals is not a tactical one; it is basic. These are incommensurate phenomena, and they require different methodologies and facilities for their investigation.

When we do look at the environment of behavior as a phenomenon worthy of investigation for itself, not merely as an instrument for unraveling the behavior-relevant programming within persons, we find that it is *not* a passive, probabilistic arena of objects and events. This discovery was forced on us; when we made long records of children's behavior, we were surprised to find that some attributes of behavior varied less across children within settings than within the days of children across settings (Barker & Wright, 1955; Barker, 1963b). We found that we could predict many aspects of children's behavior more adequately from knowledge of the behavior characteristics of the drugstores, arithmetic classes, and basketball games that they inhabited than from knowledge of the behavior tendencies of the particular children. Indeed, the conformity of people to the patterns of real-life settings is so great that deviations therefrom are often newsworthy or considered indicative of serious abnormality requiring social or medical attention. Such deviancies within the settings of the town of Midwest constitute an infinitesimal proportion of the opportunities for deviancy.

A simple hypothesis to account for the conformity of persons to the patterns of the settings in which their behavior occurs is that there are, after all, some interior motivational and cognitive *constancies across persons* that interact with a *single array of environmental input* from a setting, producing similar (conforming) behavior across all the inhabitants. However, work by Willems (1964b) and by Gump (1964) shows that the everyday situations within which people live (restaurants, basketball games, band concerts) do not provide inhabitants with a limited and fixed array of environmental inputs; those authors show that, in fact, the inputs vary in accordance with the differing motives and cognitions of the inhabitants, and that in spite of this the characteristic behavior patterns of settings are generated. Our findings indicate that most of the environments in which people live are homeostatic systems that maintain their characteristic patterns (including the behavior of the inhabitants) within preset limits by means of control mechanisms. We all experience this: On the turnpike, when our speed deviates to the slow side, we receive recurring physical and social inputs to speed up, and if we do not do this sufficiently we are eventually ejected from the turnpike (by a rear-end crash or by a traffic officer); when our speed deviates to the fast side, we receive recurring physical and social inputs to slow down, and again if we do not do this sufficiently, we are finally ejected by a head-on crash, by missing a curve, or by a traffic officer. It is important to note that the turnpike is not concerned with the sources of the deviancy of its vehicular components. Slowness because of an overloaded and underpowered car is just as unacceptable to a turnpike as slowness because of an overly cautious driver. People and other entities are components of the environmental units they inhabit in the same way that a generator is a component of an engine and a bat of a ball game. These units are behavior settings, and the concepts and principles that explicate behavior settings are utterly alien to those that explicate their component parts, such as the behavior of individual persons.

Here is one of many environmental differences Midwest and Yoredale provide their inhabitants. Some settings require child components; they coerce and incorporate children into the ongoing programs. This is true of 7 percent of Midwest's habitat and 14 percent of Yoredale's habitat. Other settings do not tolerate child components; they have child-proof boundaries, and they eject any children who manage to enter. This is true of 14 percent of Midwest's and 19 percent of Yoredale's habitat. This environmental difference between the towns makes a difference in the behavior and experiences of the children of Midwest and Yoredale, and a complete analysis of the psychology of all the inhabitants of the towns would not account for it. Forces for and against children are properties of a town's settings (its school classes, its pubs, its courts, its Golden Age Club) and not of its individual citizens. Transposing the children of Midwest to Yoredale, and vice versa, would immediately transform their behavior in respect to the parts of the towns they would enter and avoid, despite their unchanged motives and cognitions. The forces of a community's settings vis-à-vis children are examples of the power of environmental units over behavior, of their superordinate position with respect to their human components, and of the need for an eco-behavioral science independent of psychology.

Facilities for an Eco-Behavioral Science

The eco-behavioral science that will answer the pressing questions society faces today requires, above all, concepts and theories appropriate to the phenomena involved. But these will not arise de novo; they will be grounded on empirical data concerning the patterns of events within the psychologist-free settings where people live their lives. Special facilities are required in order to obtain these data.

Archives. By definition, phenomena cannot be induced to occur by an investigator if his purpose is to study them under "natural," that is, scientist-free, conditions. Because many important phenomena occur infrequently under these conditions, it may require long periods of observation and be expensive to secure adequate instances of them. This is a fact that confronts every science in connection with its ecological investigations. The yield of data is low, for example, in studies of earthquakes, bank failures, and migrating birds. It is taxing and expensive to wait for earthquakes and bank failures and to search for banded birds. Nevertheless, geologists, economists, and biologists continue to investigate these phenomena. It is worthwhile asking how they do it.

For one thing, these scientists do not consider infrequent occurrence as unfortunate, as dross; they accept it for what it is, namely, one attribute of a phenomenon that must be recorded accurately along with its other attributes, one that must be taken into account by theory. For seismological theory, it is probably as important to know the nature and distribution of the earthquakes in the Middle West of the United States as of the more frequent earthquakes of the West Coast. Here, then, is a central operational difference between experimental and ecological science: Experiments alter phenomena of infrequent occurrence and make them frequent. In this state, they can be studied efficiently. Ecological investigations in which phenomena are studied in situ and "nature" is the only inducer cannot be efficient so far as frequency is concerned.

One way other sciences facilitate the study of ecological phenomena is by accumulating data as they become available over long periods of time, by preserving them, and by making them generally accessible. Archives and museums of primary data are standard research facilities of sciences with productive ecological programs. For this reason, a lone seismographer, student of banking, or ornithologist, with limited resources and but one life to live, has access to many data that are available for study in one's own way, according to one's own theories. This has not been possible for psychologists; the science has been almost devoid of data archives.

Data. Even more basic is the fact that psychology has had no methods for securing archival data. It has been almost exclusively an experimental science, and the data of experiments have little value for archives. The inputs and constraints imposed by experiments are usually so uniquely tied to the intentions of the investigator—to a particular hypothesis, for example—that a new investigator has little freedom to ask new questions of the data. About all one can do with the data of others' experiments is to try to replicate them: an essential task but nonetheless a merely technical one. The attributes of experimental data that limit their archival value are, of course, not defects. Quite the contrary, in fact; to the degree that experiments arrange inputs and channel outputs to answer specific questions, they are good experiments. Good experimental data are problem-centered and theory-guided, and their significance is usually limited by the particular problem or theory that prompted and guided their generation.

The converse is true for ecological studies. Here, the task of the investigator and the procedures is to translate phenomena without alteration into the language of data. In their most adequate form, ecological data are phenomena-centered and atheoretical. It has been heresy, in some quarters, to speak of atheoretical data. Experience has taught us, however, that even within a purely psychological context atheoretical data can be obtained and are of value. Eighteen full-day records of children's behavior and situations have been collected at the Midwest Psychological Field Station. When we made these records, we had plans, guided by theories, for analyzing them, but the plans and theories did not guide the making of the records. Our only intention was to translate the stream of behavior into a verbal record with as much completeness as possible. We made our own use of the records and made them available to others. Over the years, other studies based on these records have been made by investigators who had no part in assembling the records; most of these studies concern problems and involve theories and analytical procedures that were far from the minds of the data collectors. These specimens of individual behavior will continue to be of use in connection with problems not yet conceived. This experience has taught us that data that are dross for one investigator are gold for another.

An eco-behavioral science must have data archives. The scientists involved in this development will have much to learn about collecting, preserving, and retrieving ecological data. Undoubtedly, data suitable for archives are moldering unknown and unused in files and storerooms; on the other hand, new audiovisual and other recording techniques threaten to overwhelm a data depository with useless material. The problem of standards for atheoretical, phenomena-centered data is a difficult and important one; it deserves the best efforts of psychologists and eco-behavioral scientists.

Data analysis. One of the purposes of experimental techniques is to arrange the data that issue from data-generating systems so they will fit prevailing machines, statistical models, and concepts. Thus we have forced-choice tests, five-point scales, normalized distributions, equated control groups, and so on. These are not sins. They facilitate the purposes of experiments: to solve problems and test hypotheses that the investigators bring to the data. But if one's intention is to explore behavior and its environment, the phenomena themselves must dictate the choices, the scales, and the distributions. It is our experience that psychological measurement experts do not know statistical and analytical techniques for dealing with "natural" phenomena, even where they are available from other sciences. We need mathematical innovators and we need textbooks and handbooks of data-reduction methods culled from quantitative botany, demography, geography, physiology, and economics. When those who work on eco-behavioral problems do not have the analytical tools they need, they inevitably cast data in the molds of experimental psychology, molds that often destroy the essential nature of the phenomena they are investigating.

Field stations. Ecological scientists are not a source of input to or a constraint on the phenomena that they study; they do not instigate the occurrence of the phenomena with which they deal. They must, therefore, set up shop in regions where their phenomena are rich and accessible, and their shops must be staffed and equipped appropriately. Field stations and observatories are regular features of the establishments of other sciences. An eco-behavioral science must have its Woods Holes and Mount Wilsons. In our experience, ecological data are more difficult to procure than experimental data. Special facilities are required, and the locating, equipping, and staffing of a field station is as specialized and as expensive as establishing a clinic or an experimental laboratory.

Two different problems are involved in the collection of ecological data. One concerns specific data-generating procedures, such as observing and making records, taking photographs, making recordings, and using documents and records. The other problem relates to general policies and programs to be followed in establishing and operating a facility for gathering nonexperimental, eco-behavioral data. We shall consider the last problem briefly; we can do little more than list some of the factors we have found to be of importance.

A field station should be within a particular, bounded community or institution that encompasses the universe of phenomena to be studied. In the present state of development of eco-behavioral science, it is desirable to avoid very large and complex systems. A field station must have a sufficiently long life expectancy for the assembly of data on infrequently occurring and slowly changing phenomena. A field station is *not* a project; it is a program.

The relation of the station and its staff to the locale it investigates is of utmost importance. There must be access without interference, acceptance without reaction. The ecologist-citizen relation is not an experimenter-subject relation, not a physician-patient relation, and not a counselor-client relation. It is a new relation yet to be defined, but some aspects of it are clear. The ecologist-citizen relation is a privileged relation based on trust. The field station must operate within the mores and tolerances of the community; this is a part of the essential policy of a field station of respecting and not altering its phenomena. A consequence of this is that some studies and techniques are not admissible. The ecologist-citizen relation imposes personnel requirements on a field station. It must have expert staff members whose primary job is to maintain communication between station and community, to define the functions of the field station, and especially to differentiate the field station from common conceptions of clinics and laboratories. The station must have local staff members for field work; this provides some protection against misunderstandings. Local residence is essential for many staff members, and they must participate in community affairs. Publications must be stated in objective, conceptual terms, and they must be nonevaluative. Station-community trust and mutual acceptance are the first requirements, and these must be maintained and renewed by continual effort.

Some may think these requirements very restricting. Our experience in Kansas and Yorkshire is that they impose fewer limitations than skeptics expect. This is the case, in part, because a field station has sources of support, too. Citizens are seriously concerned with the problems on which eco-behavioral field stations work, and the field station brings some status and substance to the community.

There are, then, four facility-operations problems that arise directly from the fundamental nature of eco-behavioral research: an archival problem, a data problem, an analysis problem, and a field station problem.

These problems are great, but the possibility of arriving at scientifically meaningful and socially useful results is also great, and they justify the commitment of intellect, effort, and money to the task.

Concluding Thoughts on Behavior Settings

The ecological environment of molar human behavior, whether we consider small towns such as Midwest and Yoredale or large metropolitan centers, is an assembly of dynamic, homeostatic entities (drugstores, city council meetings, third-grade music classes, museums, concerts, and so forth) where people are essential components (among other classes of components, such as drugs, a gavel, music books, displays, musical instruments). These are behavior settings, and within them people do not act in relation to a relatively fixed, dependable environment of benefits, deficiencies, and constraints, because stores, meetings, classes, and all other behavior settings have plans for their human components and armories of alternative ways of enforcing their plans. But this does not mean that people are powerless vis-à-vis behavior settings. Quite the contrary; when people understand behavior settings and learn to create and operate them, they greatly increase their power by managing the environment that has so coercive an influence over them. As essential parts of ongoing behavior setting enterprises that are larger than their personal undertakings, they have a hand in providing satisfactions (and dissatisfactions), not only for themselves and their immediate associates but for all others involved in the setting. As essential components of behavior settings, people have significance for more than those with whom they have direct contact.

The fundamental significance of behavior settings for the behavior sciences comes from their position within the topological hierarchy of entities ranging from cell, to organ, to person, to behavior setting, to institution (in some cases), and to community. Within this included-inclusive series, behavior settings are proximal and circumjacent to people (people are components of behavior settings), and behavior settings are proximal and interjacent to institutions and communities (they are components of institutions and communities). Although we have only the beginning of an understanding of behavior settings, we can see that enlightenment must move in two directions: inward to relationships between behavior settings and their human components, and outward to relationships with institutions and communities. In both directions, there are important potential applications. People control their lives to an important extent (1) by creating and influencing the programs of the behavior settings of their communities and (2) by selecting, so far as possible, the settings into which they allow themselves to be incorporated. A person's greatest strength is at the boundary of a setting; once one "joins," it becomes necessary to cope with much greater forces than those operating at the boundary. Knowledge of a community's behavior settings should be a strong weapon in the armory of those professionals who counsel individual persons.

INTERIOR RELATIONSHIPS: BEHAVIOR SETTINGS AND PEOPLE

Behavior settings are the concrete environmental units where people engage in behavior. People do not live in poverty or affluence, in the middle or the upper classes; they live in behavior settings. The terms "poverty" and "upper class" refer to some aspects of the actual settings people inhabit. Behavior within the settings where people live is influenced by three classes of variables: their physical properties, the number and character of their human components, and their programs. All three doubtless contribute to such global qualities as poverty and upper classness.

Physical properties of behavior settings. The amount and arrangement of space, the number, location, and properties of entrances and exits, the illumination, temperature, and decoration, and the furnishings and equipment of behavior settings all contribute to their standing patterns of behavior. Paving the streets of a small town (behavior setting Trafficways) is likely to contribute to increases in the speed with which inhabitants drive their cars. Similarly, "speed bumps" are placed in appropriate locations to reduce automobile speed. The importance of the physical properties of behavior settings is suggested by the significance for baseball games of the size, shape, and boundaries of the field and by the furor in the basketball fraternity caused by the proposal to increase the height of the basket. Manipulating the physical properties of behavior settings in order to influence behavior is the province of architects, engineers, and designers. Unfortunately, solid empirical evidence or promising theories to guide these professionals have been meager. In recent years, for example, many "open" schools have been built with very little knowledge of the consequences for children and teachers of behavior settings without boundary walls. However, our ignorance of the relations between the physical aspects of behavior settings and behavior is now well recognized, and this is an area of vigorous research; this may provide a basis for new specialities, such as eco-behavioral architecture, engineering, and design.

Human components of behavior settings. Behavior within a setting is influenced by the number and the characteristics of its human components. We are relatively well informed about some consequences of variation in number of human components, especially of fewer than an adequate number of human components, of the underpopulation of behavior settings. Issues of greatest social importance are involved here, for in many parts of the world the balance is changing from scarcity or adequacy to redundancy of human components for behavior settings. In the United States, for example, in the days of the Western frontier, people were at a premium to operate the established settings. People were valued in a nation of many underpopulated behavior settings, and the characteristic syndrome of behavior on the frontier was in close accord with the derivations from behavior setting theory: busyness, hard work, versatility, self-confidence, self-esteem, responsibility, low standards, mutual support. Now the United States and many other societies are confronted with the problem of how to cope with too many people. At the level of behavior settings and their interior relations with their human components, the answer is clear: Keep the number of people and the number of behavior settings in balance so that all available people are needed for behavior setting operation. This requires reducing the number of people or creating more behavior settings with fewer inhabitants per setting. Is the latter possible? In a crisis of declining supplies of gasoline, we place constraints on large automobiles. In a crisis of increasing numbers of people, can we place constraints on large behavior settings? Much of the answer to this lies in the external relations of settings and with the institutions and communities of which they are parts.

We know very little about how the characteristics (as opposed to the number) of the human components of behavior settings affect their operations and then rebound on the components. But we do know that variety is essential for the functioning of almost all settings. Even so specialized a behavior setting as a president's news conference requires not only the president and newsmen for its occurrence, but persons with the skills of audio engineers, guards, custodians, photographers, video specialists, and so forth. Physical components are as essential to behavior settings as human components; likewise, people with strong backs and skilled hands are as essential as those with intellectual and verbal abilities. When such human diversity occurs in behavior settings, the setting itself—with its controls and interior forces—produces a functional tolerance and appreciation among its human components.

Programs of behavior settings. The point of entry for most directly influencing behavior within a setting is by way of its program of operation. When a teacher makes a new lesson plan, when a chairperson changes the agenda of a business meeting, or when the new owner of a store changes its policies, the standing patterns of behavior in the settings change appropriately: the pupils may do seat work instead of recitations, the members of the meeting may vote on issue Y before they vote on issue X, and the customers may have to pay cash rather than charge their purchases. But most program changes cannot be made easily. An established behavior setting is an interdependent, homeostatic entity in semistable equilibrium, and as such it is resistant to change. A change in program may require more space, rearranged space, and new equipment, and it may meet physical and perhaps economic resistance; it may require more or fewer human components and altered behavior and may face social and psychological opposition. Some resistance may also come from the outside; for example, permission from a reluctant zoning commission may be required. Furthermore, because of the interdependence of behavior settings, changes in parts reverberate in unexpected ways through them, and a change in program may have unforeseeable consequences, some of which may be undesirable. Kounin (1970), for example, found that a school class program that involved publicly countering certain kinds of behavior deviation had consequences far beyond the disciplined person whose misbehavior the program was intended to correct.

It is sometimes easier to establish a new behavior setting than it is to change the program of an old one. Members of a church who become dissatisfied with its program and meet resistance to change may more easily withdraw and establish a new church with behavior setting programs that satisfy them. New interests, new social policies, new dilemmas, and new opportunities require new behavior settings. Such changes were clearly documented in our studies of Midwest and Yoredale. In 1963–64, Midwest consisted of 884 behavior settings; 504 of these (57 percent) were newly established during the previous decade, amounting to 56 new behavior settings per year, on the average. Moreover, behavior settings continually cease to occur. There were 576 behavior settings in Midwest in 1954–55; in the following decade, 215 of these (36 percent) vanished, amounting to 24 a year, on the average. Because the rate of accretion of behavior settings was greater than the rate of erosion, Midwest was more extensive as a human habitat in 1964 than in 1954. Less than half (43 percent) of its 1963–64 behavior settings were as much as ten years old. During the decade, Midwest grew 53 percent in terms of behavior settings and 16 percent in terms of population, so here is one town that was not troubled with an increase in inhabitants; over this period, it created for itself a habitat where people were in ever-greater demand as behavior setting components.

Communities renew themselves by changing the programs of their ongoing behavior settings, by discarding settings, and by creating new settings. Sarason (1972, 1974; Sarason & Others, 1977) has elucidated important aspects of these processes. Such changes in community settings are at the present time in the hands of practical persons: proprietors of stores, chairpersons, band leaders, classroom teachers, club presidents, corporate officers, politicians, community activists, and so forth. These change agents are necessarily amateurs (some of them expert amateurs) because we do not yet have a science and an accompanying technology of behavior settings.

WHOLE-PART RELATIONS

Eco-behavioral science and ecological psychology deal, respectively, with whole phenomena—namely, behavior settings—and with certain parts of the same phenomena; they do this in the way that some physical sciences deal with wholes (for example, bridge design) and other sciences deal with parts (steel, concrete) of the same structure. Just as some attributes of the physical parts when in place are determined by the structures into which they are built (their compression, temperature) and some attributes of the structures are determined by their component materials (endurance, vibration), some attributes of the human components of behavior settings are determined by the behavior settings into which they are incorporated (busyness, versatility) and some attributes of the behavior settings are determined by their human components (stability, functioning level). The "whole" sciences and the "part" sciences can be pursued independently; the forms and properties of steel and concrete can be investigated without reference to their use in bridges, and the dynamics of arches can be studied without reference to the use of steel and concrete in their construction. Nevertheless, the history of science reveals a continual enrichment of the sciences of wholes by the sciences of parts and vice versa. This is clearly shown in the work at the Midwest Psychological Field Station, where data of ecological psychology, the science of behavior setting parts, led to the discovery of the whole phenomena, behavior settings. The inclusion of behavior settings in the study of problems of ecological psychology greatly explains the latter; studies of behavior differences between American and English children (Barker & Barker, 1978) and between physically handicapped and nonhandicapped children (Schoggen, 1978), and studies of physical rehabilitation in a hospital (Willems & Halstead, 1978), are good examples.

At the current stage of its development, the scientific rigor of ecological psychology is greatly increased by eco-behavioral science. Previously, it was impossible to satisfactorily identify and describe the environmental context of the naturally occurring behavior of persons under investigation. The best that could usually be done was to specify the geographical location and fragments of some of the social context. So in this respect ecological psychology was less rigorous than experimental psychology, which created and precisely described the environment (the experimental conditions) of the behavior it studied. Now, with the ability to specify the behavior settings in which actions occur, much more rigorous studies are possible (Barker & Barker, 1978; Schoggen, Barker, & Barker, 1978; Schoggen, 1978; Willems & Halstead, 1978).

EXTERIOR RELATIONS: BEHAVIOR SETTINGS, INSTITUTIONS, AND COMMUNITIES

Behavior settings are fundamental units for describing the habitat that an institution or community provides its inhabitants. On an elementary level, a simple listing of the settings and changes in the lists over time provides important information. In the decade between 1954 and 1964, the following behavior settings, among others, disappeared from the list of Midwest's settings—circus, cream collection station, dairy barn, farm practice class, ice depot, telephone exchange—and these new settings, among others, appeared—bowling games, kindergarten classes, self-service laundry, telephone kiosks, X-ray laboratory. When measures of the extents and properties of behavior settings are added, more meaningful data are obtained; the lists become equivalent, so far as human behavior possibilities are concerned, to a catalogue of the soils of a region, with their properties and extents, for plant growth possibilities. In 1963–64, behavior setting programs with high concentrations of business behavior constituted 17.1 percent of Midwest's and 28.3 percent of Yoredale's total habitats, whereas settings with high concentrations of religious behavior constituted 8.5 percent of Midwest's and 4.2 percent of Yoredale's habitat. When measures of the amount of behavior are included, the description of the town as a habitat for behavior becomes still more complete. Although Yoredale's business habitat was 74 percent greater than Midwest's, its behavior output via town inhabitants was only 48 percent greater; in fact, Midwest's business habitat produced 6 percent more business behavior per town inhabitant than Yoredale's. Midwest's business habitat was less extensive but more productive than Yoredale's.

None of the behavior settings in Midwest or in similar towns stand alone; all are subject to controls from outside their boundaries. Some are subject only to prohibitions from the encircling town. The behavior setting Women's Bridge Club II can do as it pleases except set up its tables in the middle of Illinois Street, thus interfering with the operations of other behavior settings and the rights of persons who are not members. The program, components, and equipment of Women's Bridge Club II are its own business. But other behavior settings are less free. This is true, for example, of the setting High School Algebra I Class. Its physical properties (location, duration, equipment), its human components (members, teacher), and its program (teaching methods, topics to be covered) are imposed to a great degree by the institution, the high school, of which Algebra I is a part. But Algebra I is by no means helpless. There is two-way interaction between the setting and the school, and forces from the school often elicit counterforces or resistance from the setting. This is the arena of business executives, school superintendents, city managers, management experts, community psychologists, and students of organizations.

In Chaps. 9 and 10 above, we considered one issue of general theoretical significance in the relationship between institutions and their component parts—namely, the relationship between the size of institutions (in terms of number of inhabitants) and the population of their constituent behavior settings. The studies reviewed there demonstrate that the component behavior settings of large institutions are, on the average, larger than those of small institutions and that underpopulation is more prevalent among the settings of small institutions than of large ones. In view of these findings that in relatively small, underpopulated settings more people have power and importance than in large ones, we asked if it is inevitable that large settings diminish their inhabitants in this way. Must the large, consolidated school have large algebra classes, a large football game, a large cafeteria, and so forth, where hardly anyone is missed by the setting when absent and where a crucial problem of classes, games, and services is the superabundance of people? We asked if a newly planned school could not have three football teams and games, as the small schools in the separate towns before consolidation. To most school officials, the question was ridiculous. Efficiency is the name of the school game, as it is of the business game, the government game, even the church game. The argument is that one pastor and ten lay representatives with modern technology (such as automobiles, word-processing facilities, sound systems, and audiovisual aids) can run a unified 900-member church more effectively than six pastors and sixty lay representatives can run six 150-member churches; in short, a large church is more personnel-efficient and technically superior. The one big-church pastor can be more highly selected (more intelligent, more learned, more charismatic, more spiritual) than six small-church pastors, and his assistants can be specialists (in youth work, in music, in counseling). But there is one more attribute of the large, more efficient, unified church: It greatly reduces the significance in church affairs of about 80 percent of the formerly powerful and important lay representatives and pastors and of an uncounted number of Sunday School teachers, committee chairpersons, ushers, organists, secretaries, and choir members. The six churches provide many more people than does the large church with the opportunity to satisfy their needs to be competent and approved by carrying out essential operations in valued enterprises. We observed an instance of this during our studies of Yoredale when a new local government policy was instituted by consolidating a number of rural district councils into a single, large, and presumably efficient district government. This entailed sacrificing 22 of 24 local councillors with the evaluation, "you will never be missed," in fact, "we are better off without you." Besides depriving these people of important satisfactions, the change deprived local government of the talents and devotion of many able, responsible people.

The pressures of population, technology, and efficiency against opportunities for people to be significant may be as great a threat to survival as the pressure of population against food. The former threat is as salient, or more so, in "advanced" as in underdeveloped countries. The assertion that large, personnel-efficient, technically superior enterprises inevitably produce a better product more cheaply requires searching investigation. Modern transportation and communication make it possible to share expertise among small enterprises; it would seem that reading specialists can be transported between small schools more cheaply than the bodies of 600 students can be transported to the reading specialists. And a frequent error in computing the costs of a personnel-efficient enterprise is to ignore the costs that are exported beyond its walls. A greater proportion of dropouts from a large school than from several small schools would amount to exporting problems and expenses to other institutions and settings (to courts, jails, counseling centers, dole lines), problems and costs the community must meet. The science and art of reducing the size of machines without sacrificing their output has been spectacular in many cases; we have efficient small computers, copy machines, electric motors, gasoline engines, clothes washers, television sets, pumps, generators, and so forth. There would appear to be a similar opportunity to contrive efficient, small behavior settings where people are important. Small is indeed beautiful to people who want to reduce the risk of being helpless and expendable.

At times during the past 30 years of research on ecological psychology and behavior settings, it seemed that the research findings reduced the importance of people and increased the importance of the environment. Finally, however, it has become clear that eco-behavioral science enhances the power and importance of people to the degree that we understand and make use of behavior settings.

Reference Matter

Appendix: Occupancy Time Code

See pp. 141–43 and Tables 7.4, 7.5

Interval	Code	Score	Interval	Code	Score
0–1	1	0.25	5,526–6,201	26	5,857
2–5	2	2.50	6,202–6,930	27	6,559
6–14	3	8.75	6,931–7,714	28	7,315
15–30	4	21.00	7,715–8,555	29	8,127
31–55	5	41.25	8,556–9,455	30	8,998
56–91	6	71.50	9,456–10,416	31	9,928
92–140	7	113.75	10,417–11,440	32	10,920
141–204	8	170.00	11,441–12,529	33	11,976
205–285	9	242.25	12,530–13,685	34	13,099
286–385	10	332.50	13,686–14,910	35	14,289
386–506	11	442.75	14,911–16,206	36	15,549
507–650	12	575.00	16,207–17,575	37	16,881
651–819	13	731.25	17,576–19,019	38	18,288
820–1,015	14	913.50	19,020–20,150	39	19,770
1,016–1,240	15	1,123.75	20,151–21,750	40	21,330
1,241–1,496	16	1,364.00	21,751–23,431	41	22,970
1,497–1,785	17	1,636.25	23,432–25,195	42	24,693
1,786–2,109	18	1,942.50	25,196–27,044	43	26,499
2,110–2,470	19	2,284.75	27,045–28,980	44	28,391
2,471–2,870	20	2,665.00	28,981–31,005	45	30,371
2,871–3,311	21	3,085	31,006–33,121	46	32,441
3,312–3,795	22	3,548	33,122–35,330	47	34,604
3,796–4,324	23	4,054	35,331–37,154	48	36,860
4,325–4,900	24	4,606	37,155–39,555	49	39,212
4,901–5,525	25	5,206	39,556–42,055	50	41,662

Interval	Code	Score	Interval	Code	Score
42,056–44,656	51	44,213	207,466–214,861	86	212,012
44,657–47,360	52	46,865	214,862–222,430	87	219,494
47,361–50,169	53	49,621	222,431–230,174	88	227,150
50,170–53,085	54	52,484	230,175–238,095	89	234,983
53,086–56,110	55	55,454	238,096–246,195	90	242,993
56,111–59,246	56	58,534	246,196–254,476	91	251,183
59,247–62,495	57	61,726	254,477–262,940	92	259,556
62,496–65,859	58	65,033	262,941–271,589	93	268,112
65,860–69,340	59	68,455	271,590–280,425	94	276,854
69,341–72,940	60	71,995	280,426–289,450	95	285,784
72,941–76,661	61	75,655	289,451–298,666	96	294,904
76,662–80,505	62	79,438	298,667–308,075	97	304,217
80,506–84,474	63	83,344	308,076–317,679	98	313,723
84,475–88,570	64	87,376	317,680–327,480	99	323,425
88,571–92,975	65	91,537	327,481–337,480	100	333,325
92,976–97,151	66	95,827	337,481–347,681	101	343,425
97,152–101,640	67	100,249	347,682–358,085	102	353,728
101,641–106,264	68	104,806	358,086–368,694	103	364,234
106,265–111,025	69	109,498	368,695–379,510	104	374,946
111,026–115,925	70	114,328	379,511–390,535	105	385,866
115,926–120,966	71	119,298	390,536–401,771	106	396,996
120,967–126,150	72	124,410	401,772–413,220	107	408,338
126,151–131,479	73	129,667	413,221–424,884	108	419,894
131,480–136,955	74	135,069	424,885–436,775	109	431,666
136,956–142,580	75	140,619	436,776–448,865	110	443,657
142,581–148,356	76	146,320	448,866–461,186	111	455,867
148,357–154,285	77	152,172	461,187–473,730	112	468,299
154,286–160,369	78	158,178	473,731–486,499	113	480,956
160,370–166,610	79	164,340	486,500–499,495	114	493,838
166,611–173,010	80	170,660	499,496–512,720	115	506,948
173,011–179,571	81	177,141	512,721–526,176	116	520,288
179,572–186,295	82	183,783	526,177–539,865	117	533,860
186,296–193,184	83	190,589	539,866–553,789	118	547,667
193,185–200,240	84	197,562	553,790–567,950	119	561,709
200,241–207,465	85	204,702	567,951–582,350	120	575,989

Glossary

Action patterns: functional attributes of the standing patterns of behavior settings in terms of eleven descriptive variables: Aesthetics, Business, Education, Government, Nutrition, Personal Appearance, Physical Health, Professional Involvement, Recreation, Religion, and Social Contact.

Actones: molecular acts.

Attendance: a behavior setting attribute referring to the extent to which different population subgroups or classes are subject to pressure to inhabit or avoid them; for example, six-year-old children in Midwest are required to inhabit the behavior setting First Grade Academic Subjects (or an equivalent setting) and are excluded from the behavior setting Boy Scout Troop Meeting.

Authority system: a behavior setting with power to control only its own behavior patterns or those of a number of other behavior settings. Authority systems are grouped into five classes: Private Enterprises, Churches, Government Agencies, Schools, and Voluntary Associations.

Autonomy: a measure of the locus of control of behavior setting operations. It reflects the extent to which decisions with respect to officers, membership rules, agenda, meeting places and times, space, equipment, budgets, etc., of the setting are made within the town, the school district, the county, or the state or at the national level.

Behavior mechanisms: modalities through which molar behavior is implemented within behavior settings, such as Gross Motor Actions, Manipulation (fine motor actions), Verbalization, and Affective Behavior.

Behavior objects: natural and manufactured things with reference to which behavior of persons is transacted; the ordinary objects of behavioral commerce within behavior settings, including other persons as social behavior objects—for example, book, cup, chalk, leaves, grass, stone, cloud, shirt, teaspoon, pencil, brother, Mary, Mr. Green, telephone, typewriter.

Behavior output: the amount of behavior generated within behavior settings as measured by person-hours or occupancy time, inhabitant-setting intersections, and claim-operations.

Behavior setting: one or more standing patterns of behavior-and-milieu, with the milieu circumjacent and synomorphic to the behavior and with a specified degree of interdependence among the synomorphs.

Behavioral environment: Koffka's term for the environment as perceived by the behaving person.

Beneficence: a behavior setting attribute referring to the extent to which the setting serves different population subgroups or classes more or less equally; for example, children are the intended beneficiaries of school classes, meetings of the Cub Scouts, and Santa's visit to the town square.

Centiurb (cu): 1 percent of an urb. Measurement of habitat extent in terms of centiurbs is a measure of the at-handness of habitat supports and coercions for molar actions; it is a temporal-spatial proximity measure.

Claim-operation: a special type of inhabitant-setting intersection (ISI); it is an ISI in the operating zones 6, 5, or 4 of a behavior setting—that is, a unique combination of a particular behavior setting, a specific habitat-claim in penetration zones 6, 5, or 4 of the setting, and a particular human component implementing the claim.

Deviation-countering circuits: one of two types of routes within a behavior setting by means of which the setting is maintained with its program and goal circuits intact; errors or inadequacies that interfere with the operation of program or goal circuits are corrected. See also vetoing circuits.

Distal objects: objects separated from the perceiver by physical distance; objects not in direct contact with the perceiving organism, such as a fly ball in a baseball game.

Dynamic interdependence: the degree of influence between entities; the extent to which a change in one entity, such as a particular synomorph, is accompanied by change in another entity, another synomorph.

Dynamic interdependence test (K-test): reflects the degree of influence or functional interdependence between synomorphs—that is, the degree to which change in one is accompanied by change in another. Potential behavior settings that pass the structure test—synomorphs or synomorph complexes—must also pass the test for dynamic interdependence.

Eco-behavioral science: the name suggested by Barker for a new science, independent of psychology, that is concerned with the ecological environment; such a new science is necessary because the ecological environment is governed by laws that are incommensurate with the laws of scientific psychology, making it impossible to understand the ecological environment with the concepts and theories of scientific psychology.

Ecological environment: the objective, preperceptual context of behavior, including both social and physical-geographical-temporal components of the real-life, everyday settings within which people engage in goal-directed, purposive behavior.

Ecological psychology: the study of individual molar behavior in natural, real-life situations—that is, situations not contrived by the investigator for scientific purposes—using unobtrusive, noninterfering methods such as direct, nonparticipant observation.

Ecological units: occur without feedback from the investigator (they are self-generated), each unit has a time-space locus, and an unbroken boundary separates an internal pattern from a differing external pattern. The nature of the units with which ecology deals is the same whether they are physical, social, biological, or behavioral units.

E-O-E arc: the environment-organism-environment continuum identified by Brunswik; also referred to as the psychological unit or behavior unit. It includes three major sectors: the ecological sector of objects and physical events that become stimuli; the organism or intrapersonal sector of receptor, central, and effector processes; and the behavioral sector of actones and molar behavior achievements that occur, again, in the ecological environment.

Extra-individual patterns of behavior: setting inhabitants display stable patterns of behavior—such as teaching, reciting, and reading in a school class—that continue more or less unchanged over time despite turnover in personnel.

Genotype: a class of behavior settings with similar programs; two settings are of the same genotype if their operation could continue largely undisturbed after the interchange of their most central operatives. For example, one attorney could exchange practices with another attorney without extensive delay, but an attorney could not exchange practices with a dentist; therefore attorneys' offices and dentists' offices belong to different genotypes.

Genotype comparator: a standardized form for use in comparing two behavior settings to determine whether they belong to the same or different genotypes.

Geographic environment: Koffka's term for the objective, physical-geographical environment.

Goal circuits: routes within behavior settings by means of which setting inhabitants can reach goals that are personally satisfying.

Habitat-claims for human components: the loci, slots, or positions at any level of penetration within behavior settings that require human components for the setting to function; habitat-claims are stable structural and dynamic features of the habitat provided by a community or institution.

Habitat-claims for operatives: the loci, slots, or positions within behavior settings at penetration levels 6, 5, or 4 that require human components for the setting to function; for example, the position of secretary of 4-H Club Regular Meeting requires an appropriate human component, one with the necessary knowledge and skills.

Habitat extent: the size of either the whole or parts of a community or institution in terms of the numbers of opportunities and obligations for engaging in different kinds of molar behavior; habitat extent is measured in centiurbs.

Habitat variety: the number of different kinds of behavior settings reflecting the diversity or the homogeneity of molar behavior resources and the range of molar behavior opportunities among the behavior settings of a community or institution; habitat variety is measured by the number of behavior setting genotypes.

Inhabitant-setting intersection (ISI): a unique combination of a particular behavior setting in any of its occurrences and a specific human component in any penetration zone of the setting during one or more of its occurrences.

Interjacent: interconnected via intersecting physical or temporal boundaries. For example, the fountain and the drugstore are interjacent; the Sunday morning worship service and the Presbyterian church are interjacent.

K-test: A procedure for measuring dynamic interdependence between two synomorphs (potential behavior settings).

K-21 behavior setting: a synomorph or synomorph complex that passes the K test for dynamic interdependence at the selected level of 21; a behavior setting that passes the K test at the level of 21 or higher is considered sufficiently independent of other synomorphs or synomorph complexes to qualify as an independent behavior setting.

Life-space: Lewin's basic unit for the analysis of individual behavior consisting of the more or less differentiated psychological person (inner-personal regions and the motoric) and the psychological environment (the person's subjective representation of the environment).

Maintenance circuits: deviation-countering and vetoing circuits within a behavior setting by means of which the setting and its goal and program circuits are maintained intact.

Milieu: the objective, nonpsychological environment or situation; the constellation of nonbehavioral (physical, geographical) parts of a setting, such as buildings, streets, basketballs, hymn books, soda fountains, trees, flowers, sunshine, rain.

Molar behavior: goal-directed, purposive behavior of the whole person, such as getting dressed, having breakfast, going to school, or working on an arithmetic assignment. See molecular behavior for contrast.

Molar ecological environment: those naturally occurring phenomena outside a person's skin with which the person's molar actions are coupled but which function according to laws that are incommensurate with the laws that govern the person's molar behavior.

Molecular behavior: automatic, routinized behavior of subsystems of the person, carried out without awareness, such as pulling on socks, chewing food, taking a step in walking, or turning the page of an arithmetic book. See molar behavior for contrast.

Occupancy time (OT): the total number of hours spent by occupants of a behavior setting (or class of settings) during the survey year; also called person-hours.

Operating zones: penetration zones 6 (single leader), 5 (joint leaders), and 4 (active functionaries).

Operational range: the extent in centiurbs of the behavior settings in which members of a particular inhabitant subgroup or class are operatives or performers (zones 6, 5, or 4).

Operatives or performers: inhabitants who occupy behavior setting operating zones; they are the most immediately essential inhabitants of behavior settings because they are responsible for maintaining the setting as a structural unit and operating its program.

Operator data: data produced by a data-generating system in which the psychologist functions both as a transducer and as an operator; the psychologist is coupled into the psychological unit as an operative part of it, regulating input, and/or influencing interior conditions, and/or restraining output. Most traditional research methods in psychology—such as experiments, tests, and interviews—produce operator data. See transducer data for contrast.

Penetration: the power that different parts of a setting exert over the operation of the entire setting ranging across seven zones—from zone 6 (single leader), the most central and most powerful, to zone 0 (potential inhabitants), the most peripheral zone and the one with the least power over the setting.

Person-hours: see occupancy time, above.

Preperceptual: refers to phenomena as they exist independently of any particular person's perception of them, such as the objectively measurable wave length of light or sound; the objectively observable (ecological) environment of behavior.

Primary habitat: the behavior setting of a town where a given attribute is prominent; for example, the behavior settings of a town where Education is prominent make up the primary educational habitat of the town. The extent in centiurbs of the primary habitat is a measure of a town's major habitat resources for generating behavior possessing the particular attribute.

Program circuits: routes within behavior settings by means of which the program of the setting is implemented by inhabitants.

Prominent attribute: a behavior setting attribute (such as the action pattern Education or the behavior mechanism Gross Motor Action) is prominent if it occurs in connection with 80 percent or more of the standing pattern of a behavior setting; an attribute is secondary if it is present but not prominent.

Proximal event: the perception of an object or event at the receptor surface of a person, such as the image of a moving fly ball on a baseball player's retinas.

Psychological ecology: Lewin's term for the study of the interrelationships between psychological processes within the person and the nonpsychological environment or foreign hull. This term was also used by Barker and Wright in connection with their early studies of behavior and naturally occurring environments in the Midwest studies, but they have preferred the term "ecological psychology" since about 1968.

Psychological environment: a person's subjective representation of the ecological environment; the environment as perceived by—as it exists psychologically for—a particular person at a given time. It is part of the life-space as defined by Lewin.

Standard behavior setting: a behavior setting that occurs continuously throughout the year; its dimensional values as percentages of the dimensions of the standard town (urb) serve as convenient weights for determining the measurement of habitat extent in centiurbs of any town, part of town, or single behavior setting. Its extent in centiurbs is 1.25, the mean of the dimensional values of 0.147 percent (per year), 0.662 percent (per day), and 2.932 percent (per hour).

Standard town: an urb (see urb, below).

Standing pattern of behavior: a bounded pattern in the behavior of persons, en masse; a discrete, extra-individual behavior entity, such as the game-playing of basketball team members, the refereeing of the officials, or the leading of cheers by the cheerleaders. Each standing pattern of behavior has specific temporal-spatial coordinates (that is, each has a precise and delimited position or location in time and space), such as a basketball game, a worship service, or a piano lesson.

Structure test: a potential behavior setting must pass the structure test showing that it is a behavior-milieu synomorph; it must show that it is (1) a standing pattern of behavior, (2) in a particular milieu complex, (3) at particular time-space loci, (4) with behavior and milieu synomorphic, and (5) with milieu circumjacent to the behavior pattern.

Synomorph: an instance of congruence or fittingness between a particular behavior pattern and specific parts of the milieu, such as the behavior-milieu configuration of the pastor reading or preaching from the pulpit, the physical dimensions of which fit and support the behavior patterns—reading from the Bible or notes for the sermon.

Synomorphic relation: similar in structure, form, or shape; standing patterns of behavior are synomorphic with the physical-geographical-temporal components of a behavior setting. For example, the furniture in a classroom and the behavior patterns of studying, reciting, and writing are similar in shape or structure; the desks and seats fit the sitting and studying behavior patterns.

Territorial range: (a) the sum of the prominent and secondary extents of a behavior setting attribute, such as the territorial range of the action pattern Education is the extent in centiurbs of the habitat in which education is either prominent or secondary; (b) the territorial range of a class of inhabitants is the extent in centiurbs of the behavior settings that members of the class enter at any level of penetration, from zone 6 through zone 1.

Transducer data: data produced by a data-generating system in which the psychologist functions only as a docile receiver, coder, and transmitter of information about the input, interior conditions, and output of psychological units; there is no input from the psychologist to the data-generating system. Direct, nonparticipant observation is the most commonly used method of producing transducer data. See operator data for contrast.

Urb: a unit for the measurement of habitat extent derived from a hypothetical standard town whose dimensions in terms of number of behavior settings per year (680.5), mean number per day (151.0), and mean number per hour (34.1) were obtained by calculating for each of these dimensions the mean of four values: Midwest in 1954–55 and in 1963–64 and Yoredale in 1954–55 and in 1963–64. For convenience, the dimensional values of a town, part of a town, or of an individual behavior setting are calculated and reported in terms of percentages of the urb values, or centiurbs.

Vetoing circuits: one of two types of routes within a behavior setting by means of which the setting is maintained with its program and goal circuits intact; errors or inadequacies that interfere with the operation of program and goal circuits are dealt with by ejecting the deviant component from the setting. See also deviation-countering circuits.

Zones: see penetration, above.

References

Abelson, R. P. (1981). Psychological status of the script concept. *American Psychologist*, *36*, 715–29.

Adelberg, B. (1977). The activity ranges of children in urban and exurban communities. (Doctoral diss., University of Kansas.) *Dissertation Abstracts International*, *38*, 3462B.

Allen, V. L., & van de Vliert, E. (Eds.) (1984). *Role transitions: Explorations and explanations*. New York: Plenum Press.

Allport, F. H. (1955). *Theories of perception and the concept of structure: A review and critical analysis, with an introduction to a dynamic-structural theory of behavior*. New York: Wiley.

Allport, G. W. (1964). *Pattern and growth in personality*. New York: Holt, Rinehart & Winston.

Argyle, M., & Little, B. R. (1972). Do personality traits apply to social behaviour? *Journal for the Theory of Social Behaviour*, *2*, 1–35.

Arnold, D. W., & Greenberg, C. I. (1980). Deviate rejection within differentially manned groups. *Social Psychology Quarterly*, *43*, 419–24.

Ashby, W. R. (1956). *An introduction to cybernetics*. New York: Wiley.

Ashton, M. (1964). *An ecological study of the stream of behavior*. Unpublished master's thesis, University of Kansas, Lawrence.

Baird, L. L. (1969). Big school, small school: A critical examination of the hypothesis. *Journal of Educational Psychology*, *60*, 253–60.

Barker, R. G. (1960). Ecology and motivation. In M. R. Jones (Ed.), *Nebraska Symposium on Motivation* (vol. 8, pp. 1–49). Lincoln: University of Nebraska Press.

——— (1962, March). *Roles, ecological niches, and the psychology of the absent organism*. Paper presented at Conference on the Propositional Structure of Role Theory, Columbia, MO.

——— (1963a). On the nature of the environment. *Journal of Social Issues*, *19*, 17–38.

——— (1963b). The stream of behavior as an empirical problem. In R. G. Barker (Ed.), *The stream of behavior* (pp. 1–22). New York: Appleton-Century-Crofts.

——— (1965). Explorations in ecological psychology. *American Psychologist*, *20*, 1–14.

────── (1968). *Ecological psychology: Concepts and methods for studying the environment of human behavior*. Stanford, CA: Stanford University Press.

────── (1969). Wanted: An eco-behavioral science. In E. P. Willems & H. L. Raush (Eds.), *Naturalistic viewpoints in psychological research* (pp. 31–43). New York: Holt, Rinehart & Winston.

────── (1978a). Need for an eco-behavioral science. In R. G. Barker & Associates, *Habitats, environments, and human behavior* (pp. 36–48). San Francisco: Jossey-Bass.

────── (1978b). Return trip. In R. G. Barker & Associates, *Habitats, environments, and human behavior* (pp. 285–96). San Francisco: Jossey-Bass.

────── (1979). The influence of frontier environments on behavior. In J. O. Steffen (Ed.), *The American west: New perspectives, new dimensions* (pp. 61–93). Norman: University of Oklahoma Press.

────── (1987). Prospecting in environmental psychology. In D. Stokols & I. Altman (Eds.), *Handbook of environmental psychology* (vol. 2, pp. 1413–32). New York: Wiley.

Barker, R. G., & Associates (1978). *Habitats, environments, and human behavior: Studies in ecological psychology and eco-behavioral science from the Midwest Psychological Field Station, 1947–1972*. San Francisco: Jossey-Bass.

Barker, R. G., & Barker, L. S. (1964). Structural characteristics. In R. G. Barker & P. V. Gump (Eds.), *Big school, small school* (pp. 41–63). Stanford, CA: Stanford University Press.

────── (1978). Social actions of American and English children and adults. In R. G. Barker & Associates, *Habitats, environments, and human behavior* (pp. 99–120). San Francisco: Jossey-Bass.

Barker, R. G., Barker, L. S., & Ragle, D. D. M. (1967). The churches of Midwest, Kansas and Yoredale, Yorkshire: Their contributions to the environments of the towns. In W. Gore & L. Hodapp (Eds.), *Change in the small community* (pp. 155–89). New York: Friendship Press.

Barker, R. G., Dembo, T., & Lewin, K. (1941). Frustration and regression: A study of young children. No. 18, *University of Iowa Studies in Child Welfare*, Iowa City.

Barker, R. G., & Gump, P. V. (1964). *Big school, small school: High school size and student behavior*. Stanford, CA: Stanford University Press.

Barker, R. G., & Hall, E. R. (1964). Participation in interschool events and extracurricular activities. In R. G. Barker & P. V. Gump, *Big school, small school* (pp. 64–74). Stanford, CA: Stanford University Press.

Barker, R. G., Kounin, J. S., & Wright, H. F. (Eds.). (1943). *Child behavior and development*. New York: McGraw-Hill.

Barker, R. G., & Schoggen, P. (1973). *Qualities of community life: Methods of measuring environment and behavior applied to an American and an English town*. San Francisco: Jossey-Bass.

Barker, R. G., Wright, B. A., Meyerson, L., & Gonick, M. R. (1953). *Adjustment to physical handicap and illness: A survey of the social psychology of physique and disability*. Bulletin no. 55 (revised). New York: Social Science Research Council.

Barker, R. G., & Wright, H. F. (1949). Psychological ecology and the problem of psycho-social development. *Child Development, 20*, 131–43.

────── (1951a). *One boy's day*. New York: Harper & Row. (Reprinted by Hamden, CT: Shoestring Press, 1966)

——— (1951b). The psychological habitat of Raymond Birch. In J. H. Rohrer & M. Sherif (Eds.), *Social psychology at the crossroads* (pp. 196–212). New York: Harper & Row.

——— (1951c). *Maud Pintner: A full day study.* Unpublished manuscript, University of Kansas, Lawrence.

——— (1955). *Midwest and its children.* Evanston, IL: Row, Peterson & Co. (Reprinted by Hamden, CT: Archon Books, 1971)

Barker, R. G., Wright, H. F., Barker, L. S., & Schoggen, M. (1961). *Specimen records of English and American children.* Lawrence: University of Kansas Press.

Baron, R. A. (1971). Aggression as a function of audience presence and prior anger arousal. *Journal of Experimental Social Psychology, 7,* 515–23.

Barthell, C. N., & Holmes, D. S. (1968). High school yearbooks: A nonreactive measure of social isolation in graduates who later became schizophrenic. *Journal of Abnormal Psychology, 73,* 313–16.

Bates, F. L., & Harvey, C. C. (1975). *The structure of social systems.* New York: Wiley.

Bauer, R. A. (Ed.) (1966). *Social indicators.* Cambridge, MA: MIT Press.

Bechtel, R. B. (1977). *Enclosing behavior.* Stroudsburg, PA: Dowden, Hutchinson, & Ross.

——— (1982). Contributions of ecological psychology to the evaluation of environments. *International Review of Applied Psychology, 31,* 153–67.

Bechtel, R. B., & Ledbetter, C. B. (1976). *The temporary environment: Cold regions habitability* (Special Report 76-10). Hanover, NH: U.S. Army Corps of Engineers Cold Regions Research and Engineering Laboratory.

——— (1980). *Post occupancy evaluation of a planned community in Arctic Canada* (Special Report 80-6). Hanover, NH: U.S. Army Corps of Engineers Cold Regions Research and Engineering Laboratory.

Bechtel, R. B., Ledbetter, C. B., & Cummings, N. (1980). *Post occupancy evaluation of a remote Australian community: Shay Gap, Australia* (Special Report 80-29). Hanover, NH: U.S. Army Corps of Engineers Cold Regions Research and Engineering Laboratory.

Bem, D. J., & Allen, A. (1974). On predicting some of the people some of the time: The search for cross-situational consistencies in behavior. *Psychological Review, 81,* 506–20.

Berk, L. E. (1971). Effects of variations in the nursery school setting on environmental constraints and children's modes of adaptation. *Child Development, 42,* 839–69.

Berk, L. E., & Goebel, B. L. (1987). High school size and extracurricular participation. *Environment and Behavior, 19,* 53–76.

Bevans, G. E. (1913). *How working men spend their time.* New York: Columbia University Press.

Biddle, B. J. (1979). *Role theory: Expectations, identities, and behavior.* New York: Academic Press.

——— (1986). Recent developments in role theory. *Annual Review of Sociology, 12,* 67–92.

Biddle, B. J., & Thomas, E. J. (Eds.) (1966). *Role theory: Concepts and research.* New York: Wiley.

Borchert, J. R., & Adams, R. B. (1963). *Trade centers and trade areas of the upper Midwest* (Urban Report no. 3). Minneapolis: University of Minnesota.

Bower, G. H., Black, J. B., & Turner, T. J. (1979). Scripts in memory for text. *Cognitive Psychology, 11*, 177–220.

Bowers, K. S. (1973). Situationalism in psychology: An analysis and a critique. *Psychological Review, 80*, 307–36.

Brewer, M. B., Dull, V., & Lui, L. (1981). Perceptions of the elderly: Stereotypes as prototypes. *Journal of Personality and Social Psychology, 41*, 656–70.

Bronfenbrenner, U. (1979). *The ecology of human development*. Cambridge, MA: Harvard University Press.

Brough, J. (1963). *Auction!* New York: Bobs-Merrill.

Brunswik, E. (1943). Organismic achievement and environmental probability. *Psychological Review, 50*, 255–72.

—— (1947). *Systematic and representative design of psychological experiments*. Berkeley: University of California Press.

—— (1955). The conceptual framework of psychology. *International encyclopedia of unified science* (vol. 1, pp. 656–750). Chicago: University of Chicago Press.

—— (1956). *Perception and the representative design of psychological experiments*. Berkeley: University of California Press.

—— (1957). Scope and aspects of the cognitive problem. In H. Gruber, R. Jessor, & K. Hammond (Eds.), *Contemporary approaches to cognition: The Colorado Symposium* (pp. 5–31). Cambridge, MA: Harvard University Press.

Bureau of Economic Analysis (1981). *See* U.S. Department of Commerce.

Bureau of Labor Statistics (1981). *See* U.S. Department of Labor.

Burr, W. R., Leigh, G. K., Day, R. D., and Constantine, J. (1979). Symbolic interaction and the family. In W. R. Burr, R. Hill, F. I. Nye, & I. L. Reiss (Eds.), *Contemporary theories about the family: Vol. 2. General theories/theoretical orientation* (pp. 42–111). New York: Free Press.

Burt, R. S. (1976). Positions in networks. *Social Forces, 51*, 93–122.

—— (1982). *Toward a structural theory of action: Network models of social structure, perception, and action*. New York: Academic Press.

Campbell, W. J., Cotterell, J. L., Robinson, N. M., & Sadler, D. R. (1981). Effects of school size upon some aspects of personality. *The Journal of Educational Administration, 19*, 201–31.

Carlstein, T., Parkes, D., & Thrift, N. (Eds.) (1978). *Timing space and spacing time: Vol 2. Human activity and time geography*. London: Edward Arnold.

Chapin, F. S. (1974). *Human activity patterns in the city*. New York: Wiley.

Chein, I. (1954). The environment as a determinant of behavior. *Journal of Social Psychology, 39*, 115–27.

Clinard, M. B. (1968). *Sociology of deviant behavior* (3d ed.). New York: Holt, Rinehart & Winston.

Cohen, S., Glass, D., & Singer, J. (1973). Apartment noise, auditory discrimination and reading ability in children. *Journal of Experimental Social Psychology, 9*, 407–22.

Dickman, H. R. (1963). The perception of behavioral units. In R. G. Barker (Ed.), *The stream of behavior* (pp. 23–41). New York: Appleton-Century-Crofts.

Dollard, J., Doob, L. W. Miller, N. E., Mowrer, O. H., & Sears, R. R. (1939). *Frustration and aggression*. New Haven: Yale University Press.

Downey, R. G. (1978). Differences between entering freshmen from different size high schools. *Journal of College Student Personnel, 19*, 353–59.

Duckro, P., Beal, D., & George, C. (1979). Research on the effects of disconfirmed client role expectations in psychotherapy: A critical review. *Psychological Bulletin, 86,* 260–75.

Durkheim, E. (1938). *The rules of sociological method* (8th ed.). S. A. Solvay & J. H. Mueller (Trans.), G. E. G. Catlin (Ed.). Chicago: University of Chicago Press.

Economic report of the president (1987). Washington D.C.: U.S. Government Printing Office.

Eddy, G. L., & Sinnett, E. R. (1973). Behavior setting utilization by emotionally disturbed college students. *Journal of Consulting and Clinical Psychology, 40,* 210–16.

Ekehammar, B. (1974). Interactionism in personality from a historical perspective. *Psychological Bulletin, 81,* 1026–48.

Elder, G. H., Jr. (1974). *Children of the great depression.* Chicago: University of Chicago Press.

Endler, N. S., & Magnusson, D. (1974, July). *Interactionism, trait psychology, psychodynamics, and situationism.* Reports from the Psychological Laboratories, no. 418. Stockholm, Sweden: University of Stockholm.

Enright, R. D., & Lapsley, D. K. (1980). Social role-taking: A review of constructs, measures, and measurement of properties. *Review of Educational Research, 50,* 646–74.

Fawl, C. L. (1978). Disturbances children experience in their natural habitat. In R. G. Barker & Associates, *Habitats, environments, and human behavior* (pp. 146–68). San Francisco: Jossey-Bass.

Felson, M. (1979). How should social indicators be collected, organized, and modeled? [Review of Karl A. Fox (1974), *Social indicators and social theory: Elements of an operational system.*] *Contemporary Sociology, 8,* 40–41.

Fischer, C. S. (1973). On urban alienations and anomie: Powerlessness and social isolation. *American Sociological Review, 38,* 311–26.

——— (1975). The study of urban community and personality. *Annual Review of Sociology, 1,* 67–89.

——— (1976). *The urban experience.* New York: Harcourt Brace Jovanovich.

Fisher, C. D., & Gitelson, R. (1983). A meta-analysis of the correlates of role conflict and ambiguity. *Journal of Applied Psychology, 68,* 320–33.

Forgas, J. P. (1979). *Social episodes: The study of interaction routines.* New York: Academic Press.

Fox, K. A. (1983). The eco-behavioural view of human societies and its implications for systems science. *International Journal of Systems Science, 14,* 895–914.

——— (1984a). Behavior settings and eco-behavioral science: A new arena for mathematical social science permitting a richer and more coherent view of human activities in social systems: Part I. Concepts, measurements, and linkages to economic data systems, time-allocation matrices, and social system accounts. *Mathematical Social Sciences, 7,* 117–38.

——— (1984b). Behavior settings and eco-behavioral science: A new arena for mathematical social science permitting a richer and more coherent view of human activities in social systems: Part II. Relationships to established disciplines, and needs for mathematical development. *Mathematical Social Sciences, 7,* 139–65.

——— (1985). *Social system accounts: Linking social and economic indicators through tangible behavior settings.* Dordrecht, The Netherlands: D. Reidel.

——— (1986). An eco-behavioral approach to social systems accounting, time-allocation matrices, and measures of the quality of life. In A. J. MacFayden & H. W. MacFayden (Eds.), *Economic psychology: Intersections in theory and applications* (pp. 549–81). Amsterdam: North-Holland.

Fox, K. A., & Ghosh, S. K. (1981). A behavior setting approach to social accounts combining concepts and data from ecological psychology, economics, and studies of time use. In F. T. Juster & K. C. Land (Eds.), *Social accounting systems: Essays on the state of the art* (pp. 131–217). New York: Academic Press.

Fox, K. A., & Kumar, T. K. (1965). The functional economic area: Delineation and implications for economic analysis and policy. *Regional Science Association Papers, 15,* 57–85.

Fox, K. A., & Miles, D. G. (Eds.). (1987). *Systems economics: Concepts, models, and multidisciplinary perspectives.* Ames: Iowa State University Press.

Fuhrer, U. (1986). Review of G. Kaminski (Ed.), *Ordnung und Variabilität im Alltagsgeschehen* [Order and variability in everyday happenings]. *Journal of Environmental Psychology, 6,* 359–69.

Fuhrer, U. (in press). Bridging the ecological-psychological gap: Contextual theorizing. *Journal for the Theory of Social Behavior.*

Gans, H. J. (1962a). *The urban villagers: Group and class in the life of Italian-Americans.* New York: The Free Press of Glencoe.

——— (1962b). Urbanism and suburbanism as ways of life: A re-evaluation of definitions. In A. Rose (Ed.), *Human behavior and social processes* (pp. 625–48). Boston: Houghton Mifflin.

George, L. K. (1980). *Role transitions in later life.* Monterey, CA: Brooks/Cole.

Gergen, K. J., Gergen, M. M., & Barton, W. H. (1973). Deviance in the dark. *Psychology Today, 7,* 129–30.

Gibson, J. J. (1979). *The ecological approach to visual perception.* Boston: Houghton Mifflin.

Goffman, E. (1959). *The presentation of self in everyday life.* New York: Doubleday.

——— (1974). *Frame analysis.* London: Penguin.

Goode, W. J. (1960). A theory of role strain. *American Sociological Review, 25,* 483–96.

Gordon, C. (1976). Development of evaluated role identities. *Annual Review of Sociology, 2,* 405–33.

Gottfredson, D. C. (1985). *School size and school disorder* (Report no. 360). Baltimore, MD: Center for Social Organization of Schools, Johns Hopkins.

Grabe, M. (1981). School size and the importance of school activities. *Adolescence, 16,* 22–31.

Graesser, A. C., Woll, S. B., Kowalski, D. J., & Smith, D. A. (1980). Memory for typical and atypical actions in scripted activities. *Journal of Experimental Psychology: Human Learning and Memory, 6,* 503–15.

Grannis, J. C. (1983). Ecological observation of experiential education settings: A quantitative-qualitative instrument. *Environment and Behavior, 15,* 21–52.

Greenberg, C. I. (1979). Toward an integration of ecological psychology and industrial psychology: Undermanning theory, organization size, and job enrichment. *Environmental Psychology and Nonverbal Behavior, 3,* 228–42.

Gross, B. M. (1966). The state of the nation: Social systems accounting. In R. A. Bauer (Ed.), *Social Indicators* (pp. 154–271). Cambridge, MA: MIT Press.

Gump, P. V. (1964). Environmental guidance of the classroom behavior system. In

B. J. Biddle & W. J. Ellena (Eds.), *Contemporary research in teacher effectiveness* (pp. 165–95). New York: Holt, Rinehart & Winston.

———— (1967). Persons, settings, and larger contexts. In B. P. Indik & F. K. Berrien (Eds.), *People, groups, and organizations: An effective integration* (pp. 223–49). New York: Teachers College, Columbia University Press.

———— (1969). Intra-setting analysis: The third grade classroom as a special but instructive case. In E. P. Willems & H. L. Raush (Eds.), *Naturalistic viewpoints in psychological research* (pp. 200–220). New York: Holt, Rinehart & Winston.

———— (1975a). Environmental psychology and the behavior setting. In B. Honikman (Ed.), *Responding to social change* (pp. 152–63). Stroudsburg, PA: Dowden, Hutchinson, & Ross.

———— (1975b). Operating environments in schools of open and traditional design. In T. G. David & B. D. Wright (Eds.), *Learning Environments* (pp. 49–67). Chicago: University of Chicago Press.

———— (1982). School settings and their keeping. In D. L. Duke (Ed.), *Helping teachers manage classrooms* (pp. 98–114). Alexandria, VA: Association for Supervision and Curriculum Development.

———— (1987). School and classroom environments. In D. Stokols & I. Altman (Eds.), *Handbook of environmental psychology* (vol. 1, pp. 691–732). New York: Wiley.

Gump, P. V., & Adelberg, B. (1978). Urbanism from the perspective of ecological psychologists. *Environment and Behavior, 10,* 171–91.

Gump, P. V., & Friesen, W. V. (1964). Participation in nonclass settings. In R. G. Barker & P. V. Gump, *Big school, small school* (pp. 75–93). Stanford, CA: Stanford University Press.

Gump, P. V., & Ross, R. (1977). The fit of milieu and programme in school environments. In H. McGurk (Ed.), *Ecological factors in human development* (pp. 77–89). New York: North-Holland.

Gump, P. V., Schoggen, P., & Redl, F. (1957). The camp milieu and its immediate effects. *Journal of Social Issues, 13,* 40–46.

———— (1963). The behavior of the same child in different milieus. In R. G. Barker (Ed.), *The stream of behavior* (pp. 169–202). New York: Appleton-Century-Crofts.

Gump, P. V., & Sutton-Smith, B. (1955). Activity-setting and social interaction. *American Journal of Orthopsychiatry, 25,* 755–60.

Hackman, J. R., & Oldham, G. R. (1975). Development of the job diagnostic survey. *Journal of Applied Psychology, 60,* 159–70.

Hagerstrand, T. (1978). Survival and arena: On the life history of individuals in relation to their geographical environments. In T. Carlstein, D. Parkes, & N. Thrift (Eds.), *Timing space and spacing time: Vol. 2. Human activity and time geography* (pp. 121–45). London: Edward Arnold.

Hall, E. (1966). *The hidden dimension.* New York: Doubleday.

Hall, E. R. (1965). *An ecological study of parent-child influence in behavior.* Unpublished master's thesis, University of Kansas, Lawrence.

Halsall, E. (1973). *The comprehensive school: Guidelines for the reorganization of secondary education.* Oxford, NY: Pergamon Press.

Halverson, H. M. (1943). The development of prehension in infants. In R. G. Barker, J. S. Kounin, & H. F. Wright (Eds.), *Child behavior and development* (pp. 49–65). New York: McGraw-Hill.

Hanks, M. P., & Eckland, B. K. (1976). Athletics and social participation in the educational attainment process. *Sociology of Education, 49*, 271–94.

Hanson, L., & Wicker, A. W. (1973). *Effects of overmanning on group experience and task performance.* Paper presented at the meeting of the Western Psychological Association, Anaheim, CA.

Harloff, H. J., Gump, P. V., & Campbell, D. E. (1981). The public life of communities: Environmental change as a result of the intrusion of a flood control, conservation, and recreation reservoir. *Environment and Behavior, 13*, 685–706.

Harré, R., & Secord, P. F. (1972). *The explanation of social behavior.* Oxford: Basil Blackwell.

Heider, F. (1927). Ding und Medium. *Symposion, 1*, 109–57.

———— (1958). *The psychology of interpersonal relations.* New York: Wiley.

———— (1959). On perception, event structure and the psychological environment, selected papers. *Psychological Issues, 1* (entire issue).

Hollander, E. P. (1985). Leadership and power. In G. Lindzey & E. Aronson (Eds.), *Handbook of Social Psychology* (3d ed., vol. 2, pp. 485–537). New York: Random House.

Houghland, J. G., & Wood, J. R. (1980). Control in organizations and the commitment of its members. *Social Forces, 59*, 85–105.

Indik, B. P. (1963). Some effects of organization size on member attitudes and behavior. *Human Relations, 16*, 369–84.

Ingham, A. G., Levinger, G., Graves, J., & Peckham, V. (1974). The Ringelmann effect: Studies of group size and group performance. *Journal of Experimental Social Psychology, 10*, 371–84.

Isaacs, S. (1930). *Intellectual growth in young children.* London: George Routledge & Sons.

Jackson, P. W., & Wolfson, B. J. (1968). Varieties of constraint in a nursery school. *Young Children, 23*, 358–67.

James, W. (1950). *The principles of psychology.* (Authorized, Unabridged.) New York: Dover Publications.

Jordan, N. (1963). Some formal characteristics of the behavior of two disturbed boys. In R. G. Barker (Ed.), *The stream of behavior* (pp. 203–18). New York: Appleton-Century-Crofts.

Jorgenson, D. O., & Dukes, F. O. (1976). Deindividuation as a function of density and group membership. *Journal of Personality and Social Psychology, 34*, 24–29.

Kaminska-Feldman, M. (1982). Studies on effectiveness of memorization of events in light of cognitive script theory. *Polish Psychological Bulletin, 13*, 2, 113–21.

Kaminski, G. (Ed.) (1986). *Ordnung und Variabilitat im Alltagsgeschehen: Das Behavior Setting–Konzept in den Sozial- und Verhaltens-wissenschaften* [Order and variability in everyday happenings: The behavior setting concept in social and behavioral science]. Gottingen: Hogrefe.

Keynes, J. M. (1936). *The general theory of employment, interest and money.* New York: Harcourt, Brace, & Co.

Kimberly, J. R. (1976). Organizational size and the structuralist perspective: A review, critique, and proposal. *Administrative Science Quarterly, 21*, 571–97.

Kirmeyer, S. L. (1978). *Effects of work overload and understaffing on rangers in Yosemite National Park.* Unpublished doctoral diss., Claremont, CA: Claremont Graduate School.

Kleinert, E. J. (1969). Effects of high school size on student activity participation. *National Association of Secondary School Principals Bulletin, 53,* 34–46.

Koffka, K. (1935). *Principles of gestalt psychology.* New York: Harcourt, Brace, & Co.

Kounin, J. S. (1970). *Discipline and group management in classrooms.* New York: Holt, Rinehart, & Winston.

Kounin, J. S., & Gump, P. V. (1974). Signal systems of lesson settings and the task-related behavior of preschool children. *Journal of Educational Psychology, 66,* 554–62.

Kruse, L. (1987). Environmental psychology in Germany. In D. Stokols & I. Altman (Eds.), *Handbook of environmental psychology* (vol. 2, pp. 1195–1225). New York: Wiley.

Kuznets, S. (1937). *National income and capital formation, 1919–1935: A preliminary report.* New York: National Bureau of Economic Research.

Larson, C. M. (1949). *School size as a factor in the adjustment of high school seniors.* Pullman, WA: Bulletin no. 511, Youth Series no. 6, State College of Washington.

Latané, B. (1973). *A theory of social impact.* St. Louis, MO: Psychonomic Society.

Latané, B., & Darley, J. M. (1969). Bystander apathy. *American Scientist, 57,* 244–68.

———— (1970). *The unresponsive bystander: Why doesn't he help?* New York: Appleton-Century-Crofts.

Latané, B., Williams, K., & Harkins, S. (1979). Many hands make light the work: The causes and consequences of social loafing. *Journal of Personality and Social Psychology, 37,* 822–32.

Lawrence, D. H. (1963). The nature of the stimulus: Some relationships between learning and perception. In S. Koch (Ed.), *Psychology: A study of a science* (vol. 5, pp. 179–212). New York: McGraw-Hill.

LeCompte, W. E. (1972a). Behavior settings: The structure of the treatment environment (1). In W. J. Mitchell (Ed.), *Environmental design: Research and practice. EDRA 3/AR8* (pp. 4.2.1–4.2.5.). Los Angeles: Environmental Design Research Association.

———— (1972b). The taxonomy of a treatment environment. *Archives of Physical Medicine and Rehabilitation, 53,* 109–14.

Leeper, R. W. (1963). Learning and the fields of perception, motivation, and personality. In S. Koch (Ed.), *Psychology: A study of a science* (vol. 5, pp. 365–487). New York: McGraw-Hill.

Leontief, W. W. (1936). Quantitative input and output relations in the economic system of the United States. *Review of Economics and Statistics, 18,* 105–25.

Lewin, K. (1935). *A dynamic theory of personality: Selected papers.* (D. K. Adams, Trans.). New York: McGraw-Hill.

———— (1936). *Principles of topological psychology.* (F. Heider & G. Heider, Trans.). New York: McGraw-Hill.

———— (1938). *The conceptual representation and measurement of psychological forces.* Durham, NC: Duke University Press.

———— (1943). Forces behind food habits and methods of change. *Bulletin of the National Research Council, 108,* 35–65.

———— (1944). Constraints in psychology and psychological ecology. *University of Iowa Studies in Child Welfare, 20,* 17–20.

────── (1947). Frontiers in group dynamics, II. *Human Relations, 1,* 143–53.

────── (1951). *Field theory in social science.* (D. Cartwright, Ed.). New York: Harper & Row.

Lindsay, P. (1982). The effect of high school size on student participation, satisfaction, and attendance. *Educational Evaluation and Policy Analysis, 4,* 57–65.

────── (1984). High school size, participation in activities, and young adult social participation: Some enduring effects of schooling. *Educational Evaluation and Policy Analysis, 6,* 73–83.

Linton, R. (1936). *The study of man.* New York: Appleton-Century-Crofts.

Madsen, M. C. (1971). Developmental and cross-cultural differences in the cooperative and competitive behavior of young children. *Journal of Cross-Cultural Psychology, 2,* 365–71.

Madsen, M. C., & Shapira, A. (1970). Cooperative and competitive behavior of urban Afro-American, Anglo-American, Mexican-American, and Mexican village children. *Developmental Psychology, 3,* 16–20.

Mandel, M. J. (1983). Local roles and social networks. *American Sociological Review, 48,* 376–86.

McCartney, K. A., & Nelson, K. (1981). Children's use of scripts in story recall. *Discourse Processes, 4,* 59–70.

McNamara, J. R., & Blumer, C. A. (1982). Role playing to assess social competence: Ecological validity considerations. *Behavior Modification, 6,* 519–49.

Mead, G. H. (1934). *Mind, self, and society.* Chicago: University of Chicago Press.

Melbin, M. (1978a). The colonization of time. In T. Carlstein, D. Parkes, & N. Thrift (Eds.), *Timing space and spacing time: Vol. 2. Human activity and time geography* (pp. 100–113). London: Edward Arnold.

────── (1978b). Night as frontier. *American Sociological Review, 43,* 3–22.

Merton, R. K. (1957). *Social theory and social structure* (rev. ed.). Glencoe, IL: Free Press.

Milgram, S. (1970). The experience of living in cities. *Science, 167,* 1461–68.

Miller, G. A., Galanter, E., & Pribram, K. H. (1960). *Plans and the structure of behavior.* New York: Holt, Rinehart & Winston.

Mitchell, B. R. (1975). *European historical statistics, 1750–1970.* London: Macmillan.

Moore, G. T. (1986). Effects of the spatial definition of behavior settings on childrens' behavior: A quasi-experimental field study. *Journal of Environmental Psychology, 6,* 205–33.

Moore, W. E. (1963). *Man, time, and society.* New York: Wiley.

Moos, R. (1973). Conceptualizations of human environments. *American Psychologist, 28,* 652–55.

Moreland, R. L., & Levine, J. M. (1982). Socialization in small groups: Temporal changes in individual-group relations. In L. Berkowitz (Ed.), *Advances in experimental social psychology* (vol. 15, pp. 137–92). New York: Academic Press.

Moreno, J. L. (1934). *Who shall survive.* Washington, DC: Nervous and Mental Diseases Publishers.

Morgan, D. L., & Alwin, D. F. (1980). When less is more: School size and student social participation. *Social Psychology Quarterly, 43,* 241–52.

Murray, H. A. (1938). *Explorations in personality.* New York: Oxford University Press.

———— (1959). Preparations for the scaffold of a comprehensive system. In S. Koch (Ed.), *Psychology: A study of a science* (vol. 3, pp. 7–54). New York: McGraw-Hill.

Newcomb, T. M. (1950). *Social psychology.* New York: Dryden Press.

Nye, F. I. (Ed.) (1976). *Role structure and analysis of the family.* Beverly Hills, CA: Sage.

Organization for Economic Cooperation and Development (1973). *List of social concerns common to most OECD countries.* Paris: OECD.

———— (1982). *The OECD list of social indicators.* Paris: OECD.

Otto, L. B. (1975). Extracurricular activities in the educational attainment process. *Rural Sociology, 40,* 162–76.

———— (1976). Social integration and the status-attainment process. *American Journal of Sociology, 81,* 1360–83.

Oxley, D., & Barrera, M., Jr. (1984). Undermanning theory and the workplace: Implications of setting size for job satisfaction and social support. *Environment and Behavior, 16,* 211–34.

Parsons, T. (1951). The social system. Glencoe, IL: Free Press.

Parten, M. B. (1932). Social participation among preschool children. *Journal of Abnormal and Social Psychology, 27,* 243–69.

Payne, R., & Pugh, D. S. (1976). Organizational structure and climate. In M. D. Dunnette (Ed.), *Handbook of industrial and organizational psychology* (pp. 1125–73). Chicago: Rand McNally.

Pence, E. C., & Taylor, R. B. (1978). Level of manning and responses to deviant behavior. *Environmental Psychology and Nonverbal Behavior, 3,* 122–23.

Perkins, D. V. (1982). Individual differences and task structure in the performance of a behavior setting: An experimental evaluation of Barker's manning theory. *American Journal of Community Psychology, 10,* 617–34.

Perkins, D. V., & Perry, J. C. (1985). Dimensional analysis of behavior setting demands in a community residence for chronically mentally ill women. *Journal of Community Psychology, 13,* 350–59.

Pervin, L. A. (1978). Definitions and classifications of stimuli, situations, and environments. *Human Ecology, 6,* 71–105.

Petty, R. M. (1971). *The assimilation of a new group member: A laboratory study of behavior setting theory.* Unpublished master's thesis, University of Illinois.

———— (1974). Experimental investigation of undermanning theory. In D. H. Carson (Ed.), *Man-environment interactions: Evaluation and applications, part II* (pp. 259–69). Stroudsburg, PA: Dowd, Hutchinson, & Ross.

Petty, R. M., & Wicker, A. W. (1974). Degree of manning and degree of success of a group as determinants of members' subjective experiences and their acceptance of a new group member. *Psychological Documents, 4* (Ms. no. 616).

Porter, L. W., & Lawler, E. E., III (1965). Properties of organization structure in relation to job attitudes and behavior. *Psychological Bulletin, 64,* 23–51.

Porter, L. W., & Steers, R. M. (1973). Organizational, work, and personal factors in employee turnover and absenteeism. *Psychological Bulletin, 80,* 151–76.

Prescott, J. R. (1985). A behavior setting approach to microanalytical simulation models at the community level. In K. A. Fox, *Social system accounts: Linking social and economic indicators through tangible behavior settings* (pp. 132–49). Dordrecht, The Netherlands: Reidel.

———— (1987). Community dynamics: Microanalytic simulation models with behavior settings as basic units. In K. A. Fox & D. G. Miles (Eds.), *Systems economics*. Ames: Iowa State University Press.

Price, R. H. (1976). Behavior setting theory and research. In R. H. Moos (Ed.), *The human context: Environmental determinants of behavior* (pp. 213–47). New York: Wiley.

Price, R. H., & Blashfield, R. K. (1975). Explorations in the taxonomy of behavior settings. *American Journal of Community Psychology, 3,* 335–51.

Proshansky, H. M., Ittleson, W. H., & Rivlin, L. G. (Eds.) (1976). *Environmental psychology: People and their physical settings* (2d ed.). New York: Holt, Rinehart & Winston.

Prull, R. (1976). *The behavior setting survey as a college environment measure.* Unpublished doctoral diss., Boston College, Boston, MA.

Ragle, D. D. M., Barker, R. G., & Johnson, A. (1978). Impact of the Agricultural Extension Service on Midwest. In R. G. Barker & Associates, *Habitats, environments, and human behavior* (pp. 202–12). San Francisco: Jossey-Bass.

Ragle, D. D. M., Johnson, A., & Barker, R. G. (1967). Measuring Extension's impact. *Journal of Cooperative Extension, 5,* 178–89.

Ratliff, F. (1962). Some interrelations among physics, physiology, and psychology in the study of vision. In S. Koch (Ed.), *Psychology: A study of a science* (vol. 4, pp. 417–82). New York: McGraw-Hill.

Raush, H. L., Dittman, A. T., & Taylor, T. J. (1959). Person, setting, and change in social interaction. *Human Relations, 12,* 361–78.

———— (1960). Person, setting, and change in social interaction: II. *Human Relations, 13,* 305–32.

Rommetveit, R. (1968). *Social norms and roles.* Oslo: Universitetsforlaget. (Originally published in 1954 by the Norwegian Research Council for Science and the Humanities)

Ruggles, R. (1981). The conceptual and empirical strengths and limitations of demographic and time-based accounts. In F. T. Juster & K. C. Land (Eds.), *Social accounting systems: Essays on the state of the art* (pp. 454–76). New York: Academic Press.

Rutter, M., Maughan, B., Mortimer, P., & Ouston, J., with Smith, A. (1979). *Fifteen thousand hours: Secondary schools and their effects on children.* Cambridge, MA: Harvard University Press.

Sachson, A. D., Rappoport, L., & Sinnett, E. R. (1970). The activity record: A measure of social isolation involvement. *Psychological Reports, 26,* 413–14.

Sadalla, E. K. (1978). Population size, structural differentiation, and human behavior. *Environment and Behavior, 10,* 271–91.

Sarason, S. B. (1972). *The creation of settings and the future societies.* San Francisco: Jossey-Bass.

———— (1974). *The psychological sense of community: Prospects for a community psychology.* San Francisco: Jossey-Bass.

Sarason, S. B., & Others (1977). *Human services and resource networks: Rationale, possibilities, and public policy.* San Francisco: Jossey-Bass.

Sarbin, T. R., & Allen, V. L. (1968). Role theory. In G. Lindzey & E. Aronson (Eds.), *Handbook of social psychology* (2d ed., vol. 1, pp. 488–567). Reading, MA: Addison-Wesley.

Schank, R. C. (1982). *Dynamic memory: A theory of reminding and learning in computers and people*. Cambridge, Eng.: Cambridge University Press.

Schank, R. C., & Abelson, R. P. (1977). *Scripts, plans, goals, and understanding: An inquiry into human knowledge structures*. Hillside, NJ: Erlbaum.

Schoenfeld, W. N., & Cumming, W. W. (1963). Behavior and perception. In S. Koch (Ed.), *Psychology: A study of a science* (vol. 5, pp. 213–52). New York: McGraw-Hill.

Schoggen, M., Barker, L. S., & Barker, R. G. (1978). Behavior episodes of American and English children. In R. G. Barker & Associates, *Habitats, environments, and human behavior* (pp. 121–24). San Francisco: Jossey-Bass.

Schoggen, P. (1951). *A study in psychological ecology: A description of the behavior objects which entered the psychological habitat of an eight-year-old girl during the course of one day*. Unpublished master's thesis, University of Kansas, Lawrence.

——— (1963). Environmental forces in the everyday lives of children. In R. G. Barker (Ed.), *The stream of behavior* (pp. 42–69). New York: Appleton-Century-Crofts.

——— (1978). Environmental forces on physically disabled children. In R. G. Barker & Associates, *Habitats, environments, and human behavior* (pp. 125–45). San Francisco: Jossey-Bass.

——— (1983). Behavior settings and the quality of life. *Journal of Community Psychology, 11*, 144–57.

Schoggen, P., & Barker, R. G. (1974). The ecological psychology of adolescents in an American and an English town. *Contributions to Human Development, 1*, 12–23.

——— (1977). Ecological factors in development in an American and an English small town. In H. McGurk (Ed.), *Ecological factors in human development* (pp. 61–76). New York: North-Holland.

Schoggen, P., & Schoggen, M. (1988). Student participation and high school size. *Journal of Educational Research, 81*, 288–93.

Schuster, S. O., Murrell, S. A., & Cook, W. A. (1980). Person, setting, and interaction contributions to nursery school social behavior patterns. *Journal of Personality, 48*, 24–37.

Scott, M. (1977). Some parameters of teacher effectiveness as assessed by an ecological approach. *Journal of Educational Psychology, 69*, 217–26.

Sengupta, J. K. (1986). Modeling eco-behavioral systems. *Mathematical Social Sciences, 11*, 1–31.

——— (1987). The concept of variety in systems behavior: Applications to behavior settings, product-differentiation, and representative firms. In K. A. Fox & D. G. Miles (Eds.), *Systems economics*. Ames: Iowa State University Press.

Shaw, G. B. (1949). *Sixteen sketches*. New York: Dodd Mead.

Sherif, M. (1936). *The psychology of social norms*. New York: Harper.

Shure, M. B. (1963). Psychological ecology of a nursery school. *Child Development, 34*, 979–92.

Sieber, S. D. (1974). Toward a theory of role accumulation. *American Sociological Review, 39*, 567–78.

Simmons, H., & Schoggen, P. (1963). Mothers and fathers as sources of environmental pressure on children. In R. G. Barker (Ed.), *The stream of behavior* (pp. 70–77). New York: Appleton-Century-Crofts.

Singer, J. E., Brush, C. A., & Lubin, S. C. (1965). Some aspects of deindividuation: Identification, and conformity. *Journal of Experimental Social Psychology*, *1*, 356–78.

Sorokin, P. A., & Berger, C. Q. (1939). *Time-budgets of human behavior*. Cambridge, MA: Harvard University Press.

Soskin, W. F., & John, V. P. (1963). The study of spontaneous talk. In R. G.
Barker (Ed.), *The stream of behavior* (pp. 228–81). New York: Appleton-
Century-Crofts.

Spady, W. G. (1970). Lament for the letterman: Effects of peer status and extracurricular activities on goals and achievement. *American Journal of Sociology*,
75, 680–702.

Steiner, I. D. (1972). *Group process and productivity*. New York: Academic Press.

Stevenson, R. L. (1882). The pavilion on the links. *New Arabian Nights* (p. 192).
New York: Henry Holt.

Stokols, D. A. (1978). Environmental psychology. *Annual Review of Psychology*,
29, 253–95.

———— (1981). Group x place transactions: Some neglected issues in psychological
research on settings. In D. Magnusson (Ed.), *Toward a psychology of situations* (pp. 393–415). Hillsdale, NJ: Erlbaum.

Stokols, D. A., & Jacobi, M. (1984). Traditional, present oriented, and futuristic
modes of group-environment relations. In K. J. Gergen & M. M. Gergen
(Eds.), *Historical social psychology* (pp. 441–80). Hillsdale, NJ: Erlbaum.

Stokols, D. A., & Shumaker, S. A. (1981). People in places: A transactional view of
settings. In J. Harvey (Ed.), *Cognition, social behavior, and the environment*.
Hillsdale, NJ: Erlbaum.

Stone, R. (1971). *Demographic accounting and model-building*. Paris: Organization for Economic Cooperation and Development.

———— (1975). *Toward a system of social and demographic statistics*. Prepared for
the United Nations Department of Economic and Social Affairs. New York:
United Nations.

Stryker, S., & Macke, A. S. (1978). Status inconsistency and role conflict. *Annual
Review of Sociology*, *4*, 57–90.

Szalai, A. (Ed.) (1972). *The use of time: Daily activities of urban and suburban
populations in 12 countries*. The Hague: Mouton.

Tars, S. E., & Appleby, L. (1973). The same child in home and institution. *Environment and Behavior*, *5*, 3–28.

Terleckyj, N. E. (1975). *Improvements in the quality of life: Estimates of possibilities in the United States, 1974–1983*. Washington, D.C.: National Planning
Association.

Terman, L. M., & Merrill, M. A. (1962). *Stanford-Binet intelligence scale, manual of the third revision, form L-M*. Boston: The Riverside Press.

Thoits, P. A. (1983). Multiple identities and psychological well-being: A refor-
mulation and test of the social isolation hypothesis. *American Sociological Review*, *48*, 174–87.

Thomas, W. I., & Thomas, D. S. (1928). *The child in America: Behavior problems
and progress*. New York: Knopf.

Tinbergen, J. (1939). *Statistical testing of business cycle theories: Vol. II. Business
cycles in the United States of America, 1919–1932*. Geneva: League of Nations
Economic Intelligence Service.

Tolman, E. C. (1932). *Purposive behavior in animals and men.* New York: The Century Company.

Turner, R. H., & Shosid, N. (1976). Ambiguity and interchangeability in role attribution: The effect of the alter's response. *American Sociological Review, 41,* 993–1006.

Underwood, B., & Moore, B. (1982). Perspective taking and altruism. *Psychological Bulletin, 91,* 143–73.

U.S. Department of Commerce, Bureau of Economic Analysis (1977). *BEA economic areas (Revised, 1977): Component SMSA's, counties, and independent cities.* Washington, D.C.: U.S. Government Printing Office.

———— (1981). *Revised estimates of capital stocks and related measures for fixed non-residential private and residential capital, government-owned fixed capital, and durable goods owned by consumers, 1925–1979.* Washington, D.C.: National Income and Wealth Division, Bureau of Economic Analysis.

U.S. Department of Commerce, Office of Federal Statistical Policy and Standards (1977). *Standard occupational classification manual.* Washington, D.C.: U.S. Government Printing Office.

U.S. Department of Labor, Bureau of Labor Statistics (1981). *The national industry-occupation employment matrix, 1970, 1978, and projected 1990,* vols. 1 and 2. Washington, D.C.: U.S. Government Printing Office.

U.S. Department of Labor, Employment and Training Administration (1977). *Dictionary of occupational titles* (4th ed.). Washington, D.C.: U.S. Government Printing Office.

U.S. Department of Labor, Manpower Administration (1972). *Handbook for analyzing jobs.* Washington, D.C.: U.S. Government Printing Office.

U.S. Executive Office of the President, Office of Management and Budget (1978). *Standard industrial classification manual, 1972.* Washington, D.C.: U.S. Government Printing Office.

Van Moeseke, P. (1985). Socio-economic interface and social income. *Mathematical Social Sciences, 9,* 263–73.

———— (1986). Time and cost budgets. *Mathematical Social Sciences, 11,* 129–38.

———— (1987). The dollar values of social variables: Two models of social income. In K. A. Fox & D. G. Miles (Eds.), *Systems economics.* Ames: Iowa State University Press.

Van Sell, M., Brief, A. P., & Schuler, R. S. (1981). Role conflict and role ambiguity: Integration of the literature and directions for further research. *Human Relations, 34,* 43–71.

Vecchio, R. P., & Sussman, M. (1981). Staffing sufficiency and job enrichment: Support for an optimal level theory. *Journal of Occupational Behavior, 2,* 177–87.

Voegelin, C. F., & Voegelin, F. M. (1972). Dependence of selectional restriction on cultural spaces. In E. S. Firchow, K. Grimstead, N. Hasselmo, & W. A. O'Neil (Eds.), *Studies for Einar Haugen* (vol. 59, pp. 535–53). The Hague: Mouton.

Wachs, T. D., & Gruen, G. E. (1982). *Early experience and human development.* New York: Plenum Press.

Warner, W. K., & Hilander, J. S. (1964). The relationship between size of organization and membership participation. *Rural Sociology, 29,* 30–39.

Warner, W. L., Meeker, M., & Eels, K. (1949). *Social class in America.* Chicago: Science Research Associates.

Wechsler, D. (1974). *Wechsler Intelligence Scale for Children—revised, manual.* New York: The Psychological Corporation.

Weisner, T. (1974). *Recurrent migration and rural-urban differences in Kenya: Children's social behavior.* Paper presented at the meeting of the Psychosocial Conference on Sedentarization, University of California at Los Angeles.

Whiting, B. B., & Whiting, J. W., in collaboration with Longabaugh, R. (1975). *Children of six cultures: A psychocultural analysis.* Cambridge, MA: Harvard University Press.

Wicker, A. W. (1967). *Students' experiences in behavior settings of large and small high schools: An examination of behavior setting theory.* Unpublished doctoral diss., University of Kansas, Lawrence.

—— (1968). Undermanning, performances, and students' subjective experiences in behavior settings of large and small high schools. *Journal of Personality and Social Psychology, 10,* 255–61.

—— (1969a). Cognitive complexity, school size, and participation in school behavior settings: A test of the frequency of interaction hypothesis. *Journal of Educational Psychology, 16,* 200–203.

—— (1969b). Size of church membership and members' support of church behavior settings. *Journal of Personality and Social Psychology, 13,* 278–88.

—— (1972). Processes which mediate behavior-environment congruence. *Behavioral Science, 17,* 265–77.

—— (1973). Undermanning theory and research: Implications for the study of psychological and behavioral effects of excess populations. *Representative Research in Social Psychology, 4,* 185–206.

—— (1974). *Yosemite Valley employee survey.* Claremont, CA: Claremont College Print Shop.

—— (1979a). *An introduction to ecological psychology.* Monterey, CA: Brooks/Cole. (Republished in 1983 by New York: Cambridge University Press).

—— (1979b). Ecological psychology: Some recent and prospective developments. *American Psychologist, 34,* 755–65.

—— (1981). Nature and assessment of behavior settings: Recent contributions from the ecological perspective. In P. McReynolds (Ed.), *Advances in psychological assessment* (vol. 1, pp. 22–61). San Francisco: Jossey-Bass.

—— (1987). Behavior settings reconsidered: Temporal stages, resources, internal dynamics, context. In D. Stokols & I. Altman (Eds.), *Handbook of environmental psychology* (vol. 1, pp. 613–53). New York: Wiley.

Wicker, A. W., & Kauma, C. E. (1974). Effects of merger of a small and a large organization on members' behaviors and experiences. *Journal of Applied Psychology, 59,* 24–30.

Wicker, A. W., & King, J. C. (1988). Life cycles of behavior settings. In J. P. McGrath (Ed.), *Social psychology of time: New perspectives* (pp. 182–200). Beverly Hills, CA: Sage.

Wicker, A. W., & Kirmeyer, S. L. (1976, October). What the rangers think. *Parks and Recreation,* 28–30, 42–43.

—— (1977). From church to laboratory to national park: A program of research on excess and insufficient populations in behavior settings. In D. Stokols (Ed.), *Perspectives on environment and behavior: Theory, research, and applications* (pp. 69–96). New York: Plenum Press.

Wicker, A. W., Kirmeyer, S. L., Hanson, L., & Alexander, D. (1976). Effects of manning levels on subjective experiences, performance, and verbal interaction in groups. *Organization Behavior and Human Performance, 17,* 251–74.

Wicker, A. W., McGrath, J. E., & Armstrong, G. E. (1972). Organization size and behavior setting capacity as determinants of member participation. *Behavioral Science, 17,* 499–513.

Wicker, A. W., & Mehler, A. (1971). Assimilation of new members in a large and a small church. *Journal of Applied Psychology, 55,* 151–56.

Wiener, N. (1962). The mathematics of self-organizing systems. In R. E. Machol & P. Gray (Eds.), *Recent developments in information and decision processes* (pp. 1–21). New York: Macmillan.

Wilken, P. H. (1971). Size of organization and member participation in church congregations. *Administrative Science Quarterly, 16,* 173–79.

Willems, E. P. (1963). *Forces toward participation in behavior settings of large and small institutions.* Unpublished masters' thesis, University of Kansas, Lawrence.

——— (1964a). Review of research. In R. G. Barker & P. V. Gump, *Big school, small school* (pp. 29–37). Stanford, CA: Stanford University Press.

——— (1964b). Forces toward participation in behavior settings. In R. G. Barker & P. V. Gump, *Big school, small school* (pp. 115–35). Stanford, CA: Stanford University Press.

——— (1965). Participation in behavior settings in relation to three variables: Size of behavior settings, marginality of persons, and sensitivity to audiences. *Dissertation Abstracts International, 27,* 959B.

——— (1967). Sense of obligation to high school activities as related to school size and marginality of student. *Child Development, 38,* 1247–60.

Willems, E. P., & Halstead, L. S. (1978). An eco-behavioral approach to health status and health care. In R. G. Barker & Associates, *Habitats, environments, and human behavior* (pp. 169–89). San Francisco: Jossey-Bass.

Wirth, L. (1938). Urbanism as a way of life. *The American Journal of Sociology, 44,* 1–24.

Wright, H. F. (1967). *Recording and analyzing child behavior.* New York: Harper & Row.

——— (1971). Urban space as seen by the child. *Courrier, 21,* 1–24.

Wright, H. F., & Barker, R. G. (1950). The elementary school does not stand alone. *Progressive Education, 27,* 133–37.

Wright, H. F., Barker, R. G., Nall, J., & Schoggen, P. (1955). Toward a psychological ecology of the classroom. In A. P. Coladarci (Ed.), *Readings in educational psychology* (pp. 254–68). New York: Holt, Rinehart & Winston.

Wrong, D. (1961). The oversocialized conception of man. *American Sociological Review, 26,* 184–93.

Yamamoto, A. Y. (1979). *Culture spaces in everyday life.* Lawrence: University of Kansas Publications in Anthropology, no. 11.

Zener, K., & Gaffron, M. (1962). Perceptual experience: An analysis of its relation to the external world through internal processings. In S. Koch (Ed.), *Psychology: A study of a science* (vol. 4, pp. 516–618). New York: McGraw-Hill.

Zimbardo, P. G. (1969). The human choice: Individuation, reason, and order versus deindividuation, impulse, and chaos. In W. I. Arnold & D. Levine (Eds.), *Nebraska Symposium on Motivation* (pp. 237–307). Lincoln: University of Nebraska Press.

Name Index

Abelson, R. P., 79, 254, 302–3, 320
Adams, D. K., 335–36
Adams, R. B., 294–95
Adelberg, B., 232–33
Alexander, D., 193, 234, 236–37
Allen, A., 259
Allen, V. L., 311, 312, 313
Allport, F. H., 8
Allport, G. W., 339, 360
Altman, I., 322
Alwin, D. F., 216
Appleby, L., 260
Argyle, M., 259
Armstrong, G. E., 88–89, 193, 223–25
Arnold, D. W., 236–37
Ashby, W. R., 150–51, 166, 184, 185
Ashton, M., 5, 20

Baird, L. L., 214–15, 222
Baldwin, A., 350
Barker, L. S., 15, 152, 177, 212, 256–57, 355, 371, 372
Barker, R. G.: at Clark University, 348–49; faculty appointments of, 339–54; German ecological psychologists' views of, 254, 255; at Harvard University, 339–42; and the settings of a professional lifetime, 323–56; at Stanford University, 327–34, 345–48; as a student, 327–39; at the University of Illinois, 342–44; at the University of Iowa, 335–39; at the University of Kansas, 349–54. *See also* Barker, R. G., works of; *name of specific person or topic*
Barker, R. G., works of: (1960) 20, 241, 354; (1962) 18; (1963a) 354; (1963b) 156, 354, 361; (1965) 262, 263, 354; (1968) 134, 300–301, 304–5, 354; (1969) 267; (1978a) 267; (1979) 192; (1987) 253; (and Associates, 1978) 20, 300–301, 344, 354; (with Barker, 1964) 212; (with Barker, 1978) 152, 371, 372; (with Barker and Ragle, 1967) 256–57; (with Dembo and Lewin, 1941) 11, 154, 192–93; (with Gump, 1964) 5, 20, 211–12, 215, 218, 285, 354; (with Hall, 1964) 212; (with Kounin and Wright, 1943) 343; (with Ragle and Johnson, 1967) 20; (with Ragle and Johnson, 1978), 256; (with Schoggen, 1973) 20, 70, 74–75, 82, 97, 133, 134, 138–39, 141, 226–30, 246–50, 255, 283, 284, 289, 291–94, 354; (with Schoggen, 1974) 20; (with Schoggen, 1977) 20; (with Schoggen and Barker, 1978) 152, 372; (with Wright, Meyerson, and Gonick, 1953) 346; (with Wright, 1951a) 354; (with Wright, 1951c) 156; (with Wright, 1955) 6, 8–9, 14, 20, 76, 134, 138–39, 145, 151, 156, 158, 159, 176, 317, 354, 361; (with Wright, Barker, and Schoggen, 1961), 15, 177
Baron, R. A., 242
Barrera, M., Jr., 234
Barthell, C. N., 221
Barton, W. H., 242
Bates, F. L., 310
Bateson, G., 318
Bauer, R. A., 273
Beal, D., 313
Bechtel, R. B., 211–12, 250–51
Bem, D. J., 259
Berger, C. Q., 306

Subject Index

Library of Congress Cataloging-in-Publication Data

Schoggen, Phil.
  Behavior settings : a revision and extension of Roger G. Barker's
Ecological psychology / Phil Schoggen, with a chapter by Karl A. Fox.
     p.   cm.
  Bibliography: p.
  Includes index.
  ISBN 0-8047-1543-2 (alk. paper)
  1. Environmental psychology.   I. Barker, Roger Garlock, 1903–
Ecological psychology.   II. Title.
BF353.S36   1989
155.9—dc19   88-38736
                                                                    CIP